365 Soulful Messages
The Right Guidance at the Right Time

Jodi Chapman, Dan Teck

& Over 200 Soulful Contributors

DandiLove Unlimited

This book comes from our hearts and is here to inspire you. Please know, though, that it is not a replacement for therapy or medical advice. If you are feeling like you could use some extra support, please seek out a professional in your area.

The views represented in this book are not necessarily a reflection of the publisher. Each author wrote their story in a way that they remembered the events happening. Please note that the publisher accepts no responsibility for any inaccurate information portrayed.

The authors who contributed to this book are from all corners of the world, and we have kept their native English spelling for each of their pieces. For this reason, you will see words like "color" and "colour" or "realized" and "realised" throughout the book – just depending on what part of the world the author is from. We also wanted to find a balance of maintaining consistency throughout the book while still honoring each author's belief system. For this reason, you will see that some words are capitalized in some pieces and not in others. For the most part, we capitalize words relating to God, Source, the Universe, and a Higher Power.

Ordering information available at:
www.365soulfulmessages.com.
For wholesale inquiries, please write to: info@365bookseries.com.

Printed in the United States of America
ISBN: 13: 978-0-9981251-4-5
Library of Congress Control Number: 2019903153

www.365bookseries.com

DEDICATION

We dedicate this book to five co-authors in our series who sadly passed away since our last book was published.

Tandy Elisala and Donna Hall Kater each planned to share their writing in this book, but their bodies and souls had other plans. Our hearts break that they weren't able to be part of it after all. They were both such positive souls who had so much wisdom to give.

Cynthia Ryals, Jen Flick, and Marcia Sandals were all wonderful writers with huge hearts. They each shared from the depths of their soul and truly wanted to inspire others with their words…and they did.

Each of these authors' words will continue to uplift us all forever. And they will forever be missed by those in our community, their families and friends, and everyone they touched through their soulful words and loving hearts. We're sending love to each of them and are so grateful that they were part of our lives.

Contents

Chapter 2 – Soulful Signs 39

Chapter 8 – Messages from Our Hearts to Yours 337

Introduction

T his is the fifth and final book in our 365 Book Series, and we're so grateful that you're reading it. It's filled with a year's worth of soulful messages that helped change the authors' lives in positive ways.

While it's not always easy to say goodbye or to embrace change, we both felt at the soul level that the series had come full circle. It began with the soul (our first book was called *365 Ways to Connect with Your Soul*), and it ends with the soul. And that feels perfect to us, because for over a decade our business has been about helping others listen deeply to their soul – the voice within that's connected to all that is – and take action on its whispers.

We've loved each book in this series. We've gotten to share so many different perspectives that we never would have been exposed to. We've gotten to meet so many amazing people who we wouldn't have met otherwise. And we've made lifelong friends. Over 1,000 authors have shared their hearts in this series, and we'll forever be grateful to each of them. We feel very blessed to have published books where miraculous moments were shared, pivotal life shifts were embraced, acts of goodness were celebrated, and connecting with the soul became an integral part of life.

Throughout the years, we've felt truly grateful to have received loving emails from those who had contributed and also those who had read the stories. The messages shared how the books had shifted mindsets and opened hearts and changed lives. We never expected that when we began, but we quickly realized that these books took on a life of their own. They had their own mission. And as soon as we released them into the world, they began to heal and uplift. We saw how reading other people's stories helped us all see that we are never alone. By reading the stories, we got to witness other people's pain and see how they each came through it. We got to be present when they triumphed, and we celebrated with them. We realized that the words in these books were never just words on a page (or a screen). They represented hope. They represented what was possible. They represented dreams being realized. That's what makes this series so special. And that's why we're so grateful to have been part of it.

And this book is no different. You'll find those same messages of love and miracles. And you'll also find moments of loss and pain and uncertainty. But what we love about these books is that each piece always ends with hope, with a change – whether it's big or small – that allowed the author to view their life through a different lens, to feel grateful, to feel love, to feel whole.

The 365 true stories in this book vary greatly, but they all have one thing in common: they all include a soulful message that the author either received or that they are offering to you. The stories range from the miraculous to the mundane (but still important), from the spiritual to the secular, from the subtle and nuanced to the dramatic and impossible to miss.

Like our previous books in this series, the 200+ authors who contributed are spread out all across the globe. They speak different languages, have different professions, follow different religions, are different races, have unique experiences and points of view...our list of differences goes on and on. Yet, no matter how different we are, we're continually reminded by reading each of the stories that we're more alike than different. What we continue to find throughout each of the books in our series is how much we have in common. We all want to feel loved and to offer love, to express our deepest truth, to be seen and understood, and to feel peace and happiness. We all want to embrace our time here on Earth. And we all want to connect with our soul and stay open to the magic that being part of this world can bring.

We never could have written this book on our own. We needed each of the authors to share their unique messages. We haven't walked in their shoes, but we certainly can sympathize and feel compassion for what they've been through. And, once again, as with our previous books, we're honored that the authors trusted us and this series enough to share some of their most painful moments so that someone out there will see that they aren't alone in their experiences. That takes such bravery, and we applaud them for their vulnerability and their honesty.

Examples of Soulful Messages

While this book contains a wide array of messages, there are some common themes that you'll find throughout, such as messages coming from loved ones on the other side or from loved ones here on Earth, messages coming from our soul or our body, messages appearing as signs when we needed them most, messages coming from angels and the divine, and messages coming from animals and nature.

We realized, while reading the stories, that soulful messages can appear anywhere at any time. And it's up to us to stay open and to be on the lookout for them. That's our job. And when we do that, the powerful messages will automatically appear.

How to Read This Book

As we do with all of the books in this series, we gave each of the co-authors free rein with their pieces and trusted that the book would come together in a cohesive way once we received them all. And that's exactly what happened. The pieces fell into eight categories, which became our chapter titles:

1. Messages from the Other Side
2. Soulful Signs
3. Messages from Our Body and Soul
4. Messages from Family
5. Messages from Friends…Old and New
6. Messages from Animals and Nature
7. Messages from the Divine
8. Messages from Our Hearts to Yours

There are many ways to enjoy this book: you can read each entry in order on the day it appears, or you can flip through at random and let your soul guide you. Perhaps you have a favorite day of the year (such as your birthday or an anniversary) and want to see which piece appears on that day. Or maybe a certain chapter's theme is calling to you. For example, if you're feeling like you're missing someone on the other side, you could turn to the first chapter and see if one of the pieces speaks to you. Or if you're wanting to see how beneficial and life-changing listening to your soul truly is, you could turn to any piece from Chapter 3.

There is no right or wrong way to read this book. You can read one piece each morning or night as part of your spiritual practice. Or you can read it in the carpool lane while picking up your kids from school.

Another suggestion for reading this book is to keep a journal nearby to jot down any thoughts and inspirations that enter your heart as you read the pieces – even if they don't make sense to you at first. Chances are, they will when you most need them to.

You can also read this book with your friends as a way to deepen your relationships and share your own soulful messages with each other. You can meet (in person or online) and go through the days, or you can pick and choose them at random and share what you learned about yourself after reading the stories and taking them into your heart.

However and wherever you choose to read it, know that it's a powerful book – one that we believe has the ability to help you see the magic that's happening all around you. By reading this book, you're consciously opening your heart to being on the lookout for soulful messages in your own life, and we believe that once you begin focusing on them, you'll find yourself surrounded by them!

Giving Back

Because we've both experienced many soulful messages from being around animals and nature, we'll be donating 5% of all profits from sales of this book to the Jane Goodall Institute. (You can learn more about this charity by going to www.janegoodall.org.)

Thank You

Thank you for being part of this journey with us. We hope you enjoy each of the pieces in this special book. Our hope is that each of these stories will leave you feeling inspired, amazed, moved, and deeply appreciative of the messages and magic all around, and that you'll be on the lookout for magical messages of your own!

Hugs, love, and gratitude,
Jodi and Dan

Chapter 1
Messages from the Other Side

S ometimes soulful messages appear in very tangible ways, such as while having a conversation over coffee with a friend where they say one sentence that changes your life forever or when the same song plays on the radio over and over again and you finally listen to the words and realize that it's exactly what you needed to hear. But oftentimes, messages come from beyond this realm – from our loved ones on the other side, those who have passed on but are still with us in spirit and who are forever in our hearts.

We will be the first to admit that we have no idea how this is possible or what goes on after we leave our human body and enter the spirit realm, but what we do know is that each of the pieces in this chapter shares a similar truth: that life goes on long after we've taken our last breath and that our loved ones are always looking out for us.

It's our hope that reading the pieces throughout this chapter will bring comfort to you, especially if you've recently lost a loved one or are deeply missing someone on the other side. It's our hope that you'll embrace the messages that are shared here and that you'll be open to receiving messages of your own.

What we know for sure is that we live in a world that's magical and that's filled with so much love. And what matters most is that we stay open to receiving messages in whatever way they come to us – whether they're from this world or beyond. Because we believe that how they come to us isn't nearly as important as what they convey. Usually, they're exactly what we need to hear and take into our heart and are brought to us at exactly the right time. And we think that's pretty miraculous.

Ave Maria

By Jodi Chapman

"She's gone," my mom whispered into the phone. "Thankfully, she went peacefully, and she's no longer suffering."

For two weeks, I had been dreading this call. For two weeks, the phone barely left my side. I brought it into the bathroom. I put it next to my pillow at night. I carried it from room to room. Waiting. For two weeks, I went through the entire gamut of emotions: shock that after so many false alarms through the years, this time seemed that it was finally the end, despair that I would never see my grandma again, hope when it seemed that she might pull through, powerlessness when she appeared to be uncomfortable, and relief when she slept peacefully. And now she was really gone, and the finality felt like a crushing weight on my chest that I wasn't strong enough to remove.

In a daze, I hung up the phone and climbed into my bed, not sure what to say or do. I just wanted her back. I wanted to travel back in time and be with her, hold her hand, have her ask me how my day was at school while heating up a mini pizza in the microwave for us to share. I wanted to sit at the kitchen table with her and play a hand of Rummy before heading home to eat dinner with my family. I wanted just one more moment with her. Just one.

I closed my eyes, and "Ave Maria" began playing in my mind. I had always loved this song, and I hadn't thought of it in years. I asked Alexa to play it on our Echo, and I immediately felt calmer and soothed. I felt my grandma in the room with me, letting me know that she was home, and that everything was okay. I'd heard this song hundreds of times throughout my life, but I'd never known what the words meant. In that moment, something inside urged me to look up the translation. I got goosebumps when I saw that it was the Hail Mary prayer, something that my grandma, a devout Catholic, recited many times a day.

I know that she was with me in that moment, and I know that she's with me now. I can feel her. And now I know that any time I need to feel her close to me, I can play this song and know that we're together again. She's gone. But she's still here. That I know for sure.

Shine Your Light

By Kimberley Harrington

I believe that energy never dies. I believe in magic and messages from Heaven. Often they are subtle and easily missed, like a butterfly or a feather, but sometimes they are so bright and in-your-face wonderful that they can't go unnoticed!

My father was stubborn. He did things his way and wouldn't listen to others' opinions. After my mother died, Pop lived alone at the top of a hill in the woods. He installed a motion-sensor spotlight on the back porch, aiming it at the driveway. We were blinded trying to approach the house. "We can't see! Turn that thing off." We joked that the Space Station could see it. Pop didn't want to hear it. He insisted that someday we may need that light and would thank him.

Pop died peacefully in his sleep. We gathered at the funeral home to say goodbye privately before the visitors arrived, but noticed that Pop's two neighbors, Helen and Bob, were already inside. They eagerly stood and expressed sympathy but then couldn't wait to ask me, "Exactly when did Pop pass?" When I told them Sunday, I noticed a quick glance between them. Slowly, Helen told me that Pop's spotlight had been on non-stop since late Sunday.

We stopped up at the house after the service. We could already see the tops of the trees lit by light as we slowly made the drive up the hill. The spotlight was indeed on. No amount of jiggling the switch helped. The only way we were able to turn it off was by dismantling the entire apparatus and wiring.

Years later, my work with meditation has led me to believe that we all have an inner light. We must remove worry, judgment, fear, and doubt to let it shine. Our inner light is our true self. I have no doubt that Pop sent us a message that he had arrived in Heaven. Though that light is long gone from the house, I still see Pop's light shining on me for the rest of my life. "Yes, Pop. Thank you for your light."

My Angel Brother

By Katja Rusanen

When I was little, I was curious about a photo of a young boy in a silver frame on our bookshelf, accompanied by a small, angel-shaped candle. My mom told me that the boy was my Angel Brother. I didn't really understand why he wasn't with us. Why was he an angel and we weren't?

I later learned that he had died two years before I was born. He had drowned at the age of eight in the river near our home. Even though I had never met him, I missed having him around. A big brother would have been so cool. I imagined how he would have told all the bullies to leave me alone. He would have been there for me…but he wasn't. All I had was a photo, a candle, and a grey gravestone.

One day, years later, I stood on the riverbank. I wanted the river to wash away my pain. My boyfriend had chosen to end his life, and my heart felt crushed into thousands of pieces. I didn't want to be here any longer. It felt too painful to even breathe.

The cold water welcomed me as I took the first step. I was ready to leave. I felt that I simply could not go on without my loved one. I stepped forward and the water embraced my knees, but then there was a flash of light in my dark mind. My big brother appeared in my thoughts. This was the river that took his life. I thought of my mom, I thought of my dad, and I knew I had to turn back. I could not make them lose another child; it just did not feel right. I decided to choose life.

When I look back now, I feel so grateful for that decision. It feels like my big brother was watching over me. Even though I never got to meet him in this life, I felt that he was on my side when I needed him most. It was love that saved my life.

Experiencing Heaven

By Elise Forrer

I lost my husband Jim when he was 29 and I was 26. At the time, I was seven months pregnant and already had our two-year-old son. Two feelings stand out from that August morning when I received the news: immobilizing shock and the comforting presence of God unlike anything I had felt in my life. It was as if He wrapped me in an invisible blanket of faith, and I knew that somehow everything was going to be alright.

In the weeks that followed, I wanted more than anything to know that Jim was at peace, but frustration set in as weeks turned into months and I didn't receive any assurance. I know now that God was just waiting for the perfect time. That time arrived one evening shortly after our daughter was born. I was startled awake by Jim's heart-stopping presence beside me. I could feel his muscular strength and smell his familiar scent. He pulled me onto his lap, and we sat there together in a bubble of absolute love. Without a word, he expressed profound sorrow for leaving us, and I felt the immensity of his pain. But he also wanted me to experience the pure joy and serenity of the afterlife. I was given the opportunity to release the devastating grief I'd been holding in my body, which finally felt safe to do now that our daughter was born.

As I sensed our visit coming to an end, I felt desperate for him to take me with him. The peaceful state he had reached was so inviting; it seemed a better place than even the love I felt as a mother to my two beautiful children on Earth. But his message to me was clear: I was not done; I had more to do.

Years later, that experience is still just as vivid. Jim's message to me was true – I had more living to do, and I am thankful beyond measure for the richness of this life. Our children are grown, and as I write this, I am a grandma for the first time; that two-year-old son became a dad two weeks ago. The daughter I was carrying when Jim died got married last year and is a beautiful and healthy woman. Life has gone on for me, too. I fell in love again and have shared a life with a man who has helped me through it all. This spring, we celebrated 20 years of marriage.

I would have missed it all had I given up in those early days of despair. I remember Jim's message and know that I am still not done. No wasted moments.

Don't Forget the Celery

By Sandi Neilson

The energy hummed. I sensed several personalities from the other side gather around. Despite some recent evidence to the contrary, it was at a time when I was doubting my ability to channel messages from those who had passed on.

Tuning in to the energies there, I recognized my sister's mother-in-law by her laugh. As always, it was distinctive and warm. Dulcie had passed in her 92nd year, about six months earlier.

She showed me that she watched over my sister's second son, Josh, especially while he worked as a chef. She was very happy that, through him, her love for cooking for others was still in the family. Her pride shone through as she watched him stirring something thick and rich. She spoke just four words: "Don't forget the celery."

It was a lovely imprint I was being given, but I wasn't sure I had picked up the message correctly. Was I able to pass that message Dulcie was imparting on to Josh in the spirit it was given? How would Josh receive this message? Would he think his aunt totally kooky? I wrestled with this before finally picking up the courage to text Josh and share the message as best I could.

When we got to talk about this, Josh explained how cool this message was. It made total sense to him. He had been teaching his junior that day the art of making a Neapolitan sauce for the base of his signature gourmet pizzas. His recipe had celery in it, but there had been none at the restaurant, so he prepared the sauce without it. But he had made it very clear to his junior that normally celery was added, too.

It was great to pass on that message to someone who appreciated it and could confirm its meaningfulness. It became a turning point for me. I stopped considering I might have this gift and instead claimed it. I started in earnest to learn to master it for the express purpose of sharing these messages for all the good they bring.

Windows of the Soul

By Kathleen Gleason

The phone rang. The caller ID showed the hospital. The day before, I had a mammogram. In the past, I had never received a call, just a form letter stating that my results were normal. My heart sank, realizing there must be a problem this time. I answered, "Hello," so softly it was barely audible.

The woman on the phone said, "The radiologist has requested more images of your left breast." My mind felt splintered – not both breasts, just the left? They must have found something. I had just received the call that every woman fears. I pleaded to Heaven for help from my mother, Mary Elizabeth, who had left this earth five years earlier.

I had another mammogram, an ultrasound, and a biopsy. The diagnosis was "Grade 2 Invasive Ductal Carcinoma." I had breast cancer. I was in a club that no one asks to join. I underwent surgery to remove the mass, and radiation would follow.

At my first radiation appointment, I was as nervous as a cat in a room full of dogs. In the waiting area, I sat across from an older woman. I began to feel an incredible pull towards her – a need to connect. I got up, walked over to her, and said hello. As she looked up from her book, I felt as if I was looking into my mother's crystal blue eyes. I had goosebumps from head to toe.

She took my two hands in hers and said, "It's going to be okay." I looked into those piercing blue eyes and said, "I'm Kathy."

She winked and said, "I'm Mary."

In that instant, I knew that my mother had come to me. I told Mary that I felt my mother's presence so strongly in her. She smiled and said, "Yes, I know."

As I walked to the car, I looked to the heavens, crying and laughing. I knew that my prayers had been answered and said, "I love you, Mom. Thanks for the visit."

The Red Bird

By Sonya L. Moore

I need to make a tough decision. I don't know what to do. I am scared to the point of being paralyzed at the life-changing effects this one decision will have on my family. I'm so confused. I wish I could see a sign, like the burning bush in the Bible. A sign so obvious that it gives me the answer, removing the awful feeling of doubt and helplessness that is overtaking me.

There are a million crippling thoughts racing in my head as I hold my coffee mug and slowly inhale, in the hopes that this will magically organize my thoughts.

With these tangled thoughts in my head, I look out the window and notice the beautiful blue sky and white fluffy clouds. I hear birds chirping and see squirrels jumping from branch to branch. Just like that, this temporarily takes my mind off of my situation as I watch God's creatures play in my backyard.

Then I see it. It appears out of nowhere and lands on a tree limb directly in my line of sight. It's staring directly at me. It bounces from tree to tree, but it returns to the tree limb in front of me. It's working very hard to keep my attention and is trying to tell me something. I can just feel it. Then, suddenly, a sense of calmness washes over my body.

So, what am I looking at? It's a cardinal, but I call it a "red bird." That is what my mom called it. She passed away 22 years ago. This was her favorite bird. She said, "Whenever you see one, make a wish because something special is going to happen." That has always stuck with me. So I made a wish.

That single moment changed my life forever. My "burning bush" was the red bird. It was my mother coming to my rescue and helping me make one of the toughest decisions of my life. The answer became clear to me at that very moment. My soulful message came in the form of a red bird, a direct and personal message from my mother in Heaven.

The Hoarder

By Mauri Barnes

"Look at me, living like this," I snort with self-loathing. Stuff is stacked everywhere. Every piece of furniture in the house is covered with it. I feel like I'm buried in my own home. Aisles have been created between precariously perched boxes to make a pathway from the front door to the kitchen, bathroom, and garage. Pathetic.

This is no way to live, huddled on the sofa in front of the TV with my dogs curled around me. Comfort food, blankets, and the remote are all within easy reach. I retreat into my little "cave," sometimes for days, feeling hopeless, immobilized, and broken. I wonder what happened to my dreams, to my happiness. It feels like my life is behind me, and the future looks bleak.

Reaching rock bottom, I isolate myself from others. I don't want to be seen like this, lacking energy and motivation to get up or move or do anything. The battle going on inside me drains my spirit. Depression shuts me down.

Too often, I have placed another person's wants before my own, coping with my inability to choose by holding on to everything. Now the piles are deep and I am overwhelmed. I am a hoarder.

This is not how I want my life to be! "I don't want to live like this anymore," I cry out to the universe. "I want to change! What can I do?"

And then I hear the quiet whisper of my dad's spirit reminding me, "You are everything that you need."

Understanding his loving message, I loudly proclaim, "I need to clear this space! I need to let go of the past and all of this stuff!" Slowly, I stand up, shedding my favorite old hoodie like a butterfly emerging from its cocoon.

I begin to make a pile, then another and another. "I don't need this...I will never use this again...this isn't me anymore." As the piles grow, I begin to feel the joy of letting go and finding my happiness again.

Notes in the Margins

By Tanya Levy

I was stuck in my "not good enough" story – the one where I doubt my worth, despite all the evidence that surrounds me that I help others. I was out of balance and wanting to make an impact in my life. I was seeking guidance. I fell asleep wondering what to do.

Through the night, my paternal grandmother came to me. She showed me her Bible, the one she read every day. She lived by example, leaving a legacy of love and support. She said to me, "The notes in the margins are the ones that matter. Never forget that, honey. Your interpretations are important. Sharing those interpretations, all those notes you make in the margins of your journals are the wisdom to distill and share with others." She reminded me to spread the wisdom.

Then my maternal grandmother came to me. She was at the old farm where she lived, where we used to visit her. She tended to be more down to earth in her wisdom and taught me common sense. She used to say to me, "That's my Tanya" when I did or said something helpful. She showed me photos of family times that were so full of love and reminded me of beautiful memories. Then she showed me happy people at the beach in the sun and sand. She told me to spread joy.

Then I dreamed I was driving on a dark and sleety road behind a car with its hazards on. The car was slowing me down, and I maneuvered past it and was free. Then the dream ended. The message I received was not to be afraid of the dark. I took it as a reminder to be a light in the dark.

I woke up feeling encouraged and supported. My grandmothers came to me and reminded me to spread joyful wisdom. My dream reminded me to be a light in the dark. My story of being not enough vanished in the morning light. I put my feet on the floor and reached for my journal to record more notes in the margins.

Given Hope from the Other Side

By Mary Cate O'Malley

It had been a great interview. I just had one more question. "Tell me about my competitors and what you like about them."

The chief scientist didn't hold back. "Well, one applicant is a marketing manager, and one is a director. Of 300 applicants, you are the only one without a degree."

My game face didn't falter as I shook his hand and retrieved my now-embarrassing portfolio. Later, on my couch, staring at the ceiling, I cried. What was I thinking? I had been a newspaper clerk for 17 years. What possessed me to apply to be the director of corporate communications at a start-up?

Suddenly, I distinctly heard my brother, who had died six months before of AIDS, urging me on. "Mary, I am dead and can never do all the things I wanted. You are still alive. Don't give up. Fight for what you want. Believe in yourself. I am here for you."

I jumped up startled, but the phone rang, commanding my attention. With barely time to disguise my grief, I picked up the receiver. It was the company's CEO: "You have made the top five. I would like to invite you to the next round of interviews."

With a scheduled time, I got to work. It was pre-internet, but not pre-24-hour Kinkos. I felt a super-human surge. Within a 24-hour period, I transformed my portfolio from news articles and obits to a set of marketing collateral for this start-up, and I was confident it could compete with the four-color work I was up against.

During the next interview, I placed my portfolio in front of the CEO. His look at that moment communicated, "I have already seen it. You just lost the job."

I pushed forward. "Please, take a look."

He must have been impressed. His next call offered me the job.

Sometime later he told me, "Do you know why I hired you? Because you worked harder than anyone I have ever hired before you even got the job. I knew you would work hard for me."

That job was the start of a great career.

The Launch

By Jill Alman Bernstein

Navy aircraft carrier fighter pilots are a breed unto themselves. The danger and thrill of being launched off the carrier deck, the hook catching the plane's tail upon return. My father was such a pilot in the Korean War. He dared to fly. Flight was in his soul.

The phone rang. My sister, in a thin choked-up voice said, "Daddy is in the ICU. He can't breathe on his own."

I flew to his side and prepared. I visualized his soul floating up, all our hands joined, forming a circle of love around him. I envisioned his spirit swirling out of his body, ascending to the heavens.

He breathed his last earthly breath. I heard a bark. Our trusted Labrador bounded toward him. Walking through clouds, they were greeted by a group of men in khaki Navy uniforms – my father's squadron. They were waiting, so happy to see him. And then they walked, arm in arm, into the light.

Exhausted and sleep deprived, I questioned what I saw.

Several days later, I returned home. I was compelled to read a book that had been sitting on my shelf for years (*Soul Survivor*) about a boy, James, who was the reincarnation of a WWII fighter pilot. I read so quickly, racing like the engines of a fighter jet readying for launch, something guiding me to hurry to the part where James was playing with his GI Joes, when his parents asked him why he named his little men Billy, Walter, and Leon, and he answered that they were who met him in Heaven.

Heat rushed from my chest. I felt energy vibrations racing up and down my legs. Tears spontaneously flowed. I had no doubt that I had been guided by my father to read the book, and he made sure I read until I got to that part so that I knew that what I had seen was true.

I had questioned what I saw, but he showed me and reminded me of the gift I hold. Surrounded by his love, I stepped forward, now undeniably trusting my intuitive vision.

A Father's Gift

By Sheila Sutherland

I stood at the signpost of Mile 0 of the Alaska Highway for the first time, as a dream that I didn't know I had was born. I wanted to drive the Alaska Highway into the Yukon and through Alaska. I wasn't sure how I was going to make it happen, but I just knew in my heart that I had to do it.

A part of that dream was for my dad. He had passed away the previous year, and I knew he would have loved to do this trip, as he loved the North so much. He would be able to enjoy it...through my eyes.

Exactly one year later, I was back at that signpost, getting ready to embark on the road trip of a lifetime.

What a trip it was! The vastness of the landscape, the abundance of the wildlife, and the loneliness of the open road, where sometimes you wouldn't see another car for hours. Many times on this trip, I could feel that my dad was riding with me. This gave me a big smile on my face and in my heart.

In Whitehorse, Yukon, I stopped to see the horse sculpture that stands above the city. My usual smile was replaced with sadness, as I was missing my dad so much. Then I noticed something stuck in the base of the tail. At first I was angry, as I thought it was a piece of garbage that someone had left. That quickly changed. As I got closer, I noticed a plastic bag with hearts on it. Inside there was a burlap pouch with another heart on it. Inside that pouch was a heart-shaped rock with a card that said, "Come back to your heart." I burst into tears.

I was missing my dad so much because it was Father's Day. The day when everyone is celebrating their dads, mine gave me a gift to let me know that no matter where I am, he will always be with me in my heart.

Message from Mom

By Julie Stygar

Mediums. We are the conduit between the living and the dead. Our gifts allow us to deliver messages from Spirit to those left behind.

I have been blessed to communicate, receive, and deliver many poignant messages from Spirit. The myriad of emotions clients experience include relief, surprise, happiness, and most importantly, closure. Little did I know that I would be on the receiving side.

My mother received a diagnosis that was essentially going to take her beautiful life in a very short time. We kept her at home in a hospital bed in the living room where she spent her remaining days. Though she was nearing the end of her journey and no longer communicative, I knew she could still hear me, so I whispered in her ear, "If I am doing this the right way with giving messages, would you please let me know from the other side?" (No one else heard me say this to her.)

The day after she passed, my father, with tears in his eyes, said he had been in the bathroom washing up when he saw what looked like a tiny postcard. As he bent down to read it, he heard my mother say, "Tell Julie everything is fine."

I whooped and hollered! "Yes! This is real!"

My mother came through in a way that I personally could validate! For me, this was the moment of ultimate confirmation. What a beautiful message from an amazing source, the light of her soul.

Never be afraid to reach out to your loved ones after they pass, because they see us, hear us, help us, and are never far away.

Being a medium is a beautiful gift that I am grateful to possess, and I will continue channeling, smiling all the way.

Grandfather Has Spoken

By Tanya Levy

My paternal grandfather died when I was six. He was ill with cancer before he passed away, and the memories I have are of a strong, formidable man who loved and valued family. My mother died in 2015, and my father died in 2017. Until they both passed away, I did not think much of my paternal grandfather. However, after my father's death, I felt orphaned and very alone and was worried about other family members and how they would cope with his loss. Sometimes, despite my own grief, I felt like it was my job to look after them and fix things.

One night when I was going to sleep, I prayed for my family members who were grieving, especially the men and children. My paternal grandfather came to me in a dream and said, "Stop worrying so much about them. They are my job to take care of." I continued to worry, and he came to me again and said, "I told you I would look after them. I am responsible for them, too. This is part of my legacy."

Little by little, I worked through my grief. My dad was my best friend and always knew when I needed a hug or a piece of wisdom. My mom was always checking on me to see how my life was going and shared helpful, practical advice. As I worked through my grief, I also let go of some of my worry.

Then I had another dream. I dreamed I was chasing a blue van that was floating down a river near my grandfather's cottage. As I chased the van, I could hear my father laughing. When I shared this dream with my family, I learned that the person I was most worried about had had a similar dream. It felt like a message from my grandfather again that all would be well.

Dismissing Dread and Going After Delight

By Sandi Neilson

It all looked good on paper: a brand-new marketing plan for a brand-new direction of my work. A plan designed specifically for me. One I had invested a lot in. But I wasn't excited about taking any action on it, though it was important that I did. Dread was creeping in instead. I knew I couldn't just push through or avoid this, as these options had often backfired for me.

I was about to journal about my dilemma when I sensed that someone from the other side was there with me. As I tuned in, I picked up the energy of a small, spritely male in a dark, hand-knitted, fisherman-style jersey and a pink tutu. He was smiling broadly. I could hear the laughter as I was shown a poor performance of a pirouette, or maybe it was a highland jig, with Mike, my darling brother-in-law, almost falling over in the process.

Mike, a retired tugboat operator, had passed several years earlier. He had always been one to get fully into the spirit of a social occasion. If the theme of the party was titans and tiaras, he'd turn up in a tutu, tiara, and wand, and immerse himself in the vibe of these fun times.

Mike's message was clear: Find the fun. Delight in these times. Dance out any dread. Don't just endure this – enjoy it! Celebrate it all, every step of the way.

All the tension I was experiencing evaporated as Mike's message sank in. In my focus to do right by the plan and all that was at stake, I'd lost sight of something else. Even if this was new territory for me, laughter and light-heartedness needed to be infused all the way through. I needed to relax into this next chapter of my work. I could free myself, too, of thinking that marketing wasn't my thing.

Mike's way to deliver these messages has me easily remembering them and keeps me on point. Marketing has now become a part of working for myself that I can delight in, instead of dreading it.

I'm Here

By Jan Wilson

My grandparents were spiritualists. One evening, when I was a freshman in high school, I was invited to join one of their sessions. That particular session was dedicated to connecting to my grandfather's spirit guide. The room was absolutely silent. I don't think I'd ever felt that kind of silence before.

I looked at my grandfather and allowed my gaze to move to the others in the room and then toward my lap. Then the lights went out, and I heard the words "I'm here" whispered in my ear. I glanced around but found no one there. I heard the same words again and looked around once more and saw a stranger standing behind my grandfather. He had long gray braids, a single feather in his hair, and a slight smile on his face. Having been cautioned not to speak during the session, I remained silent.

The session continued for a few more minutes, and then the lights came on. The leader asked if anyone had anything to share. My grandfather responded, "I felt something, someone, but it didn't last long." Continuing around the group, everyone gently shook their heads no, nothing to share. When my turn came, I shared what I had witnessed, emotion coming forth with my words. My grandfather beamed at me, the leader nodded, and my grandmother grasped my hand.

That was the first and last session I ever attended. During a very trying time in my life, I remembered that evening and knew it was time for me to find guidance from the spirits. Remembering what I had observed during that session so many years before, I settled into a quiet place and closed my eyes. I heard "I'm here" whispered and wasn't sure if it was just a memory. I kept my eyes closed, and once again I heard those words. Slowly, I opened my eyes and saw a face I knew well: my grandmother's.

Since that experience, I've continued to reach out and connect almost every day – sometimes for guidance and sometimes just for a smile and a hug.

Mom's Balloon

By Nora Rose

A year after my mom passed away, on a very cold February evening, the boiler went out in her business's building. I compared three estimates and decided on the company that had serviced this beast for over 35 years. They said they would take apart the old unit to get it out of the building and build the new unit on site. As I looked around the basement, I wondered what my mother would do and realized that she would have bought a new boiler.

Work moved along until a pipe cracked, making it so the contractors would have to wait for a new pipe. Massive tools and parts were scattered around the basement. Knowing that there was nothing more I could do then, I went out into the cold, dark night and began to drive home. Halfway into my drive, I stopped for something to eat and a moment of quiet as I contemplated the day's events. I sat in a cozy chair and sipped on lemon water while I waited for my food.

Decorations were still up from Valentine's Day. A balloon floated toward me, but I wasn't paying attention to it. However, it wouldn't leave, and after a while, its string began dangling right in front of my face. I followed the string and looked up toward the ceiling. There above me was a red heart balloon circling around my chair. I watched it as tears formed in my eyes. I whispered up at the balloon, "I know it's you, Mom! I fixed things at your place. Do you like it? I'm so tired." I held on to the string.

I thought about this incredible moment. She showed herself to me so many times! Who should I tell? I paid my bill and left the balloon while saying, "I love you, Mom."

For the rest of the drive home, I thought about the many ways she has offered assurance and how she watches over me. Her messages of love and comfort never cease to amaze me. She always finds a way. It's true! Our loved ones are with us. They are just on the other side in a different dimension.

Someone at My Window

By Elizabeth R. Kipp

I awoke in the wee hours of the night. I thought I had heard a tap at my window, yet no one was there. Or were they? I thought I saw my friend, felt my friend, just on the other side of the window. He had recently transitioned, and the taste of his funeral lingered in my mouth. In this moment, his presence was palpable. I felt my heart swell and the pressure rise in my throat as these words filled the room:

"I see you there. Won't you whisper to me those words I want to hear? I miss you so. Words from long ago. Oh, please don't go. I see you there, just across the way. Oh, how do I reach you? You were just here. It seemed like yesterday. Won't you come and stay if only for a moment. Can I convince you to delay? I just want to reach you and convey how much I love you. What can I do to get my message through to you? I see you there, streaming through my window, a sweet, soft soul glow. Oh, please don't go. Stay here with me. What was that you said?"

Somewhere between earth and ether lies a place not clearly seen, yet it is perceived, felt as if a kaleidoscope dimension. Such a space opened right outside my window in the night.

I lay perfectly still, breathing softly, feeling my exhale cross through into this dimension, and drew my inhale from there. I can't explain it. Such heart space defies logic and order.

In the nexus between here and there lies a mysterious yet tangible space where none feel separate, only joined interminably in the field of love. Such is the power of a window in the night, and such are the ties between souls.

Celebrating the Circle of Life

By Isabella Rose

"It's the circle of life, and it moves us all through despair and hope, through faith and love." – Elton John

I thought I had prepared myself for the upcoming two-year anniversaries: the last time Matt and I would see each other, followed by the anniversary of his transition into the spirit realm two weeks later. I thought the worst of the grieving was over around Christmastime, but another wave of grief and sorrow had surfaced, deeper and more intense this time, like a tsunami.

I had given myself permission to take time away from social media and computer technology to allow myself time to practice self-care and to honor my grieving process. I was grateful for the loving support of my longtime friend during this time of retreat and reflection. Although I felt my heart and soul were drowning in the tears of pain and sorrow, I was aware of the increased signs sent from Heaven during this time, including repeatedly hearing songs on the radio that were special to us and seeing hawks and 228 (his date of birth and date of transition).

I was still raw from this unexpected deep dive into my grieving process but wanted to do something special to celebrate Matt, his life, his memory, and his continued presence in my life. I realized I hadn't had the chance to attend Ice Castles this year, which was how I honored him last year, checking an item off our bucket list. When I finally checked my email, I was surprised to see an email announcing the final days of Ice Castles. I checked my calendar and saw that the only day I was able to attend was on Matt's Circle of Life day.

While on the website preparing to order my tickets, I could barely believe my eyes! They were having sleigh rides this year, another item on our bucket list! Matt helped me make his Circle of Life celebration extra special and extra magickal this year!

In Loving Memory of Matthew J. Adams

Love Through Eternity

By Marian Cerdeira

I don't remember how or why I first saw that lovely profile photo of a couple on Facebook, yet every time I glanced at it, I was drawn to Ez and Dixie. Above it was a headshot of him in a ball cap, his warm blue eyes causing me to linger in a certain feeling I connected with.

After their photo popped up again and again, I felt compelled to follow my intuition and tell them how much I could feel their love for one another. Dixie responded to me and sadly explained that this man with the imploring eyes had passed away.

Suddenly, it dawned on me…Ez had been trying to get my attention to contact Dixie. As a medium, I had connected with souls who had transitioned, but this was quite different. As she told me about their extraordinary love for one another, it all made sense. Ez had decided that I was going to help him communicate with her. And to this day, Dixie and I (with Ez's prompting) enjoy a beautiful friendship.

Dixie messaged me one day and said, "Hello, my friend. It has been four years today since my darlin' left." (I was familiar with the term "darlin'," which is how I'd "heard" Ez lovingly refer to Dixie.)

I told her that I had been thinking of him that very morning. I said, "I have the sense that you keep him with you in your heart and mind, and he has the strength and the energy to remain with you, Dixie. Not everyone who passes over can be with their loved ones who are here. It takes a strong energy to do that, and Ez has made himself learn to do it. A remarkable man of his word…he said he would always be with you, and he is!"

She confirmed what I was receiving and lovingly said, "I know he is. I couldn't have coped without him."

The Gift of an Angel

By Carol Metz

Life truly is a journey with pivotal destination bubbles (PDBs) along the way that create learning possibilities. Every moment, life is a process – whether it be living in the present or living from a default identity created by limiting beliefs and the conditioning of childhood.

There are moments in one's life vividly riveted in memory that can become a PDB. Father's Day on June 16, 2013, was such a day for me. I was deep in meditation when a spiritual leader asked three questions: 1) Who has been your most notable teacher? 2) Who has been your best lover, whether current or past? 3) Who has been your biggest supporter throughout your life?

Suddenly, tears of both grief and joy streamed down my face. My heart pounded. My soul was on fire. A voice inside said that my father has always been my biggest supporter in my life. At that moment, I felt his presence so strongly with his love wrapped around me. Instantaneously, I was plunged into the depths of grief and spiraled into the magic of bliss. I felt the fear, the grief, and the love, and I knew that this was where I was supposed to be.

I wondered how this could be happening. My father died in 1984.

Everyone experiences grief. It's a complicated ebb and flow. For me, this magical moment – this PDB – clarified the emotion of unexplainable love that I had consciously struggled to understand. It opened pathways and challenged me to explore possibilities within and to live fully in the moment.

What you choose to do with the PDBs that come into your life creates your future and the foundation for what's possible or even allowable in your life.

Hugs from Brandon

By Katie Jackson

I attended an incredible personal-development seminar a month after my son's death. On the first day of the event, I noticed a guy whose name tag read *Brandon*. Ahhh…a wink from God that my son, Brandon, is still with me in spirit! The second day, we did a hugging exercise. After giving and receiving many hugs (in a room of 300 people), the guy named Brandon stood before me ready for a hug. A few tears ran down my face as we embraced. No words were exchanged; we just looked into each other's eyes after the hug. One day later, we repeated the exercise, but I didn't encounter Brandon.

The following morning, I awoke with a heavy heart and my son, Brandon, on my mind. It dawned on me that I had not seen any butterflies, dragonflies, or hawks since arriving in Arizona. After Brandon's passing, I saw these creatures daily. They brought so much peace, reminding me that his spirit is free now.

Later, at the conference, it was time to exchange hugs. Providentially, I crossed paths with Brandon and we hugged. This time I got choked up and began to cry. We stepped back, held hands, and gazed into each other's eyes (as part of the activity). I felt my son staring at me. After a bit, Brandon let go of my hands and embraced me again. I cried and mourned.

That evening, I saw Brandon at a party. I asked if we could talk a minute. I explained to him that my son named Brandon had passed a month earlier. The hugging exercise was so emotional for me because I could sense my son's presence in Brandon's hugs and in his eyes.

The next morning was the last day of the seminar. One last time, while everyone exchanged hugs, Brandon appeared before me. Now he understood the significance of his hug. Once again, tears flowed from my eyes as we hugged each other.

I got to hug my son, Brandon, and look into his eyes the night before his death. I will always remember his beautiful smile and eyes and our embrace when we said goodbye for the last time. It occurred to me that instead of seeing God's creatures in Arizona, I received hugs from Brandon!

Writing to Heal

By Mauri Barnes

I began to write after my mother died. While dealing with the finality of death, I wrote in a journal as if I were writing a letter to her. It helped me to heal on those wintry New Jersey days. I was stunned, wondering where to begin with the overwhelming task of disassembling her home, her belongings, and her life. Sitting in her living room in front of a fire, I wrote to her of my despair.

She had been preparing to visit me in Florida, and everything was packed near the door for her road trip. Then she had fallen, injuring herself badly enough that she had to delay her trip. Two weeks later, unexpectedly, she died.

Admittedly, ours was not the best of relationships. One of the reasons I moved to Florida was to get far away from her influence. Now that she was gone, it comforted me to write the words I had never spoken. Anger and regret flowed onto the pages of my journal, along with stories about what was happening in my life. I had questions and asked for her help with the job she had assigned me in her will. It was my duty to pack up her condo and sell or distribute everything she'd owned. This was a terrible assignment, and I needed her help.

She began to respond. Missing things were found. People showed up with answers to questions. Letting go became easier. The burden eased as I boxed up her memories. Mom worked her magic.

Miraculously, her condo sold very quickly, even as our country slipped into a recession and real estate sales plummeted. I recognized her influence when the buyers reported that they had given the new address to their physician who recognized it as Mom's address. She had been his office nurse in Pennsylvania for many years until she retired. Without a doubt, I believe she helped close that deal.

Writing has been a healing practice for me. And now, years later, I am still writing letters to Mom.

Dad's Visit

By Karen Wythe

Where do messages come from? They sprinkle down from the heavens just when we need them. Sometimes they are premonitions, an awareness of something to come. Sometimes they are an impression from the other side of life: the thoughts of a deceased loved one guiding us, nudging us in a specific direction or just saying we're on the right track.

I recall a day after my mother had major surgery and was staying with me. We were in deep conversation when I had a strong feeling to tell my mom I really appreciated her. That felt so odd. In our family, we never made exchanges like that. Oh, we said "I love you" or "Thanks," but never "I appreciate you."

Nevertheless, I blurted it out: "Mom, I really appreciate you." Right when I said these words, I had a really strong feeling of my deceased father's approval. It felt like a warm hug, the kind he used to give me. I could just see his sunny smile filled with happiness. At that moment, there was a loud knock on the front door right next to me.

Mom said, "You'd better answer that."

I opened the door, but no one was there. My youngest daughter was working on something in the back of her car just across the driveway. I asked her, "Who was at the door?"

She answered, "Nobody."

Baffled, I inquired, "Are you sure?"

"Really, no one was there." she responded.

To this day, I believe it was my dad making sure I understood that the message was from him. I know he still guides me and is always close.

One thing is certain: messages abound. Hopefully, we are wise enough to embrace them.

The Box of Words

By Tanya Levy

I was feeling discouraged. I have a chronic dry eye condition called Fuchs Dystrophy, and I had a painful abrasion that required me to wear a Band-Aid contact lens for several weeks. I was trying to be as quiet as possible to help my eye heal, so I spent a lot of time meditating and praying. Thankfully, my eye was healing, but I was scared about the future of my vision and about the impact of my condition on my daily life and work.

One day while meditating, I had a vision. My dad, who passed away in April 2017, came to me. He told me that my power was in words, had always been in words, and not to forget that. Then he said, "The box of words – always have a box of words with you." A few days later, I saw a post on Instagram about a Word Box class offered online by a Canadian artist. It felt like another message to keep writing and creating with words.

I enrolled in the course. I painted my box of words in purple and dark blue, and I added glitter. I looked through magazines and clipped out words that mattered to me. I made smaller boxes to hold more words for specific goals.

I still pull words when I am writing or creating to focus my work. I place them on my altar or use them as a guide for writing. When my creative muse is quiet or I get discouraged about my health, I turn to the box of words. It has its own special magic – the magic of encouragement, love, and hope. Whenever I reach for my magical box of words, I feel like my dad is right there beside me, encouraging me from the other side. He always encouraged me, and that has not stopped with his passing. I feel his love every time I hold the magical box of words.

So Many Questions

By Nick Rafter

I had so many questions.

Growing up Catholic, I just kind of accepted that after death, we go to Heaven and are reunited with our loved ones.

But what if it wasn't true? One December night, it suddenly didn't make sense. If I'm reunited with my loved ones, such as my parents, and my loved ones are also reunited with theirs, that's thousands of generations.

The afterlife had always seemed to be a chance to live again. Whatever I lost in this life would return after I passed over. The traditions that ended could come back to me in the next life. If I went blind, I'd get to see again.

But what if none of that was true?

What if I never see my grandmothers again? What if after my mom passes, I never see her again? What if death is just staring into blackness for all eternity? I felt my heart race, my face sweat, my breathing get loud and heavy. I was having an anxiety attack.

While writing about this experience online to share with others, in hopes of alleviating my anxiety, it hit me like a cooling breeze on a summer afternoon.

What if the afterlife is something only *we* experience? What if we don't live parallel afterlives? You may be in mine, but perhaps I'm not in yours. My grandmother is reunited with her grandmother, but not me, since I didn't know her. Unless I wanted her there.

The concept was comforting. I wondered if this idea was planted in my mind by my late grandmothers. They were rebellious women in life, the types who would break the rules to comfort their grandson. Did they slip the truth about the afterlife to me? I needed a sign.

Suddenly, out of the corner of my eye, I saw a shadow. I jumped, thinking someone or something was in the room with me. Then, a calming feeling came over me.

It was the sign I needed from Lena and Millie. They slipped me the secret. I had so many questions about the afterlife, and those who are there gave me some answers.

Messages from the Lady in the Doorway

By Mimi Quick

It was another ordinary day for this 10½-year-old: playing with friends, having dinner with family, and then off to bed. After saying my prayers, I went straight to sleep, but something strange happened this night that I will always remember.

I woke up out of the blue and heard my name being called: "Mimi, Mimi." I peeked over the top of my blanket and rubbed my eyes but didn't see anything or anyone. I looked around again just to make sure. Still, no one. Then I felt goosebumps all over my body, letting me know there was a spirit nearby and it had a loving message for me. You see, I had been able to see spirits and communicate with them since I was three, so this was sort of normal for me.

As the energy grew stronger and thicker, I peeked out from my blanket again. This time there was someone there: a woman standing right in my doorway wearing a robe. She didn't move, but I could hear her words in my mind. She shared detailed messages of events that were going to happen in my life and said don't be afraid. She told me that I would be moving, my parents were going to divorce, and many other things that would happen.

In the morning after I woke up, I told my mom and she asked how I knew this information. I said the woman in the doorway told me last night. Her eyes grow big with amazement. My parents sat me down and shared their plans with me because they said you already know so why keep it from you. I did move, my parents separated, and everything else the woman shared with me that night came true.

We can say she was a spirit guide, an angel, or a spirit. I never saw her again, but I did see others who have had many messages to share with me and, if you're open to hear them, with you too.

Near-Death Experience, the Divine Message

By Katie Keck Chenoweth

It was the defining moment of my life, a turn of events that put me into the flow. As my temperature rose to 105°, intense convulsions gave way to fever-induced nightmares. Instead of cottony clouds, these dreams were filled with murky grays, blacks, and devilish reds. In the ambulance, I awoke to beeping monitors, tubes, a dry-as-desert sore throat, and hallucinations. I felt dead. Stillness. ICU isolation. Visitors with masks and gowns. Lying there day after day, in and out of life. The priest brought in for last rites.

Morning broke, and I became aware of my grandpa's presence in the room. I talked to him, knowing that my mother sat on the edge of the bed, not understanding. Her father had died 15 years earlier. He spoke to me clearly: "I'm here for you. There is something you need to decide. Come with me if you want; it's up to you." All I felt was love. "If you stay, there is something you must do to be of service in the world. It is your choice, no judgment." Floating in a sea of bliss between two worlds was the most peaceful I had ever felt. I wanted to release the body of pain, but something in me resonated with staying on Earth to make a difference.

After two weeks in the ICU, I was released to recover my life. One evening, my housemate and I were watching TV when Dr. Elizabeth Kübler-Ross introduced a new field of study: near-death experience (NDE). My housemate said, "That's what happened to you when you saw your grandfather – not hallucinations!" He confirmed that my chance of dying that day had been 60%.

From that pivotal moment, doors opened that were once closed. College now made sense. I became a pioneer in the wellness movement, a leader in HIV/AIDS education, and later, in therapeutic massage. What I know for sure: I was released from fear of death and introduced to the life of service that I am still fulfilling, and it all started with Grandpa's divine message: "You are always on the right path. Every path is the right one. There is no judgment, only choice."

Who Will Mourn Her?

By Kathy Sullivan Evans

As she lay on the bed in the corner next to the window, she became fixated on the blue jay perched on the roof. He was singing his heart out. Was he calling out to his mate or a fellow blue jay to come over? Or were his morning calls for the woman's benefit – to let her know she wasn't alone? Whatever the cause of this morning music, it was all she heard for a few blissful moments.

This was her second day in hospice care, and the staff was so wonderfully caring, making sure that every request was taken to heart. She so appreciated their attention, but her heart was heavy as she lay alone in this room that was meant to bring a sense of peace to all who enter but instead carried a cloud of despair.

For her, there was no family to hold her hand or sit with her. Her lifetime of healthy living with no smoking, no drinking, and a vegan lifestyle had enabled her to attain a long life as a centenarian. But as she lay there pondering her life, she questioned whether it was worth it since all her loved ones were not there for her witness and comfort. Who's left to tell her story and share her joys and sorrows from a lifetime of traveling the world, raising a family, enjoying a successful career, and having grandkids who brought her the greatest love she could ever have dreamed of?

Then, her body grew tired and seemed to fall away. She became lighter and stronger as she floated above the activities around her. She found herself flying with the blue jay, and his songs filled her head as she began to experience an unexpected bright light filled with an overwhelming love. Lo and behold, there was a pulling to the horizon where all her loved ones were there to greet her with their heavenly faces smiling. At that moment, mourning her passing didn't matter. She had her loved ones for an eternity.

The Other Side of Healing

By Chadi Hemaidan

Three years after my dad passed away, he sent me loving guidance from the other side. During a sound meditation, I felt a deeply moving energy enter my body and take over my thoughts and feelings. I sensed that I was being guided closer to something beautiful and loving.

In my mind's eyes, I saw myself in a boat, which was next to another boat with a young man sitting in it. This man was facing away from me, but I could tell that he was familiar. I waited for him to turn to face me, but he didn't. I moved my boat so that I could see his face and was startled to find myself gazing at a much younger version of my dad, looking exactly like a photo I have of him when he was just 24.

I called to him, "Dad! Dad! It's me, your son, Chadi!"

At first, he didn't answer. A few seconds later, though, he turned to face me, and we stared at each other with pure joy.

"Do you remember me, Dad?" I asked.

I wasn't sure how he could possibly recognize me, especially because I was nearly twice his age at that time. But miraculously, the look in his eyes told me he knew who I was. He didn't have to say a word; the message came through as clearly as the blue sky: It was okay. I could move on. I didn't need to carry on this path of sadness any longer. I could let it go and bring myself to a place of joy.

As the meditation came to an end, I opened my eyes and realized that tears were running down my cheeks. Receiving this loving guidance from my dad helped to take away my pain and allowed me to move toward healing. Now, thanks to this message, I've found myself more readily able to let go and cry when I need to, and I can finally let myself heal.

Turning My Tears into Goldfish

By Carolyn Boatman

"Got to get back to the land and set my soul free.
We are stardust, we are golden, we are billion-year-old carbon,
and we've got to get ourselves back to the garden." – Joni Mitchell

Joni Mitchell's lyrics are among my favorites, and I've been singing them for years. Upon the loss of my granddaughter to a heroin overdose in October 2017, I learned to allow the lyrics to grow within my soul. Grief is a journey with no destination and no arrival, just a reinvention of self. This eruption of physical emotion cascades into living richness that is an adventure in abundantly allowing.

How would I live with this darkness? Would I plant a garden or would I sink into a pit of despair? Barefoot on the earth, I began to walk every morning into fields of green grass where horses graze. The love song of birds, wind, and earth began to heal the pain in my heart. By resisting, I denied myself a precious gift. By allowing, I summoned a new way to grow my garden of joy in my soul. Physical emotion versus soul power became a new curiosity for me. My physical would forever miss my granddaughter's touch. My soul would allow her spirit to be recognized and cherished. This willingness to abundantly allow reinvented me.

One morning while standing shoreside at my favorite pond, in the brightest of magic and miracle, there came a manifestation of my granddaughter. She stood in front of me, smiling; then she turned and dove into the pond. Upon entry, she transformed into thousands of goldfish. And then, she quickly reappeared by my side. I heard her whisper, "Let your tears become goldfish, Grandma. You have much to do, and I will help you."

My tears have become goldfish. In her memory, I create meditations of awareness, compassion, and abundantly allowing. My physical still cries for her touch, but my soul visits with her spirit, and my garden blooms abundantly with joy.

Priestessing My Daughter's Death

By Debra Sawers

I want to tell you about my daughter's last hours and how we crossed back and forth as priestesses of now and before.

Jessie loved Egypt and studied and loved the ancient Egyptian goddess Isis. We knew we were from Isis's time and had probably been together then.

Near the end of Jessie's life, I sat with her each day, calling on Isis, the great physician and healer. I called her to our circle to heal, and she did. For days, Jessie had tiny improvements, but then it happened: I harked back to priestess teachings of non-interference and of the soul's desire and the contracts with Goddess.

I called on Hecate for guidance and Aphrodite for love. Jessie squeezed my hand and opened one eye as I did invocation. I called on Great Mother to welcome my child back if that is what she wanted. I told Jessie, "We know and travel the other realms. If you need to go, then go, my darling. Go to Great Mother."

The very next day when I got there, they told me her life was expiring. I asked, "How do I priestess this transition?" and it all came to be: I sang her to the other side in a language I did not recognize. I hummed the chakra hums into her tiny ear and called Great Mother. I simultaneously held space for life and death…and then heard no heartbeat.

I remember the moment her heart stopped and mine kept on.

I stayed with Jessie and bathed her as was the tradition of the olde ones. I braided her hair (another family tradition), signifying body, mind, and spirit as one. I memorized her body, thanking her uterus for my three grandsons and blessing the baby she still had inside. I traced her ears and tiny collarbone. I thanked her mouth for all the truths she told. I memorized her like I did when she was born.

As I turned her to the side, I saw a new tattoo: Anubis, there to help her cross over to Isis and Mother.

Praise be to Great Mother as she welcomed her priestess back.

Unrequited Love

By Connie Theoharis

We tend to downplay supernatural events when they happen to us. That is how we are programmed; we are ridiculed and scoffed for entertaining such frivolity.

I recently purchased a home. As I was unpacking, I began reflecting on someone who'd been in my life 46 years ago. I remembered the days we spent together at the carnival, rope swinging at the local creek. The last time I saw him, he had asked me to marry him. I declined the proposal. We never saw each other again.

The morning after I had these reflections, I received a phone call that he had died unexpectedly the day before.

I kept replaying the times we'd shared, with an accompanying feeling of heaviness and all-encompassing sadness. A deep well of hopelessness overcame me. Days passed, and the all-pervading despair persisted. I would jot down on paper in random places how desperate and heavy I was feeling.

A few days later, I was walking at a church sale. It was raining, so most tables were covered with tarps. I picked up a corner of one tarp and found the movie *Ghost*. It occurred to me that I had begun thinking of him around the time he'd died.

At midnight, I emailed a friend and medium, explaining the 24/7 obsessive thoughts and feelings. I asked if his spirit was with me. The next morning, her email arrived: "He has a message for you. Talk to him and find out what it is, and he will move on."

My initial thought was, "How do I talk to him?" I realized I had been picking up on his thoughts and feelings. His message was, "I always loved you." A few moments later, the phrase "unrequited love" came into my mind. That evening, I heard him clearly say, "I'll say goodbye now" – and the heaviness lifted. As I walked down the stairs, the overhead light began to flicker, becoming dimmer and dimmer until a very faint light remained.

The following day, a song came on the radio called "I Will Find You." My body shivered with clear feeling (clairsentience), knowing that the song was from him. I wondered: How did he find me? And I knew: Soul consciousness transmutes but never dies.

Meeting My Ancestors

By Tanya Levy

I sit quietly in my Therapeutic Touch Level Two course. We do an exercise where we ask if the blockage we're experiencing is from before birth or after birth. I am told it is from before birth. I then ask, "How many generations back?" I am told that I have been carrying the pain for seven generations. Uh-oh, so clearly I was a caretaker in the past, too!

That night, I get up to use the bathroom and hear singing. The next morning, I ask if anyone else in the group heard the singing woman in the bathroom. No one else had. "It must have been Sarah," I said. I have had glimpses before of a woman with blonde hair who told me she was my ancestor and that her name was Sarah.

Fast-forward to my first singing-bowl massage. Sarah comes to me again. Dancing and twirling, she takes me through cobblestone streets and shows me glimpses of her handsome, dark-haired husband. She tells me in pictures and nudges that I saw too much of the pain and not enough of the joy. "You were here, and we survived it," she tells me. She is surrounded by beautiful golden energy.

She takes me to meet the life scribes in our family. They sit in a circle, scribing in the sun on canvases. She tells me, "This is your legacy. You are this generation's life scribe, and you are never alone with your words." I thank her, and she is gone.

I go to finish my Therapeutic Touch Training, Level Three. I receive a treatment, and Jacob comes to me. He tells me he is Sarah's husband. He takes me down many stairs to a room. He opens the door, and there are shelves of stories. He tells me, "You can write about the joy, but you cannot forget about the pain. You must write about everything, all of it. I will give you two things to remember. First, my crystallized tear; second, this red thread to tie on your finger so you remember to write it all." I promise him I will, and he is gone.

I am truly grateful that Sarah and Jacob helped guide me.

A GPS Sent from Heaven

By Isabella Rose

"Victor, I am so sorry," I said out loud, fighting back tears of disappointment and defeat. "I really wanted to be with your mom to celebrate your birthday and show my support, but I can't find her. I don't know what else to do but to go home. I give up."

I had exhausted all possible options I could think of. I thought I had arrived at the correct location, having typed the given address into my GPS. There were cars parked in the parking area, but I didn't recognize anyone. Unsure that I was in the correct place, I sent Victor's mom a message and hoped she would receive it.

I didn't want to be late, so I backed up and drove through the cemetery gates. Toward the top of the hill I saw a gathering. I stopped and rolled down my window and asked, "Is this the Birthday in Heaven celebration for Victor?" showing the man the address on my GPS. He informed me it was not and to try the cemetery down the street.

Both sides of the street were lined with cemeteries, and as far as I could see, there wasn't a car in sight. I pulled over to the side at one of the entrances and looked up the number for the cemetery. I called the number and explained my situation to the answering service. She took my information and told me someone would call me back as soon as possible.

I decided to try the cemetery across the street. I followed the road to the end, but still didn't find the right place. I didn't know what else to do, so I began talking to Victor. I looked up and saw a woman bicycling out of the woods toward where I was parked. She stopped, and I got out of my car and asked her for help. When I arrived at my destination, I saw that she had given me the exact directions to where I needed to be. It was then I knew that Victor had sent this woman to help me.

In Loving Memory of Victor Vernon

The Guidance to Give

By Jenny McKaig Speed

"She told me to tell you she's here and she loves you."

I can't remember if my cousin broke down crying or just had relief release across his face, like the weight lifted in a moment.

"I can't tell you how much that means to me. I have been missing her so much this week."

I had felt it so clearly. We were at my grandfather's funeral, our family having lost too many too young, and then later the monarch of our family passing. We had seen so many funerals that we all sort of knew our customary way of being. We talked, consoled one another, hugged, cried, laughed, told stories. For our family, it is the going through it together that matters.

I was in such a state of flow around that time. My intuition was at one of its all-time strongest points. I was meditating regularly and trusting the intuitive guidance I received. I not only heard words but felt them. I received guidance as to what I needed to say and do at any given moment.

When I was standing in the funeral parlour with my cousin just feet from me, I opened myself to a new level of vulnerability and simply shared what I was hearing. "Your mom is here," I said.

It wasn't one of those kind-things-to-say moments. It wasn't the stereotypical "she's looking down on us from Heaven" thing to say. I really felt her. I felt her presence so strongly and received the words to say. "Tell him I'm here and I love him," she said.

My cousin melted. I don't remember if he crumbled in my arms, if he cried, or if he just melted in his energy. But I felt and saw the relief on his face.

"You have no idea how much I've been missing her," he said.

I had no idea; he was right. I only knew what I felt. Her presence was palpable, and she guided me to share with him that she was there watching over him and that she loved him.

My aunt had passed years before we stood together that day at my grandfather's funeral. But there she was, moving through me and giving loving grace to my cousin who needed it so deeply.

Chapter 2
Soulful Signs

S o many of us have received a soulful sign at one point in our lives. Maybe we asked the universe to let us know which path we should take – to send a sign that would help make our decision super clear – and we ended up receiving exactly that. Or maybe we were missing a loved one extra and asked them to send us a sign that they were still with us, and we received the perfect message from them that helped us know without a doubt that they were still right by our side.

Even though the two of us have received many signs throughout our lives, we're still always amazed when they show up. They're like little miracles that connect us to what's possible in our universe – to another realm that we have such little knowledge of but that gives us hope that something bigger than ourselves is out there. We've had our furry kids and our human loved ones send very clear signs after they passed, letting us know that they were okay and that they were still with us. We've had rain pour down and sunbeams show up and dragonflies surround us, which were always just what we needed to help us on our journey.

As we share throughout this chapter, signs can appear in many different ways, from the lyrics of a song playing at the perfect time, to rainbows appearing exactly when we most needed them to, to butterflies showing up to let us know that our loved ones are still with us, to the clock showing the perfect number that resonates in our soul. Signs are as unique as we are. And the same sign will have very different meaning for each person. That's why it's so important that we pay close attention to possible signs that may be appearing around us, ask our soul if the sign resonates, and if it does, allow ourselves to take it into our heart and keep it there forever.

Signs are such powerful messages, and we hope that after reading this chapter you'll be inspired to look for your own signs!

Butterflies Speaking

By Jenean Zunk

I was sitting there staring at the ceiling, wondering if I had just made the biggest mistake of my life. Three days earlier, I had walked away from my career, my marriage, and my home. My brain kept saying, "I mean, really – who does that?! You could have tried harder. Giving up like that was wrong. You should have…"

But my heart. My heart was telling a different story.

After years of denial, I had finally admitted to myself that the life I was living – the life I had created – was killing my soul. I *had* to walk away.

So there I sat: 38, broke and in debt, a shattered marriage, living at my parents with no idea what to do or where to go from there. Utterly overwhelmed by my situation and exasperated by the unending chatter in my mind, I did the only thing I could think to do: I called on my angels.

I shared that I needed some validation from outside my own head, and I asked for a sign – one that was obvious and undeniable, telling me that I was on the right path. I tried to think of something specific. Something that is possible to see, but that I don't see often.

"A butterfly," I said. "Show me a butterfly today, and I will know it is from you. I will know you are telling me I am on the right path."

After saying that, I thought it would be difficult, as I had no intention of leaving the house that day, but I decided that the angels would figure it out. I jumped on the computer to begin job hunting.

About 30 minutes later, fully immersed in my job search, I heard a loud noise outside. I opened the front door to investigate, and I froze. There, swarming my front yard, were butterflies – lots and lots of butterflies. There must have been at least 30-40 of them just flying around the front yard.

At that moment, in stunned silence and with tears in my eyes, all I could think to do was to whisper, "Thank you."

Ready to Shine?

By Angela Mia La Scala

Walking in the light isn't always easy. I thought it was a shortcut leading to peace, smiles, and a welcoming world of bliss that would instantly heal me and those I loved! To some degree it is, but it comes with many lessons.

I am always aspiring to be the best version of myself, lending a helping hand, an open ear, a compassionate heart, a lantern to someone drawn to my flame. So why the pockets of darkness and doubt? Why do some teachers appear cloaked in shadows? Quickly, these thoughts spiral me into an abyss of disappointment and the desire to quit.

I call out, "What did I do wrong? Why do I feel abandoned, unsupported, and cast out? Am I a fool for believing? A light trapped in the darkness?"

That night, I close my eyes and repeat the questions. Somewhere between dream state and waking, I remember someone offering me a glass of orange juice. I politely accept. I wake up startled, thinking that that was strange!

A couple of hours later, a truck is stuck in front of me on my way to work. There's nowhere for me to go, so I sit and wait. I think, "Great, another roadblock!"

In my boredom, I read the wrap on the truck, and the words strike me like a bolt of lightning: "Ready to Shine?" I sit in awe, staring at these words, which are followed by an image of a glass of orange juice!

With a flick of a light switch, my spirits lift and darkness dissipates. Smiling, I surrender and say, "Yes, I am ready to shine!"

It's in darkness that we meet our greatest teachers, and where our angels patiently wait for us to trust. That day, my angels pulled me from that darkness, reminding me of who I am and why I'm here! They showed me a piece of myself that was yearning to be rescued from the deep abyss. Its name was Doubt. Once Doubt was acknowledged and honored, it became Faith. And it's in Faith where we are ready to shine!

The Seven-Word Miracle

By Greg Lee

I sat in shock as I took in my boss's words, "Your services will no longer be needed." After eight years at this music software company, it had become obvious that for me it was more about financial opportunity than passion.

We had just moved, bought a new house, and were sending our five-year-old to kindergarten at a new school. The timing was bizarre, but even with the challenges created by this sudden loss, I felt a sense of freedom and relief.

Would this be the time I'd allow myself to follow my dreams? Or would I just paint the inside of our new house for a couple of months? The answer: yes and yes!

Ten years earlier, on my wedding day, my college piano professor had asked, "Greg, what are you going to do now?" My response was quick and simple: Music and massage.

But as we got closer to having a family, I began to doubt my ability to make enough money doing massage, and music had not turned up much opportunity. So, I got a job…and now that job was gone.

It was time to step back into the dream, and as I did, miracles began to happen. My dear wife, Antonia, had given me gift certificates for massage, unknowingly with the woman who coordinated workshops for the master Hawaiian Lomilomi massage teacher who would mentor and assist my re-entry into a successful 25-year (and counting) career in the healing arts.

I remember the first day of class when, in traditional Hawaiian form, he talked all morning, then broke for a long potluck lunch, and finally began hands-on demonstrations. Transfixed, I watched as his hands did what mine had always done but with the wisdom of ancestors and ancient times. I eagerly took it in.

Just days after the Lomilomi class, I began working with clients, placing the list of instructions on their backs as I learned this new form of what was already so deeply in my bones from birth. Following my dreams had guided me to my destiny.

I was home.

Love Yourself

By Amy Coppola

For years, I read and researched "how to love yourself." Google's reply is "to accept yourself as you are and to come to terms with those aspects of yourself that you cannot change. It means to have self-respect, a positive self-image, and unconditional self-acceptance."

Sometimes a simple (secretly soulful) message like an invitation could lead to learning to love yourself and experiencing something more significant than you ever anticipated. Decisions about these invitations could focus on finding your life's purpose. Three life-changing messages illustrate this truth.

One of my friends invited me to participate in a New Year's visioning workshop with her. There, I met the instructor who continues to support my ongoing adventure of becoming an author – including hosting a Women's Tuscan Writing Retreat, writing stories for this book, and completing my own upcoming book!

While I was living in Denver, another life-changing message arrived in the form of an invitation for a weekly meeting for Coaching & Confidence. A local life coach had set up a Meetup to provide coaching and confidence for women. The group's leader eventually became my life-coach instructor, retreat leader, and an ongoing coach in my life.

I experienced another significant turning point thanks to leadership training, which I have attended throughout my career. Because of this, I met another longtime mentor and friend. He provided an opportunity to speak in Colorado Springs, which catapulted my participation in the National Speaker's Association (NSA). There I met dynamic, successful speakers to emulate, which sparked my journey to becoming a professional speaker.

As I live my life's purpose with greater joy, I realize that loving yourself is not a one-time event. It's about being open to allowing and accepting the messages that come through an invitation from strangers who become friends, mentors, and coaches. These inspiring, soulful messages helped fine-tune and refocus my purpose to write, coach, and speak. The resulting feeling of self-love empowers me to help others take action and find joy in their purpose. One day you will wake up and realize that you're meant for greater things…to love yourself!

Smile and Savor the Experience

By Nora Rose

What is a sign from a loved one? It could be a song that played just when you were thinking about them. It could be that you found a coin or a feather, or a dragonfly flew around to get your attention.

When you love deeply and someone you love dies, you miss them and they know your heartache. They see you struggling and want to let you know they are free of pain and suffering. They want you to remember all the good parts of their life, not just the end. They don't want you to feel sad, so they give you a sign.

One day, I tried to explain this to my aunt (my mom's sister) and her daughter as we all missed my mom very much. The electric company came out to check the meters. As I signed a form, out of nowhere was a *ping* sound on one of the shovels near us. The worker said, "That was weird!" I smiled and glanced toward the shovels and immediately knew it was my mom letting me know she was here to make sure everything was going to be just fine. My aunt listened, and my cousin had a look of fright on her face.

Three years later, my aunt's husband passed away. As we visited, I asked if my uncle had given her any signs. She enthusiastically told me how she was sitting outside on the swing missing him, and a butterfly flew around her and then landed on her hand. She beamed, knowing it was him. At that moment, a butterfly fluttered past the window as if to wave and say, "I'm still here!"

Stay open to the messages. These signs provide a power within you, a deep knowing that nothing can steal your joy. You will experience an unconditional love that settles into your soul and wraps you in a hug from the other side. Death may have a new meaning.

Because you know the signs now, when you see them, everyone will feel your loving heart and see your glow.

Trusting the Signs

By Annie Price

Soulful messages can be revealed to us in a variety of ways; the timing of how and when a message is delivered depends on the person receiving it. We may not always understand the message right away – needing the passage of time to see the divine bigger picture in what initially felt like a mystery.

Since I was a young girl, I was drawn to mysteries of all kinds, including scary tales and television shows with Rod Serling. Sometimes, when my parents and relatives were visiting, the talk would shift to eerie stories that appeared to have no explanation. They were often described in detail that was intended to have you sitting on the edge of your seat – maybe with the added bonus of goosebumps and needing the lights on at bedtime.

My curiosity continued through the years, and I read much about the "woo-woo" – extraordinary capabilities and other parts of the human experience that we still don't understand. I've found that these mysteries require trust and faith in a higher power and in your own inner guidance, no matter where it may lead you.

A few years ago, I began seeing the number 1 on a regular basis, mostly on clocks. For example, I'd see numbers like 11:00, or 11:11, or 1:11. I'd also see "11" in other places at unexpected times. This felt like more than mere coincidence; it seemed designed to get my attention. I looked up what these numbers might mean and discovered that "11:11" is the number of spiritual awakening. It's a good sign, full of great potential – a sign that you're on the right path and your actions are aligned with your soul's purpose. When you see this sign, I learned, you can expect major changes in your life and should stay open and grounded, show gratitude, and ask for guidance when you need it.

Your soulful message may pull you in a direction you'd ordinarily avoid, and the true essence of the message may take time to fully process. But keep following the signs and trust that it will all make sense someday.

A Spiritual Sign to Keep Trusting

By Lindsey Gaye Walker

Most of us are familiar with the Me Too movement, which shines a light on sexual assault and harassment. I now add my voice and say "Me too" to explain the sexual harassment I experienced and why I turned away from a career in the theatre at the age of 18.

While it broke my heart to let go of my dream, my husband-to-be helped me through it. With his encouragement, I went back to school and got a BA in psychology. I also had four beautiful children with him. But our marriage didn't last, and at the age of 50, I found myself lost and alone, wondering where my life was going. As I meditated, I saw myself in a wonderful relationship, singing again, and speaking on stages to help raise human consciousness. Doubts came up, but I decided to follow the Law of Attraction teachings and did a daily visualization.

After my youngest son finished high school, we packed up my rented apartment in Vienna and moved to Canada, as he was to attend university there. Before leaving, I went online and joined different Meetup groups, one of them for songwriters. The head of that group welcomed me, and I felt a strong magnetic pull towards him. But when we eventually met, it was clear we had led very different lives, and I felt unsure. I decided to meet him one more time, thinking it would be the last. But at the train station, an old friend of his that he hadn't seen in years suddenly bumped into us and started telling me what a wonderful man and talented music producer he was. I saw it as a spiritual sign to keep trusting, so I did.

Since that time, we've come together in love and as an award-winning music duo. We call ourselves Unleashed Dreams and write original music to support people on their life path. I'm now taking steps to start a movement to help others manifest their dreams to support our world.

You Matter

By Kathy Sullivan Evans

It had been one of those days when nothing seemed to go right. The baby had been up all night with a fever. The children woke up in foul moods and didn't want to go to school. The toast burned. And just when I was about to say the words, "What else could go wrong?" I stopped myself because I know that the Law of Attraction is always at work, and whatever is put out there to the Universe will happen! But alas, it wasn't soon enough, because just as I picked up the baby and my purse to go, the baby's diaper sprang a leak and the front of my dress got soaked! Yes, it was one of those mornings that makes me wonder if there's a hidden camera somewhere and a smiling young millennial with no kids will jump out and say, "You've been punk'd!"

At work, it felt like my workspace, which had served as a respite from the daily toil of my personal life, was on the verge of chaos. I needed some quiet time to myself to recharge. At lunch, I visited the library to find a wonderful romance novel to take me away to foreign lands on an adventure with a gorgeous man who found me irresistible, despite having a faint smell of baby excrement!

As I was perusing the novels, I picked up one that looked interesting. Just as I was about to close the book and head to the counter, a small piece of paper stuck out from between the pressed pages. I opened up the book to see what it was, and there on a simple sticky note were the words that made my day take on a whole new perspective: "You matter."

It had to be a message from Spirit on that particular day to see the words that would turn my day around! Thank you to the kind soul who left this message for me. I will leave it there for the next soul who might need a reminder too!

Make Yourself Happy

By Maria Angela Russo

One day I came across a book entitled *Men Are Just Desserts: How Learning to Be a Woman with a Life of Your Own Can Enrich the Life You Share with a Man*. The author, Sonya Friedman, spoke to my search for independence within my 20-year marriage. Change threatened my husband, Stephen. He tried to do everything he could to squelch all signs of growth in me, strangling my spirit.

Repeatedly I told him I was unhappy. He finally responded, "Then find a way to make yourself happy, leaving me out of it. I'm perfectly fine the way things are." What he meant was, "Find a way that changes nothing for me."

I longed for a relationship with Stephen, but once he made it clear that he wanted to stay emotionally cut off from our life together, I knew that divorce was the only answer. This daunting decision came while in the throes of moving from Memphis to Detroit. Though I knew that counseling would help me, I didn't want to go through a string of therapists before finding a good fit. Seeking divine guidance, I prayed, "Give me a sign that will lead me to the right therapist."

Drawn to the *Ladies Home Journal* on a nearby coffee table, I recalled hearing about people who'd ask the Universe questions before opening a random book for answers. Deciding to give that a try, I picked up the magazine and dropped it on the floor. It fell open to Sonya Friedman's monthly column, which reminded me that she had a private psychotherapy practice in my new town.

When I called Dr. Friedman's office, the receptionist steered me toward her assistant, Dian, who had greater availability. I agreed to see her the following Tuesday.

Dian was exactly what I needed. She helped me face the hard questions, like "Are you sure about this?" and "How will you manage the drastic changes?" With dignity and compassion, she saw me through 11 months of transition until the divorce was final and my daughters and I moved back to Memphis.

Guiding by Numbers

By Ellouise Heather

I sat in quiet meditation on the cool grass with the sun on my face. Eventually, it was time to ask my question: Which path shall I take? Two equally appealing personal-growth courses, enrolling at the same time. When I opened my eyes, a bee was humming immediately before me. This creature was an archetype that one of the courses in question drew upon, and the archetype I most identified with at the time. Not only that, but bees had held symbolic meaning of my grandpop since I was a young girl.

This was one of the many anecdotes my mother had told me about her father, who sadly passed away when I was three months old. He'd been unwell for a long time and put up a noble fight. My mother would often recount that he had hung on just to meet me. I was preparing to arrive on this earth just as he was preparing to depart – a bittersweet synchronicity that would forever connect us.

Confident that my choice was made and curious about the exact investment I'd be making in myself, I decided to search online for the exchange rate of US dollars to my currency, British pounds sterling. I could hardly believe it when I saw the numbers! Not because it was expensive, but since the four digits were my grandpop's birthday!

This was not the first time his birthday digits had shown up in my life. Whenever I'd had a decision to make or had felt like I'd needed comfort or support over the previous two years, it had appeared like a great cosmic 2x4. Looking back over my life, I could recall specific periods where it had been there, such as the call-in telephone number for a favourite childhood television show.

Since taking that course three years ago, which I benefitted from immensely, there have been countless times I've seen those four digits and felt sure that my grandpop was there, encouraging and guiding me. Despite his physical absence, I am supremely grateful for his continuing presence in my life.

Rainbows from Heaven

By Angie Carter

Bella was only 19 months old when she died suddenly and unexpectedly. A few days after her death, the brightest, most beautiful rainbow appeared over the lake across from our house. I ran outside with my son, who was five years old at the time, and we both felt Bella's presence. In that moment, I felt my family was together again.

This was the first of many rainbows. For months after Bella's death, I would see one almost every day. They would appear not only in the sky but also in our home or other random places, sometimes with no logical explanation. I knew in my heart the rainbows were signs from Bella in Heaven, yet I needed reassurance.

Desperately wanting to connect with my daughter, I spoke with a medium who confirmed that Bella was communicating with me through rainbows. He also mentioned a piece of Bella's artwork, and I immediately knew he was referring to a drawing of a rainbow. I had assumed someone had drawn it for her at the daycare, but when I inquired about the drawing, I discovered that at 18 months old, Bella had independently drawn the rainbow herself with a mysterious rainbow crayon that was found at the daycare weeks later!

Rainbows continue to surround me and always appear at key moments, such as when we placed Bella's memorial bench by the lake, as we left the hospital after our ultrasound when we found out we were expecting a baby girl, and after our first dance on our wedding day.

I was struggling to cope as the fifth anniversary of Bella's death approached. Two days before the anniversary, I was leaving to say goodbye to my grandmother's house, which my family sold after she passed away earlier this year. As I left my driveway, I saw a huge double rainbow in the sky. I drove toward the rainbow and was in awe when I saw a second rainbow in the bottom one. I couldn't believe my eyes: a triple rainbow!

I can always count on my daughter to send me a sign when I need her most.

Christmas Sign and the Big Kahuna

By Kristy Carr McAdams

She was elegant and could talk to a shoe and get it to smile. I called her the "Big Kahuna," which Merriam-Webster defines as "a preeminent person or thing or a Hawaiian shaman." She was under five feet tall, and her love for people was so big. Meeting people gave her joy, and she would always strike up a conversation with strangers, giving them compliments.

She was my Nana. Over 50 years separated us, yet she was one of my best friends. Witty observations of life kept her going when the going got tough. One time as I was helping her get her winter coat on, she said to me, "This coat attracts more lint than men!" She also told me, "If someone ever offers you mint or gum, you should take it!" (In case you have bad breath and they are being polite about it!)

Two weeks before Christmas in 2016, we got the call from Florida, telling us she had passed away. In the numbness of mourning, I felt guided to go to a store I had never shopped in. I resisted but finally entered and wandered around aimlessly. I was ready to leave when I saw the mysterious reason I was guided there: a wooden sign reading, "Santa's watching, and so is Nana," tucked in among angel statues.

I wept openly, right there in the middle of the store. I literally had received a "sign" from Heaven. And it was placed in the middle of angel statues, to boot! (I teach angel workshops.)

As I stepped up to the register to buy it, I saw a tub of red and white mints. I had to smile through tears as I paid the cashier. From Heaven, I was getting reminders that there's love, light, and sometimes humor, even through the darkest moments.

I know that I will offer and accept mints unabashedly, with a smile, and remember that love lives on, infinitely. Big Kahuna wisdom.

A hui hou kakou ("Until we meet again" in Hawaiian)

Forward-Moving Memories

By Shannon L. Brokaw

*"We flicker on a screen; we fold and unfold upon the mind's eye.
Brittle as wings, eternal as a heartbeat. And even when the heart falls
silent, we do not cease to be, because in the end, we all become
memories." – Call the Midwife*

My dad had gone in for a simple, routine medical procedure and was to be released the next day. What happened next was not "in the plan." I found him in the morning, unresponsive and not breathing. He was gone.

Everything happened so fast that my family didn't have time to process what was happening. As the months passed, my family was repeatedly stung by the shock of despair and heartbreak, and I found myself stuck in a bubble of depression. I was missing him and couldn't see past the fog and ugly memories of the sound of his frail ribs cracking while I performed CPR. I kept reliving the moment when I came home and saw his empty hospice bed. Those memories were the only ones I could focus on.

Grief consumed me. It ate me up. I figured it was useless to look back on his memory because it was too painful, and he wasn't here. I smiled just so people thought I was doing fine.

One day, I hit the bottom and had had enough. I prayed for guidance to help me heal. While suffering from a bout of insomnia, I happened to come across a TED Talk on grief. The lady who was speaking said to talk like the person was still here, because you were actively keeping their memory alive. You weren't moving on; you were moving forward. I'm a huge believer in signs and knew that this was from my dad.

Ever since I watched that video, I've felt such a calming peace, and I've been able to talk freely about him, knowing that, although not in the physical, he still exists in forward-moving memories.

Billboards by the Roadside

By Martina E. Faulkner

Signs aren't always big billboards on the highway of life. Today, I see signs all the time, and I've learned to take notice. However, that's not how it used to be. I used to only recognize the glaringly obvious in the midst of the subtle. Thankfully, one blatant sign changed the entire trajectory of my life.

As I was going through a divorce and beginning a new relationship with an old friend, I questioned everything. He lived half a country away with an established life while I was stuck in the throes of instability.

Though far apart, we worked to build a life together. I started planning, researching, and making connections to move to his city. Then we had a big fight, and moving was off the table. Why, I asked myself, would I make such a complete change in my life for one man, especially knowing what I had been through in my marriage?

But instead of feeling resolve, I fell to pieces because I knew somewhere in my heart that I was meant to be there with him. As it turns out, the "with him" part was false, but necessary. The truth was that I was meant to be there to meet other people who would help me change my life forever, and forever be part of my life. I needed him to make me notice an actual sign in order to make this critical move.

When we met at 19, he was a member of a youth organization I had never heard of before. So, when I was running an errand sometime after our fight, and I saw a small cardboard sign advertising this organization on the side of the road, I took note. In that moment, I resolved to move to his town. The message from the Universe was unmistakable, because to this day I have never seen another sign for that organization.

It didn't work out with this man, but that wasn't the point. I made lasting relationships in my new town while also getting a master's degree, all of which altered the course of my life, putting me squarely back on my soul's path.

My "Angel" Song

By Jean Hendricks

I would look for signs that my angels were communicating with me. Usually I connected to them by either knowing or getting a feeling.

I began to notice that after a particular song played on the radio, something pleasant would happen to me. I felt it was a new way for the angels to get a message to me, to lift my spirits, to send hope and good vibes to my soul. I began journaling after I heard my "angel" song to track events and outcomes. My idea seemed correct!

One day, I was going to a job interview at a doctor's office near my home. I was excited about this job because it was a door opening for me in a field I was enamored with, and getting hands-on experience made my soul sing. My "angel" song came on, and I joyfully sang out loud, feeling reassured, relaxed, and not worried or nervous.

I arrived a few minutes early. Getting out of my car, I saw a distressed woman standing in front of her car that wouldn't start. I had to either choose to leave the woman stranded and be on time for my interview or help and risk being late. I chose to help her. We got her car started, and she left with a hug and good wishes.

I was late. And I entered the building thinking that this didn't look good. I began to worry but quickly recalled my "angel" song. I believed there was a higher purpose and a specific reason why I was delayed and shook off my doubts.

Sometimes we are faced with complex choices, but my soul said that I had made the right choice. I believed hearing my "angel" song was instrumental in keeping me positive. I apologized for being late to the interview, and although it was short, it went well. And with a handshake, they said they'd call to let me know either way. On the ride home, my "angel" song played again.

At the end of the day, the phone rang. Humming my "angel" song, I answered, listened, then said, "Thank you…I accept."

Mind Your Messages

By Karen Wythe

Do you know you are constantly sending messages to the Universe and that they are always heard? What influences how they are received is the tone in which you send them. Every day in every way, we project our innermost thoughts, ideas, and dreams as wishes that can come true. We generate so many that they can overlap and cancel each other out. This is why it is essential to know what we want to create in our lives and to develop sincerity, clarity, and focus. When we do, all the powers that be come together to support that magical miracle of creation.

One of my serendipitous creations came about in a very surprising way. I was a young, married mother of two girls. I did all I could to make ends meet. We got by, but I kept finding I didn't have money left over to buy myself new clothes. I was buying for growing kids and my husband. Putting myself last was not intentional; I just put them first.

One day, I sat daydreaming about having lots of money and putting myself first. I even remember the moment I said out loud, "What I need is a way to have money to spend only on myself."

Around that time, I read a magazine article saying that women need to empower themselves and create their own credit line to establish their financial viability. So, when a credit application came in the mail to a very high-end women's clothing store, I decided that it would be a safe card to have because I would never use it. I filled out the application, sent it in, and very quickly received my brand-new credit card.

Three weeks after receiving the card, I got a phone call from the store. "Ma'am, you opened a credit card with us."

I quickly interrupted by saying, "I haven't even used it yet." I was sure they wanted to tell me they made a mistake and canceled the card.

I could hear the smile in the woman's voice saying, "No, no, we don't want the card back. You were entered into a drawing, and you have won a $1,000 gift certificate, which has been applied to your credit card!"

I was shocked and overjoyed as I realized I could only spend this money on myself. To this day, I live in gratitude, knowing that what I sincerely ask for I receive in the most unexpected ways.

The God Who Sings

By Joy T. Barican

The challenges life throws at us can sometimes be too overwhelming to put into words. Whenever this happens, I find that the silence in my heart is a prayer only God can hear.

During one of these times of feeling overwhelmed and alone, I quivered in fear as I seated myself at a church service that was already in progress. The choice of hymns is usually based on the church calendar, so imagine my surprise when this service featured a hymn outside of the traditional theme or season. There is no doubt in my mind that it was indeed in response to my situation. With the title "Be Not Afraid," it felt like it was being sung just to me and for me. The lyrics are simple but the message so reassuring: "Be not afraid, I go before you always. Come follow Me, and I will give you rest. Know that I am with you, through it all."

Another challenge I faced at a different time caused me to sob uncontrollably at home, praying for divine protection. The radio station we listen to does not play Bob Marley's songs. As serendipity would have it, however, on this day they played his song with the exact lyrics I needed to hear just then: "Don't worry about a thing 'cause every little thing gonna be all right." I made this song my ringtone to serve as a regular reminder that God is watching over me with messages of love and reassurance.

I am certain that I pray to the God who sings, as He has a knack of choosing songs that are so apt, and His timing is impeccable.

Follow the Signs

By Sandi Neilson

It had been a magical two days. My mind drifted off the task of unloading the dishwasher and onto the last 48 hours.

I was reminded of an archetypal profiling session I'd had several months earlier. I hadn't resonated at all with the descriptions. A few hours after this recollection, I decided to re-listen to the recording, but I remained unconnected to the details supposedly about me.

Later that day, I came across an article describing people who have what has been termed a "rainforest mind." Their brains are wired differently. They perceive and respond to much in the world in a more intricate, multi-dimensional, and multi-layered way than most folk.

It was as if the article was speaking directly to me about me. It tugged at an unease I had long held about being faulty somehow because I wasn't like everyone else.

When I related this information back to the descriptions in the recording I had listened to earlier, I found myself in a new world of me. The profiling session details were on point. I now understood myself more. It was a breakthrough moment. I had been resisting this aspect of myself because I didn't want to validate this weakness I believed I had.

As I processed this over the next couple of days, several random yet delightful things happened. First was an offer – complete with a huge loyalty discount – to work privately with an expert I greatly admired. Then someone I hadn't heard from in over 18 months got in touch. Their input had been immensely helpful then and would be perfect again for the next focus of my work. Lastly was finding a kindred spirit and a new friend as a result of a chance conversation with a stranger.

As I put away the last of the dishes, I gave thanks for it all. I felt so blessed. My higher self spoke then: "You will always be looked after – just follow the signs."

Living aligned to this has brought me deep peace. Life now is simpler yet more enriching at the same time.

Marvin's Pennies

By Diana L. Hooker

Marvin was a thrifty man. "A penny saved was a penny earned," he would always say. If he saw even a single penny lying on the ground, he would stop everything to pick it up. Of course, most people told him that it was "just a penny." But when questioned, Marvin would proudly declare, "One penny could add up to many pennies."

When Marvin passed away, his wife was lost. He had been her soulmate and the love of her life. They had done everything together for as long as she could remember, so for the first time in a lifetime, she was alone. She slipped into a deep depression.

Then one day, while she was walking down an aisle at the local grocery store, she saw a penny. But a penny is never just a penny. One by one, she started finding pennies everywhere she went. She felt they were from Marvin, telling her that he was still with her. She saved each and every penny in a box that she kept on the mantle, and before long, one penny added up to many pennies that gave her happiness again. Everyone started referring to her box of pennies as "Marvin's Pennies," bringing a smile back to her eyes.

When we lose a loved one, it is a wonderful reassurance when we receive signs that they are still with us. Even if it's just a memory, a feeling, a song, a smell, or just a penny.

Time to Turn Wounds into Wisdom

By Iona Meade

"Look at the time; it's 13:33!"

I bolted upright, pointed to the clock in the car, and urged my soul partner to pay attention before the time changed. He had just picked me up after my last day at my soul-sucking day job, and we both knew the significance. Why? It's that moment you know that your loved one is close. I knew it was my son whispering, "Mum, it's time to turn your wounds into wisdom again."

I'll back up a little to give you my soul's perspective on this confirmation of divine timing. I'd faced many challenges in my life, hitting rock bottom and being forced to rise above adversity on many levels: emotional, spiritual, intellectual, physical, and financial – including bankruptcy, divorce, and homelessness. But nothing compared to that phone call to say my 19-year-old son had just passed away at the roadside after being knocked off his motor bike.

After that, I took myself offline in order to heal. I didn't know that this was the start of a three-year spiritual transformation that would lead me to sowing the seeds of my soul-work in the world as an Earth Angel for Soul Legacy Leavers.

After three years, I sensed that I'd reached a turning point when I heard a speech by Oprah where she said to "turn your wounds into wisdom." I realized that, contrary to popular belief, time does *not* heal all wounds. But that didn't mean my life couldn't be positive. After all, only in the darkness can we see our north star and begin navigating our way out of dark times. I also realized that my wounds didn't condemn me to a life of darkness. As Rumi says, "The wound is the place where the light enters you." I knew that it was time to raise my vibration in order to be a beacon light that blazes a soul path for others to follow.

The next day, after getting the message of 13:33, I looked up the meaning of that number and learned that my guardian angel of faith was guiding me. My son was still with me; my faith and my soul were still strong. This message was all I needed to reaffirm what my soul already knew: it was time to turn my wounds into wisdom.

Pilot's Halos

By Karen Koven

At the zenith of my career, I received news that I had been selected to lead the market launch of a new training product. At the same time, my personal life was in turmoil: my marriage was disintegrating. As a consultant, not an employee, I could choose to accept or decline the project. Pondering the consequences and repeatedly asking for guidance, I felt led to embrace the challenge. Awaiting me would be a rigorous professional gauntlet.

My husband dropped me off at the airport for the flight to my client's location. We said a heart-heavy goodbye. For practical reasons, my training coincided with his move. Many of the cherished artifacts of our shared history would go with him. I would be returning to a half-empty house.

Aching for what could have been, I questioned the wisdom of taking on a monumental task at such a critical personal juncture. Had I truly listened to guidance or just heard what I wanted to hear? Silently, I implored the Divine for comfort, for a sign, for something.

Once on the plane, all I could muster was the strength to look out the window, straight down at the dense cover of clouds. It was overcast and depressing on the ground, yet cheery and luminous above the clouds. My eye caught a spectacle of color: red, orange, yellow tinged with blue and green against the expanse of white. Gently cradled on the surface of the clouds was a small, gossamer-sheer, round rainbow. The Frisbee-sized circle was both confounding and comforting. Between Florida and Minnesota, 17 round rainbows appeared, a repeated message of divine confirmation. The promise of the rainbows was the promise of a new beginning.

The next morning, I strode into my client's headquarters and conducted the training in a flawless rhythm to smiles and accolades. The rainbows reinforced that it was safe to move forward in my life.

Did you know that round rainbows are often called "pilot's halos"? They are typically only seen by pilots, and on that one day, by me.

Dog Signs

By Valerie Cameron

Have you ever noticed that we are constantly being triggered or confronted by signs or synchronicities? Messages come to me in many forms and tend to show up when I'm in an emotional circumstance or situation and trying to find out who I am.

My very first experience with signs was with animals when I was living in a small northern community. It came in the form of attracting dogs. My husband brought the first small dog home who had been wandering the streets one very cold winter (-35 to -40°C).

Over the next two years, I ended up helping four other dogs. The second dog came to me on one of my walks. She had been injured, so I brought her home to help her heal. It turned out she was pregnant, and I knew that I could not give her away until after the pups were born. My heart was broken. At first, I could not understand why I was attracting these dogs yet having to find homes for them in the end. Then I realized that all the dogs I had been attracting were messengers for me. I just didn't know what their messages were at the time.

The message came to me while when I made a wrong turn on a trip to the city and found myself lost. I was extremely upset, but in that moment I realized that the message that had been given to me wasn't about me abandoning the dogs by finding them good homes; it was me who had abandonment issues.

So, thanks to this message, I learned to pay extra attention to the signs, no matter what forms they come in. I also learned that when we ask the Universe, there will always be an answer, but it may not always arrive in the way we expect.

Prayer with Dish Soap

By Joy Resor

Praying at the sink, my entire being asks to be of service in ways that use my gifts.

Although my husband and I had agreed before marriage that I would stay home with our children as his career unfolded, our youngest has just started kindergarten.

My heart, soul, and mind need more than laundry, cleaning, and groceries in an unending rhythm.

A few days after praying, this happens...longtime travel plans shift, giving me a realization that I can attend a church gathering I would have missed.

Reaching for a skirt to dress for the meeting, a vision flashes inside...I see myself walking down the stairs from the church office when the minister calls to me.

How interesting. Even more interesting is how this plays out exactly like my vision. After the luncheon, I scoot up to the church office for a tape of a service we missed, and as I begin to walk down the stairs, the minister calls to me.

Rev. Norling invites me into his office, where he says that my name has arisen to his wife and to him. They wonder if I would be willing to edit the church newsletter, which they'd like to discuss over dinner.

Yes! I'm in awe that my prayer has been answered with perfection and swiftness. Since high school, through college and in my first job after school, I've adored interviewing and writing.

What a great fit...until it isn't. When the Oklahoma bombings occur, I realize that I'm unable to feel the tragedy; I'm on a newsletter deadline, and my heart is unable to engage. This episode invites me to stop creating the entire newsletter and to lean into healing modalities.

I carry on, however, with the heart-centered page I was led to create – Share the Joy! – about souls whose lives have been touched by God.

I'm in service, using my gifts because of a soul-deep prayer at the sink.

Trust and Follow Your Inner Guidance

By Isabella Rose

"God, Goddess, Angels, Matt, Universe, please take everything from me. Please clear my plate. I am exhausted and can't keep doing everything by myself anymore. It just isn't humanly possible. I know that my life wasn't saved in the car accident to live like this…" I prayed one night and continued to surrender my worries and fears. I had finally had enough and knew there had to be a better way.

For two years after a car accident and the tragic loss of my fiancé two months later, I had been trying to do everything by myself. Although I had made improvements in slowing down and listening to my body – remembering the importance of self-care and the reminders of my friend Jodi, "to be gentle with yourself" – I was stuck in the constant cycle of doing and pushing myself forward until I couldn't anymore. I had a hard time letting go of guilt and thoughts of what I "needed" to do. I also struggled with sticking to my boundaries and saying no to the demands and expectations others placed on me.

I was hearing my body, mind, and spirit screaming out for rest to rebalance and restore; however, I wasn't following this wise guidance. I was even aware of the signs the Universe was giving me to rest, but I ignored those, too. I have too much to do, I argued. I don't have time to rest.

The morning after I prayed, the angels and my higher self continued to get my attention through oracle cards and my daily creativity practice. I had drawn the Rest card and, later in the day, the Retreat card from a different oracle deck. The message became even more loud and clear when I tuned in to the message of my artwork through automatic writing: "TRUST! Trust your inner guidance! REST, rest, rest. Retreat and rejuvenate. All is in order. Everything is the way it is supposed to be. Trust divine order. Trust the process! You are safe. You are loved. All is well. Rest."

Finally, I got the message – and finally, I listened.

How Synchronicities Saved My Life

By Chanin Zellner

"Oh, no! I cannot move my head!" I exclaimed in a panic.

One day in August 2017, I awoke with my neck unexpectedly "stuck." Over the next five weeks, I saw multiple health practitioners and took many pharmaceuticals but still suffered with little relief.

Three weeks prior to this, I had joined a free Facebook group that my now-mentor, Dr. Alison J. Kay, had created for her vibrational medicine business. We had graduated high school together, but we didn't know each other. I discovered her on Facebook through mutual friends and learned about her endeavors. I was intrigued and had no idea how she would change my life!

At the end of September, I did research into holistic medicine and determined that my throat chakra was blocked. I wasn't sure what that actually meant, but that was my self-diagnosis. I then went to an acupuncturist and to a guy who reads energy, and they diagnosed the same thing! I seemed to be on to something! I also listened to Alison's monthly free live call. Not knowing who I was, she "randomly" chose me to work with that night. I told her briefly about my neck restriction, and she determined that my throat chakra was blocked – the fourth confirmation of this! Now I had to know more about this chakra system. And I knew that the Divine had a much grander plan for my life, even though I didn't know then what that entailed.

Utilizing energy medicine to clear my chakras, along with mindfulness coaching, Alison helped me recover from my trauma. Throughout this process, I realized that my passion is to help veterans and first responders move beyond trauma that has caused blockages in their chakras. It's apparent that the Divine was guiding me to my higher purpose via these various synchronicities.

I am now a certified Dragon Master in the Vibrational UPgrade™ System, so I can fulfill my mission to help others recover, too. If it weren't for my "unfortunate" neck problem, I probably wouldn't have looked into the chakra system or participated in that live call. I'm so thankful for Divine synchronicities!

A Soothing Beat Frees My Soul

By Lori Thiessen

My marriage of 21 years ended. Along with that came a myriad of repercussions and reverberations. I quit homeschooling, had a crushing falling-out with what had once been my deep devotion to my Christian beliefs, stopped going to church, and lost my social circle. Then, employment with the company I had worked with for 20+ years ended abruptly. I felt like I was in free-fall. And I had five teenagers to finish raising. As much as I knew this was the right direction, I would be lying if I said I didn't have times of overwhelming confusion.

My mind so easily spiraled into clouds of uncertainty. The questions I asked myself were endless and unanswered. "What's your plan now? How are you going to manage all this? Where's the money going to come from?"

My soul became all tangled up in fear. Now I was a single parent with the responsibilities of raising teenagers, finding work, and rebuilding what felt like everything.

The first time I heard the song was during one of those moments of despair. Driving alone, I turned the radio on and heard, "Oh, give me the beat, boys, and free my soul. I wanna get lost in your rock and roll and drift away…"

My wild and fearful heart slowed. My breathing relaxed. My shoulders started swaying to the soft rhythms. I had cried out for answers and direction, and I got a song that had neither. But it had a healing balm for my soul, and I knew everything would be just fine.

That moment stayed with me awhile, but life moved on and once again I found myself in that place of lost despair. And the song came back. As I stood in the kitchen alone late at night, it played on the radio. As I walked through the grocery store, wondering what I could afford to buy, there it was again: the background music playing softly.

Again and again, at the moment I needed it most, the song brought a message of comfort at exactly the right time, allowing me to move forward with hope through a very uncertain place.

Highway Hope

By Carole "Lisa Lynn" Gilbert

My mother died when I was nine, and my brother died just five short years later. These two were my main world. I also lost other close family members on an average of one per year for 10 years. This decade was a dark time in my life.

Later, as an adult, I would have days of feeling down, unsettled, and depressed. I would wonder why I felt this way. Then one day it hit me: there were so many days of the year that brought me sadness, either because it was around the time that someone died or because it was the birthday of someone I had lost. I know from Psalms 34:18 that God is close to the brokenhearted. I kept telling myself this, but it was still hard. I had to fight these feelings.

One day as I was driving down the highway close to my house and having one of those sad days, I noticed a billboard. It had been blank for a while but someone had gotten up on it and put up a nonprofessional message that didn't even fill the whole billboard. The message looked like words from a Scrabble game. It read, "Feeling down? Just look up. God."

I knew instantly it was meant for me! I thought about my sadness, and I thought about Jesus and how He could've been sad every day of His life but was filled with joy and love.

I see this billboard often and am reminded how I only have to "look up," to look toward God and know He loves me. This gives me the same uplifting feeling as hearing a favorite meaningful song. It just fills my heart with happiness and my eyes with tears of joy. And it's not the billboard and what it says but the One I'm looking upwards to. It's my God! Then I can put the sadness away and simply smile. Thank you, God, and thank you, Jesus.

The Magical Energy of 333

By Joanne Angel Barry Colon

On March 11, 2019, I shared two Facebook Live videos about the energy of the day based on numerology – and I ended up receiving a powerful message from an unexpected visitor.

In numerology, 3 (for March) represents communication, creativity, and manifestation. The 11 is a "master number," which vibrates at a higher level and translates to a 2 (1+1), which means partnership in any area, such as with self, God, Universe, family, friends, and significant others. When you add the year 2019, it equals 3, and when you add all the numbers from the date, you get 8, which means abundance.

During the morning session, I spoke about the powerful energy of the 8, how we communicate about abundance and our relationship with money. That evening, I was inspired to speak about the 11 energy as a master number, which means the portals are open to help connect to angels, spirit guides, and loved ones. As I was relaying that information, I suddenly saw my mother sitting across the table from me. I welcomed her in and informed my Facebook viewers that my mom had just joined us (reminding them that she is spirit). I then shared with my viewers that it was the eight-year anniversary of her crossing over.

I then realized that the number for the following day (March 12, 2019) equals 333, which means the angels have opened the gates for all your desires to manifest. Although my intention for my Facebook Live was to speak only of the 11 energy, my mom encouraged me to offer a single card reading from my *Chakra Balance Numerology Cosmic Energy Forecast* deck. My mom and I shuffled the deck together (as I felt her hands on my hands), and we pulled card #66, "Healing."

The message I received from this card is one of healing and communication (since 66, also a master number, transfers to the single digit 3, which is all about communication). My mom came to me to let me know that I was on the path of speaking to a larger audience and helping many more people heal with my work. From that point on, any time I see 333, I know that I'm on the right path and the spirit gates are open, helping me manifest my desires.

No Turning Back on a Dream

By David Hipshman

I had made a decision: I was going for my dreams. I would start and grow a business as a coach for entrepreneurs who wanted to make an impact in the world. I had been in a program where, to get certified, I needed to have paying clients and for them to get results. That experience awakened a desire to support others in realizing their dreams and also to have it be my business.

But how would I grow my business? I was learning that it's more about my inner being – my desire and commitment – than about the strategies.

As I was starting to grow my coaching business, fears and doubts came up – mostly about being more visible and embracing marketing myself and my program. Like most coaches, healers, and consultants, I loved the work but not the marketing of myself. But I knew that in order to grow my business, I would need to be more visible.

During this time, I was offered a job to go back to an old role in the high-tech world at a startup. It paid well and would be interesting and innovative, yet it felt like going backward. But to say no to it felt scary – like I'd be passing up an opportunity for security. I felt like I was being tested in my commitment. I knew that a coaching business is easy to start, but also easy to leave, especially if it's not comfortable.

Just as I was going to take the job, the startup was absorbed by another company. The position I was offered was no longer needed, and the offer was rescinded. At first it felt like the rug was pulled out from under me, but then I saw this as a sign. This experience rekindled my commitment and got me in touch with why I wanted to grow my coaching business in the first place. Now there was no going back, no matter what I had to face and no matter how long it took. And that freed me to embrace it more, to enjoy it more.

Since then, I've built a deeply satisfying six-figure coaching business that I continue to grow!

Three Charms

By Jody Wootton

Call it intuition or superstition, but I knew he was the one for me. He is all a girl would want in a man. Our souls crossed paths by chance…or someone had a plan for us.

Shortly after we met, he had to travel for work. He was off to Taipei. Before he left, he asked, "Is there anything that I can bring back for you?"

I replied, "You and the three things."

"What three things?" he asked.

"You'll know when you see them," I said.

He seemed puzzled. I guess he wasn't sure how to digest my vague but specific request. And I didn't know exactly either, but deep down, on a subconscious level, I did know.

The trip was relatively short – two weeks – during which there wasn't much communication between us. Maybe it was the time difference or that business trips are busy or that we had just met. On the day he returned, I decided to take a train to the airport to surprise him. The two of us were happy to be in each other's company again and to catch up during the long car ride home together.

Our conversation began typically enough for someone returning from traveling. I asked how his trip had been. "Okay, but busy," he replied. I was almost reluctant to ask if he had stumbled onto anything of three. But I guess he sensed my impending question because he said, "I have three things for you." And then he told me the story:

One year earlier, he had stayed at the same hotel. This time, shortly after he'd checked in to his room, he heard a knock at his door. It was one of the hotel's customer-service representatives. "Good evening, sir," she said. "When you last stayed here, you left three charms in your room. I have been holding them for you, and it is my pleasure to return them to you."

Livin' the Dream

By Katie Jackson

On July 3, 2019, 13 days before my son's 28th birthday, I received the call I hoped I'd never get. The police detective notified me that Brandon had a fatal overdose. Brandon had battled a heroin addiction for many years, and the hope that he'd find a beautiful life in recovery was no longer a possibility.

Brandon experienced much suffering and hardship in his short lifetime. In recent years, he often had no job, money, food, or home. Yet he experienced much love and laughter amidst his daily struggles. His sense of humor and beautiful soul touched everyone. Whenever asked how he was doing, Brandon replied, "Oh, livin' the dream!" with a big smile and laugh. His humor made us all laugh! Brandon's obituary ended with, "In his own words, he was 'livin' the dream.'"

At Brandon's wake, a school therapist, Sue, shared that she was in Chicago after Brandon passed and had seen a guy walk by wearing a shirt that said, "Living the Dream."

Then, the day after Brandon's funeral, Sue sent me a text: "You won't believe this. Went camping in the park with family…was packed up and realized my niece dropped a pillow she had. I had to take a picture. I had no idea she had it until it fell out and I picked it up this morning." The picture was a pillow that read, "LIVIN' THE DREAM."

During this time, Brandon's sister, Grace, was looking for employment. She sent a picture of a help-wanted ad: "Our team is living the dream!"

Then I received a message from my old friend Anni: "Today while window shopping in the Ogilvie Transportation Center, I saw a plaque that read, 'Living the Dream.'"

The following day, my cousin's wife, Tracey, was dropping her son off at college. The next-door neighbor had a mat in front of his door. Guess what it said… "Living the Dream."

I love this! Brandon is *everywhere*, and his sense of humor hasn't changed! There's no doubt that he's truly livin' the dream! I am so grateful for the messages from beyond that tell me all is well with his soul.

Joice

By Cathy Raymond

Joice took her life when a mix of alcohol and antidepressants created a chemical death spiral she couldn't escape.

Mourning a relationship gone sour and prescribed an antidepressant, she attended her flight-attendant graduation party. Drinking heavily and in a chemical haze, she went back to her hotel room to call her absent boyfriend. Later she was found hanging.

We were stunned! She had just passed a rigorous training program and was ready for "take-off"! Even more puzzling, we had found a load of wet clothes in her washer. Who puts in a load of wash before they commit suicide? It didn't make sense.

Joice had tried to take her life before, but they were only sad, staged cries for help and love. How would I know if this was intentional or an accident? I asked for a sign.

Sure enough, the next day on my walk, I discovered a little yellow farm finch lying lifeless on the sidewalk outside the salon next door.

Many folks see unusual but comforting bird signs after the death of a loved one. Was this mine? This colorful bird was far from home. Joice, too, was far from home. Horrifically abused as a child, she bravely fled Brazil and started a new life in Atlanta. Strangely enough, I had often thought of Joice as a little broken bird and encouraged her to see a therapist. I got a fuller answer when I turned and saw an oversized poster in the salon's plate glass window directly above the bird that read, "Brazilian Blowouts."

I laughed out loud in relief since I had asked God to make the signs big and bold so they were unmistakable. This was definitely my sign, and understanding poured through me!

Like the colorful bird, my exotic Brazilian friend found herself in a strange land, far from home. Just as the bird was unaware of the dangers of plate-glass windows, Joice was unaware of the dangers of mixing alcohol and antidepressants. The answer was clear to me: the little bird did not mean to die, and neither did Joice.

The Barn Owl

By Theresa Franson

Life is filled with aha moments where the universe reveals just how perfectly everything works out. It can be difficult to remember that experiences are happening as they need to for the good of all. I finally realized this during an amazing moment of discovery after seeing a client one day.

The idea of being late used to cause me sheer panic, and on this particular day, I seemed to be delayed by everything and ended up running 10 minutes behind – leaving me frustrated. However, as I was driving, I saw a bright-green car with the license plate "BARN OWL." Thinking this was cool but odd, I said, "Thank you," not knowing of its significance until later.

I thought about the license plate and the owl, wondering about its importance. I find animals so beautiful and love learning their messages of support and guidance as they come in and out of our lives. So, naturally, I was curious about this.

I felt inclined to share this after my client's session and was pleasantly surprised to learn that the owl had been showing up randomly for them over the last couple of weeks. After looking up the owl's meaning, I shared it with my client, who was grateful to hear the information. It provided them with some much-needed comfort, peace, and realization at a time of great transition.

My aha moment of discovery was when I realized I was never actually late. I was in fact exactly where I needed to be in order to see that license plate and bring the owl's message to my client.

Since then, I've had many more experiences that remind me I'm exactly where I need to be. Now if I feel overwhelmed, frustrated, or happen to run late, I simply breathe and remember the owl.

I find it truly astonishing how everything is in perfect vibrational flow, made up of extraordinarily perfect moments. I'm so grateful to be a part of this miraculous journey. Here's to you finding your own aha moment!

Someday Freedom

By Demetria

It is a hot, humid summer morning in a suburban Ohio town. A 10-year old girl is asleep in her bed, dreaming of pink houses, lavish swimming pools, tea parties, and playing dress-up with her friends. She is awoken from her dream at 4 a.m. by her father who is driven by a different dream. A dream so powerful, it would pull him from a remote and rugged mountainous village in Greece into this suburban town to open a restaurant.

The father's dream would come to be known as "The American Dream," and it promised a someday freedom that came through hard work, sweat, and maybe even tears. It was so compelling that it led the father and daughter to endure countless hours of long, labor-filled days and years.

The young girl would overcome her frustration at being woken up from her dream, knowing that her father would make his famous hash browns for breakfast and provide her an allowance. She learned to work really hard for what she wanted. After decades of hard work, however, she discovered that no amount of it brought her the freedom she yearned for. Her body and bank account became so burned out from years of stress and the continuous desire to achieve more that she didn't know what to do next.

Then one day, she decided to turn on the TV (something she rarely allowed herself to do) and noticed a commercial about a book titled *A New Earth: Awakening to Your Life's Purpose* by Eckhart Tolle. The book contained a message so simple and profound, it would change her life forever: There is only now, you are not separate from the whole, and love is who you are.

In a flash, the struggle was replaced by peace and a knowing that we are all part of one loving universe, guiding and providing us with exactly what we need when we need it. All we have to do is allow it to take the lead. Now that is true freedom.

Blue Money

By Nora Rose

One day my business took a downward turn into financial crisis. I was stuck in a "lack of" state of mind, and I worried about paying my bills. To help turn this thought process around, my friends suggested I start looking for "blue money" – money that came out of the blue, that I didn't earn and didn't expect to receive. A coupon or discount also equals blue money. If you bought a $300 purse for $150, that would be $150 of blue money. A free car wash would be $7 of blue money. My hope was that in looking for blue money, I would teach myself to see the abundance all around and pay attention to it…and bring some extra money in.

I had 10 days to notice the blue money around me and try to reach $1,000. My friends talked to me every day and held me accountable. I had a lunch date, and my friend paid for my lunch. That was $20 in blue money. My daughter mailed me a framed photo gift. That was $100 in blue money. The neighbor unexpectedly mowed my lawn, which was $40 in blue money. I was well on my way!

This type of thinking helped me create a positive mindset and think about money in a peaceful, abundant way instead of from a place of desperation and lack. It allowed me to search for the little things that add to financial gain. Like attracts like, and abundance attracts abundance. For a powerful shift in finances, I also started writing down affirmations like, "Money comes to me easily" and "My income is constantly increasing."

Just by shifting my mindset around money, I was seeing that all kinds of money was coming to me. I realized the more we dwell on what we don't want, the more we get what we don't want. We can retrain our brain to think about things differently, in positive ways. What we put our attention on grows. Realizing this made a big change in my subconscious mind and made life easier and happier to cope with the next steps I needed to take for my business.

Signs from the Universe

By Kianne Lei

About a year ago, I made a leap of faith and started an online coaching business. I hit roadblocks at what seemed like every turn. And no matter how hard I worked, little changed.

Feeling defeated, I arrived at my favorite park to hit the trails and clear my head. That morning on my run, as my feet penetrated the earth below me, I pleaded to the Universe, "Give me a sign. Please. I feel so stuck. Am I where I need to be?"

I came up around the corner where one path split into two: the first, a paved walkway, headed back in the direction of my car. The other winded to a narrow, overgrown, wooded path. Out of the corner of my eye, I noticed a blue jay sitting on the branch at the narrow path's edge.

I came to a stop and in an instant felt a connection to this tiny blue bird. No sooner did I go to take a step toward the bird, it flew up into the thick of the trees, beckoning me to follow. I followed the bird in a little ways, where I discovered it perched on a tiny branch, basking in the sunshine peeking through the limbs of the trees above us. It was then that I knew I had found my sign.

Since then, blue jays have appeared to me in many instances. And not only blue jays, but the significance of the color blue. Paths I've hiked following a particularly difficult week would have blue trail markers. Or the color blue would appear in my dreams. All subtle signs from the Universe guiding me on my journey.

I am not where I want to be in life or in my business yet, but I've grown so much over the last year. If anything, these little gifts from the Universe have served as reminders that although only I can ultimately decide which paths I choose to take and which lessons I choose to learn, I am never truly alone. The Universe will always have my back.

Connect with the Universal Messages

By Wendyanne Pakulsky

I believe that one of the most beautiful gifts the Universe can give us is the ability to understand that angels are always with us if we truly connect with the awareness. Sometimes angelic messages appear through seeing a butterfly or consecutive numbers, such as 111 or 333. Sometimes a message will stand out in a book, or an Earth Angel will say something that resonates deeply. I am a great believer that these messages are sent to help guide us along in the most loving, nurturing way.

Recently, I've received a series of angelic messages about the changes I'm going through in my life. First, a message came through a quote about "unbecoming" everything we are not and becoming (or growing into) everything we are meant to be. After reading this quote, I saw a butterfly – a symbol of transforming into the higher self. That same afternoon, everywhere I looked I saw the number 111, which in angel messages symbolizes intuition, high energy, inspiration, self-expression, and spiritual awakening and enlightenment.

Some may dismiss these as mere coincidences; however, I believe they are true angelic messages. They're among the most beautiful gifts I've ever received, helping me stay on my path of truth – the path where things just feel right and flow like the ocean rolling onto the shore. Staying on our own path of truth can take tremendous courage even at the best of times, but thanks to angelic messages, I can comfortably say that there is no turning back because the universe has spoken to my soul.

Whatever form they take, angelic messages can make us smile, help us grow, provide comfort during times of uncertainty, and remind us that we are never alone. Once you connect with the energy of these messages, you can remind others that they are also never alone if they are willing to just take a deep breath and work with the inspiration of angelic love.

The Elevator Message

By Gretchen Oehler Hogg

We had just finished working a prominent event, highlighting several transformational and spiritual visionaries, when I received a mysterious elevator message.

I had escorted one of our favorite speakers to meet her driver as she left the hotel. Before the event, she had expressed concern that her six-month-pregnant daughter was experiencing cramping and bleeding and was hospitalized. Having worked in obstetrics for many years, I offered comfort while silently praying that everything would be fine.

That morning, this speaker had shared that she'd awakened in the middle of the night with a powerful lucid dream. In the dream, scores of Buddhist monks reassured her about the well-being of her grandson and daughter and encouraged her to release worry. The monks revealed that her grandson is a revered, old soul from their lineage who's choosing to reincarnate during these critical, transformational times.

Shortly after our speaker's departure, I stepped into the elevator and into what felt like an alternate reality. Standing before me were three striking Buddhist rinpoches, dressed in their customary red and gold silk ceremonial robes. They stood alongside an interpreter, a local emissary, and a hotel manager. The emissary eagerly shared that these Buddhist rinpoches were here to perform a sacred ceremony in town. I acknowledged their presence and felt their penetrating eyes gaze as if they were communicating directly with my soul. I smiled, touched my Buddhist prayer wheel pendant, and bowed toward the rinpoches with a namasté prayer gesture, which they returned in kind.

As they exited the elevator, I knew beyond a shadow of a doubt that this was confirmation that the speaker's beloved grandson and daughter were going to be just fine, and I conveyed this magical encounter to her.

Despite her daughter's challenging pregnancy, her grandson greeted the world with a smile of pure joy and an enlightened, soul-eye gaze.

I know with absolute certainty that this synchronistic encounter occurred so I could share this reassuring message with the speaker. Her daughter and grandson appear to be divinely surrounded and protected by immense love and eternal wisdom.

The Miracle Breakdown

By Kimberly Lucht

It was 2 a.m. when I got up to use the bathroom. I stepped out of bed, headed toward the door, and began shaking uncontrollably. I was seizing for the first time in my life. I was fully conscious, but I couldn't control a limb in my body. Frantically, I tried to reach the walls and stabilize, but the convulsing rendered those efforts futile. It was as if my body was protesting...the question was, against what?

A year earlier, I had moved abroad to be the director of a non-profit. I thought I had it all together. I had the dream job, the dream boyfriend, and to many people looking in, the dream life. Logically, these puzzle pieces fit my vision for a dream life...but spiritually, I felt dead, numb, and devoid of life.

This seizure was a metaphor. Just like I was completely conscious and had no control over my body as I seized, I lived each day aware of what was going on but had no agency over how my life was unfolding.

Even though I was running an incredible organization, it still wasn't mine and it wasn't my dream. I didn't consciously choose this life. I settled for it.

My body was desperately trying to wake me up as it shook me back and forth. "This life isn't for you! You were meant for something much greater than this!"

But I didn't know what that something was. It seemed easier to keep going through the motions of my "dream life" than to throw it all away and try to discover what I'm really here for.

Easier...but also soul-sucking. It finally clicked. All this time, I was listening to my mind, not my heart. My logic, not my soul. My brain, not my body.

"It ends now," I thought. I surrendered, fell to the floor, and the seizing immediately stopped.

A Message from Red-Tailed Hawks

By Valerie Cameron

My husband and I were on a road trip, and as I was gazing out my window at the beauty of the landscape, I realized I had seen four different hawks: the first was sitting in the trees with blackbirds diving at it, the second was flying (also with blackbirds flying and diving at it), the third was peacefully sitting in a tree, and the fourth was coasting and flying freely above the landscape.

It dawned on me in that moment that they were giving me a synchronized message: The first two hawks were showing me that it doesn't matter what comes at you in life; even with all our obstacles and challenges, we can still find balance. The third was showing me that in stillness I could find peace within myself. The fourth hawk was showing me that one can rise above anything and not get caught up in the drama of life. It also revealed to me that I can see things from a different perspective. Considering what I was experiencing in my life at the time, these were the perfect messages for me.

It is important to be aware of the sometimes-subtle signs that the universe may be showing us through the various messengers that show up in our life. When we begin to do so, we will see that the messages are truly perfect for what we are going through or in answer to our request for guidance. I often receive messages through the animal kingdom, so I always pay close attention to nature's messengers.

Do you know that the universe loves you so much that it will continue to keep sending you messengers to repeat the message to you until you finally get what is being said? Once acknowledged, the universe then can take note that you have received the message and will move on to answering your other concerns through the natural messengers in your life and in the world. Love yourself enough to become conscious today of the messages all around you.

Ask for Help

By Melisa Archer

The time has come for me to share my time and gifts in a more structured manner. There's a fine line between giving freely and overgiving to the point of feeling taken advantage of. A common problem with healers who want to give is that there's always someone or something in need. When people expect to take time, energy, and healing, it's harder to set boundaries. Wanting the best for people does not always work within an hour, and the lines between sessions and friends often blur.

Recently, I stood on my porch and I cried to the heavens: "I've given in faith, so how do I find myself now battling for my health? Have I not given enough of myself?" The sky responded with a downpour. Along with the heavy rain, one small white feather drifted down and landed in front of me. As soon as I noticed this angel feather, the rains stopped and the sun beamed brightly. In that moment, I knew I was not alone and that everything would be okay.

During the next few days, angels on Earth and from above seemed to step forward. My path eased, and my health improved significantly.

It's hard to acknowledge that I've put my energy into distress through my own doing. But I'm reminded that I have free will, and it's up to me to set healthy boundaries, which ensures that I feel excited to give and also to receive, and to ask for help when I need it. Sometimes this means asking for assistance during energy work so it's easier to receive it for myself and others. And sometimes it means asking for a sign from above.

Upon reflection, it seems that the ones you give to are not necessarily the same ones you receive from. In a cosmic web, there are connections we do not get to visually see, but I can feel strongly that they are there. I thank all those who love with their whole heart, and I send love to those in need.

Skin in the Game

By Kimberly A. Elliott

A few years ago, while employed by a major retailer, I felt creative and energized. Well, one thing that is constant is change! Corporate initiatives came and went, and I began to feel discontent and uneasy – feelings that I eventually labeled as "boredom." I rationalized I was no longer challenged and lamented over feeling devalued.

What came next was a major announcement: a new CFO and major corporate reconstruction. Yep, massive reductions, which included *me*. Suddenly, I couldn't find a job on LinkedIn, Career Builders, or by word of mouth that sounded worth the leap from "wound licking." Hey, you fall hard when the rug is pulled from under you, *even when you know it was time to move.*

I can hardly explain what happened next. It started with an invitation to chat with the executive team of a prison ministry that I was volunteering for. In the months prior, I had begun assisting there with multiple functions. Then, just months after hearing, "Your position [which you thought was your career] with our organization has ended," I was asked to consider a new role...no longer as a volunteer with the prison ministry but to actually help lead the organization as Executive Director. I could only say yes...despite the fact that I felt grossly underqualified, and oh yes, I knew I'd assuredly be underpaid! And of course this meant voluntarily going into many prisons.

Dealing with addiction issues within my own family has been traumatic. I've experienced more than one individual I truly love continually devalue the gifts I know are in them; and sitting in a prison visiting room is unfortunately familiar...and *hard*. But the very thing we feel will take us down for the final time can often be the life preserver we get to toss to someone else, while learning to tread water and eventually swim. Now, I completely empathize with others, like my own son, who wish that we would just "get it" and realize that their pain is connected to something far deeper than the problems that surface. In fact, I know that God chose me because I have "skin in the game"! Who would know better how important it is to help provide needed resources to families who are often suffering in silence, and I feel truly blessed that I get to do what I do.

Sleepless

By Barbara Friedman

When I was diagnosed with Parkinson's Disease, I was told it was incurable, that there was no direct cause, and that it could be managed with medication. This was unacceptable to my scientific mind and offensive to my nature-based organic lifestyle. Unfortunately, it turned out to be true. Moreover, no one warned me of the many additional challenges PD created, one of which was insomnia.

I have never had healthy sleep patterns, often working through the night in my darkroom or on the computer, but as PD progressed, sleep disturbances worsened. Some nights I lay awake till 5:00 or 6:00 a.m. Most nights I awoke every two and a half hours, often unable to return to sleep.

One such night, I opened my well-worn copy of Louise Hay's classic, *You Can Heal Your Life*, to look up Insomnia. The Probable Cause was Fear. Not trusting the process of life. Guilt. Oookay. Nothing new there.

But as I closed the book, I noticed the word "Incurable." Right between "Incontinence" and "Indigestion." The Probable Cause was defined as "Cannot be cured by outer means at this point." It went on to suggest that we must go within for the cure, that the disease came from nowhere and will go back to nowhere. The New Thought Pattern stated that miracles happen every day and suggested I go within to dissolve the pattern that created this problem and that I now accept a Divine healing.

This was exactly the message I needed! It reaffirmed that I was on the right path to healing by looking into my psyche. I began recalling experiences that imprinted me with the fear that destroyed my trust in life. I could feel that – at some deep, deep level – lack of trust undermined my health and well-being. Using my resources in psychology and energy psychology, I began to release that fear and its stories.

The insomnia persists for now (as a reminder to stay awake), but the Parkinson's is not progressing. I'm on an inner journey to release embedded fear and to benefit from the shift to trusting the process of life.

Sunrise

By Jenny McKaig Speed

"Whatever it takes."

The words rolled from one side of the cylindrical rotating back of the truck to reveal themselves one word at a time. Then, so clearly, the rest of the message. "Make it happen."

The glow of the sunrise glistened on the land for our carwash. I was stopped behind a line of traffic, my favourite place to be on that road, because I knew I'd get to glance at our land, feel the energy of it.

At that time, we were under contract on the land where we'd build our carwash. We hadn't yet solidified the closing, and while we were much closer to owning the land and being ready to build, we had one major challenge to surmount. This carwash meant solidifying our financial and time freedom, two things my husband and I have been blessed to experience, but not sustainably at the same time.

"Whatever it takes. Make it happen."

That truck, and the tap on the shoulder to look up at that exact moment, gave me everything I needed to know we would overcome our obstacle and make it happen.

The sun glistened. It was a magnetic kind of morning. Music blared from my speakers. I danced and sipped my coffee as I drove. I felt complete flow and joy, appreciating details like the trees, the clear sky, and even the clouds – all of it God's creation.

Later that afternoon, I talked with my husband and he told me about a meeting he had just scheduled. "I think this is going to help us with what we need."

My heart swelled and tears rose to my eyes. I felt it clearly – the universe was delivering. We would find the solution we needed for the final detail, close on the land, and build our carwash.

That morning – with the rise of dawn, sun glistening on the land we had worked so hard to secure, putting everything on the line to make it happen – I read those words and felt the courage I needed to trust. All was aligning to give us everything that we had dreamed and visioned.

Chapter 3
Messages from Our Body and Soul

Our soul is constantly speaking to us, as is our body. They're always sending messages. Sometimes we listen, but oftentimes we don't. It can feel easier to look outside of ourselves for the answers – to look to our loved ones or a doctor or someone in a position of power to tell us what to do or how to heal or what the next step will be. But what we've found is that the answer is always within us. And to get to that answer and to really be able to hear it, we have to slow down, get still, and listen closely.

Sometimes we make things harder than they need to be. We complicate things and end up confusing ourselves in the process of doing so. When we get into the practice of listening to our soul, we find that our lives tend to flow much more easily, a weight lifts from our shoulders, and we feel better.

Jodi has been struggling with her health this past year. She's gone to many different doctors and healers and has tried many different remedies to try to make her well again. And she's realized that what she really needed to do first was to ask her body what it needed, to ask it what she could offer it to help it heal. And from that knowing, she could move forward – whether to visit a doctor or healer or simply get more sleep and eat better and stress less (or all of the above).

One thing we've learned over and over again this past year is the importance of listening to our soul and our body – they really do have the answers, and it's up to us to slow down so that we can hear what they are. Throughout this chapter, you'll read stories of people who did exactly that, and you'll see how their lives improved because they listened.

A Siren's Call

By Karen Wythe

Messages come in many forms. They can be inner guidance that leads us to a synchronistic moment. They can enrich our lives or save us from disaster. And they can show up in ways we'd least expect.

I once received an unexpected message while driving on the thruway. My brother, a couple of friends, and I were heading home after a beautiful day in Lilydale, NY. The sun was shining, and the blue sky was filled with fair-weather clouds. It was a picture-perfect day.

As I drove, we were chatting and having fun. Then, in the distance, I heard a siren. I said, "Do you hear that?"

"What? I don't hear anything," they all said.

Oddly, the noise just got louder and louder until it sounded like it was right on top of me. There was no choice: I needed to pull the car over quickly and get out of the way for the emergency vehicle that I could hear but couldn't see.

Naturally upset by the swift action, my friends questioned me, shouting, "What are you doing?"

"Pulling over. I heard a siren," I shouted.

My brother exclaimed, "WOW!!! Good thing you did! We would've been killed!" He saw a tractor trailer recklessly speeding onto the thruway. We sat there stunned. It had all happened so quickly.

This situation reminded me to always pay attention to my impressions, no matter how I perceive them. And it taught me that messages are indeed calls to action, lessons to learn, gifts from the ethers, and blessings to be received but never ignored.

Opportunity to Be Me

By Misty Proffitt-Thompson

We all receive guidance from many sources at different times throughout our day. Being present to receive the message and being able to discern whether that direction is for your higher good is key. When you receive guidance from at least two different sources at two different times, it's likely an indication that this is a direction you need to take – one that provides an opportunity to expand your mind, body, and spirit. We are blessed with free will, and it's up to us to choose whether or not to accept these opportunities.

Most of the messages I receive are from my Spirit Team. These messages often show up for me during meditation or by what I call a "download" from my guardian angels, my loved ones who have transitioned, or directly from Source. Once these messages are brought to my attention, they often reappear in the form of conversations with other people, television shows, magazine articles, and my clients.

I wish I could say that I always act immediately on the guidance I receive, but this isn't always the case. I've found that the bigger the message, the more fear seems to creep in and find shelter within me. And when I ignore these messages, they tend to appear in larger ways.

Recently, I've had many opportunities to choose whether or not to follow messages, including one particularly massive one that was presented to me continually throughout this year. Knowing that it would involve a life-altering decision, I did my best to disregard it; but the more I tried to ignore this message, the more fearful I felt and the more frequently it would appear in different forms. Eventually, I could no longer ignore this message to divorce my second husband.

This message has been difficult, and it is one that I am still working through. Feelings of failure have surrounded me, along with fear of being alone and sadness over losing the fantasy of what our lives could have looked like. But I've also been filled with excitement, knowing that I'm free to be me. To be happy in this life, we both must now move on. No matter how difficult this message has been to receive, I know that it's the right guidance at the right time.

Karmic Guidance

By Kimberly Brochu

"One step at a time," Karen tells me. "Your soul has designed it this way."

I feel my body tighten as I reject her words. I'm angry and anxious, not with Karen, but with the thought of taking life so slowly after everything we've been through.

I'm almost 40 and now find myself a single mother of three. After decades of building what I thought was our life, it has turned us upside down and dumped us out, and now she's telling me my soul wants me to take things "one step at a time."

Taking it slowly is the last thing I want to do.

Karen explains that according to the placement of planets and signs within the houses of my astrological chart, my soul's mission is to create a stable and serene foundation, one that I would ever-so-slowly build upon.

Ugh!

She asks me to try to understand that in order to rebuild my life, I need a strong and secure foundation, one that requires me to be gentle with myself and to connect more spiritually.

"A farmer turns the soil," she says, "then takes time to consider its color, texture, and density; only at that point does he begin to plant the seeds."

So I sit with what she said and go over it again in my mind and reread the notes I took as she spoke. I push the words away from me, annoyed because I don't want to do it that way. And after a short time, I pull them in to see how they feel.

I let the feelings move through my body, and then, as the farmer would do, I simply look at the soil I have tilled.

I realize that only by gradually planting seeds one by one will I grow a garden that will nourish and feed my children and myself. A grounded life that we will stand firmly upon.

And now, years later, what we have is an abundant and fruitful life that I am proud of.

Intuitive Healing with Nutritional Harmony

By Julie Wheeler

The cells of my body said to me, "Each morning, go to the organic produce department at the grocery store, and we'll show you the nutrients we want." It didn't seem so radical at the time, considering that my other option was to have a complete hysterectomy and be thrown into instant menopause at age 41 due to ovarian cysts, endometriosis, and cancer staging. A failed laparoscopic surgery had left my body screaming in pain for answers and defiantly opposing further surgery. "NO MORE punctures to the skin or cutting inside!" yelled 37.2 trillion cells as I took another pain pill and requisite anti-nausea medication.

My heavy-pain body – accustomed to suffering childhood migraines, fibromyalgia, stroke, trauma, anxiety, and depression – had finally hit a wall, pushed through into a sacred-wisdom portal, and connected with some other deep part of me. In this new space of peaceful awareness, my body further instructed that ultrasounds and other non-invasive imaging were acceptable, as were blood draws, but absolutely forbade further cutting of the skin. In a deep place, I knew that this rule was inviolable, so I asked, "Well then, how are we going to heal?" That's when nutrition intuition stepped up to the plate – in perfect timing – and said, "We'll show you, joyfully!"

The art of food harmony clicked inside me, and I saw the true beauty of all our plant friends and their healing abilities. My healing journey included meditation, visualization, energy healing, gentle stretching, mineral and herbal supplements, deep rest, cuddling with my pets, and nutrition-focused medicine. For several weeks, I exclusively ate raw fruits and veggies, including apples, broccoli, sweet potato, stone fruit, and berries. After that initial "high raw" state, I was led to add in freshly ground peanut and almond butters, then plant-based protein, then some dairy, and so on.

Your journey will be unique to you and your body's needs; listen closely and quietly while ignoring well-meaning advice from others who are also on their own unique journeys. Blessings on your good health!

March 26

Inspired to Follow My Heart

By Donna Godfrey

For many years, I had the honour of owning Healing Home, a healing centre in my community. This centre allowed me to share space with countless other practitioners while providing the public with a place where they could come to feel safe and comfortable. My experiences there were also a huge part of my own path of healing, altering my perceptions on spirituality and what it means to be of service to humanity.

One day, I decided I was going on a trip. I didn't have a mapped-out destination, timeline, or agenda. I just packed up my van with the little bit of camping gear I owned and headed off! This journey last three months and took me through Alberta, three states, BC Island and Interior, then home.

During this trip, I wanted to break the paradigm of doing things a certain way or within any particular timeframe. I would randomly stop to sightsee, go for nature walks, dine, or stop to camp whenever it felt right. After I'd been travelling awhile, I began to notice that at every stop I made, people would approach me and share personal life experiences. I trusted my inner guidance about how to respond. Sometimes I was guided to give information, and other times just to listen. Before this trip was complete, I knew in my heart that these encounters were not random but were showing me what service to humanity really means. Most of all, I felt this was preparing me for the next shift that was about to happen for me.

When I returned, I was able to surrender the Healing Home, as it was time to let someone else call it their home!

Through my travels, I learned that each and every experience can lead us to a greater understanding, which can evolve naturally without any expectation about how this should look or transpire. Love yourself and know that you are always exactly where you are meant to be!

Alchemy of Conscious Conception

By Eva Kettles

It seemed I had lost my innate ability to give life, along with my womanhood, as I got the devastating news that I couldn't get pregnant.

I had dreamt of experiencing the sacred alchemy between two people creating life. I thought it would be expressed in hot steamy ecstasy. But the universe had other plans.

The in vitro protocol is very rigid and dictates the egg to shape up perfectly in 3-7 days before it can be implanted. The seventh day had arrived, and we were told that the little egg would be sadly released that day. I begged the doctors to wait just one more day. It was very unconventional, but they gave in.

That day, I received a message from Spirit to transmute energies for the baby's soul. The soul wanted to free itself from burdens of the past. As I started the ritual, I lit the candles and invoked the violet flame of transformation and soon saw an image of a little embryo shape appear in the flame right above the wick. The miraculous transformation occurred right in front of my eyes.

The next day, the doctors couldn't believe what happened: the embryo was ready for implantation, and the shape had completely caught up with its evolutional process the day *after* it was supposed to be disposed.

We tried to consciously observe the process, which included me staying in bed for two days, but a wildfire threatened our home and we had to evacuate. When we eventually returned home, I received another message from Spirit that I was to stay in bed for four days. I listened again and was blessed with a vision. I saw a beautiful golden essence, arms spread wide; we embraced each other and merged spiritually and physically – pure awareness of this conscious creation in this moment!

I created my dream, experienced true alchemy of souls, and conscious creation. Science created the bridge to making my dream a possibility, and I learned that there are infinite ways to make your dreams come true.

My miracle daughter was born, and I am forever grateful.

Body Talk, Soul Whispers

By Bonnie L. Boucek

Living in pain is horrible. It often leaves one alone to contemplate the mysteries of life. Or to dwell on the fact that you're miserable and trying to find your way…again. This happens a great deal during the life of a chronic-illness survivor. Fate, however, can take you on an adventure.

I begin and end my day in pain – even on medication. It's my "norm." I accept this. I live with fibromyalgia, chronic pain, and several other illnesses. Each day, I listen to cues from my body: Where does it hurt? What aches? Is that a new pain? Yet, through all this pain, I still strive to improve my life. One way is by practicing meditation – a practice that led to a wonderful and terrifying discovery.

One time, I was feeling worse than normal but couldn't figure out why. After several months, I mentioned it to my doctor. Tests were ordered and I was referred to an endocrinologist for more tests. Diagnosis: primary hyperparathyroidism. Solution: surgery.

Decision time: surgery or no? I was told it would help with approximately one-fifth of my health issues. One-fifth! After filling my head with scary information from the web, I decided to schedule the surgery for the spring of 2019. Surgery: no issues. Recovery: sleep. Medications: ineffective.

It became an interesting guessing game to learn what was working or not. My body was a computer whose CPU had rebooted. I kept records of my illnesses to help me understand what was happening with my body, and I used the medical portal to obtain my copy of the reports. Surgery Report: sent specimen to pathology. Pathology: specimen tested. Result: shock. Reason: malignant. Time: acceptance.

Listening to my body through meditation, being stubborn, and forcing my doctors to find out why I felt miserable, I saved myself from a death sentence. Now, each morning, I take the time to be grateful for the things that touch my soul: good, bad, beautiful, and even ugly. This journey has caused me to re-evaluate numerous parts (clinical and spiritual) of my life. Regardless, it has made me aware of one thing: Life is more precious than many realize.

Discovering My Guiding Inner Voice

By Gigi Florez

I can vividly recall every single event in my life, ever since I was three years old. Maybe it was a gift. Maybe it was a curse. I couldn't tell. But my rather extraordinary ability to remember every moment made it very difficult and almost impossible for me to forgive and forget what was done to me.

Fighting a constant battle against my memories and how they affected my life every day was a difficult endeavor. Constantly asking myself "Why?" didn't help either. I wanted to find some meaning in this vicious thought process that poisonously mixed the past, the present, and even the future.

I began to read. I spoke to people. I read articles that came my way. I tried to interpret and perceive any message that the universe sent my way, to understand my life. In the process, I was able to unearth an inner voice, a voice that began to speak to me, like how a GPS instructs a device about where it is and where it must go.

It was an extraordinary awakening for me. No longer was I steeped in worry, anxiety, and stress caused by my past. I was able to live in the moment, taking every moment for what it was, and nothing more. Living life in the purest present is an extraordinary phenomenon. I was able to love myself. I was assured that I would find the direction I needed to go in. Life couldn't be simpler.

I was able to truly understand that only I could make myself happy. I only had to listen to the universe. I only had to be grateful for the messages being sent my way, harnessing purpose and meaning from them, to help me find myself.

Don't Hug a Cactus

By Jeanette St. Germain

I remember his smile, the kind that crinkles the skin just under the eyebrows. I remember his laugh, head thrown back like a lion as his humor hopscotched across all other conversation. I remember his warm, honeyed eyes staring into mine as early rays of dawn crept slowly through the bedroom window, that morning glow pale in comparison to the energy between our hearts.

There was a time, before grinding jaws and clenched fists, when I couldn't imagine a safer, more peaceful place to rest. Sometimes I would catch glimpses of that memory, when he chuckled at a funny video or helped our youngest make his daily smoothie. Small moments of laughter and mirth, but the surface happiness did little to soothe the anger gnawing at his core.

I spent years wearing down the muddy path inside my head, moving between "stay" or "go." Those on the outside usually advised the latter – easy to say without three young boys, a broken heart, and a mountain of bills in tow. I ran the gamut of counseling, separation, self-care, and spiritual enlightenment. Still, I loved a man who could not love himself, where one spark of anger could build a wildfire that choked the air from my throat.

One day in meditation, as I sat questioning how to embody love more fully, I noticed a blooming cactus in the front yard. I observed the spiked thorns, the soft pink and yellow flower petals, the bees reaching down through open buds. I noticed a cactus wren making its home in a hollowed-out edge and the footprints of baby quail at the base. Even with sharp barbs covering every surface, life blossomed.

I felt a warm, expansive energy of appreciation for the beauty before me. In that moment, I realized that somewhere along the line, I had convinced myself that it was impossible to leave something I loved, as if abandoning love itself. With a deep inhale, I let the truth sink in – gratitude is love, and it is possible to love without hugging the cactus.

I See You

By Kathy Sullivan Evans

I awoke this morning with what appears to be another message, a thought that came to mind as soon as I woke up, along with an urgency to write it down before it's quickly forgotten. The message was simple: "I see you." I wondered what it could mean.

"See" – a simple three-letter word with so many meanings. Webster's Dictionary's definitions of the word include "to perceive with the eyes; to look at; to scan or view; to perceive mentally; to construct a mental image of; recognize; to foresee; to ascertain, learn or find out; to make sure; to meet and converse with; to receive as a visitor; to visit; to court or keep company with," to name just a few.

When I was a child, my mother used to yell out at us girls from beyond any possible line of sight, "I see you!" We would look at one another in amazement that our mother was "all-seeing" and someone to be in awe of for having such powers!

At my monthly writer's class, we begin the session by taking a long pause and actually looking at each writer's eyes, seeing their innermost being, and smiling. I see you! It's said that if you look at someone with your third eye, you will see that person's aura and can gain insight into that person's persona by the color reflected around them.

The popular movie *Avatar* invokes the sense of "I see you" when Neytiri of the Na'vi tribe looks into Jake Sully's eyes for the first time when they realize their soul connection. Leona Lewis sings their theme song, appropriately entitled "I See You." Just beautiful!

So when the sun begins to peek above the horizon this morning, I will rise up from my writer's mode, go to the window, bask in the witness of another new day – a day of new possibilities, new connections, and new experiences – and say, "I see you!"

A Glitch as the Messenger

By Helen Ferrara

I had looked everywhere I could think of. I was holding the Third Eye Chakradance™ class on my own tonight, but the notes for it were missing. While I'd found those for all the other workshops in the cycle, these remained elusive. The text to my colleague, asking her to email them, had finally reached her hours after I'd sent it, just when she was waiting to board her flight home and couldn't access her computer.

At long last, with only minutes to spare before needing to leave, I located the original flash drive I'd received the notes on. Yes, they were there! Happy to have finally found them, I went to print them out, but my printer kept jamming on the first page. I tried printing six times – clearing the paper and resetting everything. But nothing worked.

When the echo of my colourful expletives had faded, I finally heard the "little voice" inside me trying to tell me that I wasn't to take any notes with me. I was being told to trust my intuition and act on my insights, thereby truly living the message of the Third Eye. So I trusted and spontaneously said what I felt called to say during the workshop.

Later, a number of participants shared that I had spoken some very significant phrases, different for each, that had caused major shifts within them as they danced. If I'd had the notes, this couldn't have happened.

The next morning, I had mixed feelings about trying to print something, because now I would find out whether it had all just been a coincidence, an unlucky happenstance. Opening a document on my MacBook and almost holding my breath, I tentatively sent it to be printed. It worked perfectly on the first try.

I felt elated, as well as hugely grateful and humbled. I don't easily lose my cool, but the printer jamming that many times was really exasperating; it had certainly served to make me pay attention. Now the message had been confirmed: my intuition and higher self connect me to the Universe with a strength that I would never have imagined.

It Pays to Heed My Inner Voice

By Joy T. Barican

Work and other priorities have kept Mum and me from fulfilling our dreams to travel and explore. It took a milestone birthday to compel us both to make our dreams a reality.

As Mum and I are not seasoned travellers, we engaged the services of an experienced travel consultant from a reputable agency with branches worldwide. This gave us peace of mind that everything in the guided tour packages we purchased would be taken care of.

We could hardly contain our excitement as we counted down the months, then the weeks, then the days. Not even rain dampened our spirits as we marched to the travel agency to collect our branded luggage tags, printed itineraries, and vouchers. The travel agent briefly walked us through each document, which appeared to be in order.

Mum and I boarded the plane for the first leg of our flight filled with elation for the six-week journey. As I settled myself down, I felt a nudge to review the itinerary. I tried to pacify the inner voice by telling myself to relax and that all was well. However, the inner voice got louder and this time with urgency. Although I was an unwilling participant, I found myself reaching out for the papers from my bag, which was stored under the seat. The task was daunting, as it was six weeks' worth of details to review, but the voice remained insistent.

Just when I thought the review was redundant, I could not believe what I was seeing. Imagine my shock upon discovering that the travel agent failed to make a hotel reservation in London for the extended days we had planned for prior to returning home. To say that I was not impressed would be an understatement. However, the feeling of gratitude overpowered my feeling of dismay. My soulful message saved us from the inconvenience and the panic that would have ensued when realising at the last minute that we were without accommodation.

Heeding my inner voice enabled course correction, ensuring that the entire trip was the kind of holiday dreams are made of.

Just Ask

By Rand Allen

Our conversation was deep and enthralling, like it always was whenever Robehr and I got together. You know, one of those slingshots past the moon right into a wormhole, then off to another galaxy-type conversations. During this conversation in particular, I had one of those exuberant yet burning rhetorical questions about why things in my life are the way they are. And Robehr just smiled and said, "We'll ask."

To which I replied, "Ask WHO?"

He smiled and said, "Just ASK" again, but this time he gave me a gentle poke in the chest as he pointed to my heart, meaning ask your inner self, or as he put it later on, "Ask your true Center Soul for the answer with reverence and love."

I immediately grinned because a part of me already knew this was true. So I started doing exactly that, and interestingly enough, the answer to what I was asking just floated to the surface of my subconscious and popped right into my conscious mind, which never failed to make me smile as my newfound connection to spirit gave me the answers I had never expected to receive. And truth be told, it usually wasn't much of a wait either.

Some might also call it my subconscious or even super-conscious mind or say that I'm accessing the Akashic Records through spirit. Whatever the case, as I learned to fully embrace this process of communing with my true Center Soul, many of the answers I had been seeking found resolution, and a calmness set in because I realized that truth is never that far away. It really is right there hiding within us, guiding us and helping us on our journey. I found that it also worked for lots of things, like lost keys and remembering forgotten things when your mind gets ahead of itself. So whenever I am pondering life's great mysteries, I close my eyes, put my hand on my heart...and just ask.

The Power of a Question

By Christine Callahan-Oke

I awoke from a dream with a question dangling clearly in my mind: "Are you a storyteller?" I didn't know who had asked it or where it came from, but it was prominent enough to stay with me for days.

Am I a storyteller?

I rarely remember things from my dreams, so this felt important. What did it mean – storyteller? I had blogged for years and pictured myself writing a book in the distant future but always imagined it would be inspirational non-fiction. I never envisioned writing short stories or novels.

After a while, I let the question settle in the back of my mind.

A couple of weeks later, a Facebook friend posted about a sale on an app for book writers. It caught my attention. Since I planned to write a book at some point, I decided to order it. I downloaded it to my computer for "someday" and resumed my usual activities.

Shortly afterwards, seemingly out of the blue, ideas started trickling into my mind for a story. Then they came more quickly. I woke up with ideas. More ideas emerged in the shower. Several more ideas popped up one day while I was vacuuming. The story, an empowering adventure story for kids, clearly wanted to be told.

I looked up, shrugged, and said loudly, "Okay, I'm listening!" And I started writing. And writing. So, I'm now working on the manuscript for my first book.

Looking back, I realize it could have been so easy to dismiss any or all of those signs – the question from my dream, the app, the story ideas – if I hadn't been intuitively guided to sense that a divine thread connected them.

I had been given a beautiful gift from the universe – an invitation to stay open to signs, play with the possibilities, and see what emerged.

We are all given breadcrumbs from the universe. What we choose to do with them is up to us. If we stay open to them and decide to follow where they lead, there's every chance for magic to unfold.

No Ordinary Feeling

By Karen Wythe

The car was packed, the weather was great, the sun was shining – everything pointed to a beautiful time on the road. We were ready for the three-day getaway we'd been looking forward to for weeks.

Bill and I were standing at the back of the van, preparing to close the hatch, when we looked at each other apprehensively. I said, "I don't know why, but I really don't feel like going."

He quickly responded, "I don't either. Let's just stay home."

We walked back into the house and sat down. "Why did we change our minds?" we asked ourselves. We had no reasonable explanation; however, we agreed that we'd totally lost interest in venturing away from home. No feelings of doom. No thoughts of anything going wrong. We just had no desire to leave. So we went out, unpacked the vehicle, and settled back into a normal day at home.

Later that evening, while in the utility room doing laundry, it looked like it was going to rain any minute. I reached over and closed the window when I heard a hissing noise. Directly behind me in a box was a can of green spray paint. I must have pushed something onto it that caused it to spray. Panicked, I was able to finally reach it, but not before the whole can emptied. My hands were completely covered in green paint!

Running to the nearest sink, I found myself in a frenzy trying to wash the paint from my hands. I turned on the hot water, but the water was cool. I changed sinks but that water wouldn't heat up either. Bill checked the hot water tank and saw water leaking everywhere. We went through an hour of pure chaos and were without hot water for a day while we waited for the new tank, but we considered ourselves very lucky to have avoided major home damage.

We are happy we listened to that mysterious feeling and are very thankful that we finally understood the message.

The Importance of Silence

By Kenneth I. Laws II

I have come to understand the importance of silence, not only while alone but also when shared with someone else. I am an observer, a thinker, an analyzer – sometimes even an overanalyzer – and I sometimes misinterpret my wife's silence as meaning that there's something wrong. In these moments, I must remember to shut off my brain and open my heart.

When I just listen to the silence with my heart, it has no questions, no judgments, no assumptions. In these moments of quiet, my heart opens. When I accept my wife's silence as simply silence (with no hidden meaning or agenda), I feel closest to her.

I have learned that this comfortable type of silence is okay and that the deepest connection between two people happens when there are no words used at all. Sometimes shared silence is the only way to just slow down while in the presence of another – sitting closely, holding hands, and just being present without words spoken. When I genuinely listen to the silence, it is reciprocated in many other ways: sitting even closer together, holding each other, or offering a gentle kiss with an even deeper loving look into my eyes. There is nothing quite like it.

I try to learn from these little lessons in life, guided by my heart, that teach me to be a better listener, a better husband, and a better friend. When I fail to recognize my faults and flaws – and, more importantly, own them – then I have become unteachable. I must always be willing to take a look in the mirror and remain teachable.

So, what has my heart taught me? Silence is just as important as spoken communication. Words tend to cloud our feelings and emotions, if not alter them altogether. But in silence, the most tender moments can be felt, experienced, and cherished, uncomplicated by words.

Being with What Is So

By Bianca Lynn

My father and I were very close. He was a man with a sharp wit who loved a good pun. I could always count on him for support and guidance.

He was a well-spoken man who started to lose his words in his late 80s. Over the course of several years, I watched as his abilities eroded. It started with a little forgetfulness. Then speaking became a huge effort. In February, my father suffered an event that took away his ability to walk.

Watching his deterioration, I grappled with questions about how there could be any mercy in the universe if this were allowed to happen. There were days when all I could do was sit in my car and weep as I left him, trying to release the heavy burden of his decline.

A few months later, I found myself in the desert. Sitting under a juniper tree, a message came: "Be with what is so, and there is no suffering," it said.

Be with what is so, and there is no suffering? Interesting, then…*B.S.!*, I thought.

Nonetheless, I could not shake the message. It had been so clear and so strong. So I brought it home and back to my father's side. At this point he was completely cared for by others, something I imagine he would have hated had it been just a theoretical idea.

I began sitting with my father from the place of being with what is so. As I did, a different reality began to unfold before me. He did not seem to be suffering at all. In fact, he actually seemed fine. Was it possible that I was suffering but he was not?

He passed away almost a year ago. I got to share the last few months with him, not from a place of suffering but from a place of *all is well*. "Be with what is so, and there is no suffering" allowed me to release myself and my father and simply experience the love that is underneath all.

My Hero Is Me

By Suzanne M. Fortino

I left home at 14. My boyfriend's parents took me in and embraced me as though I were their daughter. They were my heroes. They loved God, life, and *A Course in Miracles*. They became my teachers, and though I had not yet understood the concept or fully embraced living life as a student of the Course, my life was forever changed. Their unconditional love and the introduction to *A Course in Miracles* became beautiful pieces of my life puzzle.

My boyfriend and I eventually married, had children together, and stayed together for 13 years. Over time, however, our relationship became extremely dysfunctional. After my mother-in-law helped me escape an abusive lifestyle, I set out on a mission to find a man that had the same qualities as my father-in-law. I decided I needed to find a man with the same astrological sign as him, and I managed to find myself five Aquarians, but none of them ended up being my hero. I finally realized it was not the astrological sign that made my father-in-law so special.

My mother passed away when I was 29, and six weeks later, I met a man who lit up my world. Although he was an Aquarius, he managed to fail the three test questions I had for him. But I tossed my criteria aside and fell madly in love. I finally realized that even though he is my Aquarius, he is not my hero.

The quest to find my Aquarius was really a quest to find myself. I viewed my father-in-law as my savior, my hero, and I knew I had to find my own hero. For years, I looked outside myself, but the hero I have been looking for was here all along. My hero is inside me. My hero is me. I am my own savior. With the help of my adoptive parents teaching me the Course and showing me unconditional love, I finally understand that I am the one I have been looking for my whole life.

Meant to Be

By Amy Coppola

"Love is the master key that opens the gates of happiness."
– Anonymous

My career requires me to travel extensively throughout the USA. One business trip took me back to Cocoa Beach, Florida – the place where my ex-husband and I once vacationed. Driving in the rented car down the familiar road to the ocean, I nostalgically soaked up the day's sunshine mixed with memories of our emotional storms. Suddenly, reaching the main stoplight in Cocoa, I realized that I could turn left to visit our former condo. I did. In minutes, I arrived in the condo's parking lot, where I was joined by anxiety and nervousness, along with all our memories – good and bad.

His motorcycle was parked in its spot, and for a moment, I thought about knocking, but my intuition yelled, "Don't open that door!" – so I listened and left.

Back on the road to the hotel for business, I felt waves of relief and confidence from that decision. As I walked into the hotel, gratitude flooded me as I met my coworkers gathered in the lobby. These colleagues and the healthy friendships we shared were now my life. The next morning during the business meeting, it became clear how much stronger I'd become over the past seven years. Everywhere I went that week, a new guy was always near and it felt great – he had exceptional energy.

During that same week, my grandmother transitioned to the other side of life, making it more meaningful. She had always wanted me to meet a man who would look out for me, and I genuinely believe that this new man was a gift from her.

My intuitive guidance reminded me that when a relationship door is closed to keep it closed – this creates space for someone better! I realized that when you least expect it, someone special may walk into your life. This is what happened to me, and the guy I met on that business trip continues to be the trusted partner who helps me on my path in life. Whether you are loving yourself or loving someone special in your life, love is the key needed to open the door to happiness.

The Process of Self-Love

By Ayeesha S. Kanji

For a change, I was just sitting and listening to music. No downtown, no night out, just Netflix with Harvey Spector. I was scrolling through my Instagram feed on my laptop, reading old posts, and a post from February caught my eye. I had written a post about self-love. In that post, I took a selfie of myself in a dress because I felt physically amazing and liked how I look in that dress.

It dawned on me that I had not put on that dress since then. I pondered the possible reasons why I hadn't worn it. Was it because I had once again fallen off the bandwagon of juicing, exercising, and meal planning? Or because I put so much pressure on myself about feeling physically good enough to meet standards?

I realized that it's both, and now I realize why. I'm so busy with all the happy chaos that my self-love will go up and down. I know it's not just me either. Yes, I fell off the bandwagon, and yes, I did pressure myself. It is time not just for me but for everyone to accept that self-love is a process. It will have ups and downs. Is self-love perfect? No. Humans are not perfect, which is why self-love is a process.

The process of self-love is showing up, continuing to try, and not giving up. That's how I got through it; and even today, it's exactly what I do to feel good, dress up, and carry my boldness with me.

In your own process of self-love, remember to show up and carry your boldness and your strength with attitude because self-love starts there, with showing up and not giving up.

I Am

By Alyssa Canella

I often wonder if I exist. If you asked me who I am, there's only one answer I could give: *I am Alyssa*. I am. Everything else – my favorite songs, movies, smells, colors, clothes, foods, places – I can't claim as mine. I'm the hoarding heaps of miscellaneous people I've let become as much a part of me as I am. I keep people safe that way: by preserving them like a rose pressed in book pages.

I preserve the memories of friendships and romances as they were before we grew back into strangers; my golden retriever, Copper, before he went blind; my grandpa before he started forgetting. Compounds form when two substances chemically combine to create something new and indistinguishable from what it was. I am who I am because of everyone and everything I've encountered. Each encounter holds a life lesson.

When I was little, I used to believe the lie my parents told me about where babies come from: "When two people love each other very much…" I thought that out of love, life was made. I assumed this life was a child; I didn't know that *I* could be reborn through love and its destruction.

When I was three, I went on a nature walk with my aunt, picked up a leaf, and asked, "Why is it that it is what it is and not what it is not?" about the autumn leaf. I learned that when chlorophyll breaks down, leaves' green disappears and yellow-orange colors become visible before they fall. Through my changing seasons, I need the serenity to accept the things I cannot change, courage to change the things I can, and wisdom to know the difference.

I do exist: through the preservations of those I love. Love is a circle of power, as Black Elk's poem "Everything the Power of the World Does Is Done in a Circle" describes. Love is a bruise, sore and sweet, demanding to be felt; giving without expecting anything in return; knowing the whole of someone (even yourself). Love is. After everything, love still is, and so am I.

The Divine Nudge

By Jody Doty

It's during rough patches in life when mortality holds up a mirror and you pray to find small blessings in everyday moments. One of those blessings came to me in the form of an intuitive, divine nudge.

I had been at my mother's hospital bedside for days. What began in the ER culminated in a miraculous recovery and her return from death's doorway. My heart was grateful, but my body was tired. I planned to stay late when I heard the message that I needed to leave now.

All my life, I've received flashes of insight and intuitive visions. I've learned to listen to the whispers of my soul, so that's what I did that night. Mom and I shared I-love-yous, and I headed to the elevator.

When the door opened, I saw a woman holding a hospital bag. I assumed it contained personal belongings. She was quiet; I could see tears in her eyes, and I sensed she was alone. We stopped at the lobby and began the silent walk to the parking garage. Divine providence took over. I looked at her and said, "Do you need a hug?"

"Oh, yes, please," she said. We stood there for a long time, hugging each other while she cried and I held her. She said, "Thank you. I just lost my dad. I know it was meant to be. He was sick for so long, but it hurts my heart, even knowing it's for the best."

I was moved. "I know it's not the same," I said, "but I feel, sense, and see his spirit here with you."

She smiled knowingly and said, "Yes."

It was no accident that we came together that day. We needed each other. We understood and we cared. The spirit of love touched our hearts; we were filled with compassion.

Upon reflection, I was reminded that a healing presence in this world is more valuable than words. Social media, texting, Twitter, and Instagram are a poor substitute for a touch, a hug, a nod, or a smile and will never replace human love or our soul-to-soul connection.

You Are the Key

By Michelle Berube

My eyes began to well up with tears, and I knew it was only a matter of seconds before the floodgates would open and there'd be no stopping the deluge. Rather than feeling negative, however, this sensation felt freeing, refreshing, and full of life. I, however, felt suffocated and trapped – like a bird in a cage trying to spread its wings and soar – plagued by a gnawing feeling that grew stronger with each passing year.

I was stuck and no one could help. For years, I shied away from doing what felt right to me, too afraid to follow through on my desires. And what I did do always seemed to backfire, creating more strife. This pattern left me exhausted and spiraling out of control emotionally, mentally, and physically – until the day I fell to my knees under a radiant poplar tree, feeling that I simply couldn't go on like this.

Sobbing uncontrollably, I sat with my back against the tree. In that moment, a strong sense of peace encompassed me. As I began to regroup myself, the sweetness of the birds singing swept through my body and brought a smile to my face. I looked up and noticed that the clouds had begun to part, uncovering the sun, which shone intensely upon me. With my eyes toward the heavens, I asked, "How do I get out of this cage? Where and what is the key?"

The sun's intensity engulfed my whole being with peace and serenity, and I heard the words, "You are the key." Within my mind's eye, I was shown the most beautiful key I have ever seen, which has been embedded in my mind since that day. I felt deeply supported and connected to everything. I knew that it was okay for me to unlock the door that I had yearned to unlock, to answer my heart's calling.

We are all our own key. We all have the power to unlock the doors we choose to walk through, to answer the call of our hearts.

Energy in Motion

By Robyn Ringgold

After deciding against driving eight hours round trip to Pittsburgh to join friends for a ceremony where three rivers meet, I woke up with an overwhelming urge to go.

Upon arriving at the boardwalk, I found a bench where I could meditate while waiting for my friends. I noticed a man and a woman in the distance. The man was taking a few labored steps one leg at a time while grasping the railing, and the woman was pushing his wheelchair beside him. After a few steps, his energy was clearly depleted and he would sit down and she would push a bit, and then they would stop again and he would try a few more steps. I was amazed by his determination.

I began to meditate and felt a calming sense of peace wash over me. When I opened my eyes, the couple was in front of me. Our eyes briefly met, but we didn't speak to one another. That's when I heard a voice inside of me say, "Give energy healing to him."

My heart sank, my throat closed, and my stomach began to knot. How could I give healing to a stranger? What would I even say to him? By this time, they had passed me, and I decided it was too late. Immediately, I felt a wave of disappointment wash over me. This was a Divine request. The disappointment was unbearable. I felt ashamed of myself.

The couple sat down on a nearby bench. Here was another chance. I walked over to them. "Hi, my name is Robyn, and I do energy healing. Would it be okay if I shared some energy with you?"

The man's face lit up, "I'll take all of the help I can get!"

I gently lifted his hands, and an incredible wave of energy came through my body and into this man, unlike anything I had ever experienced. Our eyes met and the tears welled up, connecting our souls beyond words.

The voice spoke. "His soul accepted the healing, and he will walk again."

My First Yoga Class

By Gabrielle Taylor

Being quite accustomed to following my mom on her artistic and creative ventures, I accept her invitation to come to yoga class.

The yoga centre is on a busy Montreal street, near my elementary school. Yet recently, since the first hint of puberty, my still-childish imagination sees it as an alien land, a concrete jungle, bustling with serious adults. Unlike me, these "butchers, bakers, and candlestick makers" each have their place and identity in the order of things.

Over the past year, new hormones have been transforming my 11-year-old body's shape and size in ways that are uncomfortable. I've become increasingly awkward and uncoordinated, and my body feels foreign and unfamiliar.

Whereas beforehand I'd played freely, now a voice inside whispers that I should restrain myself, refrain from being too impulsive or carefree. There's pressure to be more acceptable and pleasing, in both personality and appearance. Whereas previously I'd been curious, confident, and agile (and one of the first chosen for the dodgeball team), I now feel trapped between childhood and a grown-up world in which I'm forever doomed as a misfit.

The yoga studio is welcoming, peaceful, and quiet. The instructor has us lie down on mats and simply breathe. Within moments, the heavy weight of judgment and expectation begins to lift as I allow the breath to flow through my lungs and belly.

She leads us through a simple sequence of poses, ending with deep relaxation. As I lie there with my eyes closed, I imagine myself swimming in a lake, the fresh, clear water caressing my skin and enlivening each pore. I see myself in a meadow of wildflowers under a blue sky, with the solid nurturing earth supporting me beneath. I feel vital energy pulsate through my entire body and soul.

The constraining labels dissipate, and once again I can sense and embrace some ease in my changing female body. For a brief moment, I get an inkling how, just like a rare and beautiful flower, I may find ways to remain myself and grow into who I am to become.

Self-Love

By Barbara Yager

Do you love yourself?

There are countless articles about self-love and the importance of loving yourself. Honestly, I believe that most of us think we love ourselves and routinely dismiss the importance of this topic.

If you had asked me several years ago if I loved myself, I would have answered with a resounding "yes." But the truth was that I really didn't. I now know this because when it came to taking care of my health, I was not doing a loving job.

For decades, I abused food, which led to a lifelong weight problem. I was well over 100 pounds overweight, and I had fooled myself into thinking that I would find the magic potion, diet, or vitamin that would help me lose the excess weight.

Year after year, I struggled to fit into clothes and into life. I endured so many embarrassing situations. Frequently, I was forced to settle for less than what I truly wanted because of my large size.

Despite the embarrassing and anxiety-filled moments, I continued to abuse food, failing to acknowledge the void of self-love in my life.

Then one day it all changed. I woke up feeling terrible. I ached all over and could barely move. For the first time, I felt my health was in true jeopardy. Over the years, I had promised myself that when my weight started to affect my health, I would get busy and do something about it. Well, the day had arrived. Sitting in the morning silence, filled with fear, I asked myself, "What do I need to do to deal with this weight?"

The guidance came in the form of very clear words: "You have to fully love yourself to make it happen." In that moment, my life changed with the Divine realization I was given. I stopped abusing food and never looked back. I reminded myself over and over that making good food choices was the biggest act of self-love.

Today, I am 120 pounds lighter and am fully loving myself!

The Power of Love

By Keyon Bayani

While reading *The Alchemist* by Paulo Coelho, I got to a part that took my breath away. What I took away from it was that my soulmate was out there in the world, waiting for me, just as I was waiting for him, and that one day, our paths would cross and we would just know.

Ten years later, I was at work, and the new guy at my job walked past my office. As he did, I heard my higher self tell me loud and clear, "You're going to marry him." I told my work colleague who was with me at the time, and we both laughed.

I didn't really think twice about what I had heard. The new guy started dating another woman in the office, and I was dating other people. But we became friends, so when I broke my foot in a freak accident, he came and visited me in the hospital. Still, after that initial message from my higher self, I never really thought about us being anything more than friends.

After I was discharged from the hospital, I was invited to a friend's party. I asked the new guy to go with me, to sit around and keep me company because I was on crutches. After the party, when we were alone, he told me that he wanted to be in a relationship with me. I couldn't believe what I was hearing. It sounded like his voice was a million miles away; it was surreal, and I was scared.

It took him two weeks to convince me to at least give us a try.

I fell in love with him one night when I was picking a fight with him, expecting his reaction to be the same as I had always gotten from past partners, but he shocked me: he didn't react in the same way. Instead, he said, "Keyon, I love you." Those words disarmed me, and today, as I write this, we are celebrating our 12th wedding anniversary.

I Had to Go Deeper

By David Hipshman

I got caught in the real-estate bubble burst, which I feared would happen, and I found myself two million dollars in debt. A friend said that that takes powerful manifesting. My trusted mentor said my soul wanted this to happen. Why, I thought, would I want this? I was in overwhelming fear, and not just about the money but about the shame of what people would think.

My number-one strategy in life had been to think my way out of challenges. But that was not going to work in this situation, as I didn't have a solution for paying back that two million. I had to go deeper.

Fortunately, I had recently started participating in an amazing meditation community. I participated in an "active" meditation almost every day to move out deep feelings of anger, fear, and shame. I really had to, to not go crazy. I went to a retreat where I surrendered and cleared out all the pain and dismantled my ego. Once I did this, I was guided to explore filing for bankruptcy. Freer of ego and shame, I was able to focus on solutions.

I did file for bankruptcy and removed most of the debt; but more importantly, I was free of the shame and the anger. I was able to move forward with a new life that eventually included coaching business owners.

This "dark night" ended up being a gift that transformed me. I remember thinking, as I overcame those challenges, that I would later help others overcome overwhelming challenges, too. And that is what I do now: help others as I had envisioned, and a big part of it is to be healed from any feelings of shame about failure. That is a key to success for those growing a business or wanting more from life than comfort. It's my business and a devotion: living a life of abundance, regardless of the external, material conditions.

Guided to Share Miracles

By Lottie Grant Cooper

With bravery, I announced to a large audience of business coaches, "I am available for healing work."

One woman at the seminar shared that she had been having chronic hip pain for over 25 years. She'd already tried physical therapy, chiropractors, traditional medicine, healers, and everything she could think of, all to no avail. We went to source energy.

With her permission, I connected with her, intuitively read her space, and asked her deep questions. Using all my knowledge from understanding family systems, psychology, family constellations, loyalty patterns, subconscious repatterning, the need to belong, soul retrieval work, working with colors, and more, we found out she had hidden resentment toward her mother from an incident she had forgotten about at age five. Although she had consciously forgotten this incident, her body kept the pain as a reminder. So I helped her facilitate releasing trapped, suppressed emotions, helped her untangle from her mother's energy and beliefs, told her inner five-year-old that she is now safe and can let go, did some soul retrieval work, and more.

The pain on a scale of 1-10 was about an 8 when we began; it dissolved into 0 by the time we were done with the process.

To this beautiful woman, it was a miracle to have 25 years of chronic pain gone. My miracle: she became my long-term transformational coaching client.

I let my voice out in front of hundreds of people when this ball of energy entered into my gut and compelled me to get up, raise my hand, and speak. I now have the courage to share my gifts in more circles, be on the radio, become a public speaker, and more. Now, thousands of people have worked with me and experienced internal miracles, relieved pain, resolved internal conflicts, found inner peace, released addictions, restored love, mended broken relationships, repaired self-esteem, expanded their businesses, and gotten unstuck in their lives.

I have seen that with the correct information, the body, mind, and soul can heal. And with awareness, listening, asking, receiving, skill, deep presence, and taking action, miracles occur.

It's Time

By Kara Kissinger

I ducked out of my office and into the dimly lit hallway to take the call I'd been expecting. The soft male voice on the other end said, "I'm sorry; it's positive."

I stood there clutching my coworker's hand as I sobbed and heard terrifying words like "grade, testing, surgeon." I had breast cancer.

The next weeks were filled with devastating emotions and sickening fear. My husband and I muddled through surgical and oncology visits to understand my stage, prognosis, and treatment options. Our hearts broke as we told our kids.

Five weeks after my diagnosis, I had a double mastectomy and scheduled a treatment plan including reconstruction surgery. I was incredibly blessed with a boss and coworkers who held me up during those weeks. I didn't have to worry about missing work or a paycheck. I was free to heal.

Eventually, I returned to work and every day I would pass that same hallway. Sometimes I'd look away because it was too painful to remember. Sometimes I'd look directly at it and offer up a prayer of gratitude. Because of the news I received there, I was taking better care of myself in all ways than I ever had in my 48 years. I was also grateful for coworkers who had become family.

A few months later, as I walked past that dim hallway, I felt the words "it's time," and a peace that filled every limb and space in my body settled into me. I'd never felt so certain that I'd received a divine message. It was time.

Time to finally take courage and leave for the career opportunity I'd held in my heart for so long while making excuses as to why it wouldn't work. It was time to say yes to the unfolding and to the very specific vision I'd held about where I wanted to spend my days sharing my talents with the company whose mission sparked passion in my heart. I'd laid the intentional groundwork a year prior, but it wasn't time then. But now, it was time.

Release from the Mind Prison

By H. Michelle Spaulding

Two years ago, my friend and I became empty nesters and decided to embark on a wellness plan. After years of "mothering," we were practicing self-care by embarking on a diet and exercise program. My friend – who was eating healthfully, working with her trainer, and losing weight – suggested that I come and use her pool so I could exercise and move pain free without hurting my joints. I was excited about the idea and the freedom that getting into the water would provide. But I was scared that I would get hurt, that it would be too hard to get into her pool, and that I couldn't do it without assistance. So, for a long, time, I didn't take her up on her offer.

Recently, however, my friend gently reminded me that I still could use her pool to exercise in. This time my pain overrode my insecurities, and I said yes. The next emotional hurdle I was presented with was finding and wearing a swimsuit. I purchased swimwear from a plus-size catalog. The main reason I hadn't swum much in the past was fear of being body shamed. This time I was determined to persevere. I became very frustrated and dejected after trying on two swimsuits that didn't fit. I kept searching until I found one that fit and also felt comfortable. At that moment, I realized that for over 30 years I had put myself in a mind prison. I had been holding myself hostage over unfounded fears and body-image insecurities.

Luckily, my friend had a handicap access to her pool. As I slowly walked into the water, I felt a freedom I hadn't felt in over a decade. My joints were relieved of carrying the weight and pain of my body. A feeling of bliss shot through my chest with every step I took toward the deep end of the pool. When my feet could no longer touch the bottom, I felt as though I were floating through the air. My spirit was free, and the water released my burdens.

I had escaped from my self-created mind prison.

The Perfect Gift

By Maria Angela Russo

I awakened to the smell of freshly brewed coffee as the morning sun rose. Sitting up with a start, I felt oddly joyful. Then I remembered. "It is New Year's Day, 1983, the year I turn 40." Excited, I recalled how I'd spent my first 20 years trying to please my mother and the next 20 trying to please my husband, Stephen. "If I am lucky enough to live another 20 years," I practically shouted, "then I am claiming them for me!"

I decided that I would give myself the best possible birthday present that year, and I had eight months to figure out what that might be. Up until then, I had been the dutiful wife and mother with no sense of who I was or what I wanted. Stephen was a General Motors executive who brought home the money while I cared for the house and our three children, which included helping everyone get adjusted to the out-of-state transfers we experienced about every two years.

My childhood groomed me well for this role. My dominating, non-negotiable mother stifled all signs of independence in me from the very beginning. I thought when I got married I'd be free to become myself, but instead I discovered I was living with a young male version of my mother with his own strong convictions about how I should live my life.

"But now it is my turn!" Ignoring all opposition from Stephen, I started going to workshops and weekend retreats that could help empower me. The only thing I ever did for myself was to take a single college class here and there to satisfy a longing since high school for a college education. As summer approached, it became increasingly clear that that dream had never died, and I discovered the perfect gift.

Within six months I had enrolled in a community college, despite Stephen's fury. I transferred to the university halfway through the first year to enroll in a four-year Psychology Program, and two weeks after graduation, I entered graduate school. Today, I am well into my second set of "another 20 years," doing what I love, just being me.

Just for Today, Do Not Worry

By Hue Anh Nguyen

I will never forget January 14, 2017. I received a call from my son's bike coach. "You need to get to the hospital now!" During a race, my son had crashed face down and had a seizure. My heart stopped. I started shaking as I told my husband. My mind was spinning, as I worried about the condition my son was in and whether I would have to face life without him.

I quickly stopped my worried thoughts. I told myself, "I need to pray and stay calm." I sent out a message, asking all my prayer warriors to focus on him. That was all I could do now. I remembered the Reiki precept I had learned: Just for today, do not worry.

I got a call from the medics. "We have your son. He's alert and awake!" I breathed a sigh of relief. The medic continued, "I wanted to verify some information. Is it true that it's your son's 17th birthday?"

"Yes, it is his birthday today!"

We reached the hospital and found my son waiting for an MRI. He appeared to be fine, even though he looked like something out of *Nightmare on Elm Street*. He wanted his photo taken, to see what his face looked like. (Teenagers!) He texted his group chat to find hundreds of texts from his friends, wishing him well.

Later, he told me, "Mom, you know I didn't feel okay this morning about racing, and I didn't listen to that instinct. I'm sorry."

Every mother worries about her children's safety. When the worst happens, we need to trust and focus on staying in the very moment. We *can* prevent worry from taking over. With "Just for today, do not worry," we can learn to trust our intuition. As we practice, we can discern if our worry should be heeded or if we need to simply trust.

My Time to Shine

By Michael Brewer

I receive messages from my soul every day. I wake up and my soul will say, "This is going to be a beautiful day." And the day flows smoothly. I meet beautiful souls, and I have the opportunity to do some of my favourite things, like watching the sunrise, swimming in the ocean, or listening to a relaxing meditation. It is just a beautiful day.

On other days, my soul will say, "Be careful today." On these days, I will ask Archangel Michael to protect my energy as I go through the day. There may be little hiccups, and I will meet people with low vibrations. I do my best to make these days good days, too.

I know that my life can move so quickly that sometimes my soul's voice does not have the opportunity to be heard. At these times, I can feel that something in my life is not quite right. It is important for me to find time to be still and be one with my soul. My soul knows what is best for me.

My soul's voice has been telling me for many months that it is time to let go of who I have been and step into my true purpose (in this life). I have been afraid to let go and embrace the uncertainty of life. This has caused a great deal of angst and worry. I stopped trusting myself to make the right decisions. I have been stuck in a job that I no longer love doing.

In recent days, I have decided to follow my soul. I am going to quit my job. I have booked a six-week holiday to Hong Kong and the United Kingdom. I am still not 100 percent certain what my future holds. I am taking a chance on life. It is time to share my true, authentic self with the world. I believe I can feel that the best of my life is yet to come. I will be following my soul's messages into my glorious future.

Cancer's Message

By Tara Leduc

I have lived with cancer for 19 years. I have known for some time that it was trying to catch my attention. Yet I have never thought to ask it: What is your message? This is a conversation, a journey, we recently had: "Cancer, what would you have me know? What would you have me do? We've been together for a long time now. Tell me your purpose."

***

Coyote tore at the left side. Pancreas, liver, spleen, then breast, shoulder, leg. Left is the feminine side. Soft, yielding, nurturing, gentle. Weak?

A void remained after flesh ripped away. Coyote brought me to Ocean. At the shallow pools, the liminal edge of soil and salt, the anemones grew. The seaweed bloomed. Otter came. Remake me, Ocean.

So I can know my bigness, my vastness. My power. My rage. Yes, the rage. To transform, to change. You can effect change. Bigger than you think. Transformation of hurricanes, of tornados, of meteors.

The feminine side is the power. Power of Kali, the Destroyer. She who destroys with cataclysmic violence. And who creates with tenderness, gentleness, vision. Vision for the future of the earth, the planet, of humanity. It is possible. Peace is possible. Massive change, teardown, destruction is necessary. To renew. To bring in the New Era, the New Way.

As we are reborn, we come this time with wisdom, tolerance, compassion, grounded hope. Aquarians, you are summoned back. Assemble the starfish, the otter, the salt, and form a Council of Knowing. The yin is not weakness; it is softness. It is the flowing, gentle, rage-filled power of the Ocean.

This is the message of the Cancer. The disease to shift you to dis-ease. To create action and change for different, for better. It is time. Start here. Start now. Start small. To create Peace anew.

***

This is the message for me from the cancer that resides in my body. Have you thought to ask *your* disease why it brings dis-ease? What would it have *you* know?

The Everything of Life

By Tanya Levy

My son's father had died. I was studying away from home when I got the call, and my support system was four hours away. I took a break from my studies to travel home for the wake. I felt very alone as I was packing and decided to travel the next morning since it was late when I found out.

That night I dreamed I was going door to door selling a business product. The person who answered the door said, "I am not buying anything, but I am a painter. Why don't you come and see what I am creating today?" He took me to a beautiful wooded area, and I saw a canvas that he had painted on the path ahead.

The canvas showed two baskets. One had beautiful orb-like eggs in a brilliant teal color. The other was full of orb-like eggs in many bright colors, including purple, pink, blue, orange, yellow, and green. I asked him why the first basket was filled with teal orbs. He told me that this is the basket of hope. I asked him why the second basket was filled with so many colorful orbs. He said that this is the basket of everything. He then asked me which basket I choose. I told him I choose the basket of everything, and the dream ended.

I thought about the dream on my trip home. I realized that in my grief, I had dreamed support for my loneliness. It was as if the painter reached out to remind me that I could focus only on the loss of my son's father and seek hope, or I could focus on everything in my life and allow all the other experiences to hold the grief.

Loss is never easy, but the painter's message was clear. Every time I got stuck in the messiness of my grief, I would close my eyes and imagine a beautiful basket of colorful orbs and remember that grief is part of the everything of life.

Challenge Accepted

By Michelle Griffith

Stay on the straight and narrow. Follow the rules. Keep your nose to the grindstone, and you will be rewarded with happiness and satisfaction. This philosophy guided me right up a sparkly corporate ladder and landed me in the office of an orthopedic surgeon.

The doctor was explaining herniated discs. He said epidural steroids would numb the pain until I could get scheduled for surgery. Looking back through tears of pain, I gathered enough focus to ask if there were any other options. He laughed and told me physical rehab may resolve the issue, but people who start that way always end up getting surgery. Then he said, "You will never make it."

Challenge accepted! I was outraged. I felt judged and vulnerable. I was in pain and felt powerless. I decided this must be a sign – one that I didn't welcome and couldn't ignore. "You will never make it" got branded into my brain that day. That was 20 years ago. I made a full recovery without surgery.

The physical process of recovery helped me find my ability to pay attention. When I started to notice and acknowledge the little things, I was grateful. With each moment of gratitude, a little bit of that "you will never make it" brand on my brain started to erode.

The mental part of my recovery was wildly practical. For every time the ugly words "you will never make it" popped into my head, I stopped to think about some tiny little victory in the moment. Making it was not some global standard. The ability to bend over and tie my shoes was one powerful demonstration of making it.

Most importantly, for my emotional and spiritual well-being, I had to reconsider my philosophy of life. I chose a new path defined by my own desires and goals. This path is paved with happiness, and it isn't straight or narrow. And yes, I *am* making it.

Morpeth's Ripple Through Time, 1837 BC

By Katie Keck Chenoweth

In the region of the ancient world known as Mesopotamia, the women in my family were healers. Now it was my turn. My mother and grandmother were fine teachers. The Fertile Crescent oasis sprouted medicinal herbs found nowhere else; our soil was naturally fertile from silt. Intuitively, I knew that each plant contained healing essences – expectorants, sedatives, energizers, unguents – all planted according to moon cycles.

On one delicious but fateful morning, I was entangled in the high emotions of my 13-year-old self. Having waited years to share my knowledge and graduate from apprentice to healer, I was alone on the path leading to the garden wall. Suddenly, a gut-wrenching sound pierced the morning silence, shattering the luminescent air. That gut-wrenching bellow came from me!

Paralyzed with fear, I lay motionless. Pebbles, which only moments ago had been dancing beneath my skipping feet, now jabbed my unresponsive body, rendering me helpless. The unthinkable had happened – an accident that changed lives. Like a stone thrown into the Tigris or Euphrates rivers, this moment moved endlessly through time.

It was months before I realized what had occurred. The morning had not yet begun for most villagers, except for the drunken farmer who had never made it to bed. He had hitched his oxen to a dilapidated cart to carry his wheat to town. Careening around a curve, he lost control. The team broke free, and the wagon rolled over me, dislocating my arm, shattering my spine. These changes rippled into the future, until now when I remembered.

Lying on a massage table, my colleague, sensing the energy around my spine and shoulder, reached for me. "I feel that this is a past-life injury. How would it feel if you were pain free?" The floodgates opened. Through my sobs, feelings of inadequacy and shame washed over me. Instantly, I realized that my body had been carrying Morpeth's pain through time. Her injuries no longer mine – I am pain free!

A Christmas Gift to Myself

By Julie Vance

The journey to leave my teaching career at the West Shore School District was a long one. I had been teaching third grade and working as a Reading Specialist for 18 years when I began to feel that there was something more I was being called to do. At the time, I had been attending a Unity church for about eight years and was beginning to get in touch with my inner voice. That inner voice was telling me it was time to leave the West Shore School District without knowing what I was going to do next!

I had always been a person who planned ahead, who hesitated to take a step until I knew where I was going. I argued with my inner voice: "I can't leave this secure position with a good salary and health benefits without knowing what I will do next. It would be irresponsible."

The voice grew stronger over time – the conflict within me got more intense as well. As I tried to ignore the promptings of my inner voice, I began to feel more and more frustrated with myself and with the work I was doing. I began to experience debilitating headaches and pain in my shoulders and back.

For months, my spiritual counselor had been encouraging me to listen to that inner voice and to take a step in the direction I was being guided to take. In September 1989, I was taking a walk when I heard: "You are to leave at the end of December. It will be a Christmas gift to yourself." I knew at that moment that it was the decision I had to make, and I was finally ready to take that step.

This was the first of many decisions I would make as guided by my inner voice, and it would lead me on a pathway I never could have imagined but that would bring me great personal growth and fulfillment.

A Dare to Follow My Heart

By Isabella Rose

My heart cried out with joy as soon as I saw the Facebook ad to become a contributing author, but my ego mind quickly took over with false belief systems programmed into my mind since early childhood: "You can't do this. You aren't good enough. No one is going to want to read what you write." But I somehow summoned up enough courage to follow my heart, intuition, and divine guidance and reached out to Jodi about my interest in contributing to the *365 Moments of Grace* book. It was a dare to myself, as deep down I truly didn't believe she would respond, never mind be interested in publishing my writing.

But she did respond! I was so surprised when I eagerly checked my email and saw she was interested in my ideas about what I would like to write about and would love to have me join as a contributing author. But then I started to second-guess myself as my self-doubt and self-sabotaging mechanisms began kicking in. "Now what I am going to do?" I thought as I began making up excuses as to why I couldn't do it: "I can't afford it, I don't know how to write, I will never be able to meet the word-count requirement, and no one will like my pieces."

Despite all these false belief systems, excuses, and doubts, I did it! I accepted that dare to myself and signed up to be a contributing author. I am so glad I did. It was the beginning of my writing career and making many more of my dreams come true. I continued as a contributing author to the 365 Book Series, stepping more and more out of my comfort zone with the love and support of Jodi, Dan, and our 365 author community, growing and expanding with each one.

Now I am about to publish my first two solo books. I didn't realize at that time just how much that dare to follow my heart would change my life.

Zentuition

By Rand Allen

Being a multitasking maestro, I prided myself on getting things done fast and efficiently. I was notorious for biting off more than I could chew, and overfilling my plate was becoming a bit of a habit these "daze," but I'd always manage to get it done in the nick of time with a triumphant "I got this."

One day my personal-assistant voice in my head sounded different, a little smoother and slower than normal, almost as if it were dipped in chocolate. With this new Godiva accent that melted right through to my third ear, it said, "Slow down and embrace the process with love."

Was it Spirit Guides? The Ascended Masters? Whatever the case, I was listening.

So I took a deep breath and relaxed into the exhale. Then, slowly, a level of clarity and intellectual confidence came over me that I'd never experienced before. My mind, although totally present and efficient in the moment, was also time traveling and working on my list of future projects at the same time and noting solutions for when I (my avatar) finally caught up. I know it sounds all quantum-field-wonkiness, but hey, I wasn't arguing the results of my new hyper-tasking brain.

I had read in the past about the Flow State mindset on the internet and found it very intriguing, to say the least, and was now thoroughly enjoying the process with an I've-got-a-secret smile transfixed upon my face. The more I honored and enjoyed this process, the deeper and clearer my mindset became, as well as getting far more done, with virtually no stress.

My voice decided to call it my Zentuition. All I had to do was Zen into it, or better yet, Zen Intuit.

Life gets noticeably easier when you learn to embrace your own Zentuition and resonate into the process! I just hope you let your spirit guide you, as mine did, to that special place of infinite wisdom and knowledge that's been hiding right there inside of you all along.

Just Breathe

By Amanda Dale

I sit here at sunset, taking slow, mindful, deep breaths. My intention is to listen with presence, peace, and poise. I hear the wind blow and feel a soft breeze. My heartbeat becomes known, as if meeting for the first time – though we've lived together for 39 years. The feel and sound of this heartbeat is like communion with an old friend. My smile radiates joy.

I breathe in and expand my intention. I now want to connect my mind with my heart. Many teachers talk about the heart connection, and I want this deepened experience for myself.

A warmth fills me. Chills, tingles, and joy rapidly sprawl throughout my body. I have an inner knowing that I am aligning with the unified field of sacred energy. I focus on this idea, this awareness of wholeness within me. Immediately, I feel a gentle, enveloping energy throughout my entire being. My awareness expands, and I feel guided to continue focusing on my inner connectedness. My "beingness" feels abstract and transcendent.

My intention expands my awareness. And my expanded awareness charges my connection within and to my Divine. My breath seems to be my momentum, my flowing catalyst, my moving energy. I am revitalized!

Finally, I am in the space that I desired desperately to know: that of the sacred Divine flow – the space of restoration, where answers freely appear.

I just created my own sacred space. I feel well. In fact, I *know* I am well and that all is well within and without. This experience that I resisted for so long was actually quite simple. I must remember that creating my own sacred space is as easy as taking one breath.

Divinely Guided to Sin City

By Leah Grant

"Move here now."

I was driving alone to my Las Vegas hotel when I heard it. I recognized the voice. It responds when I ask for guidance, always delivering short, succinct phrases. This time, however, I hadn't asked.

I ignored the message, even though I had spent the last six months looking for a place to live in Los Angeles, and two places had fallen through for unusual, unpredictable reasons. I loved living in California. I didn't want to move to the desert.

"Move here now."

I rolled my eyes when I heard it again driving to my hotel. I reasoned that because the voice had only said it twice, if I could get through tomorrow without hearing it, I could pretend it didn't happen.

"Move here now."

I cringed and groaned. A third time meant I was being guided.

With the energy of a two-year-old's temper tantrum, I sat in my hotel room and wrote a list of what I desired in a place to live. I included things that were out of my budget in California – large two-bedroom townhouse in a gated community close to the airport, but not in the flight path, with giant closets, sunken tubs, a two-car attached garage, an on-site fitness center, all appliances, a leasing office that would accept packages, a nature view, and more, all for a set price.

I was convinced that the power behind the voice would not deliver everything I wanted, but, just in case, I thought I was definitely securing my stay in SoCal by only allowing one day to find my ideal home.

I was wrong.

The next day I signed a lease. Two weeks later I moved to Sin City. My home contains everything I'd asked for and was $500 less than my named budget.

That was five years ago. From my perfect place, I founded Ecstatic Meditation, released a CD, was published in a fiction anthology, and got involved in a regenerative technology project.

Ironically, once the receiver of the unwanted message, I've become the messenger, frequently saying to others, "Move here now."

My Lotus Journey

By Kimberly Brochu

Locust?

My morning meditation has deepened my connection with spirit, which leads me to believe that the word I've just "heard" must have insight or a message in it for me. I open my eyes, feel the rays of the sun on my face, and slowly blink as the window in front of me comes into focus. Having been startled out of such a peaceful state, I close my eyes again and take a moment to ground myself, quiet my mind, and listen to this inner voice.

Rolling the foreign word around in my mind, I wonder: "Locust, isn't that an insect?" However, I then hear the word *lotus* loud and clear.

Curious about the purpose of this word coming to me, I head straight to my computer and conduct a search. After scrolling past all the Lotus car sites, I come across the flower and its inspiring story: growing from mud, submerged in murky waters, rising up in the morning to miraculously bloom with vibrantly colored petals, leaving the muck behind as it reaches high above the water and basks in the sun. I'm mesmerized as I read of the significance attached to this flower: *spirituality…awakening…emergence…cycle of birth, death, and rebirth*. Not only do these words resonate with me, they permeate my entire being. They speak of my journey and offer me hope of what lies ahead. They are the words that describe where I have been and where I am going.

The analogy of the journey of the lotus and my life has been accurate, and today I continue to surround myself with lotuses, for they are the perfect spiritual and soulful message. They are my reminder that we can all push through fear, insecurity, darkness, and karmic lessons to a place where the radiant sunlight awaits us.

A Life-Changing Wake-Up Call

By David Hipshman

Many years ago, I realized it was time to leave my job. It had been in the back of my mind and then slowly surfaced to be in my daily thoughts. My job paid well, I was treated well, and it had interesting aspects to it. I was comfortable doing it, but I did not love it.

At this time, I was experiencing an awakening. I was starting to ask what was my truest, deepest purpose? Was I living it? What was I passionate about? I really didn't know the exact answers yet, but I knew it was not what I was currently doing.

And then the comfort went away as I started to experience severe sciatica – a pain shooting through my legs when I sat for too long. I was paid to think, and it was getting harder to do this with the pain. I remember wondering if a higher power was trying to get my attention.

I decided to let it all go and give notice, but I wasn't really sure what was next. Once I acted on that decision, I felt inspired and relieved. But the truth was that I was also scared and didn't know what to do next. I had money saved, but I was used to the security of a steady paycheck.

Looking back, I realize that was one of the most important decisions I've made in my life. My family and friends thought I was crazy, and I even questioned it myself (especially after my first business endeavor that I tried after I left ended up failing). But like the song "God Bless the Broken Road," it led me in the direction of eventually living my purpose with the successful coaching business I have today.

I feel so grateful as I look back on the trust and courage it took to act on that true guidance. I'm even grateful for the pain of the sciatica that motivated me, which healed after I acted on that decision!

Magnificently Ordinary

By Angela Mia La Scala

"What is my life purpose?" This question nagged me every day. I trekked through life, exploring every twist and turn in the road, looking up, down, peering over fences, searching for inklings. I thought, "Maybe I don't have a purpose. Maybe I'm just meant to flounder through life, searching aimlessly for something that doesn't exist." The more I searched, the more I withered. My faith of finding my life purpose diminished with every breath.

As I busied myself with the never-ending search on the outside, there was one place I never thought to journey: the inside. Day after day, my soul was busy at work, projecting my life purpose, but the perpetual self-questioning distracted me from the seeing the obvious.

I was trapped in an illusion of diminished self-worth from being taught that unless we lead a life of martyrdom, self-sacrifice, and heroism, we're nothing but ordinary.

Ruminating on what a person "living their purpose" looked like, I learned that it's someone who does their work humbly, hidden in the corners of everyday life. Immediately, I called off the search for my life purpose, realizing that I was already living it!

It became clear, as expressions of gratitude came rushing in: some from family, friends, many from acquaintances, and even more from strangers across the world – some written, some spoken, some silent but nonetheless expressed. It's kind words that fall from my lips at the right moment and the encouragement for another's dream. It's a loved one's burdens carried on my shoulders and the sacrifices made for another's benefit. It's the hand extended without being asked and the time given to listen even when my ears are full. It's acknowledging the light in someone that's cloaked in darkness. Most importantly, it's teaching from my own life experiences, giving hope to others, and the inspiring messages posted daily that reach even one heart at the right time.

I'm not claiming to be special, but I do believe that one doesn't have to live a life of martyrdom, self-sacrifice, and heroism to be living their life purpose. Life purpose can be magnificently "ordinary"!

Chapter 4
Messages from Family

We oftentimes receive soulful messages from those who love us and who know us the most: our family members. Sometimes we're so close to our own lives that we aren't able to have perspective – to see what needs to be changed or how to change it. That's where our family can help. Because they know us so well, they can swoop in from their vantage point and offer just a few words that will change our lives forever. Maybe you've been uncertain about a relationship or a job or your next steps, and you mention it to a family member who says exactly what you need to hear to give you clarity and strength to do what's needed for your own soul's growth.

We've been blessed to have had each other to go to for wisdom for just about 20 years now, and we're constantly giving and receiving messages to and from each other. Whenever we feel stuck and are too close to a problem to know how to get ourselves out of it, we turn to each other for support. And we've found that when we do, magic happens, mountains move, and miracles occur.

Throughout this chapter, you'll read uplifting stories from so many people who are blessed to have supportive family members in their lives – from parents and siblings to spouses and children. When the authors needed them most for soulful guidance, their loved ones came through in beautiful ways to support them, uplift them, and help them get to exactly where they wanted to go.

While reading these stories, we loved seeing that it truly doesn't take much to receive a message from a loved one – to know that they have your back, that they are rooting for you, and that they want you to be happy. It was refreshing to witness, and it's our hope that you'll feel uplifted after reading these stories, too.

A Father's Wisdom

By Lori Thomas

Picture this: Mt. Lassen National Park, 1991. Volcanic mountains, narrow trails, pristine lakes, sweeping vistas, no people. I'm lying next to my dad in a tent, in the inky black found only deep in nature. We've been hiking for three or four days, and my nerves are still frazzled.

I was living in Germany at that time. My husband was an abusive alcoholic, and his verbal assaults had left me feeling battered and diminished. I was at my wit's end. I'd tried talking, counseling, compromises, making agreements. He turned everything into my problem. When he was angry, nothing else mattered; he'd yell and destroy things, and I had no recourse. His spending put us in debt – nothing I couldn't fix, although it was enough that I didn't feel I could afford to go on vacation. But I really had to go. I deserved this. I needed time away from my car crash of a marriage to gain a new perspective and rediscover myself. So I bought a ticket and flew to California.

So now here I lie, after three healing days of trekking through the wilderness at 6,500 feet, with the one person who has always supported me. We get into a conversation, discussing the day's events and wandering onto other topics. At some point, the conversation comes around to my marriage.

My dad addresses the situation that he sees. With great sadness in his voice, he says, "I've never seen you so unhappy. Your smile's gone. You seem so frustrated."

And with all the pain in my heart, I reply, "I've tried everything, but he won't cooperate. He doesn't seem willing to do anything differently. I keep waiting for him to change. Because if he won't change, I can't live like this."

There is a pause, and my dad says, "I think you've got your answer."

I have to absorb those words for a moment. Then, with a brilliant flash of clarity and insight, I feel all the pain and anger dissolve into peace. He's right. My husband's never going to change. I'm done. This marriage is over. I'm free.

Thanks, Dad.

A Card from Heaven

By Lori Reeves

I was driving home after spending the week sorting through my mom's things. She had died the week before, and my grief was raw. In that moment, I was surprised by my questioning of the afterlife, feeling overwhelming doubt of where she had gone and wondering if I was fooling myself by believing that we go anywhere after we die. I now desperately wanted and needed her reassurance that she had always given me when she was alive. Did she still exist somewhere?

Pulling up to my overstuffed and rain-drenched mailbox, I grabbed my mail, barely noticing the bright-pink envelope that was soaked through and coming unglued at its seams. I dashed through the rain to my house. I grabbed only the stack of wet mail, leaving the many boxes of my precious memories of my mom in the car.

Hours later, I noticed the still-damp mail sitting on the kitchen table. I peeled the bright pink envelope from the top. It was delivered to me by mistake and belonged to someone in my neighborhood. It was impossible not to look at the contents, as the rain had opened the envelope for me.

I received a card sent for another, but truly the message was for me from Heaven, from my mom. In that moment, Grace wrapped its arms around me.

The card read, "Daughter, You Amaze Me! Although I've known you since before you were born, somehow you still continue to amaze me. I've watched you go through change after change. And I've seen you navigate through tough times with your heart as a compass and your strong spirit to carry you through. Simply put, I couldn't be prouder of you. You've grown from an adorable girl into a most remarkable woman. A woman I admire, love, and respect more every day. When I held you as a baby, I knew you were special. When I see you as a woman, I realize just how special. More so than I ever could have imagined. Love, Mom."

Faith restored. Thanks, Mom!

Let's Do Lunch

By Clare Ann Raymond

My daughter stopped by for a visit and upon leaving said, "Let's do lunch." These three words changed my life forever.

"Great! I want to see your new office."

The following week, we toured her office as the new director of alumni relations at Eckerd College, then we had lunch. Afterward, she invited me to meet a colleague. Little did I know that her friend worked as the Admissions Counselor for PEL (the Program for Experienced Learners). This degree, designed for non-traditional students with life experiences, could further job advancement – or, for someone like me, make the dream of attending college possible. This program felt like a perfect match, as I indeed qualified as "experienced," so I mustered up the courage and enrolled at age 56.

For three decades as the wife of an Air Force officer, I had lovingly supported my husband's career, which included moving around Japan and the USA, setting up households in foreign cities, and navigating military politics – all while raising three children who had graduated and attended college. Now it was my turn!

Even after all my travels, college was unlike any stage of culture shock that I had experienced. Learning (and competing) with younger minds left me feeling intimidated, despite many students being helpful and welcoming. Our ages and experiences sharply contrasted, especially in the computer class. (I didn't even own a computer or use email.)

Meanwhile, my once-immaculate *Architectural Digest*-like house didn't get cleaned, and meals showed up sporadically. Instead, the joy of learning how to research, study, and write papers (longhand), became my happy routine. To survive, my husband hired a maid.

After 30 months and a lifetime of dreaming, I finally graduated in 1990. Family, friends, and grandchildren celebrated my long-awaited diploma.

Imagine taking the journey of "doing lunch" to college enrollment to graduating with a B.A. degree! I want everyone, everywhere to realize that it is never too late in life to follow and obtain their dream!

Thanks, dear daughter. Let's do lunch again. Maybe we can discuss a PhD.

The Heart-Shaped Pendant Necklace

By Lupe C. Ramirez

Every Mother's Day, I look forward to my children sending messages of love and sentiment. I understand that we all have free will and we only hurt ourselves when we expect others to bring us happiness, but this year I especially needed those sentiments because my heart felt dispirited. The previous months had been heavy and sorrowful due to a failing 11-year marriage. I felt grief stricken, and a wave of tears overtook me that Mother's Day morning. Only one month before, while in New York, I had gained confirmation that ending the relationship was the best thing to do. The last attempt to recollect why it should continue failed miserably. Deep-seated insecurity and unappreciation remained. The future was unseeable.

I received a loving text from my daughter and two of my three sons wishing me a Happy Mother's Day. My youngest son, PJ, was attending badminton practice that day. Whenever I think of him, I beam with pride and admire his fastidious manner. He readily shows up in everything he does. When he returned from practice, he ran toward me, smiling with excitement, and handed me a sweet card, a bouquet of a dozen red roses, and the most beautiful heart-shaped pendant necklace that I've ever seen. The delicate pendant was gold plated with cubic zirconia on one side of the heart. The tenderness that came with his thoughtful gift flooded my heart with joy and gratitude. My blues seemed to dissipate like smoke. He placed the necklace on me, and I haven't taken it off since.

At a time when I felt undervalued and in the throes of sadness, his gesture of love liberated my spirit. It reminded me to never forget how much I am loved, regardless of the circumstances. Since that day, whenever I feel indisposed or uncreative, I hold the pendant mindfully. It marks my challenges and insecurities as unsubstantial.

A significant reminder of our worthiness comes when the light is brought to us by someone else, unexpectedly. That day, PJ unknowingly gifted me more than a beautiful heart-shaped pendant necklace; he gave me hope for a happy future.

Rose's Kiss

By Maria Angela Russo

Looking up from my sandwich, I did a double-take at the woman sitting in the next booth. She looked exactly like my Aunt Rose. Flooded with loving memories, I thought about how I longed to move back home and live near Rose again. She would soon be 90 years old, and I knew now was the time.

I was 10 years old when my mother sent me to live with Rose and her family for three years. But even after I moved back home, for the next 10 years, Rose was the one who loved and nurtured me more than my mother ever had. She was the first one I told when I decided to get married. She said, "I would love to make your wedding dress." A gifted seamstress, Rose had been sewing my clothes for school and special occasions for years.

Now an adult, I made the decision to return to my roots. I lived with Rose for a month until I settled into my own place. For six happy years, we enjoyed each other's company with long, often reminiscent conversations, family dinners, and time in the kitchen where she loved to cook.

Then a twist of fate left me with mixed emotions as I toyed with the idea of moving across states again to be near my daughter Jennifer and her family after she gave birth to my first grandson. But I didn't want to leave my aunt. Sensing my hesitancy, Rose urged me to follow my heart.

The following summer, at age 97, Rose died. My circumstances didn't allow me to make the trip for her funeral, which left me with a heavy heart, slightly consoled by the remembrance of the quality of the six years we'd spent together. Leaving work that day, I started my car. The radio blared. In an instant, the presence of my beloved aunt permeated my being as Seal sang the words to "Kiss from a Rose." I know for certain it was her way of assuring me she was okay and our spirits would be forever entwined.

What Middle-School Lockers Teach Us

By Jill Pepper Montz

My only child starts middle school this fall. This milestone has brought mixed emotions from both of us. She is nervous about locker combinations, finding her classes, and changing clothes for P.E. But she is excited to see her friends, attend school dances, and possibly be deemed "old enough" for a phone. I am sad to see my baby girl growing up so fast, needing me less and less, and watching her morph from an elementary school child into a young woman. But I am so proud of the kind, smart, funny, outgoing, and independent person she becomes more and more each day.

At orientation, she got her class schedule (which she compared with her friends' to see if they had any classes together) and was assigned a locker and given her combination. Her dad gave the first demonstration on how to open her locker. With excitement, she piled her school supplies, locker decorations, and backpack inside then slammed the door. She informed us in her best middle-schooler voice to give her some room as she attempted to spin the lock to open the door all by herself. (I stood by, slightly impressed and slightly concerned at how quickly she had achieved a middle-schooler's personality.)

After several frustrating and failed attempts, my preteen banged her fist on the door, then spun around with crossed arms and whined, "I give up!"

Standing there sweating from the Texas heat in August and the pressure of trying not to help, I took a deep breath myself and declared, "You can't. And do you know why?"

Without looking up she growled back, "Because all the important stuff is inside."

And she was right. Whether it's a middle-school locker or life in general, we can't give up because the "important stuff" is inside all of us. We must continue to press past the frustrations and failures to find our purpose and greatness within.

My sweet (yet irritated) child might have been referring to her binders, pencils, and class schedule, but at that moment she spoke to my soul.

The Gift of Alzheimer's

By Jean Hendricks

In 2008, on Easter weekend, my mom was diagnosed with colon cancer. It was a scary time as we waited for her surgery. My dad had passed years ago, so I was there to support her.

She was the definition of a mom; her love for her children was unconditional. We had a close relationship. She was my cheerleader, my sounding board, my biggest fan, my confidante. I wanted to be all that and more to her, especially now. She loved helping others, always sharing what she had.

Fortunately, she is now cancer free, but with that came a diagnosis even more frightening because her memory began to deteriorate. After numerous doctors and tests, she was diagnosed with Alzheimer's. As her advocate, I fought for her and for her memory. It took some time to realize it was a verdict we could not reverse. When I realized that my love, stubbornness, or determination couldn't cure this for her, no matter how many doctors or prescriptions, I finally surrendered, finding peace in my mind, my heart, and my aching soul.

That's when I realized the tremendous selfless gift of love that she offered me – an opportunity to grow, to be in the world in a whole new way. She teaches me to live in the present moment, to be grateful for each day we have. When we're together, I let go of the past and forget about the future because with her, all we have is the present. These are magical, special visits. She loves to sing, so we sing together. I read once that singing is like praying twice.

As her memory declines, each visit with her is a gift. Weekly Sunday suppers with her are cherished moments. Sitting with her, holding her hands keeps us connected. Giggling while making silly faces and blowing bubbles in milk with a straw lights up our faces. Instead of being mad at the universe for what this disease has caused, I found a treasured gift: to slow down, be present, listen, laugh, and make memories. We only have this moment; we have to discover its gifts.

Don's Writing Mission

By Catherine Frink

Life delivers hardship to the sweetest people, doesn't it? This happened to my beloved brother when ALS consumed him.

ALS is a disease that prohibits signals from reaching the body; eventually all movement stops, except the person can blink their eyes. However, their mind is absolutely clear, so they are aware of it all.

I lived 2,500 miles away when I heard that this was Don's horrifying fate. I desperately prayed to ease my brother's progressively sad days. The answer came to send him daily letters on pretty paper, allowing him to share my life without writing back. I purchased a beautiful hardcover journal with lines and lovely drawings, adding scissors and stamped envelopes, and tucked them into my car to write while on the move.

At the same time, my brother's first love, Pat, whom I knew and loved, also found out Don had ALS. She received the same idea: to send him a letter every day. Pat sent memories from their relationship, clinical trial information, and natural supplements. Don wrote back to her through hospice volunteers who came to help. We were not aware we were both writing him at the same time.

Don eventually died, and a few weeks later I received a letter from Pat, which told me how Don had come to Pat, telling her that our writing to him gave him a wonderful quality of life for his last horrific years. He confessed that before we started writing to him, he had spent his days contemplating how to commit suicide.

He asked if Pat would contact me and if we would make it our life's mission to tell this story of writing daily so that fellow ALS sufferers – or anyone with an isolating, debilitating disease – would receive the same love he had.

Don said because of our writing, he knew we loved him and he loved us. He was included and had something special to look forward to every day.

Pretty paper, envelopes, a book of stamps, and willingness is all it takes to change horror into heartfelt quality of life, according to Don. Simple, loving, kind: a mission anyone can do.

A Flamingo Named Otto

By Liz Uhlaender

My son was born with unilateral microtia atresia. When he was old enough to notice the difference between his ears, I wrote him the following story:

Otto the flamingo was born with one long straight leg and one short bent leg. Doctors told Otto's mommy that he'd never be like the other baby flamingos if he didn't get a new leg right away! But Otto's mommy was not so quick to change her beautiful baby flamingo. She thought Otto was perfect just the way he was.

Sometimes, other birds would stare at Otto and his little bent leg, and sometimes they would laugh and say mean things. But Otto's mommy told him that his little bent leg made him extra strong and special. Soon, Otto would show the world just how strong and special he really was.

When Otto started playing baseball, no one expected him to be any good. His teammates groaned, "We can't have Otto on our team! With his little bent leg, we'll lose for sure!" This really hurt Otto's feelings, and sometimes he thought he should just give up. But all that grumbling from his teammates actually pushed him to work even harder than the other birds! Otto worked so hard at becoming a good baseball player that he eventually became not only his team's star pitcher but their star batter too! His legs were perfect for pitching and for sliding into bases. Otto didn't make his team lose because of his leg; he helped his team *win*!

There were still some birds who teased Otto, and it still hurt his feelings, but his mommy would tell him, "Those mean birds are actually very sad birds because they're unhappy with themselves. If you don't want to be a sad bird, you must love yourself for who you are and love other birds for who they are too!"

Soon, birds started coming to games just to watch Otto play, and one by one, the other flamingos began to stand on one leg to be just like Otto! Eventually, *all* flamingos would stand on one leg.

Some Things Do Come in Threes

By Donna Godfrey

Shortly before my grandmother passed away, she gave me a beautiful hand-stitched blanket made by my aunt, who had crossed over 35 years earlier. As much as I appreciated that my grandmother gave me this blanket, my heart told me that I should give it to my aunt's youngest child.

Growing up, our families never had any kind of relationship with this side of the family; therefore, I really had no clue as to his whereabouts. I only knew that some of them were living in British Columbia, and there was a possibility the youngest was somewhere in the area where I lived. Even though I made some unsuccessful attempts to locate him, I still felt that this blanket belonged to him. My first thought was, "Just let it go. If it's meant to be, it will happen." I wrapped up the blanket, put it in a storage closet, and after a while, forgot all about it.

Much later that summer, I was driving down the road when I heard my inner voice say, "Stop at that garage sale."

I calmly replied to myself, "I don't do garage sales anymore."

Then I heard it again: "Stop at the garage sale!"

I couldn't believe I was actually arguing with myself, but again I said, "I'm not interested!"

It wasn't until later that day, when I had to drive by that area again, that I heard the voice a third time and I finally agreed. "All right," I thought. "I'll stop, but I'm not buying anything!" Well to my surprise, at the very back of this garage sale, where the owner was holding on to items with sticky notes marked "sold," there on an old dresser was my cousin's name and phone number! Needless to say, he now has the amazing blanket that was so lovingly made by his mother many years ago.

My experiences that day reminded me that some messages do come in threes, true listening comes from within, and sometimes that can lead to unexpected but divinely guided outcomes.

The Life Not Chosen

By Lucy V. Nefstead

It was December, 1964, and life was perfect. I had just graduated from college a semester early with three majors, high grades, no student loans, and a scholarship to graduate school that fall. My friends, teachers, and family rejoiced at my accomplishment and good fortune. What could be better? And what could go wrong with the stars aligned so beautifully in my favor?

I was over the moon with happiness until I saw "the love of my life" – my long-distance boyfriend of two years – who did not share my joy of graduate school. He had other plans for us: a Christmas engagement followed by a January wedding and a 600-mile move to his hometown. What? No graduate school? What had just happened? My ideal world crumbled. I had to choose between two entirely different lives. But how?

HELP! God, angels, guides…I called on anyone who would listen. Confused and distraught, I prayed and prayed. My prayers were soon answered in the form of my Aunt Gretchen.

Calm, lovely, loving, and serene, she laughed at my confusion and smiled at my dilemma, which she explained was really no dilemma at all. To her, my choice was obvious. I could attain advanced degrees any number of places at any time. Education was easy to come by, but not love. How often do we find true love and happiness? If we are lucky enough to find love, we shouldn't let it get away. It's very elusive, and we may never find it again.

That sealed the deal. I had found love and wouldn't abandon it for all the scholarships in the world. My choice was made. I married, moved, matured, and later got advanced degrees.

I made the right choice. I never regretted my life's most important decision. Yet lately, whenever I happen to go through my "Scholarship City," I wonder what other paths I would have taken or what might have been had I picked "The Life Not Chosen."

A Special Journey

By Valerie Vestal

Death is never easy, but the worst part of losing my mom was that she never really lived.

When I was five years old, Mom converted from Methodist to Pentecostal and vowed to follow the church's practical commitments. In her journey of Christianity, she became stuck in rules, regulations, and rituals, and she developed a debilitating mental health condition called Scrupulosity. Sufferers of Scrupulosity have persistent unwanted, intrusive thoughts. They fear they aren't devout enough and will be punished. In order to calm her terrorized mind, Mom would pray excessively. This routine persisted for decades. Dad would be enraged because Mom had neglected household chores to pray or, worse, left us to live paycheck to paycheck, giving away a significant portion of the family income.

Mom was convinced she was a bad person who didn't deserve anything good in her life. With only a high school education, she was blessed to have a job as a postal clerk, but she became obsessed with the question, *Does God want me to quit my job?* She spent many days in prayer and sought validation from religious elders. Finally, she couldn't take the anguish and quit her job.

Finalizing the details of her funeral, I told the pastor that my cousin would be singing. I wasn't prepared for the words on the other end of the phone. The pastor wanted to validate the appropriateness of the music selection. His words were a distinct reminder of the controlled lifestyle my mom led. Anger welled up inside me, but after a few more minutes into the conversation, the anger began to fade. My heart softened. I was gifted with a soulful reminder that my mom's journey was and will continue to be a blessing to others. Every day when I look at my clients who struggle with mental health issues, I see Mom in their eyes. Traveling this journey with Mom has given me insight and compassion to be better prepared to help the brokenhearted.

My Eulogy

By Suzanne M. Fortino

I have had many nightmares throughout my life, and one in particular significantly changed my life. I woke up panicking and sweaty, took a sip of water, and tried to make sense of my nightmare. In it, I had died and my five beautiful children were all sitting around trying to figure out what to write in my eulogy. I saw so much concern on their faces, not just because I had died but because they could not figure out what to write. One of my children said, "I don't know what to write about Mom because she never did anything with her life." That statement was what woke me up from a sound sleep.

I was devastated, not because I had died but because my children felt that way. That day, I decided I needed to do something to make myself and them proud and to make it easy for them to write my eulogy when the time comes.

Within a week, my cousin shared a book opportunity with me on Facebook for people who wanted to be collaborating authors. I knew that this was a sign. You see, I had always wanted to be a writer. I had written my own personal journals for years, but I was always too scared to share my inner feelings with anyone. I decided this was my opportunity to show my children who I am. I signed up for one submission, and this gave me the opportunity to write one story. This book turned into a series, and I have been a contributing author in all the books.

What started out as wanting to show my children who I am has blossomed into showing myself who I am as well as the world. I do not fear death or my unification with the Holy Spirit. And I no longer fear that my children will not know what to write in my eulogy. I am a writer, and I am on this planet to share my love and light with the world.

My Prince Charming

By Catherine M. Laub

When I met Tony, he quickly became my Prince Charming. He opens doors for me, cooks, cleans, and shops. He became my caretaker due to my many hospitalizations and major surgeries. He is my rock and supports me, both financially and in all my efforts to create a spiritual business. Together we have seven children, 15 grandchildren, and three great-grandchildren.

Tony is always there to help others, too, and receives widespread respect. As an employee of a large company, Tony had many friends. He hosted yearly summer parties attended by at least 75 people. We also set up our house and backyard for birthday and anniversary parties. It was a lot of work, but Tony never complained.

This Easter, I took Tony to the Northport Veterans Hospital in New York with severe abdominal pain. After many tests and procedures, Tony was diagnosed with colon cancer.

For almost three weeks, Tony endured a lot while in the intensive care unit. He had never been sick, so he wasn't a great patient. I suggested he just take things as they come because cancer and its treatments are all very unpredictable. He took my message to heart, and things have been getting better for him. Now, he even manages to find the positive aspects of his situation – for instance, he raves about the great care he receives at the VA, expressing his gratitude for the excellent chemotherapy nurses and the caring doctors and other staff who spend time with us and answer our many questions without rushing us out. Tony also keeps a positive outlook by looking forward to the future: he lives to ski, and he plans on overcoming the cancer to continue skiing. And we both find strength in our faith: we believe that the amazing power of prayer will help in his healing.

Tony keeps his positive thinking and says he just has to keep pushing through it until he is healed. He continues to do yard work, fix things around the house, and work in his business. Tony's office is in the basement, so he gets a lot of exercise going up and down the stairs.

My Prince Charming still struggles through his illness but keeps moving forward. And through it all, he continues to support me so that I can live my life in peace and we can live happily ever after.

A Beekeeper's Story

By Melissa Monroe

I was barely 22 when I heard her say, "You catch more bees with honey than you do with a net." That was 25 years ago, and its meaning has unfolded, expanded, and transformed throughout the years.

When my mother-in-law said this, it struck me as an insider's tip for getting what you want. Although I didn't know her interpretation, my younger self connected sweet words and actions with desired worldly results. I thought this approach would make it easier for me to get a preferred job, money, friends, possessions, and outcomes. However, my soul wanted something more than external benefits.

By nature, I am reserved, reflective, and introverted. But striving for likeability quickly shifted into engaging new conversations and more courageous living. I engaged friends, family, and strangers with attentiveness, openness, and presence. In turn, these moments nourished my spirit and propelled a lifelong journey into what it means to connect.

These genuine moments were as essential to my life as breathing – while I am alive, I must do it. But after 25 years of practicing attentive presence, my understanding of connection changed again.

In 2018, I became an Ayurveda student, a choice that took me into a deep interior journey. I expanded my spirit and along with that, the ability to see abundant soulfulness and connections all around. I understood others as fellow travelers – souls evolving and growing in consciousness together. I perceived everything in life – myself, others, nature, all living things – as a collective whole walking together in healing, expanding, and awakening.

I no longer approached conversations as roads to external rewards but as pure joy and opportunities to be with another spirit. Instead of looking at what I can receive from others, I wonder, "How am I contributing to move us forward? What am I giving? How can I serve?"

A Parting Gift

By Gabrielle Taylor

The room is filled with hushed and muffled tones: the shuffling of nurses' shoes outside, an occasional gurney squeaking by, and soft sounds of the nearby patient wheezing as she sleeps. In spite of the bright, sunny September afternoon, it feels dark inside the hospital, only a few flickering reflections of light through the dappling trees outside.

I look at my grandmother's face – a faint resemblance of the lively woman I knew, now pale and almost ghostlike, her eyes closed and mouth open. As she takes her last breaths, my aunt and I (speaking hardly a word) provide much-needed moisture to her lips.

I remember a time when my grandmother and I would sip tea and laugh heartily as she told me stories of her youth in Belarus, where she grew up in the woods, making friends with bear cubs, squirrels, horses, and wolves.

My teenage self could never comprehend living through two world wars, being the wife of a foreign diplomat, raising three daughters through the most troubled times of the 20th century. But I'd always sensed my grandmother's audacity and courage, her fierce love of life, and her fiery nature.

She now looks so different from even just a few months ago, when she'd laughed off my complaints about the heat one afternoon. She taught me the trick of relaxing into it (as opposed to resisting it), something she'd learned during her time in the Far East.

The life now seems to have seeped out of my grandmother. But as I hold her long, emaciated fingers, I feel a sudden gush of energy leave her body and, like a torrential current through my hands, fill mine. In that instant, the room is buoyant with a powerful presence, swelling and pulsing with life.

Tears come suddenly, and my aunt looks at me with surprise. The message is loud and clear, although I don't hear it in words. It says, "Live with a full heart and full soul. Live with audacity."

Experiences Create Opportunities

By Donna Godfrey

My mother took ill for the last 10 years of her life. I spent a great deal of time with her then – especially during her last few years, when her condition worsened, until she crossed over. Though there were many moments of sadness, tears, frustration, and anger, this experience heightened my awareness and knowledge of my true self. I knew in my heart I had to make some lifestyle changes and knew there had to be a greater purpose than just living out life as is.

In one of my moments of deep sadness, I felt the urge to just surrender. Sitting in my living room, I just got down on my knees, raised my arms, and said, "Okay, I'm ready! Bring it on!" I knew that I was ready for a shift that would lead me to a greater understanding of my purpose – however that may look or unfold, or whatever direction it was going to take me.

Well, I honestly have to say…be sure and clear about what you ask for! In that moment, I began an incredible multi-year journey filled with many huge changes – some more challenging than others, but all with great purpose. Aside from the external changes, I gained the incredible gift of awareness that even during our most difficult emotional experiences, our awareness can be heightened from our love, compassion, and understanding. And if we're open to it, we can always receive guidance from our innate wisdom of what that experience can mean on a much deeper level of consciousness.

My mother's long illness and transition of crossing over was truly the greatest gift she could have given me. It showed me that every moment is filled with opportunities and choices that can inspire us if we choose to see it that way. And the entire experience inspired me to embrace what I truly enjoy. After her passing, I opened up a Healing Home for myself and others to use this sacred space for growth and healing. Thank you, Mom!

The Gift of Time

By Carol Metz

The greatest gift you can give someone is your time. In doing so, you are giving them a portion of your life that you will never get back.

Nearly 2,500 years ago, Aristotle contended that time is the most unknown of all unknown things, and arguably not much has changed since then. In North American society, there are fewer and fewer cultural traditions to safeguard family time, more and more distractions and expectations, and things that threaten to pull families apart. Preserving what's important takes initiative. Not choosing to carve out time and space and giving in to the busyness of life and the expectations of others will leave us reacting to what's urgent instead of honoring what's important.

For several years, I contemplated a non-materialistic "gift of time" Christmas that focused on building a tradition that would be fun, priceless, and experiential. It did not have to be perfect, but it had to be important to the family.

I put it into the practice in 2018 with my 11-year-old grandson when I asked him for the gift of time. On Christmas morning, he could hardly contain his excitement as he blurted out, "Grandma! When are we going Frisbee golfing?" We put our normal Christmas Day festivities on hold and ventured onto the ungroomed Frisbee golf course in the pouring rain. Straight-line Frisbee throwing requires continual practice, and Frisbee golfing is a skill to learn and master. Amid much tree climbing to retrieve the Frisbee; running through sandy, mucky greens; and sporadically making a hole in one, we finished the game. My grandson and I embraced each other, laughing loudly at the muddy mess we were.

On the way to retrieve our car, we stopped, turned and gazed into each other's eyes, exchanging a heartfelt connection. Truly a gift of time.

What will be your gift of time to yourself, your family, and your relationships?

My Brother's Voice

By Cath Edwards

My only brother died from a brain tumor many years ago.

During his time in hospital, he had lost his will to live and attempted to end his life as his loss of function increased. He was unable to walk or sit and had limited movement in his arms and fingers.

One night, in a desperate and anxious state, he believed that if he could roll himself off his hospital bed it would end his life. His reward for this futile attempt was a smashingly sore head and no relief from his emotional pain. He was lost and very sad.

During radiation treatment, his life was put at immediate risk. He was moved to a holding bay where he waited with uncertainty about what would happen next. In that time, he heard a voice speak to him. Was it hospital staff or patients? Was it God? It was a voice speaking softly to him. It was a voice of kindness and compassion.

What he heard was, "I love you."

It was my brother's voice.

This event in his life was so profound and powerful he booked a therapy session with me to talk about what this could mean. He asked me who could have been talking to him. He secretly knew it was his voice, but it didn't make sense.

As we talked, he realized with intense overwhelm and gratitude that it was his soul speaking ever so softly and kindly to him. It wrapped him in love and gave him safety. He found comfort in the notion that he was able to love himself, perhaps for the very first time.

What a gift it is to understand that you love yourself before your death, that your soul is safe. It took him 60 years to feel this most remarkable state of being.

I said goodbye to my brother knowing that he was loved by the essence of himself.

Miracles Are Real

By Suzanne M. Fortino

Years ago, my mother was diagnosed with inoperable lung cancer, and the treatment she chose left her body with no immunity. One day during this time, she went on a boat ride with a friend, and while in the boat, water splashed on her face, making her ill. This illness grew worse over the weeks that followed, but my mother's rebellious nature made it almost impossible for us to convince her to go to the hospital. Finally, however, she gave in and allowed us take her to the emergency room. Once there, she became weaker, and within a half hour, she slipped into a coma.

The days and weeks that followed were agonizing. At the time, I was seven months pregnant, going to school full time, and working part time. I also had a six-year-old sister the same age as my second child, both of whom were waiting for Mama to come home. I was determined to make sure that happened. My brother and I formed a pact to save our mother. We played her soothing music and recordings of nature sounds. I brushed her hair, and he rubbed her feet. I spent all my spare time at the hospital with my mom, telling her about my days, telling her about our family, and telling her how much she was loved.

Despite all our care, weeks went by without any sign of improvement. My mom was still on life support, and the doctors had no hope. They took me into the chapel, stated that it would take a miracle for her to wake up, and advised me to consider pulling the plug. I told them they were wrong and I believed in miracles. "She will wake up," I said. My brother and I continued our loving interaction with our mother, and after a few weeks, she woke up.

"Where is my dad?" she asked. While in a coma, apparently she was with him, although he had passed from cancer several years earlier. This experience affirmed to me that miracles are real and that the unconditional love that my brother and I showed her – with help from our grandfather – helped bring her home.

My Greatest Teacher

By Maria Angela Russo

My father suffered a psychotic break over 70 years ago. I was five years old. A psychiatrist diagnosed him with paranoid schizophrenia and committed him to a state mental hospital. Skilled care, shock treatments, and medication restored his mental health. However, due to the archaic 1940s laws, he remained a patient with a pass to spend three days a week at home.

Years later, my husband surprised me with theater tickets for *Man of La Mancha*. Difficult memories of my late father attempting to share his feelings about Don Quixote surfaced. Being a teenager, I had refused to listen and walked away. But as I sat in the theater on the night of the performance, my father's words flowed back to me. With tears streaming down my face, I listened to Quixote question the meaning of life and what was considered crazy. Wasn't it crazy to lock up people who thought differently and pursued seemingly impossible dreams?

Thinking about what I had missed with my father because I shunned him, my sadness overwhelmed me. Fortunately, therapeutic journaling and weekend retreats helped me heal many of those wounds.

Once, at a Kentucky retreat, someone referred to *Man of La Mancha*. Immediately, I felt my father's presence. He stayed with me all weekend, influencing my journaling and meditations. Before I fell asleep on my last night there, I prayed, "Dad, what should I do with all this awareness? Is there something you want me to know?"

Entering the Zendo on Sunday morning, I waited for the usual soft music of flutes to usher us into morning meditation. Instead, the lyrics to "I Hope You Dance" filled the room. Tears welled up as I listened once again to my father telling me to long for my dreams and to appreciate all of life because winning isn't the point, living is.

These messages echoed how my dad lived his life. A woodworker, artist, and musician, he created things of beauty with his many talents. He lived in the present moment and knew that life was worth living, never letting his illness define him or interfere with his appetite for life.

My Shining Star

By Amado F. Ramirez

My friends threw me a birthday bash around the time my baby was due. Her mother and I were disconnected and living apart. After the party, an alarming call was received from the baby's aunt. Complications from a C-section revealed the umbilical cord around the baby's neck, causing a blockage and pneumonia. I drove as fast as I could. My newborn daughter, fighting for her life, was connected to a respirator. Her little chest expanded like air forced into a little balloon. "Oh, my baby!" I exclaimed. "Please, God, don't take her."

I couldn't believe what was happening. I had considered leaving the child alone in this world. How selfish! With a 50% chance of survival, a priest gave her last rites, baptized her, and gave me a rosary. I prayed for God's intervention.

Her doctor suggested a new procedure that could circulate the baby's blood, allowing her lungs to rest and antibiotics to fight infection. I agreed, and a few hours later, she seemed at peace. A tube coming from her right jugular vein remained. The pneumonia subsided, but she remained on the respirator.

Reciting the rosary, I fell into a deep sleep. I had a dream where a bright, warm, omnipresent light shined upon me and my daughter. The loving light whispered to me, "Do not worry." I was awakened suddenly by the nudging of the nurse who told me to go home and rest.

The next morning, I felt a fresh sense of happiness and hope. To my surprise, my girl was off the respirator and breathing on her own! I cried with joy, knowing that a miracle had occurred! According to the nurse, my baby had yanked the tube out of her mouth, as if to say, "I don't need this crap anymore; I want to live!"

Her mother, Julie, and I finally had a chance to hold this beautiful little miracle from Heaven. Her birth was one of my most beautiful moments of our lives. Our baby girl, Devon Estrella Ramirez, born February 6, 1990, is a testament of love, faith, and a miracle.

Just Come Home

By Fiona Louise

"So that there might be no disharmony in the body, but that its parts should have the same concern for each other." – 1 Corinthians 12:25

I lived the high life that included a corporate career, fancy house, and world travel. I met a myriad of people and had incredible experiences. However, none of it fulfilled me. I always felt empty. I suffered severe depression for more than a decade and pushed a lot of emotions deep down inside where I thought I would never have to deal with them.

However, just after my 30th birthday, my body collapsed. I had been running on empty for quite some time, and it finally stopped working. The negative emotions resurfaced as four autoimmune conditions. My body was literally attacking itself. I was gravely ill and could no longer work, so my parents took me back into their home. Depleted, ashamed, and broken, I was bed-bound for six months.

However, with much-needed rest and nutritious food, my body became strong enough that I could take control of my mind for the first time, realising its power to make me ill or heal me. I purged the negative self-talk and silenced the inner critic. Once I had grieved deeply and allowed emotions to come up and out of me, I could finally hear my soul sing. My soul wanted to learn new things, have fulfilling experiences, and most of all, share love with others. So now I am studying at university, running chronic-illness support groups to help heal others, making new friendships with kindred spirits, and cultivating important existing relationships.

With my body, mind, and soul in harmony, I am able to see the illness as a gift – a gift that enables me to rest, recuperate, and rediscover my true self. I am content and confident, knowing that the next chapter of my life is blessed with love, passion, and purpose.

It is with gratitude that I realise that this journey was made possible by the simple message uttered by my mum when I first became ill: "Just come home."

Lessons of Compassion

By Matthew Tischler

In March 2019, I was told I had six weeks to live. My diagnosis was PEL, a rare and aggressive form of leukemia. This devastating diagnosis brought up feelings of sheer panic and fear within me, and the tears flowed – a lot of them!

Soon after the initial shock wore off, I decided that the doctors were wrong and began to fight for my life by changing my diet; incorporating meditation, prayer, chiropractic care, and inner healing into my daily life; reading and listening to Dr. Joe Dispenza's books and tapes; and starting chemotherapy.

The driving force for my being able to fully embrace my cancer experience as a blessing had a lot to do with my mom. Through her own battle with cancer and the struggles she had with chemotherapy, she taught me lessons of compassion. Even though she ascended from this planet in May 2019, I have never felt a stronger connection with her. It was (and still is) her loving, spirit-filled energy that changed how I am living and creating my future.

As a chiropractor, I had learned by treating patients with "dis-ease" in their bodies, like cancer, that when we prioritize how we feel, our attention moves away from the physical and toward our highest vibration, where we have access to the quantum field of infinite possibilities of healings.

After my cancer diagnosis, I learned to choose a high-vibe "Matt-i-tude" regardless of the circumstances. I now choose to be grateful for just waking up each morning – to be alive! I love more, have grown and cared more, and have created and given more. I bring my "Matt-i-tude" with me everywhere – especially to my chemo treatments! And whenever I need a reminder, I feel my mom's compassionate and loving energy surround and uplift me.

In each precious moment, regardless of the circumstances, we choose our thoughts and how we are going to create and experience our lives. Every time we choose to overcome, we love ourselves and we love others even more. I will always hold my mom's lessons of compassion within my heart, knowing that love heals all.

The Gratitude Picture

By Jerri Eddington

I was looking forward to spending the last weekend in 2017 with my friend Tandy. We were preparing for 2018 by doing our Reflection of 2017 (a Medicine Wheel Oracle Card reading) and creating our new vision boards.

My husband, Bob, also had an action-packed weekend planned: he and his friend Gordon were attending the Fiesta Bowl and taking a road trip to California to see the Rose Bowl.

Tandy and I spent New Year's Day focused on creating our vision boards using the Feng Shui directions and colors. I had all my pictures laid out the way I wanted them…except for a gratitude picture. I didn't know where it should go, so I put the picture aside and went to bed.

The next morning, I woke up early, eager to complete my vision board. As I looked over the board I heard a voice say, "Add the gratitude picture to your Love and Marriage area." I thought about the message I received. Had I been taking my relationship with Bob for granted? I decided I could use more gratitude in my relationship.

An hour later Bob shared the following post on Facebook: "Great night's sleep in Palms Springs after the Rose Bowl overtime game. My business enterprise surrounding this great game is off and running well. Thankful for having that vision four years ago. Jerri has been a great partner not only in this endeavor but in our walk through life itself. Wow…I don't usually go this deep on Facebook, but feeling very grateful starting out 2018. Happy New Year to All!"

Tears of gratitude came to me as I read Bob's post. Adding more gratitude to our relationship area definitely was the answer!

The Strongest Person I Know

By Lupe C. Ramirez

The years following the onset of menopause were somewhat of an uphill battle. Not only did I have to research compatible supplements and adjust to physical changes, such as body aches and itchy skin, but society told me to accept being past my prime. I dissented. After all, I enjoy the things that I did when I was younger, like dancing, laughing, and riding a bike.

Our face and body change, but I believe that our natural state of being is the personification of our soul or inner child, where a reflection of nonjudgment lives. We get propelled there when we make art, blow bubbles, or hug our puppy.

At the end of a relationship, I had gained 40 pounds. I was stuck in an emotional place that held back my sense of worthiness and empowerment, but I didn't know it at the time. I felt sluggish and unnatural. My friend shared about a six-week fitness challenge. It sounded daunting, but I knew something had to be done. Two weeks later I joined.

The workouts were timed circuits with a clean-eating meal plan. The first week, I jumped in with both feet. The second week, as my body adapted, I felt vulnerable, asking myself whether I belonged there. While on a shoulder-press machine, an overwhelming sense of exposure came over me. The tears streamed down my cheeks. Luckily, I was sweating so much that no one noticed. At the end of the workout, two trainers walking by told me what a great job I was doing and said they were proud of me.

When I got home that day, I confided in my oldest son, Vic, what had happened. He is familiar with those workouts and said they are hard and to be proud of myself for doing them. Just then, my youngest son, PJ, overheard and asked to take my sweaty picture. I allowed him to, and he posted it to his social media writing, "My mom is the strongest person I know."

By the completion of the challenge, I had evicted 16.5 pounds while unchaining my inner child.

Voices from Heaven

By Mohamed (MO) Rachadi

The world around us is full of many voices. Some are louder than others. Other voices are softer or even silent, yet they can touch your heart and your inner self. They can change your life. They can provide you with an opportunity to change the world for the better.

Five years ago, while in a prolonged coma, I heard a soft, crystal-clear voice that I will remember for the rest of my life. When the doctor left my hospital room and the last nurse turned the lights off and whispered good night, I was left alone in the dark. Suddenly, I felt a hand on my chest and heard a prayer: "God, please keep him alive; I need him." It was my younger daughter, Jaclyn, with tears and a trembling voice. I was not able to move or say a word, but I felt something miraculous happening.

The next morning, I opened my eyes and saw my wife, my two daughters, and one of the morning nurses, and we all shared a smile and hugs. The voice I'd heard the previous night was a voice from Heaven delivered by my angel daughter – a voice I will never forget as long as I live.

Since then, our lives have changed for the better. We strongly believe that things happen for a reason, and we're grateful to have the opportunity to be together and share our soul messages. My renewed purpose is to do the good that God wants me to do, which includes a mission to create and build an organization to promote understanding and peace between people regardless of religious beliefs or ethnic backgrounds. We all need each other to make this world a better place for our children.

You too will know the voices from Heaven when you hear them. Embrace them and enjoy the amazing journey.

If Only

By Angela Mia La Scala

A few years ago, life took a quick and unexpected turn on Christmas Eve morning. I never imagined "I love you" and "Be right back" would be his last words to me. "She's the love of my life," he boasted to a neighbor who was dropping off baked goods as he flew out the front door, hopping onto his bicycle.

"Hurry back! There's lots to do," were my last words to him. As if preparing dinner for our holiday guests was a priority.

If only I knew how important those final words were. If only I realized how precious that morning was. If only I would have been kinder, gentler, and more appreciative of our moments together. If only I had noticed his one chance for survival that sat on a shelf in the garage. It was these "if onlys" that changed my life forever.

I know deep in my heart that this day, this teaching, was all in the grand Divine plan from the very first moment I entered this lifetime. The earth-shattering and untimely loss of a loved one changed me in ways I never thought possible. It changed where I chose to be. Before this loss, I had been a perfectionist, a planner, a doer. I was always on the go, trapped in a never-ending cycle of completing to-do lists, only to have the list fill up over and over again. To stop and appreciate simple beauty around me, or to slow down to share a laugh, was rarely on my agenda.

I lingered in the past, burdened with regret and disappointment. I often visited the future, riddled with worry and anxiety for things that never came to be. Time was lost, wasted, and life went rolling by. I rarely lived in the present, the "here and now," the very place your loved ones live, where gratitude and laughter exist.

It took a loss to gain this wisdom, and my message now is simple: Being present is precious; and when you choose to be present, you'll never have to say "If only..."

Joyce Moments

By Heather Wiest

What a long journey, Mom. Together, we've endured your chains of depression and addiction, but now I know that you are truly free. My journal entries have been sprinkled with tears, yet comfort and peace ultimately fill my heart.

The night after you suddenly passed, your overwhelming presence energetically blanketed me with love. You gently stroked my hair and whispered, "All is well. I'm with Jesus." Oh, how I thank God for this sweet assurance! Amazing grace runs deep.

The everlasting bond we share as mother and daughter continues through "Joyce Moments," those minutes when I can see, hear, and feel you. When I recollect you affirming, "Heather, you are so brave," as I share about my traveling adventures. When Madeline, your oldest granddaughter, drives your beat-up car and proudly displays the flag of Scotland on its emblem to honor your heritage. When Dad, your first husband, speaks of you fondly, "Joyce, I remember the great times we enjoyed after I met you in London. That year was the best period of my life. May you rest peacefully now." When Jon, your son-in-love, adds to your obituary, "She never lost her adorable Scottish accent, which paired well with her fiery red hair. Her Cheshire Cat smile was contagious and complemented her love for animals." When Papa takes care of your Callie cat and spoils her with tuna treats, just because he loves you and not the cat! When your youngest granddaughter, Mackenzie, misses your fun presence and the games you played with her. When I snorkel in Belize on your one-year death anniversary because I know you would be proud of me. When you frequently visit in the mornings as a hummingbird looking at me intently through the bathroom window, reminding me to be light, joyful, and carefree.

And then I recall that hummingbirds alone have the ability to fly moving their wings in the pattern of an infinity symbol. You affirm your eternal life and our constant connection. All is well. Thank you for the joy-filled "Joyce Moments." I love you, Mom.

Soulmates

By M. Lorrie Miller

My favorite synchronicity is the story of how I met my husband, Tony, in March 1994. I had been praying to find my soulmate for a long time. Back then, before internet dating websites existed, I used to get a weekly community newspaper called *The Pennysaver*. It was mostly ads for buying local goods and services; however, the paper devoted one section to people looking for partners.

That March, I was divinely guided to create an ad. As I put pen to paper, I heard the words to write. The ad started, "Seeking Soulmate…" As part of the process, I had to record a longer message about myself and the kind of man I was looking for. Before I recorded the message, I prayed for guidance about what to say. My ad came out a week later.

The men responding also had to record a message to me. I had only listened to a couple of the recordings when a friendly voice caught my attention. I decided to call Tony that day, and we agreed to meet at a local bookstore a few days later. We gave each other a description of what we would be wearing, so we'd recognize each other. I got to the bookstore first, and when Tony arrived I saw that he was standing next to a book by the entrance that said in big, bold letters, *Soulmates*!

I couldn't believe it! Was this a sign? We talked for a while, then we headed to a nearby restaurant to get to know each other better. I liked Tony from the start. He was friendly, funny, handsome, and a real gentleman. I never responded to any of the other ads. Within a month, I felt that he was "the one." He proposed on Valentine's Day the following year, and we got married in a small, intimate ceremony that August.

Tony and I have celebrated many years of marriage since then, and I am proud to call him my best friend, soulmate, and the love of my life.

Maiden Aunt

By Marla David

She caught the corner of my eye, and I immediately turned to look. I saw a gracious woman, generously figured, with a full topping of short white hair and a smile that exuded pure genuineness. Her eyes looked watery, like she was about to cry. But what struck me most about this woman was that she bore an uncanny resemblance to my late Auntie Lilly.

Like Auntie, when this woman smiled, it was as though the back of her bottom lip was grabbing on to the bottom of the front of the top teeth. Auntie had nice teeth, despite the fact that they were false. This wasn't always the case, though. In her youth, she had buck teeth, which rendered her unpopular. But despite the poor treatment she sometimes received, Auntie didn't have a mean bone in her body. She was a pure soul who merely wanted to please and help family, friends, and even random strangers, including mentally and physically challenged people. One time, she even brought a couple into her hotel room when they were stranded.

Marriage wasn't Auntie's destiny, but she shared many wonderful times with her extended family. We often went on day trips – such as to an exhibition, the beach, or Niagara Falls – and we always ushered in the new year together. But we didn't need a special occasion to get together; we used to rub each other's backs, play cards, and just enjoy each other's company. Even though she didn't have much for herself, Auntie brought me little things she knew I would like, like tiny glasses of cream for coffee (used by restaurants years ago) to serve as teacups for my dolls, which she knit clothing for.

Someone once told me that, like everyone, I'll receive messages by way of things I notice, especially through subtleties that make me think of someone in particular. One thing I know for sure is that anything that stirs or instills a fond memory of someone who's passed is a healthy, positive thing. This was certainly the case when I saw Auntie Lilly's white-haired lookalike, who flooded me with such sacred, cherished memories and with gratitude for the special times we spent together. Now more than ever, I'm mindful of these messages and reminders. I always embrace them when I have the opportunity, and each time I do, my heart fills with warmth and love.

The Last Night of My Mom's Life

By Kris Seraphine-Oster

After 40 days of watching my mom rapidly decline from Stage 4 pancreatic cancer, and four straight days of vigil in the hospital, I was longing for home and a non-hospital meal. I needed a little break.

I went home and snuggled her dogs, heated up a can of lentil-vegetable soup, and finally got myself into a hot, lavender essential oil bath. I threw on my thick red terrycloth robe and fell asleep on the couch.

I woke up with a start, clearly hearing my name. I knew my mom was letting me know it was time to get back to the hospital. I heard a "whooshing" sound in my ears that was so loud it felt as though an earthquake was thundering through the house. The dogs began barking wildly and came running to where I was standing. My mom had come to the house to bid them farewell and give me a large download of messages.

One of those messages was for my uncle David. She said she would wait for him to say goodbye. She told me that she would be gone by midnight. I remember feeling as if I were in a dream when the phone buzzed. It was my aunt and uncle calling to ask about my mom. I told them she was waiting for him and to get to the hospital as fast as they could.

"You'd better get dressed." I could hear her voice clear as a bell. I can't begin to say how profound and comforting that was. As I drove back to the hospital, I began to panic. She spoke to me as if she were sitting right next to me, calming me. As I pulled into the parking lot, she said, "I want you to live as if you only have one year to live." It was the last time I heard her voice.

My uncle reached the hospital just before she took her very last breath. Minutes later, she passed – at 11:55 p.m. on February 25, 2017, with her family all around her.

The Mirror

By Maria Angela Russo

When my children were young, I often greeted them with outstretched arms and asked, "Have you had your hug today?"

Once my mother witnessed this and said, "I always took my kids for granted."

Hugs weren't part of my childhood. Rather, my mother held me to high standards of how to act, think, and feel, which created rage and resentment within me. Her strict rules implied I was an extension of her, stifling my sense of self. She threatened to withhold her love to ensure obedience, which I took seriously because I wanted to feel safe.

I thought moving halfway across the country would free me from her criticism. Instead, she blamed me for abandoning her. I considered severing all ties but realized I could never do that. Out of a sense of obligation, I sent my mother a plane ticket for a week's visit, which began with the usual tension between us until the third day when everything changed.

Accustomed to getting her hair styled weekly, I made her an appointment before taking her out for lunch. I noticed a mirror on the salon counter as I checked in. It was positioned in such a way that when I looked at it, I saw my mother's face as if it were a framed photograph. She stood slightly behind me, not knowing I could see her.

Up until that time, whenever in my company, my mother's countenance revealed a long-suffering life, as if I would disappear altogether if I didn't feel sorry for her. In the mirrored image, however, I saw the face of an innocent child smiling broadly in sheer delight from the attention she was getting. I saw her soul, that part of her without the roles and her life's storyline.

In an instant, a feeling of peace and forgiveness washed over me like a warm shower, dissolving a lifetime of pain and bitterness. Her childlike joy imprinted itself on my heart and left me free to love her for the divine spirit she was, going through life doing the best she could with what she knew.

You Never Know When You Say Hello

By Terry Corrao

It was July 3, 1971, and I was a young working girl, living in Berkeley, and on my own for the Fourth of July holiday weekend. My boyfriend had gone home to the East Coast for the summer, but I was planning a trip to visit him, meet his parents, and see New York City.

To beat the boredom of a holiday alone, I took a bus trip to Santa Cruz beach. It was beautiful there, but I still felt lonely and depressed. On the ride back home, I had time to think about my relationship with my boyfriend. I was unsure of our future, having seen warning signs, but uncertain about how to handle it. I bowed my head and said a little prayer to please, please let me meet someone new.

My bus arrived in San Francisco, where I boarded the streetcar for the East Bay Terminal. As the streetcar pulled up to the terminal and I exited, a voice behind me asked, "Miss, do you know where to catch the bus to Berkeley?"

I turned and found a kind-looking man with longish black hair and striking blue eyes. I said yes, I was going to Berkeley, but we were going to have to run or we would miss it. Off we flew, passing one ramp after another until we reached ours. From there we saw the backside of the bus pull out, abandoning us for the next hour. With not much else to do but make small talk, I found out he was visiting from New York, worked in the motion-picture business, and had just finished work on a movie in Los Angeles. When I told him I was going on a trip to New York, he became very excited to tell me about all the places to visit. That conversation continued over the Bay Bridge to Berkeley, over a Chinese dinner, and still continues to this day. That wonderful man, now my husband of 45 years, was the soulful messenger who answered my prayers that hot summer day.

Aviana Everleigh

By Lupe C. Ramirez

After retiring, I began volunteering at a local hospital. My shift was Friday morning, when a farmer's market was held. Views of colorful flowers, fresh fruit, and honey provided a welcome distraction – as did a piano next to the main desk, which people occasionally played during my shifts.

At that time, a discontented relationship often had me feeling sorrowful. I wear my heart on my sleeve, but some days I wish I didn't. I quickly realized how fulfilling it was to help others and feel that my service was appreciated.

My daughter, Veronica, was expecting her second baby then, which was extremely exciting. A long time had passed since holding a grandbaby. Roy Lee, my grandson, was quickly approaching sixteen. I hadn't taken any time to take it all in. At the hospital, unbeknownst to me, whenever a baby was born, a lullaby would play on the PA system. The first time I heard it, I was in the elevator. I smiled when remembering that I would be a grandma again. While browsing the gift shop, I imagined what to buy the baby.

One Friday, as I walked outside to buy flowers, a man began to play "Somewhere over the Rainbow" on the piano. As I listened, my eyes teared up and my mind wandered to images of a happy life. Later, as I walked back inside, a lullaby began to play. I was nudged to listen, and I paused to feel the warm sun on my face, which seemed to unexpectedly switch on. In that moment, a glimmer of our new little babe kindled an exchange of lovingkindness. A familiar and profound love, held in a timeless space, expanded my heart with strength. This little unborn human reminded me of an everlasting bond between us, inspiring a retrieval of joy and gratitude in me. This was a special type of communication.

The day my granddaughter was born was one of the happiest of my life. Aviana Everleigh, my cherub with the sweetest eyes, your presence in the world shines unchanging love and joy unto me forevermore. My love, I write these words for you.

Raised by a Human

By Sherry Cheek McBride

When my two beautiful children, Hollie and Mitchell, were born and placed in my arms, I remember looking at them and vowing to be the "perfect" mother. They were gifts sent to me straight from Heaven, and I envisioned the life that I would give them to be perfection. However, there was one small detail that I had forgotten: I am human.

There were days when exhaustion set in and they ate peanut butter and jelly for dinner. There were nights when I was too lazy to read to them and say a bedtime prayer. There were many days when, out of frustration, I yelled at them. There were moments when their tiny hearts were broken from harsh words, and I was too busy to notice. There were times when I missed opportunities to praise them for something small they had accomplished. There were times when I forgot schedules, snacks, teacher gifts, ball practices, or washing that favorite shirt for the next day. There were times after my divorce when I was so wrapped up in my own grief and dysfunction that I could not be the spiritual leader and role model they deserved.

There were so many times when I didn't live up to the vow to be a "perfect" mom, but what I didn't realize was that the vow of perfection is impossible…because I am a human. The only perfection in my life is my heavenly father who forgives me every day of my life for being human.

My prayer is that my children will overlook my faults and shortcomings. I pray that they know in the depths of their sweet souls that this human loves them fiercely, unconditionally, and eternally. I pray that they never experience the useless torment of guilt. I pray that they remember that we are all far from perfect but that love and forgiveness abound through Jesus Christ, our savior. And my final and greatest prayer is that we *all* can learn to forgive ourselves and one another for our imperfections because, let's face it, we were all raised by – and we all *are* – humans.

My Mother: A Strong Woman

By Catherine M. Laub

Mommy was an inspiration to her family and friends. She was the strongest and healthiest person I've ever known. She was always there to help me and my five siblings in every way we needed her. She babysat, hosted holiday gatherings at her house, helped us when we had our own parties, and even cleaned our houses while we worked.

In 2012, all of this changed when Mommy had a heart attack. Then, in 2013, she was diagnosed with a blood disease that, after two years, turned to cancer. There was no treatment, so she entered an experimental drug study, saying that if it helps others, she's happy to do it. Mommy was a trouper because although she was often in pain, she didn't want medication and hardly complained.

In February she was in the hospital for treatment and began having multiple symptoms not related to the cancer. The doctor did tests but found no reason for these symptoms, so they released her to a rehabilitation facility. Two weeks later she was back in the hospital. She declined quickly, and after another two weeks, we took her to a hospice facility where she passed two days later.

Mommy told her oncologist in February she was giving up because she felt guilty about us driving her often to New York City, two hours away. The day was long, and we got tired out. I believe that if the hospital had been nearby, Mommy would still be with us. Right up until the end, though, Mommy was always happy, even making jokes with us during her final days. When she passed, her six children, my husband, my daughter, and a family friend were with her. She smiled, so we knew Daddy had come to get her.

Since her passing, I've been noticing a lot of number twos. The angel number 22 is believed to be a highly powerful number and a sign from your guardian angel not to neglect your spiritual path and purpose. I recognize it as a sign from Mommy that she is guiding me just as I asked her to do once she passed.

A Life Lesson That Taught Me My Life Path

By Destrie Sweet Larrabee

It started with a text from my son, who had just realized that he had been a student for 35 years of his 41 years of life. It was as if a life-affirming knowing embraced my entire being in a huge flash of loving energy. I responded that I've been a student for 65 years and am still loving every minute of it. My son's answer – "Since you were 2?" – opened a portal for me, allowing me to follow a thread, connecting me to a life-altering/aligning moment that clarified my life's work!

This golden thread started when I was two years old. Early one morning, I was sitting behind a chair, lighting matches, blowing them out, and chewing off the match heads. I hadn't heard Dad come home after a long night's work. He said good morning and asked how I was feeling. I said I was fine. He then asked what I was doing, and I told him I'd found some matches and was just lighting them so I could eat them. Next, he asked me if I knew that I should not light matches. I said yes, I knew, but I couldn't eat them raw; I had to cook them first, and I knew that it was bad for kids to use the stove.

I then remembered that I'd had that very dream the night before. The experience had reminded me of my Dad's kind, patient, and loving process of first checking to make sure I was okay and safe *before* rushing to judgment, rather than assuming I was doing something bad just to do it.

When I received my son's text about being a student, I realized that the learning/living process given to me to use in my life and to put into the world – "S.E.L.F. Connections: A Process for Self-Actualization and Responsible Living" – is my dad's parenting/living model, his actual way of respectfully being with people.

I am so very grateful for this enlightenment. I continue to be a student, and my father is still connected to me. In infinite love and gratitude…thanks, Dad!

My Miracle Baby

By Jerri Eddington

Soon after I signed my first teaching contract, I learned I was pregnant. My baby was due at the end of March 1980, and I was having a very difficult pregnancy. I was hospitalized three times for early labor, and all three times I was given an intravenous alcohol drip to stop my labor. It worked because my son, Jeremy, was actually born a week late! When he was a day old, he turned completely blue due to a VSD heart murmur. I wondered if I would ever be able to take him home.

He was hospitalized for the first time at five months old with congestive heart failure and cardiac asthma. Over time, Jeremy would display several symptoms related to fetal alcohol effects due to the alcohol drips I was given during my pregnancy to stop my contractions. When he was two and a half, he had congestive heart failure again. He was hospitalized and scheduled for open heart surgery. One week before surgery, he underwent pre-surgery testing, and one test (the echocardiogram) showed the heart murmur had closed enough and surgery was no longer required! I received a clear message from the Universe: "Everything is going to be alright."

Jeremy was a delayed reader, hyperactive, and unable to follow directions. He experienced speech impairments, his coordination was poor, and he also had tactile defensiveness. Parenting Jeremy was *very* challenging at times. We worked with his teachers, therapists, and doctors to manage his various physical and emotional symptoms. When he started fourth grade, things started to come together for him, and he never looked back.

Jeremy continued to thrive in school and various community activities. Eventually, he earned a Master of Business Administration degree. He wasn't happy in the business world, so he returned to school to become a special-education teacher. Today, Jeremy is following his true passion as a middle-school special-education teacher. But to me, he'll always be my miracle baby.

Breaking Free

By Marion Stoltzfus Alexander

Since my dad turned 80, he's shared more revealing details of his life story. He was born into the Amish community and decided to remain in it after his Rumsbringa (a rite of passage during adolescence, after which a youth either chooses to be baptized within the Amish church or to leave the community). When my parents married, they both took the Amish oath and continued their life together in the tight-knit Amish community.

At the funeral of a friend outside of the Amish community, my dad heard the gospel of Christ. That experience led him to question his religion and begin his own search for truth.

Secretly, he began attending services at the local Mennonite church. One day, Dad and Mom attended a Mennonite service, and an altar call was given. Within the Mennonite church, men and woman do not sit together. Dad and Mom were unaware that the other went forward and that they were taking a risk by going up together. My dad, with tears of joy in his eyes said, "The Holy Spirit led us both forward, and there we met at the altar and were led to Christ. Not until after the service did I realize that we both accepted the gift of salvation at the same time."

This was a big step for my parents. Within their families, this is simply not done. Because they'd already taken the Amish Oath, there were consequences to this decision. My parents experienced the true meaning of being shunned. However, they were willing to break free. They wanted to accept the free gift of eternal life with Christ instead of choosing the customary traditions of a path that they felt would not lead to eternal life.

Inspired by my parents' faithful walk over 54 years ago, relatives have discovered the truth and are also breaking free. In one of our most recent visits, one of my cousins said to my dad, "You are a real soldier for Christ and have paved the way for the rest of us."

A Mother's Inspiring Power

By Mohamed (MO) Rachadi

I write from the heart to inspire my future grandchildren to be the best they can be, remain humble, and help inspire others in their generation to do what is right and live a joyful and peaceful life. I write for my late mother, Hajja Arbia, who inspired me to be the best I can be.

Here was a woman who could not read or write, who lost her husband at a young age, and raised six children against all odds. When my dad passed, I was 11 years old and my oldest brother was 13; my youngest sister was born a few months later. No one in the family had a job. The only income was from a modest pension from the French government, since my dad had served in the French Army.

The inspiration to become an entrepreneur at a young age came at night when we all sat around the table for a modest plate of couscous or a glass of tea with bread – not enough to fill our stomachs. I used to think, "What can I do to earn few dirhams to help with groceries?"

My friend Brahim and I used our imagination and God-given talents to sell different items, such as figs and boiled eggs to earn extra money for food and daily expenses.

My mother was an inspiration because she insisted that every one of us go to school so we could get the education she never received. She refused to let anyone leave school to enter the labor market at such a young age. In the end, all of us graduated with advanced degrees.

I migrated to the US, pursued the American Dream, and am now a writer and a motivational speaker with a purpose to give back to the community and the world, especially to needy children.

My mother inspired me to be my best, and I'm grateful that I get to pass on her legacy to my family and the world.

Grateful for the Gift of Memory

By Jordann Scruggs

*"Gratitude is when memory is stored in the heart
and not in the mind." – Lionel Hampton*

The jazz musician George Duhamel said, "We do not know the true value of our moments until they have undergone the test of memory." I have been blessed with a lifetime of precious memories.

Like most parents, the birth of my child is among the most precious memories in my life. My son is now grown with children of his own, but childhood memories of him are cherished gifts that my heart continues to treasure. His newborn gaze into my eyes, full of hope that I would love and care for him; the gentleness of his small hand on my cheek when he would say, "I love you, Mommy" – these memories still bring tears and touch my soul deeply. As he grew into a young man and then an adult dealing with life's challenges, the memories of our talks still play over and over in my mind, reminding me of the gifts of his love and trust. I am fortunate that he is still with me, but if I were to lose him today, my memories would sustain me until death.

I am also grateful for the many memories I have created and shared with my husband. When I married him, I never imagined the journey we would realize after 34 years. Whatever emotion one can feel has been felt between the two of us, good or bad. But through it all, we have learned love, acceptance, and what it means to honor and respect another human being who completes you. Because whether we want to admit it or not, we are not meant to live this life alone; we are charged to help and love one another. The memories my husband has given me have created my happiness, and I am grateful.

Lastly, I am grateful to the apostles, for it is through their memories of Jesus that we can know of salvation.

"But the Comforter, the Holy Ghost, whom the Father will send in my name, he shall teach you all things, and bring all things to your remembrance, whatsoever I have said unto you." – John 14:26

Do They Know Me?

By Susan M. Lucci

"Do they know me?" she asks, without any emotion other than a slight hint of anxiety that has always accompanied her for as long as I can remember.

Five years ago, this question would have broken her heart; today it breaks mine. Tears used to come easily to her; today she has no recollection of either who they are or who I am. Yet somehow she wants to know whether I have children. After more than 50 years together, my mother has no idea who I am. She looks at me with a blank, slightly suspicious stare. Every few minutes she asks my dad, her security blanket, "Who is that girl? Do we know her? Why is she here?"

It's heartbreaking beyond belief. Who are we without our memories? Without any relationship to time, place, or each other? Why are millions of us losing our minds? It's a mad, mad world, and this is a maddening disease that I may one day suffer from, as so many of us do. There's still no cure for Alzheimer's.

My mom once was a fabulous grandmother who sang every one of her grandchildren's favorite songs by heart. When she could drive, her license plate proudly beamed OMANINE. Her nine grandkids still call her "Oma," but she has no clue who she is or who any of us are. She knows not the day, the time, or the place.

And so I tell her, through tears, "Yes, Mom, I have three children, and they love you dearly. You were the absolutely best grandmother. You sang them to sleep at night when you visited. You baked pies with them. You brought them dresses and took them to the zoo."

"I did all that?" she asks, happily surprised.

And with the very next breath, she forgets everything I've said, everything I've ever said, and everything she's ever said or done, and returns to her anxious questioning.

I wonder what her soul remembers while her brain forgets. I dance in the space between endeavoring to be present with her while her body remains, while grieving the woman who was my mother.

Adding to My Bucket List

By Jamie Thomas

I sat in front of my computer screen, idly watching another video. I found myself questioning my actions for the umpteenth time – why was I sitting here? I didn't care about the video. I felt heavy, bored, uninspired.

I thought about how different things had been just two years earlier. I had been living in Idaho, where I had been mentored in primitive survival skills and was furthering my inner exploration. I thought about my journey in the wilderness school – learning to make a shelter, discovering my truths, finding my spark of life again, reconnecting with my inner child, appreciating each moment, and no longer dreading the next. I worked with natives and engaged in ceremonial sweat lodges, found a powerful support base, formed deep emotional bonds within the local men's group, lived in a communal home, explored the wilderness and grew in tune with it, drove through the entire Pacific Northwest to California on a road trip, and even met Jon Young, the man who engaged my mentors in Idaho and started the "Re-Wilding" movement.

During that time, I'd felt so alive, filled with purpose, dreams, goals, passion, and a zest for life. Yet here I was with all those memories and nothing to show for it. I was in a job I no longer cared for, feeling stuck, directionless, and going nowhere. Then I realized that I had checked off every single dream I had, and I was languishing because I was no longer following a dream.

I spoke to my mother later about my epiphany, and her words still ring in my ears: "You're too young to have crossed everything off your bucket list." She's right. There's so much more I want to do – and I can make it happen. After all, I've done it before.

Love Never Dies

By Angie Carter

I began living every parent's worst nightmare on the morning of June 28, 2014. Bella was a happy, healthy toddler; her death was sudden and unexpected. Instinctively, I held on to every piece of my child that I possibly could in fear that I would forget her. Once a parent loses a child, their worst fear becomes that their child will be forgotten.

I was terrified that I would forget the little things about Bella: the smell of her hair, the sound of her voice, the touch of her skin. I deeply feared she would lose importance to me as time passed. I knew that my memories would eventually fade, and this shattered my broken heart.

Every year on the anniversary of Bella's death, I honor her short life in some way. I expected this day would become easier with each passing year, but this year I spent the day hiding, refusing to acknowledge that my daughter has been gone for five years. My heart ached as I realized my worst fear was coming true: I was beginning to forget. I cried harder that night than I had in years. I was grieving, this time for the memory of my daughter.

I wasn't coping well and took some time off work to focus on self-healing. When I struggle, I look within for answers. This was when the message was loud and clear. I began to see the unfair expectations I had been placing on myself. I expected to never forget a thing about my daughter. I was also placing unrealistic expectations on my grief, but grief is unpredictable and has its own agenda.

The intricate details of my daughter's life may fade away, as it's humanly impossible to remember every single detail, but I will continue to remember what was important. Regardless of how much time passes, I can never forget Bella because she is a part of me. Nothing can change what she means to me, not even her death. Although memories will fade with time, my love for her will never die!

Chapter 5
Messages from Friends…Old and New

We consider our dearest friends to be part of our "soul family." They help us through the hard times and make the good times even better. They help us appreciate the beauty of life and the world around us and within us. They remind us of who we truly are and inspire us to be our best selves. And sometimes they relay messages from our soul just when we need to hear them!

In this chapter, you'll read stories of friends who shared messages that touched hearts and changed lives. Some of these friends were still living and others had already passed on. Some of them had been friends for years, others for just a few minutes. They include neighbors, teachers, classmates, and coworkers. They're people we've met through our work, in the shops and businesses of our community, and even in prison. These are soulful friendships that bridge the gap between generations, between people of different faiths, and between hearts.

Some of these friends inspired the authors to pursue their education, follow their calling, and fulfill their potential. Some of them inspired us through their words, others simply by being a positive presence in our lives. As one such friend put it, "You've saved my life just by being my friend."

The stories in this chapter celebrate a truly diverse group, but each one of these friends shares this in common: they connected with the author's spirit in meaningful ways and left an indelible mark upon their soul.

We hope the stories in this chapter allow you to not only meet these wonderful people but to become friends with them as well – to open your hearts to them and let them into your soul family. We hope they touch your hearts as deeply as they've touched ours.

Wings to Fly

By JoAnne B. Lussier

We met in high school, but it wasn't until 10 years ago that our friendship began to take shape. Mark is a talented musician and songwriter, and he invited me to join the chorus in his concert performance. I was deeply honored to be part of the magic he created on stage, especially because of a forgotten song he discovered and brought to life called "Learn to Fly." I keep his recording on my computer and listen to it when my soul feels restless.

Several years ago, Mark began experiencing serious medical issues. His days now consist of living in a rehabilitation center due to complications. Visiting him is a bit more difficult than it should be because he receives dialysis three times a week, but we try to work around it with video calls when it's possible.

I won't pretend to know how hard it must be for him to have lost his independence and mobility, yet I have never heard him complain. He always has a smile on his face, and his sense of humor can still fill a room with laughter. His eyes light up with excitement when he talks about the new technology he has that helps him pursue his passion, despite being confined to a hospital bed.

"I have limited use of my hands now," he says, "but my mind is still sharp, so I'm able to write music."

Mark has no tolerance for pity. He feels blessed despite the challenges he faces. I once asked him how he remains so positive. "My faith is strong, and the Holy Spirit lives inside me," he replied.

Conversations with Mark are like pieces of music. They are soulful, moving, and inspirational. His gentle spirit captures your attention like the melody of a familiar song and evokes a sense of peace and harmony to whoever listens with an open heart.

I've learned many life lessons from Mark. He's shown me the power of having hope and faith during hard times, but I'm most grateful for him teaching me how to spread my wings and fly.

Gifts to Last a Lifetime

By Isabella Rose

I was recovering from what should have been a fatal car accident for me. My aorta had collapsed and was torn in several places (which required surgery to restructure it), one of my lungs had collapsed, and I had a fractured shoulder, a broken humerus, a broken elbow, and four broken ribs, in addition to severe inner trauma.

My dominant arm was in a sling to allow gravity to pull my broken bones back into place, so I wasn't able to use it for weeks. Things that were once easy for me – such as writing, zipping up my jacket, buttoning my shirt, or opening bottles – now required me to get creative or ask for help. I had an occupational therapist coming to my home to help me adjust to daily living with my temporary limitations. I enjoyed our visits and shared many things with her, including my passion for holistic health and my training in various alternative healing modalities, including Reiki, angel energy healing, and aromatherapy. She encouraged me to put my knowledge and training to use by healing myself, which I immediately started to do.

I also told her about my interest in enrolling in the PhD program at Quantum University and my two previous attempts in completing the admissions process: the first time, I'd doubted myself, and the second time, I'd started the process but wasn't able to complete it due to unexpected life circumstances. She told me I had what it takes and would make an excellent doctor, and my fiancé (who was also part of the divine intervention that saved my life the night of the car accident) reinforced this message.

With their encouragement and loving support, I completed the admissions process and was accepted into the program! The car accident not only gave me the gift of life a second time but also a lifetime of gifts to share my passions for holistic health and natural medicine to heal myself, others, and the world.

GED to FNP

By Lori Love

My childhood brought challenges. I was forced to quit school at 15 due to the school burning down. By 18, I was married and had a daughter. By 21, I had a son. I had no idea how I would teach my children anything, as I had so little education. I felt ignorant, that I would amount to nothing.

In 1998, at the age of 29, I decided to pursue my GED. I studied and passed the test. I was thrilled, and a fire ignited inside me that I didn't know existed. I decided to apply to a Certified Nursing Assistant program and was accepted. I worked at a hospital in ICU and loved every minute of this position. I quickly learned that I wanted to become a nurse, but my fear of failure was so intense. How could I go to nursing school when my education consisted of only a GED?

I began to take prerequisites for the program, which I really enjoyed, and my grades were better than I ever hoped they would be. I applied to nursing school at a community college and was accepted. This is when my journey began to evolve. The program was tough, and family life was challenging. My husband became a cook, a house cleaner, and a taxi for both children. I passed, took my boards, and was now an RN!

In 2012, a coworker/friend asked me a question: "Lori, with all the gifts and talents God has given you, why would you put a cap on your education?"

This changed my life. I applied and completed my BSN program and didn't stop there. I knew where my dreams were going to take me. I applied for an MSN-FNP program and completed and passed national boards.

Fear of failure should never be an option. I am living proof that you can do anything you put your mind to if you really want it. My dreams were bigger than my fears, and I am thankful for the journey, as well as my supportive husband.

Don't Skip Lunch

By Diana L. Hooker

I am a true believer that everything happens for a reason and that the people in our lives are there on purpose. This was affirmed recently while attending a seminar. The seminar was a four-day event that kept us busy from early in the morning until late at night, providing great knowledge and delicious food.

Unfortunately, my work obligations did not take a four-day break, so I opted to skip a morning session and lunch to finish up some client work. Once in my room, the internet simply would not connect, which was imperative for me to do what I needed to do. I even tried using my phone as a hotspot for my computer, but to no avail. After spending an hour exhausting all possibilities, I begrudgingly decided that I would eat lunch after all and try again later.

A lady that I had met that morning asked if she could sit with me. We engaged in a casual conversation of pleasantries until she began to talk about her family. She told me that she was a mother of five, and her youngest complained about how much she worked. At that moment, I felt led to tell her that my youngest son had been dealing with anxiety for most of his life, and it had developed into O.D.D. She immediately teared up and said that her son had been diagnosed with the same thing!

We spent the rest of our lunch connecting over the similar struggles helping our sons through their O.D.D. I was able to tell her of a program that my husband and I had found that had a tremendous impact aiding our son with his anxiety. She told me I had given her hope with the story of our son's success with the program.

Had I actually stayed in my room and skipped lunch, I would have missed this important opportunity. It was a divine intervention because when I returned to my room later, the internet worked perfectly.

Transformation on the Mountain

By Gabrielle Taylor

It's a three-hour hike to the top of Mount Pico, and the climb starts to get steep within the first hour.

We're a party of 10 attempting to reach the summit of the 8,000-foot volcanic mountain in the Azores archipelago in Portugal. A cross-generational mix, there are a couple in their 60s, a few of us in our 40s, some 20-somethings, and my 11- and 13-year-old daughter and son.

My kids whip ahead of the older crowd as though "uphill" weren't a thing. In need of a break, the older people stop, and Olsen, one of the seniors, pulls out a bag of candy bars, which he generously offers to share.

"Candy bars!" I call out to my kids (who are way above us by this time), knowing that they're Francis's favourite.

Sure enough, he bounds down, head over heels for the goodies. But as Olsen sees this eager 13-year-old fall upon us, he pulls back his treats protectively. "None for the kids!" he growls.

My husband and I look at each other, our eyes wide, wondering what this guy has against kids. This suspicion is confirmed two hours later as we pull ourselves hands and feet up to the summit. My kids scramble ahead of Olsen, and I hear him curse under his breath.

After reaching the summit, we're ready for anything. But have you ever noticed how coming down a mountain can be more challenging than going up? Even for kids.

Francis turns an ankle slightly and needs to take it slowly. He finds himself at the back of the party, with who else but Olsen, who's seriously struggling to make it down the steep part. Francis holds his elbow and guides him down some dangerously sloped rocks.

They trail behind the rest of us, each supporting the other. And when we hear Olsen's voice, the tone has changed from irritated and callous to soft and tender. "Oh, can you help me over this part, Francis?" And then a few moments later, "Would you like a candy bar?"

The Messenger

By Jordann Scruggs

"I will give him…a new name written on the stone which no one knows but he who receives it… which comes down out of Heaven from My God." – Revelation 2:17; 3:12

One never knows how people entering our lives may change us or the impact they will forever impart – like my friends Ron and Aliyanna.

Aliyanna and I had developed a working friendship, and soon I was introduced to her husband, Ron, a Messianic Jewish rabbi who held regular services.

Regretfully, I had strayed from church but, curious, decided to attend Ron's services. As a Southern Baptist, I had focused on the New Testament; however, Ron's teachings from the Old Testament offered abundant history and a clearer understanding of God's pearls of wisdom.

After learning that Ron had brain cancer, he and Aliyanna struggled but never lost faith in God. In addition to being a teacher, Ron had become my "brother," and it was difficult to watch this once-robust man endure such agony. Over time, I stopped visiting, keeping in contact with Aliyanna sporadically.

Upon hearing that Ron's time was near, I went to visit. The cancer transformation was startling, devastation complete. Warned that Ron recognized few people, I called his name. Aliyanna said, "Ron, do you know who this is?" In that miraculous moment, Ron looked straight at me and smiled. "Of course, it's Hannah," he answered. Through his soul, I felt the love of God and instantly knew I had been given my heavenly name. Amazed, I heard Aliyanna reply, "Yes, Ron, it's Hannah." Quietly, I spoke with Ron; speaking my Christian love and thanking him for his guidance back to where my heart knew was home. He smiled and closed his eyes to sleep.

The Bible often speaks of God changing a name. Jesus met Simon and immediately changed Simon's name to Peter. When God changes a name, it implies He sees a new chapter in your life that will fulfill His plan for you. This watershed experience revealed my life's purpose, making me forever grateful to Aliyanna and Ron, my brother, my teacher, and God's Messenger.

Lightning to My Heart

By David Hipshman

A few years ago, I attended a powerful seminar where my intention was to look deeper at what I was doing, choosing, and being. At the very end, when everyone was leaving, a voice in my head said, "Turn around and talk to the person behind you." I saw a smiling, attractive woman with a lot of light. We started talking like we had known each other a long time. It turned out we were on the same flight back and lived pretty close to each other. We sat together and realized we wanted to continue to apply what we learned at the seminar and decided to be learning buddies.

I was seeing that the biggest challenge in my life had to do with letting my emotions (mainly negative) keep me stuck. I had started to learn about "emotional mastery," which included facing and feeling our emotions, to be more freed up. I wanted this, but I didn't really know how to do it. I called my new friend and asked for her advice. She told me about a meditation that addresses this exact challenge and invited me to go with her to try it. I trusted that by going to this meditation, a big breakthrough would happen for me – and that's exactly what happened! I learned tools to face, feel, let go, and heal, and I have been using these tools from the "Heart of the Matter" meditation for years now.

And something else happened after that was very profound: I met the meditation leader, whose name is Piper. I felt an intense electrical current in my solar plexus while I was next to her. It was so strong that it actually tickled my skin. It was like a lightning bolt to my heart that I could not ignore or rationalize away. I decided to do a longer retreat that she was leading. After that, I went on a "deeper" path – a calling to channel "higher power" to and through me.

Looking back, I see that I trusted each step, and they led me to my true calling!

Soulful Sunday Strolling: Spaces In Between

By Susan M. Lucci

Once in a while, I stroll around my town at the speed of soul, with my heart wide open. Sweet surprises and soulful conversations abound.

On a recent Sunday, I sat on a sunny bench reading. Looking up, I saw a trio of tots skipping toward me, their joy contagious. As I spoke, they averted their eyes until their mother said, "It's okay." Sadly, I realized a barrier of safety separated us: I was a stranger with light skin. With shy eyes, they sat down. I savored our brief connection, and they were off to enjoy a spa day with their mommy.

My next soulful encounter arose at the gym. One of the trainers shared stories about motivation, daily practice, and engaging mind, body, and soul. She works with the body; I work with the soul. We've spent enough time ruled by our minds.

Next stop, the dress shop to enjoy a multisensory experience, thanks to the way the local businesswoman arranges her textiles. We chatted about the uprising of women's voices and an uptick of women in power. Together, we imagined an event bringing together her people and mine.

In the coffee shop, I witnessed a beautiful connection between a mother and her young son. Smiling, I returned to my book. The mother appeared at my table. Having just moved to town, she was eager to connect – she loved the book I was reading. It turns out she holds women's circles, too. I can't wait to continue our soulful conversation.

I choose to live in this unique community because of its diversity of perspectives. Connecting soulfully with strangers is deeply nourishing. While the walls separating us are mighty and there's work to be done bridging our divides, my every connection with another being on this lonely planet sparks joy and hope.

What's possible when we break down the walls and connect in the spaces between us? Let's bring back the town square and make it welcoming and inclusive enough to hold all our fabulously varying views! If we aren't the people and now isn't the time, then who and when?

Judge Not

By Margaret Jane Landa

Teaching is a fascinating profession. I taught for over 46 years, and no two days were ever the same. You learn from those you teach.

One of the students who taught me a valuable life lesson was in what was then termed a learning-disabilities class. This was a young man from a group home, who I'll call Paul. He was about 15 at the time, bright, handsome, and a good artist with a pleasant, outgoing personality. His mother had mental problems and was institutionalized. His father couldn't cope with the children and earn a living, so the children ended up in the foster-care system.

The situation that taught me so much came on one of the last days of school. The weather was warm, and shorts and tee shirts were in style. Paul came into the classroom, put his foot up on the chair and there for all to see were the family jewels!

The class started, and I could feel myself getting angrier by the second. How dare he come to school like that! What was he thinking? My mind was filled with all kinds of things I would tell him as soon as the class was over about how unacceptable his behavior was.

When the class was over, I told him to stay and asked him why he had come to school dressed inappropriately. He told me that at the home, they were only allowed to wash clothes twice a week. On that morning, by the time he got his shower, there was no underwear left. Immediately I understood. The anger and judgment were gone as I realized this was a situation over which he had no control. What I had blamed him for made him feel worse about the matter.

I realized that I can never know another's problems or circumstances, and for my own mental health, it's best not to judge! This knowledge gave me the right guidance at the right time, which resulted in a quieter mind and a sense of freedom.

Women Lifting Women Higher

By Julie Ann Wylie

I'd heard tales of non-competitive, empathetic communities where women support one another during life's highs and lows, but at 47 I had yet to find one of these groups. That is, until I went to prison.

In November of 2009, our caravan pulled up to the Women's Correctional Facility in Lockhart, Texas. I was there as a respectful listener, having said yes to attending an event marking the completion of a course offered by a local non-profit named Truth Be Told. The graduates, incarcerated women, told stories of choices made and circumstances beyond their control that led them to prison. Their accounts stirred in me relatable emotions of grief, regret, betrayal, desperation, sadness, surrender, triumph, and hope. The evening left me nearly speechless; I'd never before witnessed the impact of a community of women lifting one another higher. My experience at the meeting was palpable and profound; its supportive, healing qualities impacted every cell of my body.

Combinations of circumstances beyond my control and the choices made over a lifetime had accumulated to form my own metaphorical prison, and I wanted the freedom observed in this community of women lifting women higher. That night I said yes to serving women behind bars, and while that might sound like a noble cause, it was in an act of self-rescue.

Ten years have passed since that auspicious evening, and I continue to return to prison as a volunteer facilitator. Every time I tell my story, my truth of what is holding me back from being the fullest expression of myself, I find I'm vitally engaged in life.

You, too, can create and thrive in a community of women lifting women higher by first noting circumstances beyond your control and sharing those out loud with a safe listener. Next, with that respectful witness, reflect on choices made and actions taken that shine a light on mental and emotional imprisoning patterns. Truth telling, first to oneself and then to others, is a practice that I have found naturally lends itself to freer living.

What imprisons you?

Connie's Gift

By Lori Thomas

I was meeting my friend Connie and her beautiful teenage daughter, Meera, at a regional park east of San Francisco. It was a July morning, and the air was rapidly warming as we greeted each other and decided what path to take.

We directed our walk toward the stream flowing along the border of the park. The dappled shade of the trees growing near the bank provided a cool, shady haven where we could enjoy the myriad forms of life that thrived in and around the water. We turned right onto a short path that led past a huge oak tree. Meera, who loves climbing trees, made a beeline for the oak.

As she passed me, I looked down, and directly in front of us lay a three-foot-long rattlesnake, stretched out with her head near the tree and her tail halfway across the path. She seemed unfazed by our proximity.

Connie and I savored the encounter, honoring the snake's presence and receiving her wisdom. I received a message about awareness, focus, and respect, and created a short video. Connie did the same.

As she recorded, I noticed a marked difference between our videos. Connie's words expressed love and appreciation, plus the fullness of the messages we'd received from the snake, much like a prayer. It was clear that she had received much the same message as I had but verbalized it completely, while I had not. My video had included only part of the message, and the rest, with my emotions and reverence, remained unspoken.

As our walk continued, I noticed Connie voicing appreciation to no one in particular, thanking her knees for helping her climb a large rock, thanking butterflies for their presence and flowers for their beauty. While I felt these things inside, her verbalization made them more potent and made me more aware of my own feelings of appreciation.

What a powerful practice! Verbalizing our thoughts amplifies the effects. As I carry this lesson forward, focusing on what I love and giving voice to express the beauty and good I see, I am excited to see how my life changes.

The Wisdom of Gratitude

By Nancy Merrill Justice

On our journey through life, many souls will cross our path briefly, but on rare and special occasions, a significant person will choose to walk beside us and take our hand in friendship and love. These special souls enrich our lives and show us the meaning of grace and gratitude.

I was blessed to have been joined on my path by a hero of a man named Jack. He was the father of a close college friend, and he reached out at a time when my path was clouded in shadows of grief and pain. The deaths of three family members and several close friends, a divorce, and serious injuries from a third auto accident had left me feeling unsure and hopeless. Jack offered his guiding hand – filling me with love, courage, inspiration, and the wisdom of gratitude.

Jack lit up my life every day with a cheery phone call. We would commiserate, laugh, and share stories of years gone by. He'd make certain we ended our conversations expressing gratitude for friends and family. Jack was a mentor, teaching by example that our perspective affects how we experience life – in pain or in gratitude and joy.

During this time, Jack was diagnosed with a devastating lung disease, which the doctors said would soon take his life. But Jack told his doctors he was determined to watch his youngest grandson graduate from college in three years – and that was that.

As months passed, Jack's labored breathing often required him to be hospitalized. He was a rock of character and strength – always positive, hopeful, and very gracious to all his caregivers. Beloved by all, Jack's spirit inspired and elevated the entire hospital to excellence. He became known as the "Walking Miracle" – repeatedly making unexpected recoveries from treatments and returning home to his family.

Although he passed soon after, Jack proudly lived to see his grandson graduate from Carnegie Mellon University. And I continue my journey with new perspective – experiencing more love and joy, inspired by the wisdom of gratitude.

The Dream

By Maria Angela Russo

I saw myself as a trembling child, crouched down in the farthest corner of a maze-like horse stable. It was like watching a movie. A horse with a cigar hanging from his muzzle and a straw hat on his head searched for me. When he found me, I knew he'd trample me to death. I woke up screaming.

The dream's meaning was clear to me. The personified horse represented my Uncle Carlos. For three years, I lived with him and his family, and for all of those years, I could not escape his attacks, regardless of how hard I tried. Nowhere was safe.

The abuse ended when I moved back home at age 13. I thought it was over, without leaving scars. The fact that it might have had any lasting effect on my life never occurred to me. I didn't make the connection between what happened as a child and the depression that permeated my life for the next 20 years. This secret created an emotional infection within me, and it took all my energy to keep it hidden. Though I survived by burying it all and never telling anyone, my soul knew.

I'd already thought about calling my parish priest to talk about how I'd lost my way spiritually and how trapped and unhappy I felt in my marriage. Now, stunned by the emotional impact of my childhood trauma suddenly surfacing, I knew I needed to make that call to get help with the confusion of these newly resurrected feelings. Once I relayed my story, the priest recognized my need for more help than he could provide, so he referred me to a therapist.

Therapy sessions changed the course of my life, launching me onto a path of healing, self-awareness, and personal growth. In time, I began writing about my experiences and found that the clarity writing brought was the greatest healer of all. I learned that denying my own truth meant denying the potential to live the life I came here to live.

A Friend's Just-Right Response

By Joy Resor

Have you ever heard a voice when you're home alone, knowing it hasn't come from a person?

In April 2016, while applying blush and lipstick after a quick shower, I hear a voice in the air above and behind my right shoulder: "How can you reach more people?"

Flustered due to a time-crunch feeling rising inside, I manage to say, "I can't think about this right now; I need to get to class."

Traveling the four-lane road for a journaling circle, I muse with gratitude about messages I've earlier received from Spirit: The day my mother-in-law Sarah dies, I discover her favorite cheese in the fridge with that day's expiration date; when my husband ends our marriage with words that land in my gut like a black cloud, I hear, "Take in this darkness. You need it. You're going to transmute it."

Next, a strong thought arises to stop musing, to be present on the drive. Surprising myself, I arrive early, before the students. These extra moments allow me to prepare the table and sit with my eyes closed, breathing into stillness. When Diane arrives, sitting next to me, I see that she's more serious than I've witnessed. "Joy, I don't think you understand how valuable the questions you ask are. I am growing and changing because of this class! You need to put them in a book."

Struck by inspiration, my hand rises to hold my heart, challenging me to speak right away. Sharing beyond the awe I feel, I tell her she's just given me a meaningful answer to a question I'd received. Wow.

The next two weeks overflow with events and commitments. Anytime I'm home, though, I allow powerful, playful journaling prompts to arrive through my heart and hands, adding up to a book that reaches more people.

Angels with Messages, Wherever You Go

By Gigi Florez

An angel was sent to help me hear what I needed to hear.

It seemed like an ordinary night as I did my rounds. In one room, a new patient had checked in, a rather young man. As soon as I entered his room, he asked, "So, do you know why I am here?" I told him no, as it was the first time I was seeing him, and I hadn't seen his chart yet. Without a pause, he continued speaking, saying he was admitted because he suddenly fainted on the street. He'd had a tooth pulled a couple of days earlier, and the procedure had apparently caused an infection. He had carelessly ignored the pain, and the infection in his dental cavity had reached his blood, eventually causing the fainting.

As I listened to him, something came over me. Lost for words, I left his room after managing to wish him a good night. Once in the hallway, I felt an overwhelming sense of gratitude. It dawned on me that the universe had sent me an angel in the form of this young patient, who had delivered the message I needed to hear.

As soon as I finished my shift, I hurriedly called my dentist and sought an appointment. Not too long ago, after a root canal procedure had gone wrong, I had developed an infection similar to the one in the young man's story. The infection had reached my jawbone, and I had needed two surgeries performed by three specialists. Though the surgeries saved me, I still wasn't out of the woods. My dentists had told me that it was imperative that I continue to follow up on my dental visits so they'd know for sure that the infection had fully passed. As I was feeling rather well, I had carelessly put off these appointments. But the mysterious way in which the universe had sent me a message was unmistakable, and I couldn't help but feel a sense of overwhelming gratitude for having received it.

The universe had a plan for me.

Mothers and Divine Intervention

By Lisa Anna Palmer

As a second-generation Italian-Canadian, I grew up knowing many Italian immigrants my parents' age and many second-generation Italian-Americans and Italian-Canadians like me.

After my father passed away, I felt like I had lost a big part of myself – not just a piece of my heart but a piece of my heritage, the connection back to my roots. This led me to pray to meet an Italian-born person my age – someone who I could speak my mother tongue with, who was born in Italy and had decided to move to Canada, just as my parents had in the 1950s.

A few days before my sister Emily's wedding, she, my mother, my niece, and I were standing in line at our favorite spa. In front of us were two tall, beautiful women who were speaking perfect native Italian – just like my cousins did back in Italy.

Of course, my mom jumped at the opportunity and said, *"Ciao! Ma siete del Italia?"* ("Hi! You are from Italy, right?") Next thing you know, the five of us were engaged in an excited conversation, until we realized that we were holding up the line.

At the end of our spa day, I exchanged numbers with my newfound friend, Stefania. That was seven years ago, and we've since become close friends. We've supported each other, met for dinner, and shared our visions for making the world a better place through our respective work. Stefania kept saying to me, "Lisa, we have met for a reason."

A few months ago, Stefania founded BYBS™ and asked me to help her launch her startup. The more we worked together, the more we realized that we shared a soul purpose: to help grow a generation of leaders who care more about people and the planet than they do about profits. Through our companies, we plan to collaborate on projects that will have a positive impact on young people and the future of the world.

I prayed for an Italian friend, and my prayers were answered and more, thanks to the power of our mothers' and divine intervention.

I agree with Stefania. Our friendship was meant to be.

20-Year High School Reunion

By Ayeesha S. Kanji

As I contemplate my upcoming 20-year high school reunion, the days of my youth come back to me. The days of figuring out derivatives and why I could care less about chemistry come back to me. The faces of elementary school, grade school, and junior high come back to me. The world was a different place when I went to high school, and what amazes me is how those of us who maintain contact actually agree on how different everything is.

Treasuring our youth and who we were as kids is sacred in our journey of life. I still remember what I wanted as a teenager, and I can actually say that I have achieved 80% of those goals. In the past 20 years of moving around, attending university, working, traveling, and discovering, I can say that I have lived more than I ever thought I would.

I always tell everyone the same story. I was born, bred, and brought up as a California Girl and became a woman in Canada. The years of learning values and who I was were surrounded by palm trees and warm beaches. The years when I solidified who I have grown to be were surrounded with snow and fall colours.

Most people say that we live once and to enjoy every day. But as Snoopy told Charlie Brown (in an old cartoon that I recently saw on an Instagram post), "No, Charlie. We live every day, not just once." I agree with Snoopy. Every day, treasure those sacred years of your youth – the times of becoming who you wanted to be. Remember the day you learned how to multiply, and treasure all the moments when you learn something new. Our childhood memories will always stick to us more than we are willing to admit. As I prepare to attend my high school reunion, I reflect on how adulting is overrated because the years we spent together will always be sacred.

Earth Angel Messages

By Nicole Black

Both my parents have passed on, but I still get multiple signs from them daily, comforting me from beyond. There are so many stories I could have chosen to share with you about how they answer questions or how they have kept me safe. I could tell you about the beautiful sparrow that came to visit me and didn't leave until I said, "I love you, Mom." I could share the stories of pennies with the years of significant events showing up seemingly out of nowhere. However, I wanted something deeper. Something more meaningful. With less than twenty-four hours until my deadline, I knew I needed to pick something. But which story?

I try really hard not to "hate" anything because there is always a lesson to be learned. But I have to admit, I actually hate missing deadlines. Slightly panicked I was going to miss this deadline, I went to meet a friend for coffee. A woman I don't know came over to me. She smiled and asked if she could tell me something. She had the most beautiful glow about her, and her energy was contagious. Smiling, she said, "I was drawn to you. I have to tell you how beautiful your soul is. I don't usually go to strangers and tell them when I see that, but there was something that told me I needed to tell you that."

Sometimes it isn't a penny with a specific year on it or a feather when I ask one of my parents a question. Sometimes it's an Earth Angel – a person who has no agenda and wants nothing from you – coming to tell you something good. And that is a beautiful thing.

We can all do that for others – a smile or a kind word can change another person's day. I'd like to invite each of you to find a way to make someone else smile today. You never know – you may be helping them complete something for a very important deadline.

Allowing Your Heart to Break

By Anne Bradley

My beloved dog passed away nine years ago. Sadie had been my constant companion for 11 years, and when I came home from the vet alone that day, I was shattered. I vowed that day to never love another dog. I felt all scraped out inside, and I knew if I lost another dog, it would break me so completely that I would die. I just couldn't bear to go through the heartbreak again.

Over the years, I never missed a chance to hug and pat a friendly dog. I especially loved to play with the dogs my neighbor Kate would walk by my house each day. I'd rush out and stop her and visit a moment while I patted and enjoyed the dogs. She asked why I hadn't adopted a new dog after all these years. I told her about my vow and how I was certain one more loss like that would kill me. She nodded knowingly, and went on her way.

A few days later, Kate waved me over while walking her dogs and said, "I thought about what you said. And if it were me, I'd go out and get yourself a new dog to love. And when they die, it probably will kill you. And I say that it would be worth it for all the loving days in between now and then. Your heart will be open, and you'll die happy, having the love of a dog again in your life."

The next day, I went to the shelter and rescued a nine-month-old furry bundle of love. He warms my feet as I write, and I can't believe I waited nine long, empty years afraid to love. It's been two months now, and my heart aches with the bigness of the love I feel for him. I'm happier now than I've ever been and wake with joy in my heart again.

Thank you, Kate, for your wisdom when I needed it most. I will cherish every precious moment, knowing that my heart will break again and I'll die happy.

The Power of Words

By Janet Womack

Ten years ago, it seemed like my life was in a downhill spiral. I felt l like my prayers weren't being answered, like I'd possibly wasted years of my life, and I wasn't sure what my purpose here on Earth was.

I'd gone through multiple failed IVF cycles, all resulting in a heartbreaking phone call from the doctor. Devastating news.

I struggled.

I was legitimately grieving the loss of my dream of becoming a mother. I had been defining my self-worth based upon having a child. I had pleaded with God in plenty of prayer. If I wasn't supposed to be a mother, could he please hit me upside the head with what His purpose was for me, because I sure couldn't see it through my broken heart and my tears.

Then one day I was visiting one of my closest friends. She asked me, "Do you know I feel like you've saved my life, just by being my friend?" I told her no, I didn't, and she reminded me of all we'd been through over the years as friends. It hadn't even crossed my mind that I had made so much difference in the life of my friend. It was a real *It's a Wonderful Life* moment!

Ten years ago, my oldest step-son passed away. We are blessed to be raising his daughter. She's a very wise 14 year old. I've spent the past year and a half going through multiple surgeries and chemotherapy for breast cancer, and she's been one of my biggest cheerleaders though it all. She's held my hand and assured me that it's okay when I feel like I need to cry. The most humbling and proud moment of my life was when she just hugged me tight and said, "Mimi, I am so glad I have you. I hate to think of how my life would have turned out without you."

Never hesitate to tell someone how much they mean to you, or how they have helped to impact your life in a good way. It might be just the message they need right then – as it was for me with my friend and my granddaughter – offering a light even in the darkest moments.

Broken Silence

By JoAnne B. Lussier

Several women and I gather each month to celebrate the new moon and one another. We call in the four directions, meditate, and share pearls of wisdom we've gathered along our spiritual paths. We accept each other where we are and promise to uphold a safe space with no judgment.

One evening, our circle lasted much longer than usual, as conversation drifted into the ebb and flow of worldly events and the effect on our emotions. It was hours past my bedtime when we finally closed our circle to enjoy the blessing of good food and lighter conversation, but I was eager for the night to end.

A small-framed woman, whom I had only met once before, continued to speak of a particularly traumatic event in her recent past. We continued to hold space for her, sensing she was still trying to process the harsh reality of trusting the man she loved.

As her story unfolded, it became evident that she was in an abusive relationship that culminated in a false arrest. Shame had caused her to keep this a secret despite her innocence. She couldn't understand how the lies her boyfriend told became the evidence against her. Sitting alone in a cold jail cell, her voice fell upon deaf ears. Feeling vulnerable and victimized by the institution designed to serve and protect, she felt betrayed all over again.

I felt her pain as flashbacks from my own experience hit me like waves crashing onto the shore. Reaching out, I touched her arm and began sharing fragments of my own story. With stunned faces, we all looked at one another in this ugly moment of truth. Like a floodgate burst open, we spilled our secrets one by one, recounting the patterns of abuse we had endured as women, wives, and mothers. An overwhelming sense of admiration and respect washed over me for these incredible women. Their resilience is testimony to the inner strength of all women and our ability to rise above the injustice. No longer silenced and shamed, we hold our heads high with dignity, and we honor the women we've become.

A Supportive Family

By Catherine M. Laub

Mike was a great husband, a fantastic father to four teenagers, and a welcomed member of our extended family. He always had a smile and was happy to talk with all of us at family gatherings. In 2005, we all took a cruise to the Caribbean, and Mike made sure his children (three young girls at the time) had lots of fun. And I'll always remember Mike and Margaret's wedding day; I'd never seen a couple so connected and so in love.

Last November, right around Thanksgiving, Mike was diagnosed with lung cancer. He was a fighter and wanted to be home as much as possible. His family was there for him through it all – including his wife and kids, his parents and siblings, and his in-laws (Margaret's parents, three siblings, and their families), who all played a large part in his care. They all took turns driving the kids to their friends' houses and events. They drove Mike to his doctor appointments and sat with him while Margaret was out. And they prepared (and still prepare) many meals for the family.

Sadly, Mike passed in June.

All of these family members continue to help Margaret and her children. We just attended a fundraiser for them, which was a major success. Over 350 people attended and bought multiple prize tickets to help Mike's family. The success was due to the many hours put in by all the family and friends. They walked from business to business for weeks asking for donations. There were over 200 baskets and gifts in all! Plus, in addition to donating gift certificates for the raffles, many local restaurants donated food for the event.

Margaret posted a thank-you as follows: "The love, support, and generosity the kids and I have received is beyond comprehension. Our family hasn't left our side from the day of Mike's diagnosis to today, and I don't see them leaving anytime soon." I echo those words because Margaret's family is also my family, and I'm proud of all of them for all they have done.

Journey into Dance

By Lori Kilgour Martin

The first time I walked into a dance studio, it was as though I had returned home. Placing my hands on the barre, I felt held in a warm embrace.

Those defining moments arrived after watching a friend dance in her backyard. A slumbering spark of light awakened. Following that event, God led me to a wonderful teacher who introduced me to the world of ballet, jazz, and musical theatre.

After graduation from high school, it was time to leave her nest. I auditioned for the ballet school first on my dream list; however, it was not to be. I then became unsure of my abilities and body image.

A few months later, we heard news that Canada's first prima ballerina was coming to conduct a workshop during an arts festival. With my teacher's unwavering support, I stepped through another door and found myself thriving in this woman's presence. Soon after, I was accepted into her college dance program.

It was an intense three years that brought immense growth. She was an amazing master who pulled me out of my comfort zone, entrusting me with featured roles, including the lead sylph in *Les Sylphides* and one of the four little swans in *Swan Lake*.

There was a belief in her eyes as well that I did not have. While classes, along with the rehearsal process, were demanding at times, she nurtured me through the immense fear of being front and center. Those insecurities rose up often regarding my body's ability to embrace the intricate choreography and movements. I also suffered injuries, but thankfully I always recovered.

Both of these graceful mentors instilled faith and the strength to survive through life's challenges on this journey. Together, they were instrumental in gifting me with a solid foundation. Remembering them often, the energy of dance continues to ground my soul and is part of the internal fabric of my heart – weaving its signature in everything I do.

To express without words, emotions rise from within – I move freely in unison with the music. There is love and joy. I am eternally grateful.

Three Simple Words

By Meredith Fjelsted

"You're going to need surgery."

I wanted the pain and bleeding to stop, so I believed the doctor was right. His next words felt like a direct hit to my stomach. "Schedule your hysterectomy right away." Then he walked out of the room, leaving me with a business card to call and schedule a hysterectomy. I sat there alone. Shattered. My dream of marrying and having a family of my own broke into pieces and crumbled around me.

I scheduled the hysterectomy, as directed. As the day approached, my stomach told me what my heart already knew: I didn't want to go through with it. But what choice did I have? I had to believe that the doctor knew what he was doing. I believed there was no alternative. What I had wanted was being taken away. I had wanted the chance to get married. I had wanted the chance to start a family. This dream was about to literally be pulled out from inside me and discarded.

I told a friend about my upcoming procedure and she replied with three simple words that changed my perspective forever: "Get another opinion."

I got a second opinion, and the first doctor was right. I needed surgery. But the second doctor was willing to let me keep my uterus. I wish I could tell you I went on to have children, but I didn't. However, I married a man who already had two children. Eight years, four miscarriages, no babies and many surgeries later, I had a hysterectomy.

Following the advice to get a second opinion changed my life forever. In the end, I had to give in to the inevitable, but I'll never regret it. The years in between are what made me a better person. They taught me how to trust myself. They taught me faith, hope, love, and forgiveness. They taught me how to become my own health advocate. Today I am a Health Coach, and I teach people to do the same. And, in the end, I got a family of my own.

Sight That Helps You Soar

By Kimberly A. Elliott

Thirteen-year-olds can be pretty precocious. I know I certainly wanted to believe that my personality at that age said, "Smart...determined..." Yes, I was one of those girls! But I was also well mannered. I knew no matter how "cute" I thought I could be, embarrassing *my* mama (especially in public) – *and living to tell about it* – was *not* an option. However, I definitely had a little adventurousness in me. What I didn't anticipate was "Baby, you're going to be a missionary!" rolling right off the lips of an elderly woman I met, as easy as "Now, Honey, close your mouth before you catch a fly!"

My friend, Tina, and I were at Shiloh Baptist noon-day prayer (not customary for most teen girls we knew, but we actually enjoyed it). There was something about the dichotomy of the "wisdom of godliness" and "knowledge of worldliness" that intrigued us. On this particular day, though, my life was impacted so much that 40 years later I'm still writing about it!

Honestly, I couldn't even begin to recall the woman's name who said this to me all those years ago. I do remember that she called everyone my age "Baby." Yet truer words, I don't believe, have ever been spoken over me!

I did become a missionary. And I've enjoyed serving others in my hometown, in many states across the US, and in other countries, including Haiti, Nicaragua, and even South Africa. My life's verse is "Here am I, Lord. Send me." It resonates with something inside me that confirms that my mission is bigger than me. I get to serve others and receive so much more in giving that I always have a ready reserve to give more.

I've often heard that the eyes are the window to the soul. I guess mine were like a crystal-clear lake that day...or perhaps there's a sight that sees beyond the perceived to the possible, and when the heart gets a glimpse of it, it soars!

Our Best Is Good Enough

By Chanin Zellner

"If you don't stop beating yourself up, you're going to get cancer!" Greg forcefully exclaimed. He was a tall guy with a peaceful vibe who suddenly stood up in front of me, pointing his finger.

Taken aback, I thought, "How does he know this about me?" I'd been blaming myself for "mistakes" my whole life, and my motto was, "Woulda, coulda, shoulda." My life was filled with regrets, and I joked that you would find my picture in the dictionary next to the word "guilt."

My husband and I met Greg Drambour when we married in 2008. Aside from being a shamanic healer and minister, he was a cancer survivor, so I took to heart the words he spoke during our premarital counseling session and vowed to rid myself of the guilt and shame I carried.

He introduced me to a counselor named Mavis Karn, who told me during a session, "We all do the best we can with the knowledge we have at the time." Those words changed my life.

I was born a perfectionist and "good enough" was not in my vocabulary. Whether it was schoolwork as a kid, my performance as an employee, raising my kids, or being a wife, anything less than perfection was unacceptable. I lived in constant fear of failing and disappointing others, and I suffered from low self-esteem and depression for much of my life because perfection was not attainable.

In 2017, I was guided to a compassionate mentor named Alison J. Kay who helped me heal the trauma stored in my body due to false beliefs and life circumstances. Because of the work I did with her to understand how our thoughts affect our lives, I finally embraced what Mavis said many years prior: "We all do the best we can with the knowledge we have at the time."

Thanks to persistent divine intervention, I am free of perfectionism and fear of failure. I forgave myself for the times I didn't know any better. And now I do the best I can each day, and that is good enough!

My Soul Became Whole Again

By Karen A. Hill

Who knew that joining a support group could turn out to be such a miraculous, mind-blowing experience?

At a time when I felt emptiness in my soul and had insane ideas, I reached out to a spiritual support group. In spite of my irrational thinking, fascinating changes began to happen. This group appeared to have their lives in order, and I was desperate to make changes in my life. Women and men from various backgrounds showed me some basic tools for living. I knew, way deep down inside, I needed and wanted to be a productive member of society by gaining employment, establishing housing, and regaining and sustaining a healthy relationship with my family.

My first task in the group seemed far-fetched. I was asked to show up an hour early to set up tables and chairs – and then, afterward, to clean tables and floors, wash coffee pots and dishes, and take out the trash. During each meeting, I was observant and mindful of what others were doing and saying, and I had much help from other members. I acquired basic communication skills, which allowed me to become more positive and confident when I spoke, and my self-esteem was empowered by the group. I learned how to slowly deal with my feelings through journaling and discussing it with my mentor, who also showed me simple skills to find employment.

It was a slow healing process, but miracles happened. My family gained trust as I came home on time every night and showed up anytime I said I would. After a while, they allowed me to live with them until I could support myself. While living there, I paid rent and cleaned up after others and myself. Finally my soul began to fill up with God, love, family, and friends. I gained courage and strength in everything I worked toward. I was pleased with these unforeseen rewards.

In the end, I remain fascinated by the feelings of excitement that I get by telling you my story, which still energizes me and puts a huge smile on my face. Taking selfless acts brings great reward.

When Your Career Chooses You

By Scott Fjelsted

Confucius said, "Choose a job you love, and you will never have to work a day in your life."

I was on the road to doing the exact opposite. Following in my successful brother's footsteps, I started college majoring in accounting. After a few long, grueling semesters, the thought of being confined to a desk was beginning to sicken me. My grades were suffering, as I was not interested in the material, yet I felt I had no other option. I thought, "What am I even doing here?"

But everything changed on the day I overheard Brian, one of my gym buddies, talking about his major where he got to help people achieve their fitness goals *and* get paid for it. Something lit up inside me as if I had just won the lottery. I thought, "You can get paid to do that? I've been doing that for free for years!" My career had just chosen me.

College went from something I wanted to get away from to something I couldn't get enough of. I immediately changed my major from accounting to kinesiology and fell in love with learning for the first time in my life.

Because I overheard that conversation in a weight room over 25 years ago, thousands of lives have been impacted in a positive way – lives of people like Gordy, a man in his 50s, losing 150 pounds in a year and keeping it off over seven years now, and Susan, who went from being told she would never walk again to completing multiple 5Ks. I get to work in an environment where people come to me to better their lives, one rep at a time.

I would change the Confucius quote above to "Let your career choose you, and you will never have to work a day in your life." I guess that's why I'm never going to retire – because for the last 21 years, I have never really worked.

Friendship Remembered

By Jordann Scruggs

"A friend loveth at all times." – Proverbs 17:17

The brown envelope lay on the table – dread knocking at my heart's door. The return address told me what I didn't want to know. The envelope remained unopened.

In 1966, as a teenager, I was placed in an orphanage. Teenagers innately don't trust, and I was no different – until Joann. Joann worked in administration, and we would embark on a friendship that lasted more than 50 years.

Through the years, I came to realize that Joann was God's gift to me, a rock in my stormy life, always there to comfort and advise. When I became a Christian, I struggled to understand how to live this new life. Joann simply said, "Just live your life as if Jesus were always by your side."

Joann's Christian example was evident throughout her life. She and her husband, Bill, fostered troubled children for 29 of their 47 years of marriage. The adoption of their twin daughters, Sara and Amy, was the culmination of selfless love. Joann began the first childcare facility in her small country town and taught numerous children about Jesus and His love for them.

While Joann remained where she had always been, I explored the world, always knowing I could come back to my compass, Joann, and find true north. She lived vicariously through my adventures and occasionally would have adventures of her own. But no matter how much time or distance apart, we would meet again and not skip a beat.

We talked incessantly about everything; we revealed our fears, disappointments, and dreams. We listened to each other cry and held each other in silence, never questioning our devotion. Joann's faith was solid, her family love steadfast, and her friendship true.

Finally opening the brown envelope, I realized that I'd missed Joann's funeral. Two years passed before I knelt at her grave, nestled in the peaceful hills of Kentucky. Missing from the stone's inscription of wife and mother was the word now missing from my life: friend.

An Unlikely Friendship

By JoAnne B. Lussier

While standing at the breakfast bar shuffling through a pile of bills, an unfamiliar envelope caught my attention. Inside was a child-support check from my husband's new boss. Feeling relieved, I felt compelled to call the owner of the company. After being put on hold for several minutes, my call was answered.

"Hello? This is Wayne."

"Hi, Wayne. My name is JoAnne. I'm calling to thank you for mailing my child-support check weeks sooner than anticipated."

"Oh, that's why you're calling me," he snickered. "Full confession here: I was hesitant to take your call because your divorce is a hot topic in the shop these days. I was expecting something worse."

"No, I simply wanted to express my gratitude because the money is needed right now."

Little did I know that this stranger would become such a dear friend. Wayne had recently divorced and took me under his wing. His sense of humor brightened my mood, especially when he joked about being my girlfriend. We often talked on the phone late at night after my daughters were asleep. His wisdom and compassion helped me focus on the things that truly mattered.

Wayne's children were much older than mine, so sharing his experiences helped me through many painfully dark moments.

"I'm the go-to dad," he quipped, "not a Disneyland dad. They come to me when they need something, not when they want to have fun."

"I'm not a fun mom anymore," I mumbled.

"Sweetheart, don't cry," he soothed. "It's cheap to buy smiles when nothing matters," he explained. "When children come to you during their vulnerable moments or ask for help, it's a testament to your true character because they trust you."

He assured me that someday I would see it as a blessing and not a failure, but I wasn't convinced.

Wayne passed away many years ago, and my children are adults now. I can't help but smile each time my daughters choose me to confide in or ask for advice. Wayne, in his infinite wisdom, knew it all along.

Pour Some Honey on It

By Melissa Monroe

It started with a simple piece of advice: "Eat a little something sweet in the morning – not too much, just a little."

I had only known her for two weeks when she said it, and I remember thinking, "That's all you've got? That's your big advice?"

Her name was Nima, and she was my first Ayurveda teacher. At the time, her words sounded basic, limited, faulty. Now I realize they applied not only to my digestion but to my words, actions, spirituality, relationships, work, and lifestyle.

That's because food – like our body, mind, and spirit, and everything around us – contains elemental qualities (hot/cold, hard/soft, rough/smooth). These elements constantly and dynamically affect us. With every bite, word, season, and sensory impression, our entire constitution adjusts – mind, body, and spirit. We adjust. What and how we eat, how we live, act, and speak all leave an imprint.

When we met, I had excess hard, dry, rough, and sharp qualities – a reality that showed up in my words, actions, thoughts, and physical symptoms. Nima's suggestion to add sweetness to my diet applied to my entire life.

Honey with breakfast was just the start. I added yoga, meditation, mantras, and abhyanga (self-oil massage). I nourished myself with warm, restorative foods; cozy blankets; rest; and soothing colors, scents, and sounds. Over time, the sweet taste healed every aspect of my life. This balance awakened a deep clarity, flow, and joy I had never lived. A well of love, compassion, forgiveness, and kindness opened and infused my relationships, work, body, mind, and spirit. My perspective of myself, others, the world, and my role in it shifted.

Deep self-care, aligned for your particular needs, unlocks a love that cannot be contained. I invite you to nourish your body, mind, and spirit incrementally, through practices that grow over time. Be patient. Watch how your consciousness expands, your body says yes, and your mind balances. In the process, know that I am holding space for you wherever and whoever you are. I send you love and peace.

The Text Message That Changed My Life

By Nikki Ackerman

Tired, frustrated, and feeling as if the life had been sucked out of me, I pleaded, "If I could only find a part-time social-work job and concentrate on my business."

My body could no longer tolerate working overnights full time. It was rebelling against me with increasing migraines and issues that required me to have my gall bladder removed the year prior due to poor eating habits, forcing myself to be awake during the night, sleeping during the day, and incorporating changes at the night job.

Then it came. I received a text message from a friend of a holistic counselor looking for a part-time Licensed Independent Counselor or Social Worker and possibly a Reiki and massage therapist to join her growing private counseling and wellness practice. Instantly, goosebumps lined my arms as I read the text sitting at my desk at my business. I thought to myself, "I'm a Licensed Independent Social Worker and a Reiki Master!"

I knew then that it was God or the universe providing me with an opportunity. Butterflies fluttered in my stomach. It's a scary thing to think about leaving the security of a full-time job, but I thought to myself, "It can't hurt to talk to the lady." It gave me hope.

And that's what we did. I asked to meet, just see what she had envisioned for her practice. One email led to another until we finally met. I knew this was the leap I needed to take in my life. A month later, I submitted my resignation and a month's notice from the night job.

The transition has been a journey. Sometimes it takes a lot to have faith in God and the universe to support what feels like a radical change. My wellness has improved in so many ways, and I'm grateful for this experience. I'm so happy I followed my intuition and followed up on that life-changing text message.

Sister-Friends

By Kimberly A. Elliott

Oh, how sister-friends have blessed my soul! I mean, aside from faith that grounds me, good health (which I could truly value more), adoring children and grandchildren (if this page had illustrations, surely I would have pictures), and a husband who makes me feel like I hung the moon…I am truly blessed with some amazing friends.

Now, before you turn the page concluding, "Whose life is really that perfect?" consider this: Every life has challenges (and I'm actually writing a novel about the monumental wisdom I continue to gain from those), but every glass is half empty and half full…at the same time!

I recently took a trip with my sister-friends that impacted me even more once we came home. We were all excited about the opportunity. We planned (a little). We procrastinated (*a lot*)! You see, this same group of women has known one another for more than 30 years and has rarely planned a Sunday brunch successfully. Planning for us all to depart and arrive at a getaway destination – *all at the same time* – was quite spectacular!

There's always one person (me) packing minutes before I walk out the door. There's the thoughtful one, Betty-Jo, who buys the group matching luggage. (I mean, *come on*! That requires forethought that I'll never have.) There's Aunt Lizzy, the cautiously optimistic one, who has an exit strategy in case she needs a way out of the trip (*like if one of us pisses her off*)! There's the free spirit, Deb, who would take the trip without any of us. Then, there's Bon-Bon, asking a dozen times, "What size bag can I bring?" and still ending up repacking on the way to the airport.

Our time together was so memorable, we even made new friends, but what I brought back and will never unpack is the importance of keeping your friends close. Friends who bring smiles to your heart keep you focused on the cup always being half FULL!

A Helping Hand from Him

By Reema Sharma Nagwan

Life was running smoothly. My husband, two girls, and I were content. The world kept spinning and the time came when my kids grew up. My elder daughter became serious about finding a part-time job. I hadn't realised how time had flown; in my eyes, she was still a kid running around carefree.

As a mother, I was unprepared to let her into the real world just yet. I didn't want her to buckle under the pressure of studying for her final years of high school in the coming years along with work. But as time went on, she developed a stronger, genuine willingness to work a paid job. I could see this when she applied for her Tax File Number.

I felt a conflict within me. My motherly affection was warring with my rationale. One half of me felt she was still my little baby. But my other half was unwilling to hold her back, wanting her to go for it and stand on her own two feet.

One morning, still of two minds, I woke up and, as usual, went to pay my obeisance in front of our altar. As I kneeled, bowing down and touching my forehead to the floor, an idea flickered: Why not get my husband to talk to his friend who ran a franchisee of a well-known fast-food chain? But a thought stopped me. Was he really a friend, or just a Facebook friend? I was hesitant, but a voice inside urged me to give this a shot.

After nights of discussion, my husband finally agreed to dial the number. To our pleasant surprise, his friend amiably agreed to hire our daughter for two weeks, welcoming us with open arms. While there, I saw her enjoying herself, which was an eye-opener. I realised she truly had grown up, making me believe she was ready to tackle the real world. She soon started working in a local branch of the same food chain – much to my delight!

Looking back, I realise that in the midst of confusion, He lent us a helping hand. And along the way, we made lifelong friends and my daughter got to spread her wings.

The Madeleine Effect: the Downside's Upside

By Susan M. Lucci

The "911" crisis is quickly becoming our new normal. Trauma and tragedy pervade the 24/7 news stream – from school shootings to climate calamities. I amped up my meditation practice as an antidote to all these crises. Trying to slow my racing heart by sitting still and breathing more deeply, I sense new capacities emerging within and between us – including an expansion of our collective heart. With every emergency, I see people coming together to cry, comfort, cheer, and collaborate.

Community is our very best response to chaos: it's the upside of the downside. What Maharishi Mahesh Yogi predicted in 1960 (that 1% of a population practicing Transcendental Meditation could produce measurable improvements for the whole) came true in 1974 when the crime rate fell by 16% after focused meditation. "The Maharishi Effect" describes the influence of positivity generated by conscious heart coherence.

My community recently generated "The Madeleine Effect." For six sleepless nights, while Madeleine was lost with her dog, Mogi, in Glacier Park, dozens searched the woods, while thousands of us around the country generated conscious coherence. As all eyes focused on Glacier's Bear Country, we connected our hearts. Magically, on Mother's Day, Madeleine was found alive – somehow miraculously surviving a week in the wild, without food, water, or shelter!

A massive mission of professional rescuers, psychic locators, family, and friends created a web of support woven text to text, hand in hand. We came together to find one mother's lost daughter. In the face of unfathomable fear – imagine the ferocity of a mother bear and the wilds of a melting Montana winter – we responded by holding hope in our virtual home: our collective consciousness. What could have been the worst Mother's Day ever became the best by tapping our amazing positive power of community. Our courageous and compassionate response to this emergency brought Madeleine home safely.

What a wonderful realization: We can activate our power for good by connecting in the space between us. A worldwide web of souls found Madeleine by coming together, and that is the miracle of The Madeleine Effect!

Find the Pause

By Cheryl Kedan

"I know the plans I have for you…
plans to give you hope and a future." – Jeremiah 29:11

One Friday, I hurried off to work, leaving my sick husband with no idea of the crisis about to happen. Later that day, I received a startling call from the ambulance EMT saying that my husband was in critical condition and was being rushed to the hospital.

Internally, I pleaded for answers while imagined disasters flashed in my mind. By the time I got there, he was gone. I was 48 years old, much too young to be a widow. My devastation was a ripped, gaping wound in my flesh that left me gasping for life. I laced myself together with rage and dread.

Over time, the search for actions to reanimate my shredded heart became a driving need. I relied on a mentor who gifted me with a perspective shift that I will always remember. After expressing my sadness and despair by relating how my husband had promoted, valued, and loved me for 30 years, I heard my mentor's words: "How lucky you are to have these memories. There are many people who never have a person in their life that gives them these things." How true. I had been adored by someone who had enriched my life and pushed me to accomplish and excel.

My mentor's wisdom has become a guiding principle for me to create joy in my life. She explained to me that there is a small decision point between when we feel an emotion and how we will react to it. She said that this pause is always possible in our interactions and in our thoughts. In that small moment, we have a choice: to choose joy or despair, healing or sorrow. It's up to us how we will respond to life's shifting shape. We can stop in that moment, pause, and determine the next response.

This turning point has become the beginning of actively choosing happiness when my emotions overwhelm me. Life creates chaos, and our ability to find the pause determines the actions we take to move into the reimagined future.

Autopilot

By Melisa Archer

Every day had become the same as yesterday. Tomorrow would be the same as today. There was comfort in this. Bills would be paid, the garbage taken out, meals made. But where was the passion, the physical, mental, and emotional energy? I was starving for it.

Married to an amazing man that I love, how can this be that we no longer have the "in love" passion that we once had?

Since childhood, I had wanted a baby. Year after year, I waited. Five years became 10, one decade followed another, and still I waited. Now 44, still feeling young but knowing that time is no longer on my side, I stated my intentions to my husband and made it clear: this needed to be my year to make a baby. My husband replied, "No, it is not in the plans for us. I do not want to help bring a child into this world."

Depression overtook me. Having a baby is something that you just can't create on your own. I felt abandoned by my life partner. I now realized that my dreams were not valued in this marriage.

I went on a much-needed vacation with my mom. On our walk back from dinner, I met a man who looked me in the eye and said, "You are my wife." It was a little shocking because it was something I would not have expected to hear. But I told him no, I was not his wife. The man then asked, "Are you married?" When I told him I was, the man looked puzzled and shook his head. "No, you are my wife." This seemed crazy to me, but for some reason, I did feel connected to him, from a lifetime ago.

I avoided him for a few days, but eventually our paths crossed again. The man asked if I had children, and I said no. He said, "I would like to give you a child and make a home." It was so crazy and not planned.

What a wake-up call! I realized that I had been stuck on autopilot. This gave me the motivation to make divinely guided changes in my life, and so I rerouted my destination.

Healing Words
By B. J. Garcia

One day in 1986, I was driving home from work when I found myself pulling off to the side of the road, feeling lost and alone. I had worked so hard at creating a life that I thought would give me happiness and fulfillment. I had a wonderful family, a beautiful home, and an amazing job, yet somehow there was a deep feeling of emptiness inside me. With tears running down my face, I cried out to God, "Surely there has got to be more to life than this!" In that moment, there was no answer to my cry.

Little did I know that my life was about to change in a big way. My mother, whom I had been at odds with during most of my growing-up years, had been diagnosed with cancer. When I heard the news, I knew this was going to be one of the biggest challenges for us both. I was angry, blaming, feeling trapped, and wondering how I was going to get through this with her.

One morning I was called to turn on the television, which was something I rarely did. *The Phil Donohue Show* was on, and his guest speakers that morning were Louise Hay and Dr. Bernie Siegel. They were talking about how to heal your life. It was a new and foreign concept to me but caught my attention.

Louise shared two simple suggestions: change your "I should" to "I could," and change your "I have to" to "I choose to," releasing yourself from past conditioning based on guilt and shame. In examination, I could see that my whole life had been run on "I should" and "I have to." This was the answer to my prayers! For the first time in my life, I felt that I had a choice.

Thanks to these two simple suggestions, my mother and I had two beautiful years together before her passing. Twenty-five years later, I was honored to meet Louise Hay and thank her for her healing words that changed my life forever.

Opening the Gate

By Cath Edwards

They would walk through the prison gate after overnight lock-up with their heads hung low, expecting that I would lead them into the education wing with an approach like many who had gone before me.

I shook their hands, greeted them warmly, and made eye contact. I smiled with genuine happiness. This was not the norm for them and was not well received by other staff.

I was a female teacher in a male maximum-security prison and found it to be soulless. There was either total apathy or sheer hostility with not much in between from both inmates and staff. It had its own slow but threatening pulse, pumping bleakly away with no end in sight. It felt like their souls had been torn out, never to return. Or worse still, left behind with nothing but a shadow of a life not lived.

I couldn't and wouldn't treat the inmates in an inhumane way. My soul spoke to me loud and clear that no matter what offense they had committed, I would treat them with respect and compassion. Perhaps this sounds incredibly naive and insensitive, especially to those who had locked them up or were victims of their crime, but I believed that the only way to create change was to be the change.

Over time, I witnessed these men shift that soulless, tattered energy to life. They learned that there are other human beings who can show compassion, love, and understanding.

I clearly remember the day when there were 15 inmates in my class from 15 different countries of origin, including an Australian Aboriginal man. They were locked up for serious crimes. Many of the men were enemies through culture and history and would normally be in segregated areas when not in class.

As I held the class in my arms with a curiosity about what had happened to them and where their choices had led them, I witnessed them showing curiosity for one another's lives, their unique cultures, and, more times than not, their distressing childhood traumas.

They were being heard, perhaps briefly, but a lifetime in their hearts while I watched their souls smile. They were reclaiming what was rightfully theirs.

Lunch at the Coffee Shop

By Shelia Prance

I live in a small rural town and shop locally when possible. I was recently downtown and decided to have lunch at the coffee shop. I found a seat and noticed there were several tables of men and women dressed in business attire. When my lunch arrived, one of the men commented that perhaps he needed to order the same spinach wrap.

The gentleman stated that the group was from a local church. They were talking with residents about their faith and inviting people to visit their next service. He quickly started quoting scripture to me. He also said that the current political situation in the United States was an issue and we all need to work together as citizens. I reached into my handbag to retrieve a business card that provides my name and business information. I wear many hats in my life as an accountant, an author, and ordained minister.

When I showed this gentleman my business card, his facial expression spoke volumes. It quickly became obvious that he did not respect women in the ministry. I said that I am an author and not employed by a church. I handed him my business card, but he refused to accept it, so I placed it on the table in front of him. We spoke for a few minutes, and he walked away without taking my card.

Although many people in my area are not ready to accept others because of religious, political, or social issues, I am attempting to reach out in my community to make positive changes. I use my ministry social media account to post numerous soulful articles, quotes, news items, and blogs. My goal is to plant seeds of change, nurture each one, and allow them to sprout.

The encounter at the coffee shop provided a soulful message that I heard loud and clear: We all have work to accomplish.

The Real Gift

By Margot Edge

A brilliant star has left us, but his effect on me has not dimmed.

I discovered the author Richard Wagamese thanks to a friend's suggestion, and I was immediately drawn to his writing. It filled me with such a strong sense of place that I would frequently mark passages for reference. But the real gift for me is his book *Embers: One Ojibway's Meditations*. I just touched the book and knew it would be a treasure to me. It is always within reach, well-thumbed and tabbed.

His pages are filled with sage words of his elders, guiding him to allow the simple wonders of the world to be a natural part of life. He encourages people to write daily and let the soul come through onto the paper – to sit in silence and let Creator move you to a better understanding of yourself. He suggests listening to your heart over your mind. Although it may take time to change your approach to action, he reminds us that a response of "I feel" carries more weight than "I think."

The year after I found his writing, I was in the hospital under heavy medication. It was then that I looked over and saw him in the next room. How could this be? Maybe it was the medication surfacing, but it truly seemed so real. I wanted to call out to him and tell him how much his words meant to me.

After waking from a coma and a near-death experience, I survived. Sadly, however, three months later, Wagamese died.

His writing is still my daily inspiration. He encourages me to write, as I remember his advice: Observe, listen, and see the beauty in the natural environment all around you. Warm the soul with rich thoughts. Reach new heights. Recharge and glow.

He began life in difficult circumstances. A long, dark road ended when he was encouraged to use his talent for words. Fortunately for us, they remain an inspiration to experiment and enjoy the experience.

Thank you, Richard Wagamese (1955-2017).

Spiritual Rain

By Netta de Beer

Last July I was on holiday in Mumbai, India, during the beautiful monsoon season.

One afternoon, during a break in the rains, I arranged to have a taxi take me shopping. The manager at the hotel where I was staying told the driver where to take me and to wait for me, but when I came out of the shopping mall, I couldn't find my taxi. I looked for my phone but couldn't find that either.

After a long, fruitless search, I gave up looking for my phone and went to find another taxi. There were many taxis around, so I don't know why I chose this particular one, but I'm glad I did. The young driver, Rahul, could see that something was wrong, so I told him about losing my phone. He tried to calm me down by singing me a Hindi song.

When we arrived at the hotel, he walked me to the front desk and told management what happened. I thanked him and could see that he really cared. As I went up to my room, a very strange feeling came over my body – something so beautiful that I couldn't explain.

The next morning, I was awoken by a knock on my door. It was the hotel manager asking me to please come down to the front desk. When I got there, Rahul was waiting with the biggest smile ever…and my phone! After dropping me off, he'd searched the area where he'd picked me up until he found the phone. I had left it at the coffee shop, he told me. I was speechless, and I felt the same strange feeling that I'd felt the previous afternoon. Then I understood everything. God was with me all along. I asked Rahul how I could ever thank him, and he said, "Ma'am, you already did."

Although he wasn't looking for anything in return, I decided to help Rahul start his own small business. And he helped remind me of such an important message: even more beautiful than the monsoon rain is the spiritual rain of kindness.

In the Grace of God's Presence

By Gena Livings

As a young child, I was raised in the midst of religious turmoil that sparked early questions concerning the presence of God and how to live my life in a way that would serve a higher purpose. I prayed earnestly to God to receive insight to all my unanswered questions so I could lead a more peaceful life and be a blessing to God and others. I also wrote to God in my daily journal, and this became my personal dialogue with Him in the form of poems, prayers, and artwork that expressed my thoughts and innermost feelings.

In the spring of 1992, I was introduced to Bob, a spiritually focused golf coach, who took me under his wing for 12 months and addressed many of my unanswered questions that changed the "internal course" of my life forever!

Prior to meeting Bob, I didn't know how to live in God's presence. Bob explained to me that in order for God to be present in my life, I have to be fully present for God. Being present means being fully aware and engaged in each moment, in the here and now.

Every aspect of daily life, no matter how mundane, is a moment-to-moment experience in God's presence. As we learn to live from our spirit and our hearts, we realize that we are a divine part of God, and everything in our life comes alive with light and with joy. God's presence is found in a beautiful sunset at the beach, in the sweet-smelling fragrance of a wildflower, and through the joyful sound of a baby's laughter.

God lives in each one of us, and when we remember this, we will always experience God's presence living right inside our soul. The spirit of God is everywhere – its constant presence expresses complete harmony, unity, and love.

This simple insight, communicated through Bob, shifted my perspective, and I no longer felt separate from God. I felt Her energy reach in and hug my heart for the very first time, and I felt grateful, blessed, and fully loved in the grace of God's presence.

A Seed Planted in Consciousness

By Julie Vance

Becoming a Unity minister was not something I planned, nor was there a single moment when I knew I was "called" to ministry. It was a gradual process that led me step by step to ordination.

That process began with a conversation I had with the minister of a Unity church I had been attending for about a year. Reverend Audrey McGinnis was a role model in my life. I admired her positive attitude, her integrity in living the principles she taught, and her delight in seeing others grow and evolve.

One day, following the Sunday service, she revealed her plan for my life. "After you retire from teaching," she confidently told me, "you can go to Unity Village (in Lee's Summit, Missouri) and become a Unity minister."

"Why in the world would she suggest this to me?" I wondered. I had never indicated any interest in becoming a minister. Was it possible she saw some of the qualities in me that I so admired in her?

Although I didn't say it out loud, I thought to myself, "Well, there is no way I am ever going to do that!" However, the seed was planted in my consciousness – an idea that would take almost 20 years and many experiences to come to fruition.

During those 20 years, I became actively involved in the Unity Church as a board member, teacher, speaker, and newsletter editor. I left my public-school teaching position to start my own business facilitating personal-growth workshops and seminars. I was invited to begin an outreach Unity group in a nearby community. Finally, as Reverend Audrey had predicted, I entered the Unity Worldwide Ministries program to become an ordained minister and was ordained at my church in the presence of my congregation, family, and friends.

Step by step, the seed that was planted in my consciousness on that Sunday afternoon 20 years earlier led me to fulfilling a dream that I had not yet envisioned for myself but which brought me great joy and fulfillment!

Healing Power of Circle
By Susan M. Lucci

Claiming our seats in Circle, nervousness abounds. Some know each other; most barely know ourselves. Having held hundreds of Circles, I hold hope.

An ambitious businesswoman/mother of three grown men faces cancer's second attempt at grabbing her attention. We're called together because of her impending surgery; her intention is healing for all. Next to her sits a nurse, visibly weathered by constant worry for sandwiching generations. A lifetime of putting others' needs first weighs heavily.

Women shift in their seats to avoid the sun. They will remember this ancient archetype, I assure them. Discomfort is where growth plays.

The dark face of grief is worn by a mother carrying the tragic death of her teen daughter, a decade ago today. Memories pervade the minds of these midlife mamas. I notice we each stand at a threshold. Settling into this soulful space, we prepare for a precious conversation, unrepeatable.

One tearfully questions her expectation to be the perfect mother. Another, sweaty from decluttering her childhood home, prepares to place her mother in assisted living as she launches her firstborn to college. A therapist who works with at-risk youth squirms, terribly uncomfortable. Wondering if she'll stay, I notice her catch courage as she speaks.

Trees, birds, and wind surround us; broken shards of sea glass form our center. I welcome whatever wants to move through us and light the candle. Taking three breaths – let go, let be, and let come – we share the space between. I smile, claiming courage to hold this brave space.

Soul makes herself known in a moment of grace as a butterfly flutters through. The mother who lost a daughter breaks into a smile: "If I put this stone of grief sitting on my heart down, I can fly and be free!"

The final conversation – raised with "I know this is irrelevant" – is ironically followed by a really resonant Carpool Karaoke with Paul McCartney story, ending with a new mantra for all: "Let It Be." To close Circle, we extend palm to palm – one hand giving, the other receiving. Strangers, now friends, pass transformational healing energy.

Lifting the Mad-Rush Spell

By Gabrielle Taylor

I have five things still on this afternoon's to-do list, which reads: get groceries, stop at garage, pick up mail, attend meeting, make supper.

I've got to confess: despite my love of yoga, meditation, and all things Zen, I frequently rush through my days. Sometimes I think a spell has been cast on me. Despite how intimately I know how hurrying can lead to exhaustion and even burnout, I still fall prey to it.

So, here I am today, wholeheartedly committed and convinced that if only I "get it all done," life will somehow bring me to "better things."

After picking up my ingredients at the supermarket, I eye the checkout lines, trying to gauge which one will be the shortest. I often joke with my family that whichever checkout line I choose, the next one will always go faster. On that February afternoon, I simply choose the line in front of me, which has only two people ahead, each with a only a few items.

As I approach, I notice that the man ahead is hunched over his walker, moving slowly and obviously in pain. In my rushed state (only focusing on the next thing on my list), my first reaction is one of irritation: "There I go again choosing the slowest checkout line." I stand for a few seconds, going over my to-do list for the umpteenth time, looking at my watch.

It's now the "poor hunched" man's turn. But, to my total surprise, he doesn't take his spot at the register. Instead, he turns around, smiles, and generously gestures for me to go ahead. Even with his slouched demeanor, the large awkward glasses, and gnarled hands, this angel in disguise radiates intention, kindness, and peace.

I happily breeze through the checkout, but I remain stunned at what's just happened. For the first time today, I pause and take a deep breath, noticing that my to-do list has evaporated. This brief encounter with a stranger has revealed to me the secret to lifting the spell of my frenzied life and brought relief to my soul.

The One Thing
By B. J. Garcia

Every once in a while, a simple book, with a simple title and a simple message, captures the attention of someone and changes the direction of their life forever. This happened to me while participating in the Your Soulful Book writing program, created by Jodi Chapman and Dan Teck.

On one of our monthly calls, Dan and Jodi suggested that we read a book called *The One Thing* written by Gary Keller with Jay Papasan. As Dan was describing the premise of the book, he presented Keller's question: "What is one thing you can do, such that by doing it, everything else will be easier or unnecessary?"

My internal wheels began spinning! What was my one thing? I have many things that I love to do and many gifts and talents that I love sharing with others, but what is that *one thing*?

Attempting to answer this question through my mental spinning was getting me nowhere. I finally stopped the mind and took a deep breath, and my body and mind began to relax, allowing the question to drop deeper into my heart.

Resting in the stillness, I experienced a profound and pivotal moment of realizing that the answer to my question is *Love*. Love is the one thing I can be, that by being it, everything else will be easier or unnecessary.

In this realization, there was an awareness that Love has always been here. Love had never gone anywhere; but somewhere along life's path, I had left Love. In my lifelong search for Love on the outside, I was overlooking the one thing that was always here and patiently waiting for my return.

As I put my attention on Love, embracing its fullness, my life is changing in miraculous ways. All aspects of my inner and outer world are now flourishing in this Love.

I am so deeply grateful for the gift of this simple book, with its simple title and its simple message, that has led me back to Love.

Melted Crayons

By JoAnne B. Lussier

Summer seems to last forever when you're young. Days flow into each other like forgotten crayons melting in noonday sun. Busy schedules are laid to rest and clocks no longer demand your time. Life is simple, just the way it ought to be.

On my day off from work, a friend invited me over to her lake house for lunch. With the excessive heat, we decided to eat inside where it was cooler. The view from her table captivated my attention immediately. The water rippled in the breeze, inviting the sun's rays to partner in a wistful dance. The lake was calm and soothing, and I felt my body breathe for the first time in weeks.

Eager to sit outside and feel the sun and wind on our faces, we sat by the water's edge before the afternoon rain began. Sharing similar life experiences, we are comfortable talking about topics that we rarely discuss with others. It's comforting to know that someone else has witnessed life through the same lens and shares your perspective without fear of judgment.

As the afternoon drifted by, the wind began to pick up and the clouds became heavy and dark. Although a storm was approaching, we were content to sit and wait for the raindrops to drive us back indoors. The shift in energy welcomed nostalgic conversation. My friend recalled memories of lying on the grass and watching the clouds go by while imagining them as animals or shapes. "I don't do that anymore," she admitted.

I laughed and said, "I still do!"

The sky burst open with a quick, soaking rain before turning sunny again. Driving home, I thought about my own childhood and the little girl who still resides inside my memories. She has a colorful imagination and a loving heart. She's simple, innocent, and full of hope. She's taught me that life is stormy and that in order to weather those storms, you need to watch for the sun. Like a box of melted crayons, life is messy. Yet it's the colorful days in between that create a beautiful story.

Chapter 6
Messages from Animals and Nature

This has been a tough year for us. We had to say goodbye to two of our cats, Elsie and Monkey, very quickly and unexpectedly. Our hearts are still breaking and most likely will continue to do so for quite some time. Although we can't wave a magic wand and bring them back, we have been able to open our hearts to receive soulful messages from them. For instance, soon after Elsie died, we began seeing sunbeams just about every time we took a picture – something that had never happened before. It was a perfect magical message from our "sun cat" who always found the sunny spots in the house. Monkey, on the other hand, showed up as a downpour. (Jodi shares more about how absolutely perfect this sign was in her piece about him in this chapter).

Signs from our beloved animals let us know they're still with us, which brings us some comfort. We've also found some comfort from nature – whether it's by spending time at the beach, enjoying the ever-changing tidepools near our home, or walking among Oregon's old-growth forests. Nature's magnificence always manages to put our lives into perspective, reminds us of what has lasting importance, and conveys the messages and energy we most need for our healing and growth.

In this chapter, you'll read stories of many other animals who have sent messages from the other side, as well as animals – including dogs, cats, bats, birds, bees, whales, and ponies – who are alive and well who have also shared messages in their own unique way. You'll also read about the wonders of nature and the valuable lessons they impart.

Enjoy Every Moment
By Dan Teck

On April 26, 2011, we found Elsie in a vacant lot near our house. After Jodi lured her over with a can of cat food, our new friend was more than happy to be carried home. A trip to the vet revealed that she had been spayed and seemed young (about one year old), healthy, and well cared for – so we were surprised that no one responded to the "Found Cat" posters we put up around the neighborhood and online.

Our tabby "foundling" quickly became an integral part of our family – a daughter, a friend, and also a teacher who modeled how to live with joy, love, and appreciation. She took pleasure in every little thing: a soft bed, a cardboard box to sit on (or in), a patch of sunlight (which she always managed to find), a few minutes of playing with a toy, and (as we already knew) a plate of canned food. Most of all, she seemed to appreciate just being around us. Because she followed Jodi wherever she went, we called her "Mama's little duckling."

She and I also developed a special bond. She loved sitting on my lap and kneading my stomach as I read, lying in my fuzzy guitar case as I played, and connecting each morning during our "sunshine perch" ritual, when I'd put her on top of her kitty condo, rub our heads together, and tell her how much I love her.

Sadly, on February 10, 2019, she suffered a massive stroke and passed away shortly thereafter – with Jodi and I petting her head and telling her how much we love her…forever. Shocked and devastated, we wanted to hold on to our memories of her, which we decided to write down. We had many notebooks (which we use in our business), so we got to take our pick from a number of possibilities. We considered one that was covered in hearts (fitting because of how much we love her) and one with a butterfly on the front (also fitting, albeit bittersweet, given her recent transition). But the one we decided to use felt just right because of the three simple words on the cover, which perfectly encapsulate Elsie's ongoing message for us: "Enjoy every moment."

Going Batty

By Jenean Zunk

I am grateful for this vacation. Sitting on the deck overlooking Lake Tahoe, I savor this gorgeous evening as I watch the sun set over the mountains. And I reflect on my situation over the last two years.

Every summer since I moved into my new house, I have had bats. Which, to put it nicely, isn't fun. However, knowing that animals and bugs are a common way the Universe sends me messages (and once I get the message, the critters go away), I have been desperately searching to understand this one. I talk to my angels and tell them I am open to getting the message, but I need some help.

My friend calls, and we begin enjoying a meandering conversation (as good friends do) when I happen to look up and see a flock of birds about 20 yards down on the beach. I think it is odd that birds would be feeding when it is almost dark and quickly realize they aren't birds at all – they're bats!

I tell my friend I have to go and sit down to watch them. As I laugh, I say to my angels, "Thank you for bringing them in a way that is not terrifying, but what is the message? I have searched and searched for the meaning, but they are still coming. What am I missing?"

I hear a voice that says, "Search again."

I watch a bit longer and then head back to my hotel room to search again for the symbolism of bats. I come across the same information as before, except one small paragraph jumps out at me that I hadn't previously caught – bats have singular focus, which supports them in finding their food. Then it hits me. I ask myself, "What are you focused on? Are you constantly focused on what you want or what you don't want?"

Since then, I've been asking myself this question daily, literally moment by moment, reshaping my life as I do. And thankfully, the bats have since found another home.

Miraculous Microworld

By Gabrielle Taylor

It's a few days before my 21st birthday and I'm alone, far away, across the ocean in a foreign country. After an experience of heartbreak and a devastating disappointment, I feel so sad and lost. "Is life just a random series of events, and am I just a random accident, a lone atom drifting in the universe?" I ask myself.

Thankfully, I'm with some friends of friends, who are kind enough to take me in while I regain my bearings. Unsure of what my next step will be, I could easily go into panic mode. I know that I'll soon be visiting my family in Poland, but I have three weeks till then. And with my broken heart, I have no clue as to how and where I'll fill my thoughts, soul, and time.

Sitting in my friends' garden, I pull out my travel sketchpad and black ink pen. I start to observe the tiny flowers in the grass. An entire miniature world opens up before me, and as I draw, I allow myself to get lost in it. For an insect (or for Alice in Wonderland), this could be a rainforest, filled with lush grasses, curved stems, curlicued flowers, bluebells, and giant worms that come out of the rich soil.

I draw the bright light flickering off meadow buttercups. A tiny off-white petal hovers and whispers like angels' wings over a daisy. Long blades of grass loop and dangle, twist and swirl, casting deep shadows in this mini jungle. As I discover the intricate and subtle details of this world, my eyes begin to dance with the give and take, with the delicate splashes of colour.

Like a healing balm for my flustered heart, the pulsating, alive energy and freshness of what I see permeates my being and starts to ease my troubles. Could it be that God (not the devil) is found here in the details? I'm in awe and wonder, and realize that whereas I had only a few moments before felt lost and broken, I'm now perfectly at home here in this miraculous microworld.

Sunlight on the Floor

By Lyn A. Kyrc

His name was "Picker." We lived in Nashville, so we felt it was a fitting name for our new black puppy. He was most handsome! He grew to be a 105-pound, 14-year-old...puppy!

Picker became a family member, of course. He was laid back and filled to the brim with pure unconditional love. From the time he was a puppy, we would often find him lying in a random ray of sunshine on the kitchen floor. There he'd be, on his back, legs in the air, ears laid flat. We always chuckled at the sight of our sweet Picker, all comfy in his favorite spot.

Every night when I came home from work, he'd lumber clumsily down the steps to greet me. *Thump! Thump! Stumble! Thump!* I always grinned when I heard him bound down the stairs. I knew it would be followed with a wagging tail and lots of puppy kisses! One evening there was no sound of a stumbling dog as I put my key in the doorknob. "Maybe he's just sound asleep in his ray of sunlight," I thought.

When I found him, he was indeed lying in the sunlight and appeared to be sleeping soundly. Picker had passed in his peaceful slumber as he lay in his favorite place. We gathered as a family that night and celebrated Picker's life with endless photographs, tears, and laughter as we each shared our memories.

When I came home from work the following day, it seemed so quiet as the key turned in the doorknob. There on the floor was the seemingly endless empty ray of sunshine. When I looked more closely, I noticed something else. In the middle of the sunlight was a beautiful rainbow reflection. I smiled and tearfully envisioned him lying in the sunshine on the floor.

Now when I see a beautiful rainbow, I know that Picker, our 105-pound furry bundle of love, will always be with us...in our hearts, lying in the sunshine, with his legs in the air.

The Bees' Tree

By Mauri Barnes

A swarm of bees moved in between the walls of my house next to the back door. We lived harmoniously for many years until the house began to hum and the line of bees coming and going to the hive became continuous.

It took a while to find a beekeeper who would remove the whole hive for relocation. Many had told exaggerated stories of Africanized bees that attacked and killed. They wanted to exterminate the hive with poisons. "Not my bees," I thought. "I could stand in the line of their approach to the hive, and they would swerve to fly around me every time. They're not Africanized."

The beekeeper called a few days after the removal to tell me that he had not gotten the queen bee. He advised me to keep a lookout for another swarm, as the bees would resettle nearby. Soon, I began to see bees coming and going from an old cherry laurel tree over by the fence. They weren't in the way, so I decided to allow them to make their new home in the tree.

Time passed and I needed to replace the aged and worn roof of my home. I prayed for help with this expensive project, thinking of all the overtime I'd have to schedule to finance the project.

Then, Tropical Storm Debby came through our part of Florida with high gusty winds and heavy rains. One loud crack and a thump on the roof sent me running outdoors to see what had happened. I ran into the swarm of bees in pelting rain, receiving quite a few stings around my face. It was heartbreaking to see that the bees' tree had broken right through their hive. The top of the tree had fallen onto my house, piercing a hole the size of a quarter through the roof.

The after-storm insurance inspection revealed that the entire roof would need to be replaced. It was covered by my plan.

I had saved the bees, and they gave me a new roof.

Rock Solid

By Valerie Cameron

I was really fortunate to live close to a lake with an amazing beach that spanned 12 miles. Some days I would walk out into the water, some days I would dig my toes deep into the sand, and some days I would just sit and listen to the waves and the wind. The lake had such a calming effect on me.

It was getting close to fall, and I didn't know that this was going to be the last time I would be on this beach. As I was heading back to my vehicle, I noticed a large rock to my right. I stopped and said to myself and to the rock, "Wow! I have never noticed you here before." I proceeded to take pictures of it, as I was baffled by how it got there.

As I turned to walk away, I heard a voice say to me, "Take me with you." I turned around, as I thought someone was on the beach and wanted a ride back to town, but no one was there. I looked at the rock and said, "If that was you speaking to me, then you are going to have to make yourself as light as a feather, as I have quite a way to get back to my vehicle." Thankfully, it complied with me, and I carried it to my car.

A few months later, I heard the rock calling to me. I started to have a panic attack, because we had moved and never unpacked all our belongings. I wasn't sure where the guys had unloaded my rock or if they had even packed it. I searched everywhere and was so happy to find it. It asked me to place it at my back door. When I didn't understand why it wanted to be placed there, it told me that my front and back door were in alignment, so whatever came in the front went directly out the back. It said that it would hold things in place for me. We sold the house two years later and made enough for us to be debt free.

Be aware when you are spoken to, because it can come in many forms. I'm so grateful for all the blessings that this rock has brought me.

My Chunky Sunshine

By Alissa Iida

I remember when he first jumped onto my lap. He placed his furry paws on my right shoulder and then gave me a big, wet kiss on my cheek. We were in love at first sight! Little did I know that I'd be walking out of PetSmart adopting a gorgeous ginger kitty.

In many times of needing emotional support – such as grieving a divorce, losing a family member, or suffering a major car accident – Chunky always came to my rescue. When my heart was suffering in pain and tears were streaming down my face, he would always know when I needed him. Within seconds of me feeling any type of sadness, Chunky would come running to sit on my heart. These moments were our "Heart to Heart" time together. He just knew when and how to calm me down with his majestic presence. Every day, Chunky would need to have his "Mama and Me" time where he would climb onto me and just relax by falling asleep in the crook of my neck or taking a nap next to me (but always needing to have his paws touching me or be in his favorite position: hugging me and giving me kisses).

Sadly, Chunky passed away on March 27, 2019. I will always be grateful for my handsome boy who brought so much joy to my life. Chunky, I miss holding your soft, furry body, watching you jump onto the radio and bop your head to the beat of the music, feeling your paws on my face, and most of all, loving on you. I never thought that I would miss you jumping on my head every morning, but I even miss you biting into my pajamas to wake me up for work. Best alarm clock ever!

Even now, from the other side, my Chunky always makes sure that he comes to visit his Mama every day, whether it's opening a newspaper to see "Chunky Tomato Soup," seeing another cat similar to him, or seeing something that reminds me of him. His precious message is that the bond of unconditional love between us never goes away.

I love you with all my heart, Chunky. You will always be "Mama's Boy." You have healed and comforted my heart many times over, and I am eternally grateful for the 15 years of life that we shared together. Thank you for being one of my Guardian Angels. Rest in Aloha, my Chunky Sunshine.

Orca Medicine

By Candy Motzek

Each summer, we enjoy our oceanside cabin. It's on the west "wet" coast of British Columbia, Canada, a place well known for its incredible wild natural beauty. I often sit on the rocky shore and stare out at the waves. Sometimes the ocean is a clear calm blue with only the sound of seagulls, ravens, and eagles flying by. Other times, the seas are a dark grey with white foam, as massive waves are whipped by the wind.

During a difficult and stress-filled time in my corporate life, I nervously contemplated a change to a more fulfilling career as a life coach. But, truth be told, I was scared, and I had spent weeks second-guessing and wondering what on earth had possessed me to think of a career change. On the outside, I was successful and had everything going for me, but on the inside, I was hollow and drained.

One day during this time, as I sat at the water's edge, I heard an unfamiliar sound – a deep and powerful exhale. As I searched in the distance, the sound came again, this time closer, much closer. Suddenly, three fully grown killer whales swam past, 20 feet from shore. They were moving fast; the wake from their swimming was a like a motorboat. One of these beautiful animals stared at me and, in that moment, I felt a deep connection with the soul of the whale.

I didn't have time to be afraid; I could only feel their massive presence. Only minutes later did the fear set in when I realized that this amazing predator, who hunts and kills great white sharks, could easily have attacked me as I sat at the shoreline. But the message of the orca was clear: it was time to step out of the fears holding me back and embrace my life's calling and purpose.

And I did.

Stuck in the Middle

By Marci Kobayashi

A fuzzy black caterpillar was making its way across the paved bike path to the leafy green bushes on the other side. I stopped to watch and cheer it on. Then, halfway across, it stopped, turned around, and headed back across the path toward the tree-lined side. It had only gone a short distance when it stopped and once again started back towards the bushes. I watched the caterpillar change directions over and over again. It never got far from the middle of the path. I couldn't stop watching.

So far, no one else had come down the path. It is a path well used by dog-walkers and cyclists, so I started mentally urging the caterpillar on, knowing it was a matter of time. From my perspective, either side seemed infinitely better than staying in the middle of the path.

Engrossed by the caterpillar, I didn't notice the patrolling police officer coming up behind me on his bicycle. He stopped, questioning if I was in trouble. I pointed out the caterpillar and said I was just watching. He looked at me with concern but wished me a good day and moved on. Shortly after, the caterpillar made its way all the way across the path without stopping and disappeared into the underbrush. I felt complete and continued my walk.

I think about that caterpillar every time I walk past the bend in the path where we met. I remember how indecision – or, rather, a lack of commitment to its chosen direction – was keeping this caterpillar stuck in the middle. There is nothing inherently wrong with being in the middle of a path. The caterpillar could have stayed right there. Perhaps it would have become food for a crow. Or maybe it would have died in the sun and made food for the ants. Both are worthy fates in the cycle of life.

I don't know what happened to the caterpillar after it crossed the path. What I know for sure, though, is that if it had stayed in the middle, becoming a butterfly would not have been one of its fates.

Sunshine on a Cloudy Day
By Marla David

I had the privilege of experiencing unconditional love from my little canine soulmate, Sunshine. Sunnee was a Jack Russell Terrier – a classic RCA Victor dog. She weighed a mere 15 pounds but thought she was invincible, like one of the large breeds. You know – big dog in a little dog's body syndrome. Sunnee guarded her yard and was matriarch of her pack, which at its highest count was eight, each with their own personality, special quirks, and needs. Each one adorable in his or her way. I love them all, those who are still living and those who have passed.

Sunnee was intuitive; she had a sixth sense. She just knew things, like exactly where I hurt. She'd begin to lick there. She never left my side when I was ill and slept mostly under my left arm for almost 20 years. When my mom took ill, Sunnee stayed with her, as she sensed Mom's need. She would come to me only after Mom was asleep. At the stairs, Sunnee would go ahead a few steps, wait for Mom, and then continue all the way up or down. During the gathering after my dad's funeral, the spots on Sunnee's belly completely disappeared. This lasted a few weeks then came back. Wow.

My dogs have always been faithful and devoted companions and teachers. They have brought laughter and lightness into my world and have given me unconditional love. They have taught me many things. I am grateful I was given the privilege of having these experiences.

I have two dogs now. It seems strange for me. I keep looking around for the others, but they are not within sight. I think of them often, just as I think of my family and friends who have passed. They've taught me that life is fleeting, over in a blink of an eye, just like sunshine on a cloudy day. One moment it is bright and blinding, and the next the sun falls behind the darkened cloud, waiting for the slightest chance at beaming once again. So, as Mom used to say, make hay while the sun shines.

Ocean Healing

By Jeanette St. Germain

The teal water of the Caribbean Sea splashed playfully against my scrunched-up toes. I took a slow inhale of the salty air and closed my eyes against the throbbing orange of the setting sun. The bits of sand clinging to my damp skin felt more like white silk than tiny rocks, and I stood there in complete wonder as the scene before me trembled the walls around my heart, inviting me to recognize a new kind of aliveness.

My mind was a spinning kaleidoscope, twirling with fragmented thoughts about marriage, parenthood, work, and all manner of earthly responsibilities. I didn't know which way to go, who I was supposed to be, or if I was anyone at all. I was in a kind of limbo, held frozen over a chasm of unknown dreams and unrealized potential.

The wind whipped around me, as if trying to lighten the heaviness of my mental questioning. I knew I had been called to this place of power for a reason. So I decided to listen, to see, to let go of the "stuckness" I felt in almost every area of my life. I took another breath and opened my awareness to the pulsing wildness, the peacefulness, the expression of connection all around me.

Suddenly, as I shifted into the present moment, an electric buzz ran from head to toe. With a shiver of excitement bordering on fear, I felt compelled to step deeper into the warm water. The rocking of the waves beckoned, promising to nurture and restore my life-force. I waded out until my feet couldn't reach, and then I started to float, opening my arms and my own feminine energy to the Goddess nature of the ocean.

There was safety and weightlessness, a kind of expansion where all was One and one was All. I felt the stirrings of some ancient wisdom rising within me, a kind of knowing that all experiences can be seen as rich and miraculous, as creation exploring itself. As I welcomed her, she brought me home.

Carl's Magpies

By Veronica Mather

My spiritual awakening began when my brother passed away after a car accident. Carl was three months away from his 40th birthday, and my world shattered in an instant. The thought of never seeing Carl and his cheeky grin again left my world dark and full of despair. I had always believed that when we die our journey was over, and I was having difficulty coming to terms with this reality.

After Carl's funeral, we were faced with the daunting task of collecting his belongings. Carl's friends were so amazing. They brought their trucks and trailers and helped us pack everything he owned. Words just can't convey the surreal, gut-wrenching feeling of seeing all of Carl's treasured possessions on the back of a truck.

When you lose someone, all you have left are memories and their material possessions. I brought home some seashells and rocks that Carl had collected from the beach, along with a lifelike magpie statue, a mascot for his favourite football team.

The next morning, I was getting ready for work when I heard magpies warbling loudly. I approached the back glass door, and on the veranda were three magpies. Never before had they come so close to the house! I watched as they flapped their wings, tilted their heads back, and caroled. It was like a war cry. In that moment, I was overwhelmed by the feeling of Carl's presence. It felt like he was acknowledging that I had his magpie, that he was still around, and that everything would be okay.

This beautiful moment brought feelings of comfort that although Carl and I can't walk beside each other on Earth again, we will always be connected. It was the start of ongoing communication with Carl and confirmation for me that when we die, it is not the end for our soul or our connection with those we love. It is just the opening of a door for the continuation of our spiritual journey.

Deep and Slow

By Mary Lunnen

Recently, I woke in the night with an excruciating headache, unlike any previous experience. I got up, checking as I went for signs of a stroke: my face was fine, as was my speech (as far as I could tell), and I could easily lift both arms above my head. I did have a strange dizziness, a light-headed feeling, and a sensation of numbness around my lips. I took one painkiller and went back to bed.

In the UK, we are fortunate to have our wonderful National Health Service, but that means it is hard to get an appointment to see a doctor. I tried, but nothing was available. So I just rested.

The next day, the severe headache had gone but the other feelings were the same, and I managed to get an emergency appointment. I was referred straight away for investigation at the nearest hospital, where I had various scans and tests. As I was lying on the hospital bed, about to have a lumbar puncture to double check that I had not bled in the brain, I decided to call on Source – specifically, my connection with the ocean.

I immediately received a wonderful sense of being supported. I heard the song of humpback whales and saw images of them floating in the water between the ocean depths and the surface. So graceful and such huge creatures. I had my eyes shut, and the sunlight was streaming through the window, so the colour through my eyelids was red/orange. I saw a huge whale's eye looking at me with such love and tenderness. Later, I asked for guidance and heard the words "deep and slow," a recipe for rest and recuperation.

The very same day, a kayaker took stunning photos and video of humpback whales feeding off the coast of Cornwall, a rare occurrence here. A coincidence, or part of the message?

Blue Dragonfly Angel

By Kristy Carr McAdams

"Dragonflies are sent as a sign from above to show us we're cared for, to tell us we are loved." – Unknown

The wind and rain had raged briefly yet powerfully, flexing nature's muscles, and I pondered the calm after the storm: heavenly blue skies, sun beaming brightly, and the perfect summer-day temperature of 75°. All this beauty after days of a severe heat wave of 99° temperatures, which the storm broke, along with all the old trees and power lines it knocked down. So many extremes in such a short time!

As I pulled into my driveway upon returning from errands, I parked and stepped out of my car and immediately noticed a bright blue dragonfly perched on top of a pole at eye level next to me. I was so close, yet he stayed put, standing confidently, pondering me as I pondered him.

Gazing at the stationary "Mr. Blue Dragonfly" in amazement (usually dragonflies flutter off quickly), I realized that his courageous, winged stance reminded me of an angel. It felt like Heaven was giving me a sign to have faith, as I had been going through some emotional challenges in my life.

Just that morning, I had been praying and calling on Archangel Michael, as he helps with finding my life purpose and courage. As Archangel Michael has wings and is connected to the color blue, I'd like to think that "Mr. Blue Dragonfly" was an angel in disguise, sent as a sign of support, a reminder of balance, courage, and hope.

Storms pass, change happens, and the sun shines again another day. Without change, life would be stagnant. Dark clouds help us appreciate when there are blue, sunny skies. Strength is found in the contrast. And so I whisper words of gratitude to Heaven and to "Mr. Blue Dragonfly Angel" for all he symbolizes. "Thank you for the reminder of the blessings of today, for the blessings of yesterday, and for the blessings of tomorrow."

Shadow – My Gentle Shepherd

By Jordann Scruggs

"Dogs come into our lives to teach us about love and loyalty.
They depart to teach us about loss." – Erica Jong

Gripping the phone tightly, I listened to the veterinarian explain the exploratory surgery he had performed on our nine-year-old German Shepherd, Shadow. The results caused my body to shake and sobs overwhelmed me. Shadow was the victim of an inoperable cancer. Quietly, I asked the vet to wait for us before he eased Shadow's suffering.

As we entered the room, bright sunlight beamed through a large Palladian window, warming the otherwise cold space and blanketing Shadow as she lay motionless on the operating table. Gently lifting her head into my arms, I held her paw and whispered our love. Moments later, I slowly nodded to the doctor. Surreally, I watched the pink liquid race through the tubes into her heart, and in seconds she was gone.

Sleep eluded me for weeks as I was consumed by memories and the loss of our beloved companion. I missed our moments in the garden where Shadow would sniff flowers and gaze in wonder at butterflies sharing her adventure. I missed her patience, her intense stare as she listened to me with no judgment, and her complete devotion when she would lie beside me and settle my soul. I yearned for a sign that Shadow was at peace. Then, during one of those fitful nights when sleep finally allowed me to drift off in the early-morning hours, the sign came.

Never having dreamed in color, it was captivating to see God's sign in wondrous luminosity: a field of flowers – rich purples, reds, yellows – a chromatic vision that seemed to continuously present itself in successive rows extending forever into the horizon. As each row appeared, Shadow frolicked amid the flowers and chased butterflies. Her perfect joy permeated my heart. Sensing that Shadow's happiness was complete, I realized that this was her Heaven and my consolation.

When I awoke, I thanked God for His loving message, His peace, and the gift of Shadow – my gentle shepherd.

Cloudy, with a Chance of Perspective

By Jill Pepper Montz

I grew up a farmer's daughter, so if my alarm isn't set for "dark-thirty," then I feel like I'm sleeping my day away. Most mornings, I see the sky turn wonderful shades of blue, purple, pink, orange, and yellow just before the sun peeps over the wide-open Texas plains.

Sunrises are good for my soul. They remind me that no matter how bad the day before was, today is a new day full of new opportunities, hopes, and dreams. The darkness has ended, and there is light on the other side. It's hard not to smile at a sunrise.

My favorite sunrises are those that have a few clouds sharing the canvas as God paints the morning. Whether they are wispy clouds streaked across the sky in a light brushstroke or bigger blobs dabbed onto the scene with a heavy hand, they all add another level of beauty to an already breathtaking scene.

Clouds give the day more texture and character. But some days the clouds take center stage and even the most radiant sun stays hidden behind the clouds' impenetrable gray mass.

One dreary morning as I walked around a lake, bundled up against the cool breeze, I hurried along the path in an effort to beat the rain that I knew must be moments away from dropping from the rumbling clouds. Before I could get back to my car, the skies cracked and rays of sunlight came flooding down to Earth like a search party looking for a lost soul in the blackest night.

I slowed my pace to a gentle stroll and tilted my head to the heavens. Within moments, the fortress of clouds was broken into dozens of pillowy pieces.

It was a beautiful and lovely reminder that in life, the brightest moments can follow the darkest times. The dark spots don't hinder the beauty that follows; they merely add dimension, details, and a new perspective. Cloud-free days are nice and have their own kind of wonder, but a few clouds in my day or in my life are nothing to worry about.

How My Cat Showed Me Trust

By Susan Jacobi

My daughter insisted we try the Humane Society once more. Within an hour, we bonded with our feline family member, renamed her Boudica, and brought her home. Boudica was with us for 17 months before she passed. In that time, she taught me lessons I had struggled to learn for years.

I knew that Boudica had been abused before we adopted her. She longed to love and be loved, but her fears held her back. During the first 10-12 months, she would not let me touch her head. She winced to let me know she was afraid. When she began to feel safe, she sat next to me on the sofa. I gently touched the top of her head and told her what a beautiful kitty she was. Over time, she felt safe enough to trust me. I pet the top of her head ever so gently. She learned that I wasn't going to hurt her. Eventually, she let me scratch the top of her head and then behind her ears. She held her head high while purring with contentment.

Boudica learned she was safe with me. Having her head rubbed became one of her pleasures. At night, she touched my cheek with her nose before facing the wall and settling in for bed. I gave her a pat on her back and told her to have sweet dreams. She slightly turned her head as if to say, "You, too."

I remind myself how Boudica never would have experienced pleasure had she chosen not to trust me. I look at my life and wonder where and when I don't trust people or even myself. I think about how Boudica enjoyed having her head rubbed and wonder what pleasures I am missing out on.

Boudica showed me how to be vulnerable. She taught me that I can expose my heart and be safe. Her example of learning to trust will be with me for the rest of my life. I am forever grateful to her.

Appreciation and the Gift of Two Plums

By Nancy Merrill Justice

I love nature walks among the mature trees along the coast. The sounds that whisper through the air as the ocean breezes blow through their branches vibrate a calm energy of inspiration and wisdom. On one such walk, life showed me the gifts that flow to us when we radiate the vibration of appreciation.

My dog, Laddie, and I took a detour from our usual pathway and found a secluded grove of Japanese plum trees decorated with yellowish-red plums. I couldn't resist picking the lowest-hanging fruits. Although quite firm, the plums ripened into the most divinely sweet plums I had ever tasted!

I thought how fun it would be to make a batch of homemade plum jam. The recipe called for a few more plums than I had collected, so on our next walk, I came prepared with a walking stick to knock down plums from the highest branches. As I approached the grove, imagining how delicious the jam was going to taste, my jaw dropped in disappointment – no plums!

I walked under and around the largest and most prolific of the trees but saw no fruit. To soothe my disappointment, I began talking to the trees, telling them I would bring the walking stick sooner next season.

Within seconds I realized what an amazing gift finding this small grove of plum trees had truly been. My words soon became expressions of appreciation. As I thanked the trees for the abundance of sweet plums, I felt a beautiful energy shift throughout my entire body. Laddie felt it too, and he leaned affectionately into my leg.

Upon leaving the grove, the path took us past that big plum tree I had scoured but seen no plums. Amazingly, right there in plain sight were two plump red plums hanging on the lower branches.

While on this path of wisdom, life showed me how our desires can quickly become our physical reality when we radiate the vibration of appreciation – whether we desire healing, financial abundance, romance, or just two sweet plums to make jam.

Birdsong

By Alisa Auger

It was early on the day we had planned to take a road trip and attend my grandmother's 90th birthday celebration. I had a daily routine of morning meditation and rituals that led into my creative practice: composing music. On this day, however, I decided to just do a quickie meditation. Then, instead of all my morning rituals and creative time, I could enjoy a leisurely morning – having coffee on the front porch with my husband and getting ready for the special day ahead. I've never liked to feel rushed; I prefer everything to feel spacious so I can live in full presence.

When I came downstairs, David said to me, "Oh, I heard the most amazing birdsong this morning!" and proceeded to whistle the three-note tune. Immediately, an entire song came flooding in. It was lovely, and I felt a little annoyed by the "intrusion." You see, I had recently started to "hear the music," and it had really taken over my life. I couldn't get away from constant music flowing – I had blown open the floodgates. After a few months, I was grateful; yet I also knew that I could access this abundance any time, so being a little overwhelmed, I had sort of "gotten over" the magic of it all.

I said, "I think I'll just let this one go." I had different plans for my morning and didn't want to be bothered. But David encouraged me to take the time and sit down and get it done. He reminded me that it wouldn't take long and that it was important for me to honour this gift. I wasn't too thrilled at the time, but at his insistence, I listened.

I sat down at the piano, played what I heard, and grabbed the staff paper to jot down the notes. I'm so grateful that I did because it's a lovely little song, and every time I hear it I'm reminded of my grandma and her special day when I co-wrote a song with my husband, the Universe, and a little bird.

Soaring Free from the Mountaintop

By Cath Edwards

It was an early start to a New Year expedition. I was up before dawn with three-year-old twins, an eight-year-old, their parents, and my hubby. As a family, we had promised ourselves we would tackle "Heartbreak Mountain." After years of issues with my heart, I was going to conquer my fear.

Like eager beavers and armed with cool water, we headed up the mountain track with childlike anticipation of a stunning view at the top. On the way up, a very fit and healthy elderly man glided effortlessly past us, making comments about the young twins being great walkers. Lots of smiles were shared, and on he went.

As I arrived at the top, sucking deeply for much-needed air, I was approached by a woman pleading if I knew how to do CPR. Luckily, I am trained. I headed with her to the top of the mountain. There in front me, on a ledge with glorious and breathtaking views, was the very man who had recently passed us. Having suffered a head injury from collapsing, he was unconscious and not breathing.

Medical help was coming but was still a long way off; I could hear the ambulance. The desperately ill man's family was on the ledge, helpless as they watched me begin CPR with the assistance of others. It was a chaotic scene with many onlookers.

Halfway through an hour of exhausting CPR, I noticed that this beautiful soul had taken his last breath. As someone took over chest compressions, I stepped back without breathing a word of what I had noticed and looked out at nature gently showing me its beauty.

It felt surreal. Like a camera, I captured the scene that he had witnessed before he collapsed. I drifted out to the endless blue ocean and sky, calm and happy that he had witnessed this view as the last thing his eyes would see. It created a respectful stillness within me. His life had ended with a glimpse of nature living on.

What Sophie Taught Me

By Claire Chew

"Three sunsets, then I will be ready. I need your help. I'd like to have a party before I go. Will you invite friends we've inspired along the way? Have them over to come say goodbye at 30-minute intervals so I can have some one-on-one time with them. Ask them to share what they've learned from me. One day you will teach and take my place." I carried out her last wish. We invited friends over for a daylong life-celebration party for my soul dog, Sophie. After a last supper of steak and vanilla ice cream, we took our last walk around the neighborhood.

I had no idea what that cryptic message meant. Me, teach? I was a type-A creative in advertising. Six months later, on a flight from NYC to LA, my seat was upgraded last minute, and I found myself next to an executive. We traded small talk, and when asked what I did for work, "I design heirloom keepsakes to celebrate the pet-human bond" tumbled out of my mouth. What was that about? All I knew was that for months, I had grieved the loss of the only family member who loved me unconditionally. Six hours later, I landed in LA with a deal memo for 10K scrawled on a cocktail napkin, and a new business was born. Fueled by loss and the love for my dog, I dove headfirst into a new career. From the Rainbow Bridge, Sophie inspired a collection of matching human and canine fine jewelry and accessories.

My heart sought out ways to continue to honor what Sophie meant to me. In the winter of 2005, Sophie came in a meditation when I was missing her. A pet-memorial candle with the blessing "A tribute of our love and friendship, know my spirit will always be near. Close to your heart. Always and forever" was downloaded into my consciousness. How could I say no? Soon, the candles found their way to retail pet boutiques. One day, a store manager called with a customer who had an aching heart as I once did. "Would I speak with her?" Was this what Sophie meant? As the universe would have it, I had just completed my MA in Spiritual Psychology and became certified as a grief recovery specialist. Down the rabbit hole we went.

Tens of thousands of candles and hundreds of pet-loss support sessions later, I am continuing the soul message Sophie left for me that fateful day 16 years ago, and for that I will forever be grateful.

An Unexpected Blessing

By Janet G. Nestor

My new home office was finally complete. I was excited about the prospect of writing articles and books from the desk I'd positioned so I could gaze into the woods beside the house and enjoy my beloved ancient pine tree and the marsh.

The private entrance to my office is inside the backyard fence. I wanted to make sure my guests felt comfortable walking to the back and opening the fence. As I walked down the steps into the yard, something caught my eye. I looked up and saw thousands of dragonflies swarming over the roof of my office. The swarm was so dense that the air looked gray and the sky was hidden behind a moving dragonfly cloud. I was awestruck by the swarm and mesmerized by their orchestrated flight pattern.

Time melted away. The hour I watched the swarm felt like minutes. The tornado-like spiral, created and maintained by these dragonflies, was so perfect that it resembled a wheel turning in the air. The internet informed me that a dragonfly swarm meant there was a lot of food in the area. If this is true, this swarm was enjoying the equivalent of a Thanksgiving feast. But I instinctively knew they were not eating. The gutters had just been cleaned. The roof was clean and dry, and the air was clear of summer insects. There was nothing for them to eat. So why the swarm?

It was dusk when the last few dragonflies disappeared.

On a commonsense level, I wanted a logical answer but found none. On a spiritual level, however, it made perfect sense to me. I'm convinced that the dragonflies spent half a workday creating a healing energetic vortex as a blessing for me and every client who crosses the threshold. After their blessing, the atmosphere inside my office and out felt soft and inviting, as if it had been sprinkled with fairy dust. I whispered thank you and accepted Mother Nature's gift.

Tiny Life Decisions

By Marci Kobayashi

I was standing in the snack aisle, and though I knew I shouldn't, I let my hand reach out for the package of cookies. And then I stopped. Shocked! There was a fruit fly on my hand. The message was clear. You saved my life, now I'll save yours. I shook my head, laughing, turned away from the cookies, and headed for the cash register.

Several hours before, I had been in my home office, typing an email when a fruit fly landed on the desk between my hands. I was surprised because I live on the 11th floor and my office is in a room down the hall from the kitchen. I rarely if ever see insects in the kitchen, let alone my office. Besides, it was winter, and all the windows were closed. I couldn't imagine where the tiny fruit fly had come from. It would be so easy to squish it. Such a tiny spark of life, but life nonetheless. Rather than send it off to its next life, I coerced it onto a piece of paper and transferred it over to one of my plants.

Feeling pleased with my good deed, I wrapped up my work and walked to the grocery store to buy something for dinner. I was on a strict plant-based diet alongside my husband, who was on a mission to overcome his stage-3 colon cancer without conventional treatments, such as chemotherapy. I was planning to buy fresh vegetables when I found myself in that snack aisle. The cookies I was tempted by were filled with more sugar and preservatives than plants, precisely the kind of food that leads to a slow death.

My husband is now cancer free, and we do indulge in sweet treats on occasion. Even so, I often think about the day the fruit fly saved me from succumbing to my cookie craving. Unbelievably, the fruit fly rode my hand that day all the way home from the store. When I got back upstairs, I transferred it to my plant and said a prayer of thanks.

Nature's Renewal

By Cheryl Kedan

"An early morning walk is a blessing for the whole day."
– Henry David Thoreau

The crowd hikes to the falls of Jenny Lake, but we follow the trail less traveled. We head south in the damp morning to the Moose Ponds to fulfill a wish to move into the quiet and see animals. We follow the path, and the trees whispering in the wind fill our soul with grandeur. Silently, we move to embrace the forest as it embraces us. The fallen trees look like the aftermath of giants bowling down the mountain. It opens the sky to trace the tops of the Tetons. On this day of clarity, the mountains loom above us, calling our hearts to enlarge with joy. The meadow is a carpet of sunshine from the rudbeckia exploding in front of us.

She stands in the middle of the marshy area, perhaps 50 yards away, her massive velvet head up, sensing our presence. She tests for danger then calmly returns to plunge her head into the water to eat the catkins and grasses growing on the bottom. We capture this sight of reality in our memory and watch as she rhythmically dives for breakfast then straightens up to watch and chew. Moving around a wooded area, we view her calf in the shallows. The calf waits for the cow moose while she eats her fill. There is no hurry, no impatience – just natural order. The calf, so young, waits for her mother to feed her.

How long we are spellbound, I cannot say. It seems we are a part of the natural world, that we understand the ebb and flow of life in the wild. We observe the simple connection of cow and calf with the task of living. There is simplicity and dignity in the order. Living in the moment with these awe-inspiring creatures, a sense of completeness surrounds and saturates us.

Enter the wild to walk with spirit. Hold these sacred lands safe. The oasis of nature gives life renewal.

Claimed by a Pony

By Michelle Griffith

Two nameless brown ponies with thick winter coats were standing on the far side of the paddock enjoying a bale of hay. As I pulled in, they lifted their heads for a glance and went right back to munching. Both of them were alert with perky little ears smartly monitoring the parking lot.

I was visiting their farm to meet a horse with potential to be a good partner in my coaching business. After a brief exchange with her, it was clear that she wasn't interested in my kind of work. As I walked back to my car with the farm manager, one of the nameless brown ponies came to full alert, gave a whinny, and ran full tilt toward us. He arrived at the fence with a screeching halt and pushed his head through the rails.

Most ponies don't walk away from hay to seek scratches from a random stranger. He wanted me to take him home. The message was loud and clear, so I asked, "Is he for sale?" The manager gave a chuckle and then realized I was serious. He promptly responded yes and offered up the basic information.

We finalized the purchase details while the pony stood there leaning into my scratches and claiming me as his person. As I drove away, he trotted along the paddock down the driveway until he was redirected by a cross fence. I was smitten.

On moving day, I found out this little guy had never been on a trip. Since ponies are often measured in terms of shenanigans and drama, I was concerned about putting him on the trailer. In what seemed to be a validation of his choice to partner with me, the pony walked up the ramp and stood quietly in the trailer without incident. For me, it was the sign that officially sealed the deal.

This once-nameless pony is now named Cheese out of respect for his role as chief smile officer and his affection for being photographed. Thanks for choosing me, and cheers to a lifetime of happy pony shenanigans.

Magpie Messengers

By Faye Rogers

Not long ago, I was driving to a meeting. Although I was in a rush, running late, I couldn't help but notice two magpies standing on either side of the road.

I communicate with animals, and I love being in touch with their humanity and specialness and sharing their unique perceptions with their families. When communicating with animals, I receive from them mental imaging, words, emotions, and visual pictures, and these usually are relayed as "subjective," which is seeing within.

But these two magpies were speaking to me with words that were floating out of their beaks, which is called "objective" clairaudience. And I heard their voices, just as you would if you woke to the morning songbirds singing or were having a conversation face to face with a friend. The magpies were yelling at me to be careful.

I asked them whether I should continue my journey, and they replied, "Yes, but be careful."

At every major intersection I came to, seven in total, I encountered two magpies standing on either side of the intersection, all giving the same advice to be careful. I couldn't help hearing them as they were so darn loud, their voices penetrating the silence of the countryside.

Driving on an open road that racers regularly use, I encountered two magpies sitting on either side of the road. In the middle of my side of the road sat a hawk, so I had to stop. If I hadn't stopped, I would have had a head-on accident, because a farmer had parked his tractor on the other side of the road, which was the only blind spot on the road. A car that was travelling at excessive speed crossed onto my side of the road to avoid the tractor and narrowly missed me.

There could be many what-ifs attached to this story, but I was very fortunate, thanks to the divine messenger birds.

Touched by Love

By JoAnne B. Lussier

Willow's story is short and bittersweet, just like her life. I adopted Willow much like most of my cats – she was unwanted. Her first owners singled her out as the most undesirable in the litter and were neglecting her. Without hesitation, this little ball of gray fluff made her way home with me to get the love and attention she deserved.

We bonded instantly and grew to understand each other without words. If soulmates exist between humans and animals, our connection was divinely inspired. The love in her sage green eyes captured my heart and spoke directly to my soul like soft whispers from God.

Willow had her share of medical issues. Days before her death, she was being treated for an infection. Waiting in the vet's office, I felt grateful that her issues paled in comparison to the animals who were in crisis that evening. In the days that followed, however, it became clear that she wasn't recovering. Her pained gaze worried me. Sensing that something was wrong, we made another trip to the hospital. The vet concluded she needed pain medication and sent us home.

The following evening, Willow went into acute respiratory arrest. X-rays revealed an undetected heart condition, which required immediate hospitalization. Smothering her with tearful hugs and kisses, I had to leave her, not knowing if she'd make it through the night. The vet called a few hours later to inform me that everything was done to save her life, but Willow had other plans. Heartbroken, I gripped my pillow tightly and cried myself to sleep.

Days after Willow's death, I stumbled across an ad for Reiki certification. In the past, I'd been unable to afford the course, but this class was reasonably priced and the teacher was an animal lover. This perfectly timed opportunity was no doubt Willow's gift to me to lessen my grief and thank me for being her mom. In that moment, my healing journey began.

Willow's gentle spirit lives on in me and through my hands as a Reiki Master Teacher. The essence of her unconditional love lingers upon all the lives I touch.

My Therapy Sessions Can Get Dirty

By Jill Pepper Montz

Gardening is my therapy. I use the time with my flowers to unwind my thoughts and dig around in the mud of my emotions; while my hands get dirty, my soul gets clean. At the end of a long session, my back aches and my knees are stiff, but my heart feels less entangled by the weeds of life and is looking for the sunshine.

Several people have passed my house and commented on my beautiful flowers. I thank them with a smile and a wave, knowing all too well the many hours I have spent sweating and often bleeding – doing all I can to help the delicate petals grow boldly in the summer sun.

However, every year there seems to be that one plant that simply won't grow. It starts out strong and lovely just like the others, but soon it begins to wilt and turn dark. All the petals fall to the ground, and regardless of my many efforts to save it, eventually it dies.

Every year, I am sad to see that, even with my knowledge and love for all things green, I can't make this particular plant grow. And every year, I leave the remains of that plant in my garden as a reminder.

The dead plant reminds me that in life, like in gardening, some things fail, regardless of the time, energy, or resources I devote to them. They get the same love and care, but for whatever reason, they aren't meant to thrive and bloom. So instead of watering what is dead, I simply acknowledge my efforts and focus on what is beautiful all around me.

Learning to accept what I can't change is hard. Finding the beauty that still exists can be hard, too. Seeing the dead plant every time I water my garden reminds me that not everything works out like I planned. Seeing the other flowers dance and sway in the summer breeze reminds me that just because some things fail doesn't mean all things fail, which I think both a good therapist and a good gardener would agree with.

A Gift of Enchantment

By Annalene Hart

My mother and I would often find ourselves drawn to the beach for morning walks and swims for our soul-replenishment time. One day while we were walking along Nokomis Beach in Florida, my mother pointed to something in the sand. As we got closer, I realized that it was a seahorse, moored and immobile, attempting to move itself in the sand. I instinctively picked it up by its corkscrew tail and watched it squirm and writhe in my hand. Its delicate skeletal body twisted itself for mobility, but now it was suspended in the air.

It was so amazing to lift this light-as-a-feather sea creature that was twisting itself and gently vibrating in my hand like a wind-up toy. It emanated an overwhelming sweetness that was beyond this world. This fragile presence was like a fairy-tale creature, as improbable as a unicorn. I held it with supreme care, enchanted by its energy.

I carefully put it back into the ocean and watched a wave take it back out to its true home. I thought, "It's amazing you exist at all. How do you survive in these unpredictable times and in the often-inhospitable waters of the ocean?"

I felt that I'd had a profound encounter with a primordial, other-worldly being. It was a true gift of enchantment. And I'll never forget how its sweet essence was so much larger than the tiny frame it inhabited.

Kiki

By Amy Coppola

"Heaven goes by favor. If it went by merit, you would stay out and your dog would go in." – Mark Twain

As I flew to Denver, I realized that it was divine timing that this trip had been planned months ago. Kiki, my dear friend Ana's little Yorkshire terrier, was very ill. I was on a two-week work trip from San Francisco and headed to Denver for the weekend. As I landed, I felt relieved in anticipation of being able to comfort my friend and spend time with both of them.

When I first saw Kiki, I realized how serious her situation was. She was so frail, weak, and fighting for her life. Ana and I discussed Kiki's suffering, when and how to decide to make that hard call, and what would be in the best interest of little Kiki. Who are we to play God in situations like this? That thought always runs through my mind when I reflect on this situation. How do you know when it is time to end someone's suffering? Why is it our call? I do believe that pets are our responsibility, and it was apparent that Ana's little baby was suffering.

We decided that Saturday morning would be Kiki's last car ride. The veterinarian explained the procedure and what was going to happen. Ana and I cried for Kiki, who by that point was unable to function, had no strength left in her body, and could barely open her eyes. As Kiki drifted away from us, I reflected on the way she ran in my backyard with the big dogs and would plow through the snow. For eight years, Kiki had provided so much safety and security for Ana. Her small stature but massive attitude made her fearlessly defend Ana against much larger animal adversaries.

Kiki's precious little soul of only seven pounds brought so much joy and life to everyone she met. Kiki was and will always be the smallest dog with the biggest heart and soul.

The Power of Persistence

By Lori Thomas

I was sitting on a log in the woods near my home after walking barefoot for a while. The sun was gone, and the quiet was conducive to meditation and connection with nature.

As I sat there, I felt a small creature make its way onto my foot. A quick check with my flashlight verified that it was a little brown slug. It continued on until it was on one of my toes.

Slugs are amazing, possessing a mouth that contains thousands of tiny teeth called radula. They test everything with their mouth as they move forward, and it feels like being scraped by the tiniest bit of sandpaper, or a miniature cat tongue.

As we sat there, I felt her faint, slow, persistent rasping on my toe but remained focused on my meditation. Later, I felt a flash of pain, like a pinprick, there and gone, where she had been chewing. It still wasn't enough to interrupt my meditation though. It wasn't until I was ready to leave, and the slug was still rasping away, that I looked down with a flashlight and saw that there was a tiny hole where she was lying. She had actually chewed all the way through my skin in the space of 15-20 minutes!

As a member of the cleanup crew, this persistence gives slugs the ability to chew and thus break down almost any organic matter, even though it may take a long time. For me, it was a message about the power of persistence, patience, and small, incremental changes. The slug's actions made clear to me that small changes in thoughts and actions, done consistently, have the power to transform our lives.

I am currently seeing this happening in my own life. Persistent focus on appreciation brings more to appreciate. A few words written consistently, and a book begins to take shape. A shift in perception of how I view any situation in my life gradually changes the situation.

Long-term persistence in little things is life changing over time. Thank you, slug, for your message.

Rescued

By Jessilyn Gaylor

Rocco came at a time in my life when I was feeling lost and doubting every decision I had made over the last couple of years.

I had recently quit graduate school, a school I had moved 2,300 miles away from home to attend. Struggling to make a life for myself in New Mexico, I resumed working in the restaurant business. A man I worked with was trying to rehome his dog.

"Do you want a dog?" he asked, showing me his picture.

My response was immediate: "Yes, I want him!" I had always wanted to rescue a dog, but it had never seemed like a logical time – until then.

I arranged to meet the woman who was fostering him. When I arrived and opened the gate to her yard, my eyes widened with pure excitement. Standing before me was a massive German Shepherd/Husky mix. He was full of energy, yet his demeanor was soft and welcoming. The moment our eyes met, I was overcome with a feeling of belonging and purpose that had eluded me over the past year. There was no doubt in my mind that this dog was meant to be mine.

Slowly transitioning a rescue animal like Rocco was critical. Before I adopted him, he had been a guard dog at a metal shop, and his life consisted of being tied to his owner's truck during the day then put into the shop overnight. When the shop was destroyed in a fire, the woman knew she had to rescue him. Determined to give Rocco a second chance, she took him home until she could find someone who was worthy of him.

As we walked through the dog park that afternoon, she shared bits of information about his personality while I quickly fell in love. I felt beyond blessed when I was chosen to be his new owner.

Rocco isn't a dog I rescued. He's my family and gives me purpose and joy every day. When people ask how Rocco came into my life, they praise me for saving him, but I know that Rocco is the one who rescued me.

September 9

A Magical Message

By Pauline Hosie Robinson

Moving can be a daunting experience! Although moving is in my DNA as both a military child and wife, nothing seemed to flow with relocating from Sydney to Newcastle/Lake Macquarie. Even though Newcastle was just a two-and-a-half-hour drive from Sydney, it was unknown to me. And no matter how many times I visited, I couldn't seem to get a feel for the area. Such uncertainty was a new experience for me, as I usually know when a place feels right.

The fog that seemed to surround me didn't lift as the weeks passed. Once my unit was sold, the pressure to find a home began to weigh me down. One morning, I walked outside to gather my thoughts. Moments later, I returned to my desk to check real-estate availability. Glancing at the empty cup beside my computer, I was astounded at what I saw and my heart leapt with joy! In the bottom of the cup, the fine particles had created a perfectly formed tree of life encompassed by a circle. The roots were clearly defined and in balance with the canopy of the tree. The image and the power of its message took a while to sink in. "How did such a complete image form?" I questioned. Feeling blessed to receive such a magical message, peace enveloped me. From that moment, I felt guided.

The number 11 played a pivotal role in that guidance as I relate this number to my mum, so I knew she was directing me. Every financial transaction relating to the sale of my unit and each potential property I visited contained an 11. In November 2017, I moved into 18/11 Aintree Close. The name of my complex is "Gumtrees," and the street address is 11. My home is surrounded by a variety of established trees with a small stream nearby. Birds, butterflies, dragonflies, and water dragons thrive here. My townhouse is a place of joy and tranquility.

Thank you to my beautiful mother who guided me here.

My Garden – A Little Slice of Heaven

By Marla David

"There's no place like home," Dorothy repeated in *The Wizard of Oz* as she tapped her heels in those famous ruby slippers. No matter who you are, home is something special – a place to retreat to, to be safe, to nurture, to survive, and most importantly, to thrive. My mantra is *home, health, happiness* – and I feel awful that many people do not even have a roof over their head, let alone a home, especially when home is a basic human need. As a true Taurus, my home is my sanctuary – a place for me to live my best life in the manner that serves my highest good. It has been my little slice of Heaven on Earth for 25 years.

One of my favorite parts about my home is my garden. You can often find me in the vegetable garden that I call my urban farm. I could be tying the veggies on the stakes, weeding, potting in the shed, filling the wild bird feeders, or just chilling on the covered porch. In addition to bringing me immense pleasure, my garden has also supplied homes and food for bees, butterflies, birds, chipmunks, squirrels, and raccoons – the wildlife in this area is thriving!

This summer, my property was chosen as one of the top 200 gardens in the area. This got me working to ensure that my garden would remain memorable in the minds of those who would visit on the day of the garden tour, as my home was one of 10 homes chosen to show their garden. I planted various native plant species and plants that attract bees and butterflies. I also had help creating different special areas – a mini succulent garden, a lavender patch, the perennial gardens.

Even without the recognition or honor of the garden tour, I'm grateful to have such an oasis. Just being outside in nature is therapeutic; the trees and my garden are my natural healers. But it's especially nice to share this little slice of Heaven with others and have them enjoy it too. My garden always reminds me of Dorothy's message: there is no place like home, and I'm so grateful that I've gotten to forge so many happy memories here with friends and family.

Everything's Going to Be Okay

By Annie Price

Early spring was in the air as I forced myself out of bed when the 6 a.m. alarm went off. Soon, I would see my daughter off to school and then jump in the car to arrive at Bev's before her husband left for work. I was one of three part-time caregivers, and we didn't leave Bev alone.

Several years earlier, at age 53, Bev had been diagnosed with early-onset Alzheimer's, and her primary desire was to remain in her home. This was manageable with additional caregiver support, and I'd been with her for almost four years. Bev is a force to be reckoned with, as she recently celebrated her 62nd birthday, determinedly skipping past her original prognosis.

As much as I loved and admired Bev, I'd been struggling – not just with greater care requirements, but also in having to witness her decline and see her disappear day by day. I'd heard Alzheimer's referred to as "the longest death," and it seemed understandable. Now, Bev could hardly speak and couldn't find the bathroom that she'd used every day for years. She began displaying uncharacteristic outbursts of anger, confusion, and anxiety – all understandable and expected symptoms of this terrible disease. I wrestled with wanting to leave and wanting to stay until...something changed.

On this early spring morning, as I approached Bev's front door, I heard the soft call of a mourning dove. I hadn't heard this for a long time, and I immediately relaxed and smiled to myself. Everything was going to be okay. For me, the mourning dove is a meaningful, soulful messenger, providing gentle reassurance during challenging times. Over the next few weeks, I continued to be comforted by occasionally hearing the dove's song.

Just a few weeks later, Bev's husband finally made the difficult decision to move her to a memory-care facility. It was time. I felt both relief and sadness.

Bev is already adjusting to her new place. She loves dance class and visiting the garden where she enjoys pulling weeds and communing with growing things. And she continues to defy Alzheimer's and embrace moments of joy.

One Step

By Marci Kobayashi

I was walking along a grassy section near the riverbank and enjoying the spring flowers when a small white butterfly landed in the middle of the path right in front of me. I stopped, too. I thought about taking a picture, but it flew away before I could move.

I resumed my walk and within seconds noticed a yellow butterfly flying by my side. The butterfly circled around and landed right in front of me. I stopped one step away from the butterfly. We shared a moment, and then it flew away.

And then it happened again. What was so interesting about this path? Why were the butterflies stopping on it and not on any of the spring flowers blooming nearby?

The butterflies had my attention. Since butterflies are commonly associated with transformation, I wondered if these butterflies were showing up in my path to let me know that a transformation was on the way. Or perhaps they were encouraging me to acknowledge a transformation I had just come through.

I continued my walk, actively looking for and watching the butterflies. What was their message for me today?

Once again, a butterfly circled around and landed one step away from me in the middle of the path. I stopped. A slow grin spread across my face, and I felt my heart surge in gratitude for the butterfly lesson: *Transformation is one step away.*

Transformation sounds like this big, long process wrought with pain, struggle, and monumental effort – something you want to avoid but are grateful for once you get to the other side. But what if it was as easy as taking one step? What if transformation was only one step away?

The butterfly on the path in front of me took off. I stood there a few minutes and then took the next step.

September 13

A Channeled Message from Momma Earth

By Janet G. Nestor

For a time, I met regularly with a spiritual group whose purpose was to support Momma Earth. Each night, we came together and, using imagery, covered her with our love. We opened our arms and held her in our collective embrace. The energy created was so tender and powerful that tears often filled my eyes. We also felt Momma's cry for help.

Even though our healing was for Momma, a great love developed within each of us – a love for one another and a loving connection with all living things. These weeks together were incredibly soul expanding, a benefit I had not expected.

Recently, I asked Momma Earth some questions, and she answered! This is part of our conversation:

Q: Momma, do you consider yourself a divine being?

Momma Earth (M.E.): I do believe I am a sacred, divine being. I am part of creation just like you, and I have organs similar to yours. Scientists do not fully understand me.

Q: What do you need most from your inhabitants?

M.E.: My greatest desire is for all beings to love each other, support each other, and live in peace and companionship. I need you to see me as one of you and know that I have the ability to experience love and pain. I support your life.

Q: How do you experience love and pain?

M.E.: I have a sensory system. When I receive your love, I feel safe and can use my energy for the good of all. I can take a person's misery and suffering and reprocess it through the roots of the trees who then use my soil as a healing place.

Q: Momma, when we love you, we love ourselves. Is that correct?

M.E.: When you love yourself, you share it with everything around you, including me. My waters flow, seasons flow, blood flows through the trees. The day flows into night and back into the morning. You too require flow to survive. You are a divine part of creation, and you are meant to thrive.

Cindy in Spirit

By Rhonda Lee

She was my first friend, my protector, and my first avenue to my connection with spirit. Her name was Cindy, and she was my parents' baby/dogchild before I was born. Cindy hovered over my mother when she was pregnant with me and was my constant companion throughout her life and beyond.

The first time Cindy connected with me in spirit form was the night she died. She was 15 and declining in health. After a stay at the vet's office, she had come home to make her journey to the rainbow bridge.

I'll never forget that night. Sometime during the night, I woke up to the sensation of my whole bed vibrating, and immediately the hall light came on. I heard my mother crying and knew what had happened but could not move from my bed. Once the light went off, I fell back asleep only to be awakened a few minutes later to the sensation of something jumping on my bed and the covers sliding down about five or six inches. I could literally feel Cindy on my bed, and I knew she had come to say goodbye...or so I thought. This was the start of my relationship with Cindy in spirit form.

Throughout my life, Cindy has continued to be with me through very significant circumstances. I have often seen her preceding the death of another pet or family member. I always take this as a sign that she is still constantly by my side, ready to comfort me. The week before my father's death, I saw her walking around in my backyard and then moving through my parents' house the day before he died. Later, I learned that my dad had been seeing her around the house earlier that week as well. Cindy had come to help us ease into my father's transition.

Cindy is a constant in my life and set the stage for every interaction I would have regarding my connection to the spirit world. I know that she will watch over me for the rest of my life.

September 15

Winged Messengers of Choices
By Lorraine Raymond

The workshop goal invited learning shamanic rituals and discovering my animal spirit guide from an 80-years-young Celtic shamaness. Inspired, I sought guidance to better navigate the whitewater rapids of raising a teenage daughter as a single mom on this, her 16th birthday. Other spiritual sojourners joined me in the classroom – a transformed space that resembled a post-Black Friday sale littered with pillows, blankets, and bedspreads.

As the rhythmic, heart-pulsing music began, the shamaness coaxed, "Breathe…trust yourself to go deeper within. Ask for your animal spirit guide to come to you. Be patient. Breathe…" *Boom, boom, boom*…drumming music heard with external ears slowly descended into my body to become one with an inner heartbeat. Anxiety-filled thoughts started flying about.

"What if I can't do this?" *Boom, boom, boom.* "What if no animal spirit guide appears when I ask who's here to meet me?" *Boom, boom, boom.* "I hope it's a dolphin."

Then my mind's eye landed on a pole ascending from the ground, stretching heavenward with no end. With squinting eyes, I focused on the pulsating movement blanketing the pole and saw millions of opalescent dragonflies, their ballerina-like wings waving up and down.

After silently gasping, "Oh, my!" a dark thought flew by: "What? I got an insect as my animal spirit guide?"

Yes, Dragonfly chose to guide me. Future dragonfly studies revealed metaphysical meanings with messages of power, light, and choices for my daughter and me: we shared power. Dragonfly lives a short life. Remembering this truth, we could in higher awareness live our lives fully. Worry, control, and arguing only diminished joy. We were light. Dragonfly possesses enormous eyes with a 360° perspective. We could try seeing "the light at the end of any tunnel" by forgiving. We had choices. Dragonfly represents change with iridescent wings sensitized to the slightest breeze. While transitioning from Honduras to stateside living, being less sensitive to the winds of change could avoid emotional storms.

Today, sightings of Dragonfly encourage us to ask heartful questions and then choose to accept the guidance, even if it comes from an insect!

Dragonfly Magic in Bali

By Lorraine Raymond

Dragonfly chose to serve as my animal spirit guide. I resisted. Everyone else in the shamanic workshop seemed thrilled with the guides that appeared to them during our meditation: bear, tiger, turtle, whale, hummingbird, and oh, yes, a dolphin – my secretly hoped-for guide.

It took leading a Vision Quest in Bali, the "island of the gods" and my spiritual home, a year later to embrace this 300-million-year-old magical creature. Seated cross-legged outdoors during a sunrise writing session, my peaceful envelope of time shredded.

Clang! Clang! Clang! Startled, I looked up and saw a dozen sarong-wrapped Balinese appear, peppering the rice field near the hotel; old and young family members frantically beat aluminum pots and pans with sticks. Like an unexpected tropical shower, a silvery cloud stormed with pesty, java rice sparrows. The clanging interrupted their crop-damaging breakfast of rice and dragonfly larvae, a Balinese source of protein.

Then the spectacular accelerated. I witnessed millions of garnet dragonflies ascending! While shading the half-acre paddy, the winged jewel-creatures momentarily eclipsed the sunrise. The living cloud surged upward. Looking like a movie scene, it migrated into the technicolor rays of mango oranges, pomegranate crimsons, and lemon citrines – only to dissolve.

Like unripe coconuts, mesmerizing thoughts hung suspended. What on earth?! This wasn't worldly; instead, it was divine. Reality returned via perfumed, frangipani breezes. Flashing back to the shamanic workshop, I couldn't help wondering about Dragonfly's second appearance.

Expanded dragonfly investigations inspired the future design (and logo) for my Divine Dialogue Writing System.™ Dragonfly's metaphysical messages revealed that as a water creature, it symbolized the subconscious mind that writing can reveal. Their skittering movements across the water's surface symbolized that those hidden thoughts can surface to clarify questions. Dragonfly carries deeper meanings deserving mindfulness that can find expression with a writing practice.

My students and I can write with magical words using an intuitive process that transforms our soulful messages into sacred service.

September 17

The Trust Within

By Valerie Cameron

Life is busy, the world is moving so fast, and you feel you can't stop because if you do, you'll be missing out. With so much to be done and so many things we think need attending to, it's easy to get pulled into the circus of life, but I've found that being aware is key.

One day, I was feeling really off and powerless to make any real changes, so I decided to go out into nature to meditate. I knew in my heart that if I just got out of the rat race and found somewhere quiet with no distractions, I would be able to hear what my soul wanted me to know. On my journey, I found an amazing big rock that I could sit on while listening to my heart. This became my solace every day for the next year.

The rock was positioned along the forest but wasn't close enough so that I could touch the nearby trees. I noticed three beautiful birch trees that had grown together, and I thought it would be amazing if I were closer to them. (I've always been intrigued by the power of three – as in body/mind/soul or me, myself, and I).

The next morning when I went to my rock, I sat down and noticed that I could touch the trees. In my shock and awe, I got up and looked around and realized that nothing had changed – the terrain was the same. I was confused, but only for a moment. It occurred to me that just the day before, I had wanted to be closer. At first I felt that this was how powerful we are when setting intentions, but at the same time I was also inspired to really trust in the power I held and that we all have within.

In the end, when I took the time to slow down and be aware, I discovered how powerful we truly are. We are told we can move mountains, and I started out with a huge rock!

Coyote Balance

By Michelle Griffith

Every day, nature is full of offerings that challenge my curiosity. I notice mundane things, like vultures soaring on air currents, rabbits freeloading in my garden, and even an unwelcome row of tiny ants marching near the kitchen window. I wonder if these things actually are mundane or worthy of note.

I sometimes like to reference my favorite books on nature symbolism for perspective, but mostly, I draw my own conclusions about the things I notice and how they relate to my current situation. Once in a while, nature will toss me a doozy for consideration. My favorite example is the day I pulled into my driveway in the early afternoon and a big, healthy coyote was sitting beside the pine trees. She looked right at me with no fear and no desire to move on. I felt like she had been waiting patiently for me to arrive. As I watched from the car, she sat quietly. I pulled up to the garage and turned around. She watched and waited. I sat and wondered.

As my mind raced, I got emotional and felt overwhelmed. I realized how midlife had been smacking me in the face with intermittent waves of hormone-enhanced emotion and overwhelm. At first I laughed, and then I cried. At that moment, the coyote stood up and trotted across the street to the vast open field between my house and the woods where, I imagine, she lives. She paused and looked back at me three times. Finally, she took off across the field and left me to process the awareness that had come from our exchange.

Coyote symbolism is laced with paradox, and ultimately boils down to finding balance. For me, balance is a verb. It is active and precarious, and it is my most important core value. I am deeply grateful for nature's wisdom and believe that life on the planet is a shared experience. I will continue to stay curious and seek my own balance with a sacred connection to balance in nature.

Divine Sparks

By Heidi Cohen-Barocas

People often come to me, sharing their experiences as elders. I've heard suffering, nonacceptance, and incredible wisdom. A soulful message arrived for me from the rabbi to create a spiritual meditation program. After leading seven months of my first chakra (attribute) meditations, the right guidance arrived – sacred messages coming as Divine Downloads to unfolding the essence of enlightenment:

There is another connection created for us, and it happens when we open our eyes and heart to the interconnecting of souls. May we open our physical and spiritual eyes to nature and see her Divine miracles.

Now imagine a window. Looking out the window, we see St. Petersburg. It's summer, and we're in the lightning capital of the world.

Through our changing weather patterns, we witness nature's power and the shaking up of energy. It's Mother Nature's soul, illuminating her message. She is revealing her smile ever so brightly. It's a sparking of her soul, waving to influence another aspect of light.

She orchestrates her dance almost daily, touching the earth with her magical power. She is actualizing divine light with the keynotes of thunder. Her purpose is to allow our human souls to spark faith, despite the darkness of the clouds. When a storm comes in, we often sense a misunderstood action. Something negative. What actually begins is a transformation of light, an invitation for peacefulness to come in. She is shedding the negative power. The energy breaks out of the old pattern to transform hardship, heartache, and pain.

As the lightning becomes revealed, the inner light can flow. It helps our physical consciousness awaken to another perception. Her lightning conducts a dance, drawing us inward to the "Clouds of Glory."

July is a luminous month. Longer days allow us to see the greatness in God and the integration that exists in all creation. Each day is an invitation to earthly magic, warming us to bring forth physical and spiritual pleasures.

This sacred guidance reminded me that Divine Sparks possess a power...teaching us the presence of our soul's attributes and the world of integration and the interconnecting light.

Our Monkey

By Jodi Chapman

Our 10-year-old cat, Monkey, had quickly gone from being perfectly healthy to very ill. We drove him to the nearest hospital, where he was immediately admitted for testing. We made arrangements to stay at a nearby hotel so we could visit him often.

After settling into our room, we left to spend time with him and saw a rainbow that seemed to end right at the hospital. I asked my husband if he thought that was a good sign or a "rainbow bridge" kind of sign. We had just gotten a call from the doctor saying that all his vitals were improving, so we assumed it was a positive sign. Monkey was in an oxygen chamber, so we couldn't hold him, but we could put our hands through and pet him and give him love that way. We stayed for a while and then told him how much we loved him and said we would be back soon.

The doctor called the next morning and told us that he was continuing to improve. We breathed huge sighs of relief. And then five minutes later our world crumbled. She called back, and with a shaky voice asked us to come right away. She said that he was plummeting and they were going to try to stabilize him, but she was afraid he would go into cardiac arrest soon. We got there in 10 minutes and were sucked into the most horrible whirlwind that ended with us saying goodbye to our sweet boy. They discovered that he had lymphoma, and it overtook his entire body so quickly. Our Monkey was gone.

In a heartbroken daze, we went back to the hotel, packed our things, and began the drive home. Through my tears, I said to Dan that it shouldn't be so sunny – that the world should be gloomy and rainy. Not long into our drive, we got our rain – Monkey-style – a deluge that forced us to pull over, that created rivers on the road, that came with such power, just like our force-of-nature boy. This fit his personality so perfectly. He was a thug and loved to fight. He wouldn't show us a rainbow. He would show us a downpour. That was who he was. He loved hard and fought hard.

When the rain stopped, we pulled up behind a car that had paw prints around the license plate and a butterfly sticker on the window, which seemed just right. We miss our boy so much, and we'll always be grateful for these signs.

Rock-Solid Closure

By Marci Kobayashi

The first time I visited my husband's parents at their homestead in the mountains, I wasn't a welcomed guest. His parents were not expecting me, and though I was eager to meet them, I understood their hesitation and opted to wait in the car. Their son was in the middle of an unexpected divorce, and they were confused over where their loyalties should lie. Who was this woman? Where were the grandchildren and where was their mother?

I waited with the windows rolled down, breathing in the warm summer air. I could see the rice fields and forested mountains in the distance. With nothing to do, I watched the dragonflies take turns landing on the side mirror. I slowed my breathing and sank my energy into Mother Earth. Though I had no idea how I would ever connect with his family, I knew I could connect with the land. I felt a calm wash over me as I anchored a piece of my soul.

Now, after 20+ years and many trips to that home, I don't doubt my connection to my husband's family. I made peace and built a strong rapport with his mother long before she transitioned and now watch over his father, in his 90s, as he navigates a new life with us in the city.

Even so, my heart carried residue from that first visit. Questions of whether I was worthy, of whether I belonged. A compulsion to prove myself. These feelings no longer served me, so on a recent visit, I walked over to the giant boulders lining the driveway and stood on the road where I sat in the parked car summers ago. I closed my eyes and sank my energy back into Mother Earth. I asked for help, and together we washed away the outdated fears and beliefs.

Afterward, I leaned against the nearest boulder and noticed a small edge coming loose. I lifted it away and grinned when it fit perfectly in my palm. Rock-solid closure. Thank you, Mother. A stone for my altar in honor of our exchange.

Chapter 7
Messages from the Divine

For some people, divine messages are only contained in sacred scriptures that are thousands of years old. For others, however, divine messages are a part of their current life – something they've experienced directly! In this chapter, you'll read firsthand accounts from people who have experienced divine messages.

These messages changed the way these people looked at the world. They changed the way they experienced religion and spirituality. And, in many cases, they changed the course of their lives.

These divine messages have shown up in many ways. For some, they've taken the form of auditory messages: divine whispers – or shouts – that made them sit up, pay attention, and change their ways. For others, they've shown up as a feeling, a physical sensation, or a healing energy. For some, they've come from divine messengers, such as angels, archangels, spirit guides, or God/Higher Power. For others, they've been delivered through Earth Angels who may not have been conscious that they were delivering a message at all!

No matter how these messages were conveyed, though, they all touched the hearts of those who received them – reminding them that they are never alone, guiding them to trust their intuition, and deepening their faith in this amazing, magical universe. And we hope that they do the same for you.

A Slip of the Tongue

By Jodi Chapman

Recently while showering, I felt a lump the size of a jellybean just under my armpit. My heart immediately started pounding and my mind started racing. I had Dan feel it, and he too was concerned. I made an appointment with my doctor for later that day, and he ordered an ultrasound for later that week. I did my best to put it out of my mind and was thankful I had extra work to keep me busy.

The day of the appointment arrived, and after scanning the area for several minutes, the technician said she would be right back after she spoke with the doctor. All I could hear was the second hand of the clock, which seemed to consume the entire room. Even though they had warmed the smock I was wearing, I began to shiver from nerves. After what felt like an eternity (which was only about 15 minutes), the technician returned and said I needed to get a mammogram immediately so the doctor could compare it with the ultrasound results.

The mammogram technician came into the room and said she could fit me in in about 30 minutes. I told her I needed to go tell my husband that it was going to be a longer appointment. I went out to the car where Dan was waiting and immediately burst into tears. I was scared about the urgency and worried that they saw something they didn't like. I was scared about how my life, our life, could be changed forever. We talked for several minutes and hugged for several more, and then I went back in to wait for my name to be called.

I walked up to the counter to let them know I was back, and the guy said, "Oh, you must be Jude. I'll let them know you're here."

"No, my name is Jodi," I replied, with a shaky voice.

He gave me a confused look and looked back down at my chart and apologized for his mistake. In that moment, I sensed that I was going to be okay. My name is a derivative of St. Jude. I grew up in a Catholic family, and my mom named me after this saint so that he would always look after me and keep me safe. Hearing this slip of the tongue brought me comfort and helped me feel that somehow everything was going to work out. And it did. Everything went smoothly with the test, and I got the all clear. I was so grateful for this soulful message that arrived when I needed it most, and I'll always hold it close to my heart.

The Moment I Knew

By Nicole Lee Dolan

"Bayside." Whether it was the voice of God, my spirit guides, or the wisdom of my soul, I heard the word loud and clear. At the time, though, I had no idea what Bayside was.

It was one of those moments when everything – and I mean *everything* – had fallen apart. The life I thought I knew, the one I'd worked so hard to create, was gone…seemingly in an instant. And then, right in the middle of that already-horrific time – while stuck in a traffic jam in the pouring rain – I received a message of yet another loss: a loved one had passed.

Feeling too unstable to keep driving, I pulled over, got out of the car, and yelled at the sky: "What do you want from me?!" I didn't expect the sky to respond, but it did: I heard the word "Bayside" – not just in my mind but out loud! Now I was not only angry and upset but also confused and annoyed by this seemingly meaningless response (although I must say I was also rather impressed that it had come through auditorily – a new experience for me!).

I later realized that Bayside was one of many divine messages I received on what I refer to as my very own sacred path at this time. The only meaning it had in that moment, however, was that I was either going crazy or that I had truly heard back from the sky.

Joseph Campbell said that "we must be willing to let go of the life we have planned so as to have the life that is waiting for us." This is exactly what happened to me the night I heard the word "Bayside." I found myself lost: mentally, emotionally, spiritually, and physically. And I wound up right in front of an enormous church named Bayside. Although I do not consider myself a woman who belongs to or identifies with any specific religion, the church's name was a decent start at grabbing my attention.

Bayside was my first step into a spiritual journey that changed everything. This journey led me across the world and eventually into the arms of my beloved. I will forever be grateful for the whisper in the wind that night. It was the moment in my life when I no longer just believed that we are loved and supported by the invisible forces that surround us. It was the moment that I *knew*.

September 24

Keep Praying

By Mauri Barnes

I was at the surgery desk in a children's hospital the night the call came. A young girl had been run over by her family's SUV and was being flown in by helicopter from a hospital over 100 miles away. Her parents, driving from there, were expected to arrive in three hours.

She had been helping unload groceries from the car and "horsing around" with her younger brother when the car shifted out of park and rolled backward, knocking her over. The rear tire passed directly over her chest. Multiple surgical teams were called in to attend to her expected injuries. The heart and general surgery teams started first, working together meticulously to make the necessary repairs.

I was asked to meet the parents when they arrived and escort them to a private waiting room with our hospital chaplain. Shock and fear contorted their faces, and tears filled their eyes. I could only relay the carefully worded update from the surgeon without elaboration. "We are doing the best that we can."

The night was long, and her injuries were serious. The grim final message that I was given was to "tell them that we've done everything that we can."

I had to stop for a moment to suppress my tears and gain control of my voice before I could stand in front of her family. They were holding hands with the chaplain, praying. Her mother was pale and shaky, on the verge of collapse.

Spirit spoke as these words came out of my mouth. It wasn't what I was directed to say. "I have seen many miracles in this hospital," I began. "You are doing the best thing that you can do right now; just keep praying. Your daughter is strong, and the doctors are doing everything that they can."

The miracle came in the morning when she woke up. She survived an SUV running over her small body. It was believed that her extreme physical fitness from gymnastics had protected her body from the terrible trauma.

I believe that it was the prayers.

Grace Whispered, "Surrender"

By Michelle Radomski

I remember the night. December 17, 2017. Immersed in water as hot as my body would tolerate, I was drowning. Drowning in pain, fear, depression. I had reached that dark place from which real change emerges. Rock bottom.

Certain that the pain would overcome me, I whispered the prayer that evokes angels and hope. "Help. Please, help."

The response was urgent, clear, and audible. "Surrender."

My reply was fierce. "Wait. What? You want me to surrender? Give up? Quit? No! I won't do it."

This time the response was quiet and compassionate. "No, Beloved. We don't want you to give up. We're asking you to let go. Surrender to Grace."

There I sat, in a tub that had long run cold, with no idea how to surrender. Confused, yet desperate to find a place to start, I did what all humans do these days. I grabbed my phone, typed the word "Surrender," and hit "Search."

Three hours (and numerous rabbit holes and tub fillings) later, I uncovered the meaning of the message. Seven small words that would forever change me. "I can't. God can. I let God."

"Okay," I said, directly to Grace. "I get it. I've been trying to do this alone and clearly I can't. You have the power to create miracles. I choose to let these miracles unfold. I surrender to you."

Tears flowed. Breath came. My heart cracked open, and hope seeped in. From that moment on, I had an ally. A divine, willing, loving, powerful partner. I had Grace.

Spent from the effort, yet full from the experience, I emerged from the bath and sank into my bed. As I waited for sleep to arrive, Grace had one more message for me. "Step fully in, Beloved. Trust the process as it unfolds for you."

Today, I'm no longer drowning. I'm buoyed and guided by Grace. When I feel a nudge, I check to see if my heart says yes, and then I step in. I stay surrendered to Grace, and I trust the ever-unfolding process.

And that, Beloveds, has made all the difference.

Healing Hands

By Jeffery Brochu

It was pitch black. I had been traveling for several miles down a narrow, steep country road, and I hadn't seen another car or house for miles. The only light on the road was the reflection of the millions of stars above.

I had just left an amazing transformational workshop, and my life was about to change. On a soul level, I knew it, and on another, I couldn't even imagine the impact this day would have for the rest of my life.

Earlier in the day I remembered my Reiki teacher telling me that sometimes the Reiki would just turn on. "Your hands will just heat up," she said and instructed me to place my intentions for the Reiki to be received for the highest and best use of whoever was near me.

As I was driving that night, my hands heated up, but there wasn't another car or home in my view. I came around a curve and could see the reflection of a car's headlights in the distance coming in the opposite direction. As it got closer, I realized that it was an ambulance traveling with no siren or flashing lights. The lights were bright inside the cabin, and I could clearly see an older gentleman in the back, propped up on the gurney. He was hooked up to all kinds of tubes and machines, and I could see a paramedic working on him.

I could feel Spirit guiding me. It was a new connection for me, yet at the same time, one that felt so familiar. I could see into the eyes of this man as if I had known him intimately. Spirit continued to connect me to the beautiful warm Reiki healing energy that I felt in my hands. I was able to share this with him, without question, but still wondered who this man was and how we had become connected in this moment.

Spirit knew him even if I didn't and connected us as closely as the stars above us are connected to one another.

Unknowingly Divine Intervention

By Donna Godfrey

There are no coincidences in life. Every living moment, every interaction you have with others – regardless of whether it's for a few days, a few years, or just a few moments – transpires exactly as it's meant to be.

This message was reinforced for me through my interactions with a lady I met at a fair. She told me that she and her family had recently moved to Canada from the UK. She also told me that she was extremely intuitive and very aware of her clairvoyant abilities, and she felt strongly that she had come for a reason. We exchanged cards, but I didn't hear from her until several months later, when she called and said that my card kept falling out of her hand purse every time she opened it. She booked a Reiki session with me, after which I never saw her again.

Three years later, in the summer of 2010, the publisher of a magazine called me to say a lady wrote an article about me and sent it from England. Apparently, during the guided mediation in her Reiki session, I took her to a place where she had met up with her father, who had crossed over. There were other things shown to her as well, which guided her to move her family back to England.

Initially, when I had first talked to her, she'd been adamant that she was going to stay in Canada no matter what. But something transpired in her session that triggered her to listen to her heightened intuitive side, and she returned. Once she was back home, she learned that she had blood clots in both lungs and was close to death. She felt she was given a second chance at life, and this inspired her to write about divine interventions – including the one during our Reiki session.

The beauty of this is that I had no knowledge of this until her article was published. It also showed me that we all are used divinely, whether we're consciously aware of it or not. How beautiful is that! I know innately that being of service to humanity does not always require us to know everything or understand everything! Just knowing to be heart-centred or present, for any given moment, can be more than enough!

Miracle in May

By Lori Love

On May 20, 2016, I woke up with a sudden burst of shortness of breath. I'd had surgery two and a half weeks earlier and was unable to walk. Nonetheless, I went to work just like any other day; however, it was not just like any other day.

After speaking with one of my physicians around 3:00 p.m., I drove myself to an imaging center. I couldn't breathe, and I knew something wasn't right. An ultrasound of my leg revealed a deep vein thrombosis that occluded my entire left leg. I was sent to the hospital, where I had a CT scan of my chest and learned the horrifying results: I had several blood clots in both of my lungs and was told I would probably not make it. My husband of 29 years sat in shock.

I was quickly taken to the ICU and started on a blood thinner to stop the clots. Later the next day, I was taken to interventional radiology and had a filter placed to halt any more blood clots from invading my lungs or brain. However, the blood thinner caused me to bleed profusely, so I had to be sutured to stop the bleeding.

I was in and out of consciousness for many days. During that time, many prayers were said for me all over the world, and many family members visited me in the hospital, although I don't remember. During moments of lucidity, I sensed that everyone was so upset, yet I felt a sense of peace.

That Sunday, I suddenly woke up, sat straight up in the bed, and told the nurse to call my husband and to bring my computer because I had a paper to write. (I was in Nurse Practitioner school.) The nurse looked at me, not believing her eyes, and called my husband. I wrote a paper and received a 99/100.

God performed a miracle. I began to heal and was sent to a regular room. All my physicians and healthcare providers say that I shouldn't be here, and I say, "But God had other plans."

The Magic Mirror, Loud and Clear

By Cindie Chavez

I missed our morning meeting because the kids were home from school that day.

With the phone resting on my shoulder, my hands in the bubbly dishwater, I listened as my friend cheerfully informed me of the details. Doing my best to remain politely interested, I could feel the anger rising in my chest. My solar plexus burned like the sun. I was confused – why was I angry?

For years, we four had met for tea and discussion, supporting each other as we navigated marriages, businesses, parenting – life. We'd meet in our homes, local restaurants, and occasionally at a nearby park for a sunny picnic.

The phone call was so ordinary – my closest friend calling to tell me what they'd discussed and what our future plans were. While she was telling me when and where we'd meet next, I felt my irritation flaring into a scorching ache.

"Sounds great to me," I said and rushed off the call, still confused about what I was feeling. These were not feelings I allowed myself to feel. I was the happy, laid-back, easygoing one.

As I pondered my anger, I heard the message – not quite audible but as loud and clear as the voice of God herself, "Oh, I'm sorry. I thought you wanted to be last. You always put yourself last."

I was stunned. For years, I had always deferred to everyone. When asked what I wanted, I replied with some version of "I don't care; what do you want?"

The truth hit me like a splash of cold water. I had deferred to everyone else for so long that they no longer asked if I had a preference.

The Universe was showing me how I treated myself by creating a mirror with my relationships. If I didn't respect my own preferences, no one else would either.

Today, when I'm asked what I want, I give a specific answer, even if I have to search my soul to find one. As the saying goes: how can you have what you want if you don't know what it is?

Divine Intervention

By Suzanne M. Fortino

I was born into a family of abuse and neglect. The ironic part is I always knew that my mother loved me, even when she was too incapacitated to show me. From a young age, I made a decision to fight against injustice. I took it upon myself to stand up and protect the people who were unable to protect themselves. This decision formed who I am today.

In school I was an outcast. Because I stood alone against the mostly male bullies who picked on the vulnerable kids, they called me Amazon Woman. When I got older, I continued my mission. The difference then was that I was fueled by alcohol and sometimes actually stood up for myself. By then, I had added martial arts to my street fighting repertoire, so my nickname became Ninja B***h.

I always told myself that violence was okay because it was always in defense and never offense. After I had my fifth child, I became unable to stand up to people. I started hyperventilating, being unable to speak or even confront people when an issue came up that I considered an injustice. For 10 years, I experienced this with no explanation from doctors. There was nothing medically wrong with me.

I have always believed this was divine intervention. The Holy Spirit was intervening in my life to teach me a better way of dealing with what I considered injustices. I was compelled to start using my intellect and my heart to dissolve confrontations, and I have embraced my destiny to project love to all in order to strike down the injustices of the world. I now realize that even though I suffered from abuse and neglect as a child, the love my mother had for me allowed me to be open to divine intervention.

The Voice

By Lindsey Gaye Walker

A year had passed since my divorce, and while I did my best to move forward, I struggled parenting our two teenage boys and navigating my new life. One day in August, I found myself desperately crying, "Oh, God, I'm so lost. I don't know what to do! What should I do?!"

From the depths of my inner turmoil came a voice that told me to get a book down from the shelf called *A Course in Miracles*. This book had been gifted to me years earlier, but I hadn't read it. After telling the voice that I had no energy to even open a book, I was told to leave my apartment and board a train. My brain felt so foggy from crying that I surrendered all resistance and just did what it said.

Once on the train, I was told when to get off and was then led to a beach bar where I was instructed to go inside. Concerned that some man might try to pick me up, I refused and continued down the path, but it came to a dead end and I had to turn back. As I passed the bar again, meditative music started playing, and my heart opened and I relaxed. The voice continued to say go in, so with bated breath, I did.

Shortly after, a lady entered and started chatting to me. She asked if I had ever heard of a book called *A Course in Miracles* and if I would like to join her and some friends who were going to listen to it being read to them. I couldn't believe what I was hearing. Clearly, this book had a message for me! I raised my eyes to the heavens and silently said to the voice, "You so crack me up!" It was in that moment I realized I was always spiritually guided and never alone.

I soon discovered that the core teachings of the book were to choose love over fear, forgive yourself and others completely, and trust the Voice of God. These teachings continue to guide me to this day.

Letting Things off My Chest

By Janet Womack

On March 9, 2018, I was diagnosed with breast cancer.

The two-week wait to see the specialist was torture, but he let me record our conversation as he told me my options for treatment. He held out his hands. In one hand, I'd have a lumpectomy, followed by a series of radiation treatments. In his other hand, I'd have a mastectomy, most likely followed by nothing – no chemo or radiation – considering it was such an early-stage cancer.

I wasn't rushed into making a decision, and he said I could come back until my questions were answered. I went back two weeks later. I needed more answers. If I decided upon a mastectomy, I was entitled by law to have both breasts removed, with the option to have reconstruction. It would be a very long surgery and a six- to eight-week recovery.

I was terrified and continued to pray for guidance. A month later, on April 10, 2018, I felt a heart-crushing pain in my chest. I couldn't breathe and started to panic. I drove myself to the ER.

After a bunch of tests, my diagnosis was "extreme anxiety" and "if I didn't know already, I had a 1.5 cm lump in my right breast."

I replied with "Yes, I know. It's why I'm here in this state of panic!"

A voice greater than my own kept guiding me away from the lumpectomy, saying, "It's not good enough."

With so much coming at me, I had not been listening to it. That night in the hospital, I made the most difficult decision I've ever had to make. On June 21, 2018, I had a bilateral mastectomy with DIEP flap reconstruction. I was in surgery for 10 hours and spent three days in the hospital. I had a long recovery ahead of me.

A week later, my breast surgeon called to check on me. He told me that my intuition had been right and I'd made a great choice. There was a second hidden cancer in that same breast, which hadn't shown up on any of my scans.

I know that God was guiding me along the way. I only had to listen and let go.

Blanket of Peace

By Jodie Scott

It was a blustery afternoon in the dead of winter in North Carolina. Cold, dark clouds roared through the sky. Lightning flashed, thunder was so loud it was all you could hear, and the rain was so dense that you couldn't see out the windows. I was 15 years old, and my heart was hurting bad. I really didn't know how much longer I could stand the pain. I threw myself on the thickly padded four-poster bed and cried in agony and despair. My emotions were out of control. *I* was out of control.

I had been depressed most of my life, and this seemed to be the culmination of all those years of intense heartache and pain. The pain was unbearable. I cried out frantically, "God! I don't even know if you're real, but if you are, you'd best show up right now. I am not kidding! I am dead serious! I am done! You'd better end this heartache right now, or I will! I can't take it anymore!" I lay across the bed, crying, knowing that my life was over. I had never felt so defeated. Time eluded me. I lost consciousness.

Later, I was awakened by a stillness. I felt a warm blanket being pulled up over my body, very slowly and deliberately, as if being guided by angels. With this blanket came a peace unlike anything I'd ever felt and a love I'd never known. I had no words. I looked to see who was there. I saw no one, yet I knew I was not alone, nor have I been since.

In that moment, I felt His presence and I knew that, yes, the Almighty God is real. Yes, our loving God did show up for me. I have no question about it. And yes, He is available, to each and every one of us.

As I look back through my life, I see that there were many times when God showed up for me. All I had to do was ask. I didn't know it then, but I sure know it now.

Storms may continue to rumble through life, but I will never be alone again, nor do I have to endure alone. All we have to do is ask and we will receive.

A Stroke of Guidance

By Davalynn Kim

February 11, 2019 changed my life forever. My dad, our rock, had a brainstem stroke. My healthy, brilliant dad was paralyzed on his left side and couldn't walk, swallow, speak, or use his entire left side. My purpose now burned inside my soul brighter than a thousand suns. That purpose was to heal my father.

Dad had suffered aspiration pneumonia due to his inability to swallow. My sister and I cleared his lungs day and night for two weeks. We got his physical body stable, but as the days passed, Dad sank deeper and deeper into depression over his new condition.

One afternoon, I was soul searching for the next step. Unexpectedly, a voice reverberated through my whole being: "His joy must return." This voice came with a powerful feeling. I began to focus our daily meditations on joy. I briefly thought of The Abundance Program by Edgar Cayce, but the voice emphatically stated, "Not yet."

Slowly, Dad began participating more in therapy. There was a glimmer of hope outside of a hospital bed. The therapists were giving us two weeks to cover some ground or we were going home with a feeding tube and partial paralysis. One night, I was cueing up his meditation music, and the voice came again. "Play it now!" I began to play The Abundance Program three times a night while Dad slept. After a week of the program, Dad was laughing easily and bringing joy to all around him.

We were drawing near to the two-week end date. Four days before the tentative discharge, the voice returned. "Create a specific Abundance Program for him. Tell his mind what to explain to his body." All I could do was cry. I innately knew it was going to work. I wrote The Abundant Healing Program, targeted Dad's specific needs, and played it each night. On the day of his supposed final evaluation and discharge, the supervising therapist rushed in and told us Dad had made significant progress. They were giving him four more weeks of therapy. After three weeks, the wondrous voice urged me to "give him new guidance." I recorded even more specific instructions for his mind, body, and soul.

By the time we left, Dad was eating, talking, writing, and walking with a walker. The voice of Divine Guidance weaved purpose into my soul. I am forever grateful.

Humbled by Grace

By Melisa Archer

Perspective plays a huge role in determining how we feel about things. For instance, I live in North America, where the struggles and "First World problems" seem very significant. But recently I've been messaging with a man who lives and works in the Caribbean, where they are expected to be happy to work twelve-hour shifts, twelve days in a row – in extreme heat and for minimal pay – just to have two days off.

One night, after getting very little sleep the day before, this man was bogged down with many worries, but his top priority was his extreme thirst. In a country where you cannot drink the tap water, finding potable water can be a challenge. I was concerned for him, but being in another country, how could I help? I couldn't go get him a bottle of water or order it for him online. I became extremely distressed on his behalf. When I imagined someone in pain due to thirst – in this day and age! – how small my own personal problems seemed by comparison.

As we messaged, this man of such faith actually tried to comfort *me*, saying that I should put all worry out of my mind, that he would be fine. And sure enough, within a few minutes, he sent a text with a picture of himself looking happy and excited. He explained that a Good Samaritan had brought him a bottle of water. He didn't understand how a stranger could have known that he had desperately needed a bottle of water, but he said, "It's true that God, my God, does not abandon his children."

Hearing about this encounter – and seeing him experience so much joy and happiness – warmed my heart and filled me with hope for humanity. He went on to say that for the poor, happiness lasts for a short time, but, as he reminded me, many times the men of this world have been abused, but God has blessed him in other ways.

God Always Has a Plan

By Debra Lee James

The teen years are a difficult time, and mine were no exception. I was dealing with peer pressure, bullying, and hormones run amok – but my teen years also included various types of abuse, family with substance-abuse issues, and my own mental-health issues. All these things came together in a "perfect storm" one spring day when I was 15 years old.

My school day was particularly degrading because, no matter how hard I tried, I seemed to do nothing right – from making many mistakes on my homework to wearing geeky clothes. Once I got home, my brother continued to inflict emotional torture on me – from criticizing my looks to reminding me that he's the first-born son and golden child. I called my mother at her job to complain. Huge mistake on my part.

In order to distance myself from my brother's torment, I walked the half mile to my grandmother's home, hoping my feelings of unworthiness would subside. Wrong. My two younger cousins were giving my grandmother a hard time, chaos surrounded me, and I decided I'd had enough. Enough of frustration, of disappointment, of *life*.

I went into the bathroom, locked the door, and searched for a razor blade. I held the razor to my wrist, pushed down, and drew the razor along my arm. Nothing happened. I tried again – nothing happened. The blade cut toilet paper, cloth, and the shower curtain. A third time, I drew the razor along my arm. Not even a scratch, making me think about my actions. According to my beliefs, suicide blocks my entering Heaven. On finding my body, my grandmother would blame herself. I knew beyond a shadow of a doubt that God had an important plan for my life. Why else would He prevent that razor from cutting me?

Over the years, so many people have told me what a positive influence I've had on their lives as a woman, a Christian, a mentor, a healthcare professional, and more. I'm grateful to be here.

Finding My Truth

By Stephanie Williams

I had a relationship with God that terrified me. I was raised in a faith that taught about being saved and learned that God loves us all so very much – we just have to follow a few simple rules to be good. Except those rules were not always so simple, and the consequences were dire. My relationship with God was strained, to say the least, and the little connection we had was strictly based on fear.

I found myself feeling depressed, like I was failing in every aspect of life. I yearned for some sort of spiritual fulfillment and had cried out many nights begging for a sign. Then I stumbled upon a book, *Conversations with God*. I'd had this book for a decade but had never read it.

I started reading through the pages and got an overwhelming feeling that the message in this book was written just for me in this very moment, even though it had been written long ago. It told me of a God that was not disappointed or angry but unconditionally loving and accepting of me just how I was in this moment. Unconditionally loving.

God needed nothing – no steps, no specific prayer, absolutely nothing from me to earn this love because to ask that of me itself is the definition of conditional. God is not vengeful or jealous. He/She/It is pure love, and anything made of pure love needs nothing from me to earn favor.

The moment I stopped fearing God, I was able to truly have a beautiful relationship with Him. How much more special is a bond if you choose it out of want rather than fear of what will happen to you if you don't?

You are loved no matter what. You are just where you are supposed to be right now in this moment. Ask the universe for guidance, and it will always provide, if you're open to reading the signs.

My inner truth came to me while reading a book; yours may come in the next song you hear or the next person you talk to. Your truth will speak to you if you listen.

Her Big Day

By Antonia Van Becker

My youngest daughter was getting married! We started planning in November and made a beautiful backyard design with a landscaper for a fairytale garden wedding in July.

They started in December: fixing an existing patio and starting a new one, clearing space for turf, and leaving piles of dirt and broken concrete in the front yard. Then it started to rain. The work was put off again and again, but we had faith it would get done for the big day.

The rain stopped in March, and we asked when the landscapers would start work again. They showed up for a couple days and pushed the dirt around and then left. They destroyed the irrigation system and asked for more money. They missed the wedding shower deadline at the end of May.

Then, at the beginning of July on a hot Friday afternoon, the foreman came and again asked for more money. "If you don't give us the money, we're gone." They left us with a mess of broken pipes, garbage, and less than three weeks to go.

We went into shock. That night, I was struck with the realization that we must do what we weren't accustomed to: *ask for help*. We asked our friends, our families, the universe, and especially the angels. I asked the angels for help every day. I asked out loud while driving, in prayers before bed, silently while in conversation, and in rhythm while shoveling gravel. Every day, things began to happen. We sourced materials. Strangers told us where to go when we couldn't find things. Projects got done. Miracles happened. We didn't sleep much. We didn't get enough business done, but we finished the yard.

The wedding day dawned bright and beautiful, our two brides were so thankful, and the celebration was joyous. Once more we asked the angels to give the girls peace and happiness in their marriage, and then we thanked our special angels and invited them to sit with us and enjoy the view!

Pain Has Purpose

By Nicole C. Lofton

There was a time in my life when I felt discouraged and, quite honestly, a bit depressed. I didn't understand why I had gone through so many difficulties – from emotionally challenging situations while growing up to, more recently, an emotionally abusive relationship. These experiences had left me feeling frustrated, alone, mad at myself, and plagued by self-esteem issues, which I battled constantly and allowed to hold me back. Not all my pain has been emotional, though. In fact, as I write this, I am dealing with a physical health issue. But through all these tough times, one thing has kept me going. It all started with an experience that changed my life forever.

One day I was crying and praying, and I know that God heard me because it was almost like he was right there with me, comforting me. I could hear him clearly. He walked me through all the trials that I had faced and showed me how they all connected to one another and how those trials connected me to other people. I began to see that life in general is a process that prepares us for our purpose. It is easy to get frustrated with the process, though, especially when we don't fully understand that everything we go through has a purpose. But now I could see that the trials we go through strengthen us, humble us, and teach us lessons. They give us experience and wisdom to be able to help the next person.

Now when I experience a trial, I try to find the positive in it because I know that the outcome is greater than the pain. As a life coach and anti-domestic violence advocate, I now dedicate my life to letting people know that pain has a purpose. I know that my purpose is to help them understand the purpose in their pain.

Never Alone

By Chris Anderson

Looking to find a special gift for Mother's Day, I was drawn to a small florist with an attached greenhouse out back. Perusing the rows of fragrant flowers and sumptuous greenery, I searched for something my mother would absolutely love. Instead, I found myself enchanted by a hanging basket of tiny indigo flowers. Being a single mother, I often struggled financially so I always stressed to my children that I did not need store-bought presents. My most-cherished gifts have always been those handmade trinkets, lovingly made by my children in school or at the kitchen table, and yet, I was smitten with this basket and secretly hoped they would buy me these flowers. Doubting this would happen, I reached up and put my hand on the basket. Halfway down I stopped. After all, I had come to buy something for my mother, not for myself. I thought if it was still there after Mothers' Day, I would bring it home.

Mother's Day arrived and neither of my children felt well enough to travel, so I made the long drive by myself. My mother and I spent the entire day together – going to lunch, window shopping, driving the countryside, and enjoying quality time together!

Heading home, I felt conflicted – grateful but melancholy and even a little resentful toward my children, until a warmth flooded over me. It was as if God was sitting in the car and had His arms around me. In my heart, I heard the words, "You are doing a great job. I love you!" Comforted and in awe, I let go of my harsh feelings and let the love I felt wash through me.

I arrived home relaxed and happy. To my delight, sitting on the patio were both my children – and the very same hanging basket of indigo flowers I had fallen in love with days before! Moved to tears, I wondered: if God thought enough to show up in this situation and make himself known to me, how much more does He love and care for me when I am faced with great adversity? From that day forward, I've found peace in knowing that we are never alone on our journey.

Calling All Angels

By Lisa M. Raymond

My life and faith changed forever in 2015.

With his kind blue eyes and big heart, my husband is special and funny and easy to love. Sadly, in 2015 he fell ill and faced emergency heart surgery. Due to complications, he was not a candidate for open-heart surgery and was running out of options. On the Friday before Easter, the family and I sat praying, waiting for a doctor to take his case. Desperate for a distraction, my mother-in-law and I went for coffee. Standing in line, Train's marvelous song "Calling All Angels" filled my mind: "I-I-I-I'm calling all angels, calling all angels." Embracing each lyric, I silently sang along: "I won't give up if you don't give up."

Distracted, I bumped into a nurse and turned to see a smock full of angels. Surprised and encouraged, I continued walking as the inner song resumed: "I-I-I-I'm calling all angels…I need a hand to help build up some kind of hope inside of me."

As we reached the empty elevator, a woman quickly entered. Looking right at us, she said, "Tough day?"

"Yes," I said reflexively. "We could use a few miracles if you have any."

"I will see what I can do," she smiled, disappearing into the empty corridor.

Surprised by the comment, we walked toward my husband's room. Suddenly, an image of my husband's bed flashed in my mind. Three huge men stood behind his bed with their heads hung down, looking powerful and protective. Then wings slowly wrapped around his bed. It was only a moment, but the image was so startling.

We arrived at his room moments later to see him hugging a doctor, accepted for a procedure that would save his life. Relieved and overwhelmed, I went to a nearby waiting room to call family. As I stood in the dimly lit room, my eyes caught a line on a poster in the corner: "Expect Miracles." Stunned by another message, I felt overwhelmed and grateful.

I know now that I can truly expect miracles when calling on angels!

Graceful Assurance

By Nora T. Barican

As far back in my formative years as I can recall, I have always been drawn to a prayerful life; so, as an adult, entering the convent as a Catholic nun was a no-brainer. However, given that I am an only child, I had the privilege and responsibility to care for my parents in their old age. I love my parents and would do anything for them, but there remained a sense of unease in having given up what to me felt like my calling.

Gripped with guilt and confusion, I knelt before the altar alone in my bedroom, closed my eyes, and prayed for forgiveness and guidance. I summoned Saint Therese of Lisieux's intercession to give me a tangible sign that, despite not pursuing my vocation, I remained in God's favour. (She is popularly known as "The Little Flower of Jesus" and is often pictured with the Crucifix adorned with red roses.)

The answer to my prayer was instantaneous! When I opened my eyes, a fresh red rose petal was nestled on top of my prayer book. Living a simple life, we could not afford fresh flowers at home, nor was the altar near a window. I cried in disbelief and in faithful acceptance at the same time. Heaven must have seen how tormented I was and gifted me with this graceful assurance.

Being in a state of grace has been described as the condition of a person who is pleasing to God. With the rose petal, I felt assured that, just like St. Therese who became holy by doing little things with great love, I too could do the same, outside of the religious order.

Since then, I try to consciously live my life in a standard of grace and not perfection. In my heart, my efforts in following this simple yet beautiful approach to spirituality is enough to remain in close relationship with the Divine.

Connecting with the Archangels Through Colors

By Debbie Labinski

In 2014 I prayed for something to change my awareness, something or someone to teach me how to heal and love myself again. I felt ready to look outside of church and my current relationships to truly find myself. I had given birth to three children who brought light and meaning to my life in a fulfilling way, but I was suffering from weight gain, depression, and loneliness. I started reading about angels, joining energy circles, and taking intuition and angel classes. I felt my life shift when I began to connect to the archangels through meditation, automatic writing, and wearing colors that the archangels vibrate to. Within months of inviting the archangels into my day, signs became clearer to me and I began following the feelings (clairsentience) that were coming more easily to me.

I have learned that archangels have colors that they vibrate to and that the archangels can connect with us more easily when we wear their vibrational color. I like to invite archangels in and connect to their energy, especially while getting my day started. And at the end of each day, I usually journal my archangel experiences as a reminder of how I felt during the connection and what I was wearing that deepened or strengthened my connection with that daily archangel. For example, some days I call in my creative angels, like Archangels Jophiel and Uriel, who vibrate to pink, yellow, and red. These two archangels pick out the best outfits and support me emotionally when I may be feeling insecure about my body.

I have been dressing with the archangels' vibrational colors to support my personal energy for over four years now. It has helped me to feel and hear the archangels much more easily. I encourage you to give it a try, too, and journal about your personal experiences. I am excited for you to have fun with the archangels and find out how dressing in their colors can support your overall energy.

A Walk in the Woods

By Diana L. Hooker

As often as she could, Deb would take a walk in the woods close to her home. In the woods, she found a peace that enabled her to spend time talking to God.

One late afternoon as she set out for her journey, she was interrupted by a ping on her phone, warning of an impending storm. She could see the storm quickly moving in her direction, threatening to end her walk before it could even begin. She stopped. After a few long minutes of contemplating what to do, she decided that a little rain wouldn't hurt her and proceeded down the path. Within a few minutes of her decision, the clouds seemed to clear and the sun shone brightly. Deb looked at her app again, and the storm had vanished from the radar. Though with no other human, she certainly wasn't alone.

She declared aloud, "God, you are my Friend. You are my Father. I am Yours!"

A moment after saying this aloud, Deb received another ping, this time a message from a new friend: "I know that we don't know each other well, but I felt that I need to tell you this: God says that he knows you intimately and calls you His friend, His beloved, His daughter of Zion, His chosen and anointed one. He calls you His!" Deb got chills feeling that God had replied to her gratitude and enveloped her in His love.

Even though we may be faced with impending storms, we need to persevere. God is our Friend and our Father, and we are His. He will clear the path and shine brightly upon us.

Intervention at the Intersection

By Jacine Rilea

The warmth of the autumn sun was pleasant on my face as I weaved in and out of the light traffic in my red Corolla. I was driving north through Northcote, along St. Georges Road. As a young driver, I was in my usual rush, pushing the speed limit and urging to get ahead.

In the distance, I watched as the lights of the intersection on Bell Street turned red and instinctively started to lift my foot off the accelerator. My practice was to maintain the speed that would get me through the intersection first and without stopping.

In a two-lane passage, my right-side lane was free ahead. As my inner clock counted, I kept the speed I would need to get me to the intersection at a good pace. My foot hovered between the brake and the accelerator. The cars in the left lane came to a stop. Would the light turn green before I had to use the brake? Yes, it did!

I quickly moved my foot to the accelerator, ready to speed ahead of the other drivers. In this moment, I felt a force field stopping my right foot. Something was preventing my foot from pressing down on the pedal.

No. A distinct no. I wondered, "Why not?" My foot continued to hover above the pedals as my car kept on going, and I entered the intersection first.

Just then, a black car entered my vision from the left, going at an incredible speed. I saw him. Another young driver rushing to get ahead. Black hair, long nose, and looking straight ahead. I felt him sense me coming from the right. He flinched – he was helpless – and then in a second he had passed.

I couldn't brake or accelerate and stayed in suspended animation as my car continued with the momentum it had kept from before the lights turned green. "That's why not," I heard.

As I continued to float past the intersection in a surreal state, I realised that someone had stopped me. Someone with a force, a concern, and a knowing of what could have been.

Angels and Armor

By Teresa Velardi

"I don't think I can do this anymore, God. The longer this goes on, the harder it gets to continue. But I know that good will come from this, so please send an army of angels with me as I go forward today. Thank you."

That's what I wrote in my journal as I began my quiet time. I start my day having my morning coffee with God, which includes my journal and my Bible app. That morning, I would be going to court to argue my ongoing case. The details aren't nearly as important as what happened.

Feeling a bit weary of the situation, I wrote for a bit before I opened the Bible app. The verse of the day was Ephesians 6:10-20, "The Armor of God." The armor is worn to stand against the forces of evil in the spiritual realm, and these verses describe the armor. I'd read this many times but was struck by the timing. I was comforted, feeling guided to move forward, knowing I had tools to take with me from a higher source.

A pastor friend of mine sent out daily scriptures, and as I closed my journal, I saw the morning text come in. The scripture for the day was "The Armor of God." I looked up, smiled, expressed my gratitude for the reaffirmation and confidence I was feeling, knowing I was not alone. I got dressed and went to my car, equipped with my paperwork and my spiritual armor.

The drive to the courthouse was about 40 minutes. Normally I drive in silence, gathering my thoughts, pondering my day, or reviewing my quiet time. I turned on the radio. Instead, a CD, which I didn't know was in the player, filled my car with the voice of Joyce Meyer teaching on "The Armor of God."

Don't you love it when the Creator of the Universe starts the day with you, giving you exactly what you need at the right time?

Honor Life

By Jeffery Brochu

It was a brisk fall day, and the faint sound of "Going Down the Road Feeling Bad" was playing from an old bootleg cassette. Having just completed my final exams in my first year of college, I was on top of the world.

It was cold, damp, and rainy, one of those days when you almost wished it were snowing instead – at least that would have felt comforting. Headed for home, I came around a sharp corner and completely lost control of my car. It went into a spin, and the whole scene felt like I was watching a movie in slow motion. A woman out for her morning jog jumped out of the way; the terror on her face must have mirrored my own.

A moment later, my car slammed into a telephone poll, making the loudest sound I'd ever heard. And then everything went silent. I felt myself lifted up out of the car through a shaft of light, protected and spared the pain I'd inevitably feel soon, and even the potential of death.

At first, I thought it was my guardian angel, but then I knew without a doubt that God had saved me. If the car had made just one more quarter of a turn, the impact would've been to the driver's side. Because I hit the pole head on, however, it came halfway through the car.

As the jogger began banging on my window to see if I was okay, I came back into my body and, amazingly, I walked away without a scratch on me!

The ultimate soulful message I received that day was to honor my life. At a time when I did not know who God was to me, he knew who I was and, thankfully, chose to save me anyway.

Spirit Lifeline

By Bobbie Carr

Some years ago, there was a period in my life when I went from being a generally healthy person to one who had a mysterious illness. I consulted various specialists to try to discover why I often experienced severe body aches, alternating spells of night chills and sweats, as well as a complete lack of appetite and energy. My days consisted of listlessly sitting in a chair and at night restlessly coping with the symptoms. This went on for months.

Through it all, I prayed to God more fervently than I ever had before, asking for His help to get through the illness and emerge healthy once again. In answer to my pleas during the ordeal, I believe that God sent me visions on two different occasions.

The first vision I had was of my deceased Aunt Marie calling my name, opening the door to my room, and letting hundreds of beautiful pink roses suffused with light flow like a glorious river into my room. I perceived this vision as a sign of hope.

In the second vision, my husband's deceased Uncle Lou stood at the foot of my bed, repeatedly encouraging me to "hang in there" while pointing to the other deceased people who surrounded my bed to support my getting through the illness.

With God's grace and the prayers of family and friends, after many months I finally found a doctor who was able to help me regain my health, even though a cause of the illness was never found. It took some time, but I eventually recovered and resumed my normal lifestyle.

A long while after I recovered, my husband told me that he had thought I was going to die at some point during the course of the sickness. I truly believe that my literal lifeline and lifesaver was the strength and faith I received from God.

Unexpected Change

By Patricia Peters

Years ago, I was co-partner of an incredibly successful business. I had a dream team, lovely clients, and was highly profitable with only 10 hours of work each week. I enjoyed my lifestyle and attended tons of seminars for my personal and spiritual growth.

Yet something was missing. I was grateful for the abundance and loved the business; however, I found myself feeling bored more and more often. I was clueless about what was going on inside me. Everything was perfect, and yet it wasn't.

One day, I experienced a lightbulb moment, a divine calling. I heard, "Send the Dai Komyo [Reiki symbol of divine wisdom] into the business for the greater good of all!"

I followed the calling and did the energy work, asking for the next step in my life. I felt exhilarated and curious about what the universe would conjure up.

Three days later, I knew. It hit me like a hammer: my business partner came to me with the following words: "You know, I recently lost my fortune in the stock market. I don't want to split the profits with you any longer. I want all the money. I will kick you out if you don't quit voluntarily. You have two days. I expect your resignation by Monday."

Boom!

To my surprise, I didn't feel threatened at all. Knowing he couldn't do anything to me, I felt totally calm inside. I left and drove home wondering what that was all about.

With the help of an excellent lawyer whom I found by divine guidance, I ended up selling my share to my business partner. He fired almost the entire team. Lots of clients quit because of what happened.

So what happened to "for the greater good"? The fired ones made great careers, my business partner made peace with his dad after decades of alienation, and I became the business coach and spiritual mentor I was always meant to be.

Surrender to divine wisdom! I know by experience that it always turns out for your higher good, even if it looks like your life is falling apart.

Finding Faith to Hold Onto

By Jamie Lynn Thompson

The smell of sweat and stale air filled the space. My bottom hurt from the hard bench, and I sat anxiously, not knowing what to expect. I rode with a friend to Summer Bible Camp, as my parents had just divorced, and my mom sent me to get away for a while to a positive place. Now we sat in a stuffy room filled with countless strangers waiting for the pastor to speak about the upcoming week.

I was very nervous. The camp seemed to be quite strict, based on the things we were allowed to pack. Finally the pastor told us the schedule and activities, and we were shuffled and divided into our camp houses and introduced to our counselors. Thankfully, they kept me and my friend together, and our adventure began.

My time at camp was filled with fun, smiles, and laughs along the way. My favorite time was in the evenings after dinner when we all crammed into the chapel, and the staff would perform a puppet show on the topics of the day: friendship, faith, love, and community, along with singing and prayer. I felt like I absorbed it all and prayed the loudest.

I was a confused and hurt little girl looking for something to hold onto, to keep me above the water of my life that I seemed to be sinking in. I found faith in that crowded space. I found a way to cope, to deal with my life, to feel comfort that someone or something was listening to me. I found the line to hold me up and that would be with me always. I have continued to hold onto that line after camp. I joined my church choir and the puppet ministry.

To this day, when I struggle, I go out and sit in nature – holding tightly to my line of faith, just like at camp, and know I am not alone.

Finding faith to hold onto every day makes me smile and pushes me to reach for the stars, shine my sparkle for all to see, and just be me.

In My Mind's Eye

By Mary Niemi

I raised my two boys as a single mother after my husband's death. Those boys have grown into well-balanced men living independent lives. I knew I had raised them in wisdom and courage, but I often looked back and wished that I had done some things differently.

One day, I lay on my sofa, resting in a deep meditative state, at peace but not asleep. Silently, in my mind's eye, an angel with huge feathery wings came into focus. Somehow I knew that he was Archangel Michael. He reached out his hands to me. In awe, I shoved aside all thoughts of not being worthy and laid my hands in his.

Looking intensely into my eyes, Archangel Michael gently but emphatically spoke: "Mary, do you understand what a powerful mothering ability you have?"

"Sort of," I replied, as pride in my mother-journey battled my self-criticism.

Archangel Michael spoke again with deep compassion: "Mary, you were chosen to be the mother of your boys because you had all the characteristics required to bring to them the lessons they needed. You did the perfect things right and the necessary things wrong! How could your boys learn to grow and thrive on Earth if you didn't make mistakes? Forget perfection," he said with a gentle smile. "It's not possible."

His total support and love for me filled me with a comforting sense of joy and peace. Ever so slowly, he faded away, leaving my whole self humming with the vibration of his divine presence.

In those precious minutes, my entire view of myself as a mother, and as a person, changed for the positive in a deeply profound way. I now have a new confidence that lets me be at peace being my own genuine self. When an angel tells me that I'm succeeding in my mother-journey, I finally believe it's true!

Surrender and Acceptance

By Stephanie L. Foran

Our cats, Chloe and Claudia, stole our hearts 11 years ago, and I quickly became attuned to their behavior. Last year, I noticed that Claudia was drinking too much water. She could no longer jump up high. She was losing weight and urinating more. She seemed weak and lethargic. My suspicions were confirmed: Claudia was diabetic. We learned we would need to give her insulin injections twice a day. I was devastated.

Questions raced through my head: *How will this affect Claudia's longevity? Will the injections hurt her? What if she starts to fear us?* Our hometowns and family were hours away. No more "home for the holidays." No more overnight getaways. No more evening social activities. No more sleeping in on the weekends. It felt like house arrest. Despite this, we were committed to giving Claudia the care she needed. We owed that to her.

My husband bravely stepped up and agreed to administer Claudia's shots. I compared pet-food brands, analyzed ingredients, and did endless research. I also carefully monitored Claudia's eating patterns. I bought new toys to encourage her to become more active. We had an amazing vet and diligently followed up with tests and appointments.

Claudia seemed to spring back to life. She grew stronger and healthier, but she remained diabetic. In desperate need of relief, I attended a group Reiki and sound-healing session. We shared a sacred space and spoke in a circle. I expressed how exhausted I was in my unending quest to reverse Claudia's diabetes.

Suddenly, something shifted in me. I realized there was nothing more I could do and surrendered. It was time to give it to God and accept whatever the outcome was. A sense of peace came over me.

Soon afterward, our vet told us that Claudia was "trending toward remission." We were instructed to lower her insulin dosage and retest her. Amazingly, after seven months, Claudia had gone into remission!

After doing all we can in a situation, sometimes it takes surrender and acceptance for divine miracles to unfold.

The Dream to a Road

By Joanna Werch Takes

When I was in my 20s, I thought the key to happiness was to follow the "rules": meet someone, date, and get married. In fact, I already had a boyfriend, and that seemed to be the likely direction this relationship was going – and quickly. Too quickly? Perhaps. I just wasn't sure this particular path was the right road for me.

I decided to ask for Divine help. Before going to bed one night, I prayed fervently and asked for guidance to tell me what to do with this relationship. I unclasped my hands, settled into bed, and lay my head on the pillow. That night, I had a dream.

In the dream, I had just purchased a brand-new, sleek, red motorcycle, and I was ready to take it out for its first run. In my waking life, I'd ridden on the back of my father's motorcycles over the years, but I'd never learned how to drive one myself. In the dream, however, I knew how to ride, and I had a fun, shiny new toy, one that gave me excitement and freedom. I took off down the highway, rode west of my hometown, and gained speed. Suddenly, at a major four-way intersection, I failed to stop in time and ran right into a southbound farm truck.

Luckily, in this dreamscape, no one, including me, was hurt, but my shiny new red motorcycle was bent all out of shape in the hay that had scattered across the road. It was broken beyond repair. Since it was new, however, I still had payments to make on it. The bills would keep coming, and I would need to keep paying them, even though I now had nothing to show for it.

As I opened my eyes from this dream, the words floated through my consciousness: "Slow down, or you'll be paying the consequences."

I had received an answer to my prayer, and my life took a different road.

It's Never Too Late for Happiness

By Severino Concepcion De Los Santos

Sometimes life is full of struggles that never seem to end. I would cry out to God, "Please end my life if this is my existence. I have been hardworking, providing for my four children and the mother of my children."

Living in a third-world country, I suffered in many ways to provide and be an excellent example for my children. My dream was to be with one woman in my life, to have a happy home, to have our children, to work together as a team. Often I have cried to my partner, "Please, I need your help to put food onto the table for our children." The response was not supportive but demanding for me to make money to give to her. Having given all that I can, it seems it is never enough.

I go to work, I sleep, and I try to plan a better future for our life. How can I do this when my partner works against me? While we lived together and shared a bed, I was legally notified of a judgment against me to pay child support. How is this possible? How very uncomfortable.

Moving out of my home was hard. I was pushed out of the relationship. I did not want my children to think that I had abandoned them. My life was providing for them, so nothing would change. I looked at where I wanted to be in life and how I had been treated. This made me want to be alone. I wanted a better life. How could I find happiness? I prayed to God to send an answer.

I met someone who did not speak the same language or live in my country. But I knew in my soul that the suffering was over. If I love her and she loves me, then God has made us the happiest people in the world.

Sometimes God weeds your garden of unhappiness before planting happiness, but we do not see his plans. We must hold true that something good will happen for us.

Keep Your Eyes on Me

By Susan Jacobi

When I was six years old, I met Jesus.

For the first 20 years of my life, I was a victim of child abuse. When I was six, my father came into my bedroom and began his routine of attacking me.

One clear night as the moon shone directly into my room, I found myself mesmerized by the man in the moon. I lay in bed, studying his face, focusing on his eyes, his nose, and his smile. Suddenly, Jesus appeared to me. He was suspended in air, lying on His back. He was wearing a flawless white tunic that flowed beneath Him. He positioned Himself so His eyes would be aligned with mine. As He turned His left ear toward me, our eyes connected.

I remember having no fear when I saw Him. He didn't frighten me. I knew instinctively that I was safe with Him. His eyes showed me a love that I had never experienced. It was pure. It was safe. It was warm and inviting.

As my father proceeded with his choices, Jesus, still looking into my eyes as if they were attached to mine said, "Keep your eyes on me. I will keep you safe. I will help you get ready for school in the morning. I will help you walk to school." And he did. He has always kept His promise to me.

My abuse got more intense as the years went on. My journey to reclaim my life was exhausting and tedious. As I reflect on each abusive act and the steps I took to heal, I see how Jesus kept His promise. Many health professionals have shared their amazement that I survived my history. I know that without Jesus helping me with each step, I would not be here.

I share His message. He is very much alive. Countless times a day when I feel lost or my worries are overtaking my problem-solving mind, I repeat His command: "Keep your eyes on me." That brings me peace now as much as it did when I was six.

A Seed Planted

By B. J. Garcia

*"Children contain the seed of their future and that seed can grow and
flourish when nurtured with unconditional love and acceptance.
Without these qualities, the child slowly begins to close off their heart
out of unconscious fear." – Richard Rudd, founder of the Gene Keys*

In my desperate search to know what my purpose in life was, I went to an intuitive counselor who informed me that I would know my purpose in seven years. Seven years came and went, and I was still clueless as to my purpose.

In my desperation, as I was lying in bed one night, I demanded out loud that God tell me my life's purpose. Lying still and waiting, suddenly I heard from the depths of my being: "You will work with juvenile delinquents."

The thought of this terrified me, and I instantly sat up and shouted, "No way!"

For the next seven years, I denied that this experience had happened. Little did I realize that a seed had been planted in my heart on that day, which I discovered years later while attending a spiritual retreat.

During the retreat, a prison program video was shown. The men interviewed in this video were sharing from their hearts about past criminal behavior and their awakening experiences during their incarceration as they began to know their true self as love. As I listened, their stories touched my heart, and I felt the pain of their past as if it were my own. Even though I had never been incarcerated, it triggered layers of pain inside me, from the wounded child to the juvenile delinquent to the unhappy adult. With this came a new level of awareness, compassion, and understanding for the meaning of a juvenile delinquent.

After watching this video, I knew that my true purpose was leading me to work with men and women in prison. They became my teachers as much as I was theirs. Slowly, I began to let down my defense patterns, open my heart, and heal my childhood wounding through unconditional love, acceptance, and forgiveness.

Choose Love

By Valerie Vestal

Closing the casket brings such finality. I wanted to hold on to Mom as long as I could. Dad and I had agreed that her casket would be open throughout the service. I knew she wasn't really there, but it brought me comfort. I wanted to see the face of the woman who had taught me so much. I can hear her saying, "Where there's a will, there's a way" – the words that supported me to never give up.

The funeral director had observed that the casket lid would hinder guests from seeing the pastor. She ordered her attendants to close the lid. I saw this out of the corner of my eye and immediately brought it to a halt. (I have never been known for being subtle.) I couldn't for the life of me figure out why the funeral director would be concerned about whether or not anyone could see the pastor. It wasn't *her* life we were remembering. After seeing the tattoo reading "I work for shoes" inches above her heels, it was easier to understand. Her tattoo had me question if maybe she had lost touch with the human connection.

Dad is a peacemaker and dislikes making waves. He agreed that the casket would be closed. I gently nodded, acknowledging his words. I was 44 years old when Mom died, no longer a little girl who could be punished for disobedience. My willingness to concede without hesitation was solely out of love for my dad.

Reflecting on the situation, I received a powerful sense of divine wisdom. This is how our Heavenly Father also desires us to develop our relationship with Him. Choosing to follow His word, not out of fear, but from a desire to delight in the will of the Lord with all our hearts. Choose love; follow His word with the love and wonder of a child.

When You Hear God

By Giuliana Melo

In 2011, I was diagnosed with stage-three peritoneal cancer with metastasis to all my female organs and appendix. I was angry with God and cried out, "Why me?"

I actually heard him say, "Why not you, Giuliana?"

To which I responded, "Well if why not me, then I need help! I want to heal my life." This began a great journey to learn, grow, heal, and expand.

In order to heal my life and survive the cancer, I had to change my life. I had to make big choices, and I had to take chances. I had to honour my feelings, all of them: the joy and the pain. When I realized my pain was from wanting to be liked and loved, I began to love myself. When I realized my pain came from wanting to be acknowledged, I began to see who I really was as love and light. When I realized my pain came from hoping to be special, I began to explore the true me. When I realized my pain came from wanting to belong, I recognized I was a part of God and, at a soul level, perfect, whole, and complete. When I realized my pain came from the actions of others, I began to take responsibility for my own life and got into personal mentoring and identified my old story and created a new one. When I realized my pain came from chasing those who didn't want me in their lives, I set myself free.

It is said that the Universe is continuously speaking to us. I hadn't been listening. The diabetes was a whisper, and the cancer was a scream! I was finally ready to listen and tune in to the signs that were continuously being sent to me to guide me on my life path. We all have the gift of intuition. I tuned in and listened and was guided to teachers, people, places, and things to nourish me and help me heal. I learned about angels and how they help us. I now ask them in every day, and I always pay attention and listen.

Clarity in an Instant

By Donna S. Priesmeyer

Several years ago I was restless. I had always loved my chosen profession, but due to circumstances beyond my control, my career path had become a source of frustration. Rather than feeding my soul, my work situation was difficult. I was emotionally and physically drained. After months of dealing with challenges and disappointments, I had a gut feeling that it might be time to move on.

One day as I drove to work, I was dreading going into the office and feeling a sense of angst about my future. I began to pray earnestly for divine guidance. I asked for clarity regarding what I should do – should I stay, in hopes that things would get better, or resign and forfeit the generous salary and benefits I had accrued from years of work and dedication?

Then, in the midst of morning rush-hour traffic, an inner voice clearly spoke these words: "...set yourself, stand ye still, and see the salvation of the Lord." This was a Bible verse (2 Chronicles 20:17) that had often brought me comfort in times of stress and confusion.

"I understand," I said out loud. "I'll take no action until I'm certain it's the right action. I'll continue to do my best every day, maintain a good attitude, and move forward, trusting that I'll know beyond the shadow of a doubt when it's time to go."

Then the car in front of me made a left turn, and the license plate on the car that was now in front of me spelled CLARITY! I was so grateful to have confirmation of my answer in an instant!

I worked another six months, and then, due to budget cuts, my position was eliminated. The amazing thing about this outcome was that I was able to leave my job free from stress and financial worries because I received a severance package and my yearly bonus.

I'm so glad I prayed for guidance that day and really listened. It made all the difference in beginning my new life on a positive note.

Dancing with the Divine

By Julie Vance

As I was reading *Falling into the Arms of God: Meditations with Teresa of Avila* by Megan Don as part of my meditation time, I was drawn to the idea of letting go of expectations of what happens during meditation and relying on Spirit to guide me.

With gentle music in the background, I relaxed into the present moment and asked Spirit to lead me – to take me where I needed to go. I found myself dancing – not with a human partner, but dancing through a field of green – leaping into the air, feeling a gentle breeze blowing my hair, feeling free and at ease with myself and with my life.

I said to myself, "This is how it feels to dance with the Divine in a dance of life." Focused on the presence of Spirit within me, I felt I was part of the rhythm and flow of all of life and one with all that is.

Dancing has always been part of my life. I remember, at the age of five, whirling around the living room with an expression of pure joy on my face, feeling uninhibited and free.

It would be many years – years that took me through the awkwardness of adolescence and junior-high dances, discomfort with my "non-athletic" body, and fear that I might make a mistake – before I would again feel that sense of freedom through the medium of ballroom dancing and years before I would understand that this same freedom comes from "dancing with the Divine" and letting Spirit lead me in my life experiences.

I have talked about my "dance with the Divine" often in the last few years in my writing and through inspirational messages, but this morning, my Inner Spirit reminded me of what it feels like to let go, trust, and dance with the Divine. It was exactly what I needed today!

Beneath the Desk

By Carole "Lisa Lynn" Gilbert

Have you ever relied on yourself to do something, only to wish later that you'd relied on God? I have become a firm believer in seeking God's guidance first.

One particular day, I didn't notice the writing on the wall; I simply jumped in full force. We had bought a house with many remodeling needs, and I had one thing left to do before we moved in: remove a large desk in the laundry room. It was an odd place for a desk, and it had to go. The job looked easy enough, so I grabbed my tools of choice (a crowbar and hammer) and went to work.

My time to remodel each day was limited because I went back and forth between this house and picking up the kids and showing our other house. I spent three hours trying to pry that desk from the wall that day, and it wasn't budging. My time was up. I would either get it out then or I'd have to leave it for another day. I'd already put three holes in the wall that I would now have to fix, but I was determined. So I tried again.

After two more holes and frustrated exhaustion I sat down. I couldn't muscle it anymore! I started to cry. Then I prayed, "God, I can't get it! Will you help me?"

All of a sudden, I felt as though someone was forcibly turning my head to an awkward position, but as I looked forward, there it was: the nail! And then I felt my head being turned to the other side, and there was a second nail! Those two nails beneath the desk were the only things holding it to the wall!

I have no doubt that God showed me those nails that day! It's amazing what we can do when we know Jesus and let God's guidance work through us.

Enjoy the Ride

By Lisa R. Cohen

This prophetic message was received during a meditative writing session:
"So, where do I begin?" I ask.

"Begin with that which you want to avoid."

"Why?" I inquire.

"Because it is causing you undo distress, and you, my dear one, need to be clear minded at all times so that I can speak directly to you without the distraction of anxiety. Remember when I explained that life is analogous to the kiddie ride with the vehicles that spin around, the one in which each child is placed in their assigned fire engine, truck, or car?"

"I do," I reply.

"Each presumes they're in control, but in reality, the operator is regulating the ride. They've yet to figure out that their vehicle is being ultimately controlled by someone other than themselves and can't begin to fathom all that goes on behind the scenes to arrange for them to have this fantastical experience. That's not so different from life, is it?"

I peer through the eyes of a child.

"Have you ever imagined the impact of those who push others aside or relentlessly complain? Have you considered the possible consequences of hesitating, refusing to board, or escaping mid ride?"

I shudder.

My perspective expands as our lively discussion continues. Our gaze shifts, resting upon those eagerly waiting their turn, intuitively trusting that they will not be overlooked. Playfully engaging friends along the way, they explore with reverent curiosity, boldly boarding in divine time.

"The moral of the story...?" I tease.

"Be courteous to those with whom you share the road. Mind your fuel. Celebrate passengers, realign, and maintain balance. Yield to change. Your prayer flares, high beams, and hazard lights summon our imminent assistance."

"Anything else?" I smiled.

"Enjoy the ride!"

Mala Messages

By Heather Wiest

Not many material things catch my attention, but this particular mala bracelet set instantly captured my heart! The striking smoky quartz strand promoted grounding and healing. Unconditional love flowed out of the delicate rose quartz piece. And the beautiful iridescent labradorite string fostered balance, insight, and transformation. The meanings of these semiprecious stones sealed the deal, as each one deeply resonated with my personal soul intentions.

After years of faithfully wearing this dynamic trio of bracelets, the smoky quartz strand broke. Was God confirming grounding and healing in my life? Was complete healing from decades of trauma, fear, self-protection, and controlling behaviors even possible? After years of working through layers of traumatic childhood experiences and the unhealthy coping behaviors adopted as a result, God was gently whispering, "Yes, my precious daughter." I smiled at these thoughts but soon had the smoky quartz restrung.

Months later, the smoky quartz and labradorite strings both broke; beads scattered all over the floor. This mala moment urged me to level up. As I processed another layer of healing, an ultimate breakthrough occurred, and I experienced clarity and renewal. I felt alive! I bowed down in awe and immediately sought the Lord for wisdom and affirmation. I always search the Scriptures for confirmation of messages given. My heart rejoiced as I read, "Jesus turned around, and when He saw her He said, 'Daughter, be encouraged! Your faith has made you well!' And the woman was healed at that moment." (Matthew 9:22, NLT) Wow! It was time to fully live in this deep knowing that I was wholehearted and free! Definitely not perfect, but guided to move forward representing faith, hope, love, and complete healing.

The rose quartz bracelet still adorns my wrist. Along with a newer rose quartz mala around my neck, they remind me that Divine Love never fails. God's unconditional presence, grace, and forgiveness have ultimately transformed me from the inside out, and my purpose is to share this hope that anchors my soul. Let us all HEAL: Heed, Experience, Awaken, Live!

Just Believe

By Michele B. Drzymala

I first met Brenda in 1995, when she lived a few houses down from me. She had an infectious smile, and we shared the joy of having newborn sons. The first time we met, she invited me to her son's first birthday party that same day! At the party, we knew that our boys would end up being best friends, which has remained true for the last 23 years. Over the next two years, we each had a second child and became the closest of friends.

Soon after, Brenda was diagnosed with pre-cancer and was successfully treated. She was subsequently diagnosed with breast cancer and after two surgeries was cancer free.

In 2012, Brenda called to tell me that the cancer had returned and was now in her liver. Amazingly, she remained as positive as always.

On Good Friday of 2016, the Lord called Brenda home. At her viewing, I had never seen such an outpouring of emotion as people gathered together to celebrate her life.

For me, a deep grief set in, and I found myself unable to do anything. I withdrew from those I love and ended up seeking professional help to deal with my complex grief.

In 2017, I attended Relay4Life with my family and placed a luminaria bag at the finish line of the track in her honor.

Later that year, my doctor told me to lean into Brenda and my husband, Jeff. That night, Jeff and I were looking through an old photo album, which contained photos of a time without cancer. I rose to my feet and began to cry tears of joy. As my husband comforted me, in my mind I saw the Relay4Life track. I was breaking the finish-line tape with God and my angels circling the track. The last thing my mind showed me was the luminaria bag. The strong grip of grief released me, and I was free.

Blessed Mother Mary's Invitation to Peace
By M. Lorrie Miller

My husband, Tony, and I were on our way home when we passed a sign for Emmitsburg, Maryland. I felt an immense peace come over me that lasted for hours. I took this as a sign to explore the town further.

Soon after, we drove to Emmitsburg's National Shrine Grotto at Lourdes, a replica of the original Lourdes in France, where Bernadette saw apparitions of Blessed Mother Mary. When we visited, I experienced the same profound serenity as before and received messages from Mary to guide my life.

Several years later I was in a car accident that turned my life upside down. I prayed to Mary for healing and direction. She instructed me to write the script for my desired life, as if I were already healed. She also asked me to write the book *An Invitation to Co-Creation: Blessed Mother Mary's Invitation to Humanity to Co-Create the Way to Inner and World Peace.*

Mary said that this invitation is inclusive of all faiths and spiritual paths based on love, and it is offered to everyone desiring divine help to create joyful, purposeful lives. The goal of Mary's invitation is to heal ourselves, our communities, and our world. Healing occurs as we experience inner peace, which we then extend to the world. The path to peace also involves seeing the world as an "us," choosing love and respect for one another, and appreciating our diversity.

My own invitation to co-creation has been an opportunity to look at what needs to change in order to align my life with my soul's purpose. This has included coming out of the spiritual closet, speaking my truth, and living more authentically. I am tremendously humbled that Blessed Mother has entrusted me with her writing project and am immensely thankful for her help in finding my voice and sharing her message of peace and oneness. I have experienced so many positive life changes on this journey. My healing continues, and I cherish Mary's ongoing love and support as she guides me to peace, purpose, and wholeness.

My Forgotten Prayer

By Carole "Lisa Lynn" Gilbert

I wasn't always surrounded by beauty. When I was a little girl, my mother was tragically killed. It was the murder that shook our small country town. After that I lived in different homes with different families, averaging a move every six months. During that time, I saw the evil side of this world that I never knew existed. I prayed and begged God to give me back my safe, loving home, but He didn't answer. This was a big prayer for a child.

Fast-forward almost 50 years, and I can say I've lived in the same house for the past 20 years. I now pray for others and hear about their answers from God, but I had long forgotten that childhood prayer of mine that God never answered and I had long stopped praying it.

One day as I was walking through my house looking out toward the lake, I realized that God is answering my prayers every day! And the answer to that long-forgotten childhood prayer of a safe, loving home was all around me. God had never forgotten! That day I understood Psalm 37:4 about God giving us the desires of our heart if we take delight and hope and seek Him. I now see how God answers our prayers, our desires, in the small things and in small ways, too. Things like that secure comfort of our homes, being able to pursue the creativity of our talents that also come from God, and every color of everything we see, like the landscape out my window that I look at daily.

God wants us to have enjoyment, to have the desires of our hearts, even the desires we've long forgotten. God wants to answer our every prayer. The signs of God are there. We just have to look. I hope you seek God and see how He wants to give you your desires. I know He gives me mine.

Receiving the Holy Spirit

By Jodi Cross

While on a retreat in North Wales with a group of energy healers, we were taken to visit a Franciscan monastery, nestled in a pretty valley at the edge of a steep wooded hill. The monastery had a beautiful woodland walk, spiraling up past the stations of the cross, each with a small vista of its own, until it reached the summit glade where an ancient wooden cross stood proud and strong. After our picnic lunch at the foot of the huge cross, we were asked to spend time in contemplation and meditation. It was suggested that we could stay on the hill or explore the monastery and rose gardens, then we'd meet at the appropriate time to return to the retreat centre.

I spent time wandering the rose garden, drinking in the heady aroma and the explosion of colour, snapping photographs as I slowly made my way across to the chapel. As I entered the little sunlit chapel, a huge sense of calm washed over me. I was completely alone. I walked slowly across the back of this sacred space, enjoying the peace and tranquility. As I turned to walk up towards the altar, I felt guided to a certain spot just to the left of the altar table. My angels and guides were surrounding me. I stood in silence, connecting to Jesus, St. Francis, and God. The energy was incredible, palpable, holy.

I have no idea how long I stood in that sacred space, but I was aware of the click of the door and a person's footfall, followed by the creak of an oak pew, somewhere in the midst of pure peace, pure love, pure calm.

After a while, I felt the energy release and the holy presence gently recede. I stepped back and bowed my head in reverence. Turning to leave, I noticed a fellow student who beckoned me to join him. He turned to me and said, "I've just witnessed something amazing: I just saw the Holy Spirit enter your body as a Pure White Dove!"

My Father's Hand

By Jordann Scruggs

*"Fear not, for I am with you; be not dismayed, for I am your God; I
will strengthen you, I will help you, I will uphold you with my
righteous right hand." – Isaiah 41:10*

When I was a somewhat rebellious child, my Southern Baptist
grandmother would drag me to church, but the only thing I received
from those sermons was chewing gum offered for my silence.

Sometime later, my parents abandoned the responsibility of our
family, and my siblings and I were sent to an orphanage. Church
meetings were mandatory – no excuses! Like most adolescents, I slept
through the services. However, one Sunday I was awakened by a "fire-
and-brimstone exhortation." Fear of "burning in hell" made me race
down the aisle to accept Christ, without completely understanding the
significance of the act.

Fortunately, I heard the invitation of salvation again and, being
somewhat older, clearly understood the commitment of accepting Jesus
as my personal Savior.

That summer I attended a church camp at Kentucky Lake. In the
mornings, we would slip into the silence of the woods and meditate
upon the Word. At night, lined up in front of a bonfire, we sang hymns
and praised God. One evening, I managed to be at the end of the line,
away from the others. In childlike sincerity, I asked for God's help in
finding His path for my life. There in the stillness, I felt a large, powerful
yet gentle Hand press down on my right shoulder. In an instant, the
Hand was gone. Startled, I looked around, but no one was near me. His
answer to my prayer had been assuring and simple.

I still marvel at the simplicity of God's salvation. John 3:16 tells us,
"For God so loved the world that He gave His only Son, that whoever
believes in Him shall have eternal life." Believe in God, acknowledge
your sin, and you will spend eternity with God. It's that simple.

God has always been faithful and kept His promises to me. And
after all these years, I still feel My Father's Hand.

There Is Only One Message

By Lindsay S. Godfree

Angels are present all around us and want nothing more than to be of service to each of us. You only have to ask and messages appear.

As an Angel Oracle, I have a message for you at this perfect time. When I asked the question, "What is it that they most need to hear now?" this was the angels' answer:

Remember that your life is just a picture of Source energy as it moves through you and presents as experience for translation into the physical world. Your interactions with others are the bounceback of the energy.

Everything every day is a sacred practice. It can't be any other way; it is all energetic information. Just be open and pay attention. Be loving and kind.

We know that you want your life to be meaningful. Everything *is* meaningful – that is the magic. It is all around you, in every breath you take. So do not concern yourself with "meaningful."

It (the meaning of your life) is what you say it is. Take whatever meaning you want; make no judgment of it but only delight in it.

It is like the play of light on the water. See how it sparkles and moves. Feel how it delights you, that simple pattern and the shifting of the forces of nature.

Now you get the picture. All of it is the play of the light.

Be easy about the journey. There really is no race to be run, no finish line to cross. Everything just *is* and is perfect, just as that water and wave and that reflection of the light. It is as perfect as the energy dancing.

We will give you this message over and over, and you will resonate it for others who will resonate it for those they touch. All of life is sounding off as the harmony and melody and all the various overtones of Oneness.

There is only one message – the message of love, of praise, and of glory to God.

The Window in the Sky

By Heidi Cohen-Barocas

My words illustrate my journey as a spiritual seeker, looking at acts of nature that never duplicate. These powerful messages come from God's paintbrush. The meanings are generated through the eyes, mind, heart, and soul. Reality ultimately belongs to the individual self.

A real window of light appeared surrounded by the dark rain clouds. These small miracles began to inspire Divine Downloads; the action taken was to sit on the bench and receive these messages:

What is it I see from the window? I see what is not seen through my eyes alone. There is this beautiful world of pleasure and pain. I see them both expressed. The window may appear small. To me, this is my glimpse of Divine Light.

I see the light and the darkness. There is so much that is hidden in those strange clouds. This is my chance to realize that the clouds have their purpose, that everything has a purpose. What is contained within and behind those clouds? There is so much uniqueness there to take inside my heart.

This is when I hear God speak – the creation of the window reveals a purpose within everything. My eyes continue to look up. My focus sees what's unique, Divine Light. I realize it is time to look inside my heart.

All of those clouds are hiding the essence of light. From my human perspective, I know that my heart and soul contain Divine Light. It is hidden and not seen with the eyes. It is expressed like the sky does with the weather. This really is all an expression, revealed in its own particular way.

My pose demonstrates the light and darkness in my mood. It is communicated by my heart's expression. Can I see my purposeful human perspective? Yes, it is the realization of Divine Light. I realize that our kindness contains the light.

After reflecting on the messages, I discovered the evidence of inner light in an individual. These magical moments enclothe us with radiance. They show the human potential and reveal a bit of brightness within the darkness of the clouds.

I Never Leave You

By Lisa R. Cohen

This prophetic message was received during a series of meditative writing sessions:

Unto you I give life. Amongst the flock yet once again…

Thus in essence you travel in new vessels of which vestiges of time know no limits. A course of study, lest you know sorrow and pain, bearing ripe fruit from which all shall eat.

Unto you I sing; unto you I bring my glory in all that is, was, and will be. For you, as well as all those who accompany you are instruments of divine healing, purposeful mighty harbingers of change delivered unto this world to please me.

Forget not from where'th you came and know that you have not traveled too far from my gaze, never too far from my grasp. You are forever within my reach.

For within I placed a natural navigation system orienting you toward my light, the light of your redeemer. You are luminous!

Know from the source of that which you came. It is my wind that set your wings on a trajectory. From where you are to where you go, I steer clear of harm and wrongdoings.

From that which I came, unto that which I go, is one and the same, a continuum of sound from that which I compose and play magnificent music for all to hear the sweet sounds of your soul, the signature sounds of surrender to all that is, was, and will be.

Little ones, come and listen to my song of peace, intricately woven with the dynamics of sounds in motion, delicately put in place for you to partake in.

Still now, little one; although our waters appear to part, that is yet another illusion.

So sleep, rest, and I will come to you in your hour of need. For you who know only to drink from my cup that overflows with love for all, which I quench the thirst of. Share your desires with me. Meet me in your dreams; I shall be there and in every wakeful moment. For I never leave you during your absence, brief or lengthy, I wait for you to return to my loving embrace.

Angel Helpers

By M. Lorrie Miller

It was the Friday before Memorial Day, and my husband, Tony, and I were ready to celebrate at our favorite seaside restaurant. We decided to go for a late lunch, since the place is always crowded. Before we left, I said a prayer to get us safely to and from our destination. I also asked our angels for help with parking and a table with a view. When we got to the restaurant, the parking lot was packed. However, just as we pulled in, three cars pulled out. We got a great table with the same ease. Service was prompt, and lunch was delicious. We savored the afternoon and the amazing view.

After lunch, we ran a quick errand, and then we were back on the road. We had only gone a few miles when we heard the disheartening *flop, flop, flop* sound of our tire blowing out. We were on a busy highway with no shoulder, and it was rush hour. Luckily, my husband managed to pull into a nearby side street. He checked our spare tire, and it was flat too. Ugh! On a holiday weekend, we could wait hours for a tow truck.

Tony called AAA and told them our dilemma. They said they would call back with our estimated wait time. While we were waiting, my husband remarked that we could see through the houses to the next street where Angel Park is located. Angel Park is a playground, and Tony was one of the volunteers who helped build it a few years ago.

This seemed like a fortuitous sign, and I said another prayer to the angels to help expedite our wait for the tow. Soon afterward, we got notice that our tow was scheduled to arrive shortly. It was less than twenty minutes from our initial call for help until the tow truck showed up! Before we knew it, we were back home again.

Thank you, Angel Helpers, for a delightful day out and for getting us back home safe and sound!

As Doors Slammed Shut

By Joy T. Barican

When you are doing well in your job and have been handpicked to execute a work program with the enticement of a promotion, it is gut wrenching when you're denied the promotion, especially after successfully executing the role for two years and receiving two nominations for the RISE Award (Recognising Inspirational Service Excellence). This experience was quite unpalatable. In spite of keeping an open mind, I could not help that a sense of distrust, injustice, and resentment started to develop.

Mum reminded me not to focus on the hurt but to trust that whatever is behind the door God had shut was not meant for me.

With my career progression hampered, I was left no choice but to contemplate exploring opportunities outside the organisation. As this door slammed shut, I refused to linger regretfully upon the closed door, as I might miss seeing the one that would open for me.

I prayed for divine guidance. Not long after, the answer came in the form of an opening in another department. As I generally like the company, I thought it was worth giving it a second chance. After all, what had transpired was not necessarily a reflection of the entire company's values and policies but of a few individuals' shortcomings.

I applied for the position, but, yet again, it was not meant to be. Although I felt despondent, I recalled Mum's advice and accepted that rejection is God's protection.

I again prayed for divine guidance and strength. The answer to my prayers could not have come at a better time. Indeed, missing out on the promotion was a blessing in disguise. Synchronicity played a huge part where my role was made redundant, qualifying me for an amount that served as an enabler of dreams.

Time and again, God has demonstrated how no one can open the door He closes, and no one can close the door He opens.

Don't Give Up

By Michelle Anne Gould

For years, my life had been a beautiful party of friendships, variety, and enriching experiences. I felt like a master of the Law of Attraction – surrounding myself with brilliant people at the top of their fields, becoming a leader in my own right, and tapping into my free spirit and independence. I cherished every single breath of life. But after I had my first child, my life took a 180° turn.

Motherhood itself was amazing, and my love for my child was boundless. However, my health suffered, and my relationship with my baby's father rapidly deteriorated. Piece by piece, my world seemed to crumble around me. My joyful, vibrant self descended into fear, and the lightness in my heart shut down. I felt like I'd landed in a foreign place where universal laws no longer worked – like I'd been hurled into someone else's nightmare.

I tried to pick myself up, deciding to be a beautiful role model for my children, and enrolled in studies that would allow me to support my family and create a beautiful avenue for my heart to soar and shine. But this just turned out to be another wrong turn, leading me through an even darker door. Every step forward resulted in 10 backward, until I felt like malevolent beings were attacking me at every corner as I walked through the shadow of death. I prayed, cried, and screamed at God daily until I finally gave up and surrendered, which is when I actually died in my sleep, hearing myself say the word "over."

Miraculously, the Holy Spirit brought me back and gave me new life. Upon awakening, I didn't know where I was, but I found peace in a sign that read "Don't give up; even Moses was a basket case."

Now I tell myself this message: Don't give up. Keep your eyes on love. You've got this.

The Redeemer

By Lorre Leigh

The pain from infidelity can be crippling. It stops your heart from beating and your mind from reasoning, and the world as you know it seems to stop spinning. I was frozen in heartbreak and anger.

During this time, I was gifted a book, *The Blessed Marriage*, by a close friend. I was hesitant to read it because I felt I was not the one in this relationship who needed this enlightenment, but when I did, the words hit me instantly. "Marriage is the image of God. Two become one, just as He is One, bringing Him ultimate glory and channeling abundant blessing to their union and family. This is the blessed marriage."

These words resounded so loudly because, from the moment I accepted Jesus as my Saviour, all I desired was for His character to be seen in me, to bring Him glory. Now I had to consider that perhaps I was not as blameless in the condition of my marriage as I thought. Perhaps my own character was not reflecting what it should. I read further. "Your relationship needs a redeemer. The redeemer is the one who dies first."

The next paragraph challenged me to commit to doing my part and accept my husband's responsibilities, even if he did not. I immediately became defensive.

"Absolutely not! This isn't fair! Why should I be the one to die?! I didn't do anything wrong! I won't do it!"

Then, a gentle voice said, "Interesting. What if Jesus had said that? What if He had said, 'No, this isn't fair; I didn't do anything wrong'? Where would you be if that was His attitude?"

"Well, I'm not Jesus!" I shouted.

Silence.

After a long pause, I asked, "Why me?"

"Because you asked to reflect my character. This is my character."

So I forgave someone I had vowed to love for better or worse. It didn't save my marriage, but it created in me the understanding that I will live my life through forgiveness, as I have been forgiven.

Can You Hear Me?

By Jean Hendricks

Our beloved cat passed away, leaving me devastated. My husband knew I needed to wait before we adopted another one. I needed time to heal.

Occasionally he would ask, but I wasn't ready. Then one night while watching TV, I heard Archangel Michael's voice inside my head. Although I didn't have the gift of hearing, I understood him perfectly and tried to ignore him because he told me it was time to get a cat. Appeasing him, I said, "Sure, during Christmas vacation." Heck no. Michael wanted us to get a cat *now*. Sigh.

He guided me to a local pet store's website. I grabbed my laptop and did as asked. As I scrolled through the pictures on the page, I saw *the cat* – I knew. I asked him, "This one, right?" Yes. Turning the laptop toward my husband, I asked, "Want to adopt this cat?" He started crying, nodding his head yes.

I then heard Michael say not one, but two cats. Huh? We ended up adopting both Harvey and his sister Wendy. We brought them home, but Harvey wasn't well. The vet said he was very, very sick and had to stay for treatment. I cried on the way home from the vet and, between the sobs, yelled at Michael, "Do you hear me? How could you ask me to adopt a cat that might die?" My heart and soul knew the Michael wouldn't do something like that, but the human "me" doubted.

Thankfully, Harvey is fine now, a spitfire who chases his sister. Michael restored my fear of losing a loved one. Harvey's recovery strengthened my faith. Michael blessed me by allowing me to keep my clairaudience, and we've since had countless conversations. But even more importantly, Harvey is healthy.

My husband calls Harvey my tail. That's true: we are linked. We have a deep soul connection. He's my teacher who meditates with me. I've learned much from him. He's taught me to keep the faith, take time to play, and not to give up. Every time I look at his face, I melt and my soul shines. Thank you, Michael. I heard you.

A Gracious, Loving Presence

By Noemi Grace

I sat on the window seat and reached for the weathered book. Its title, *An Autobiography of a Christian Mystic*, was barely visible. The spine cracked as I opened it, and mustiness filled my nostrils.

The sun's rays danced across the page, highlighting a single sentence: "I sought to know a gracious, loving presence." The words lingered as I read them aloud and looked at my parents' smiling faces. My heart filled with love and appreciation for them as never before.

As I relished the moment, I heard Karen Drucker singing, "I am healed, whole, and healthy. I am well." I sat upright, dazed yet acutely aware of every nuance of that dream.

Then, in a flash of insight, I understood that my parents and I wanted the same thing: to know the gracious, loving presence of God. Suddenly, the difference in our approaches didn't matter.

Those few seconds transformed my relationship with my parents. I stopped judging them and started sharing myself more authentically, even though I expected them to judge me. But they never did. Then I realized that the judgment I experienced in our relationship mostly came from me.

Every day, I also began to affirm, "I want to know the gracious, loving presence," and those words filled me with joy. When I shared the dream with a friend, she said emphatically, "*You* are the gracious, loving presence you seek to know."

That shocked me, and I protested, "I'm not that gracious or loving." But I decided to do a test and created a new mantra: "I am a gracious, loving presence." I encountered internal resistance but affirmed it anyway. To my surprise, I became more gracious and loving toward myself and others.

This one dream dissolved the volumes of judgment I'd held toward myself and my parents. It also enabled me to know myself as a gracious, loving presence and to know them as the kind, generous, loving people they are. What an amazing gift from the only dream I can remember in years.

More Than a Dream

By Jamie Thomas

I arrived one warm spring day at a small lake with a friend and met with another friend of hers for an event they were hosting. It ended up being the three of us on a little wooden dock, a scraggly tree listing up from the water's gently rolling surface.

The trees hid homes and park benches behind their leaves, as green as the grass that grew from the ground and shone in the sunlight. We were all standing, hands in the air with fingers and thumbs forming a circle as my friend and I followed our sandy-haired acquaintance in a t'ai chi movement. I vaguely caught a glimpse of my friend's dark, curly hair and smiled, reflecting on how we likely looked and how little I cared in relation to the contentment and peace I felt, when I froze at a realization: I had dreamt this before.

All of it. Not a moment of déjà vu. I remembered every detail from my dream, from my friend's dark, curly hair and the clothing she wore over her olive skin to her friend's sandy hair and our movements as we looked out over the water from the dock, with the tree to our right. I had dreamt this – and remembered the familiarity I had felt with these people from the dream, even though I hadn't known them then.

Here I was, living in a dream I'd had years ago. In that instant, every belief and thought I had about what was possible, what was real, was shaken to its core. I felt a stunning, almost cold realization that much of what I doubted, despite my upbringing and various gatherings I had attended, could be very real. Suddenly, all the spiritual so-called nonsense I heard from some people didn't seem so impossible anymore.

Since then, I've experienced so much that many would write off as hallucinations, night terrors, or tricks of the mind. But after that dream and several others like it, I seriously question those assumptions and just how much of what I've experienced is momentary delusion…or something far more significant.

In My Father's House

By Jodi Cross

Walking through the gate as it creaked and groaned open, I grabbed for my granny's hand. Her kid gloves felt as soft as a kiss. I needed her support for this very special event. Looking up, I realised that the black metal gates were even taller than my granny: huge, strong, and grand, guarding the way to the most important building in the village.

St. James Village Church stood at the top of the hill, a place of quiet contemplation and reverence, and this was my first visit to Sunday School. This was my granny's church, and I was allowed to attend this very special class, as I would be four years old very soon.

Walking up the hill towards this majestic, honey-coloured stone structure, Granny had explained to me the importance of the church.

"It is a place for people to connect and talk to God, to say their prayers to him, sing hymns to him, and join in communion with the village to thank God for all our blessings. Because it is God's house, you must be very respectful and listen carefully to the Sunday School teacher who is going to teach you all about Jesus, God, and Heaven."

Holding tightly to Granny as she turned the huge metal ring to open an enormous oak door, I felt that something important was about to take place. As we stepped over the threshold, the cool air within was filled with a strange yet comforting perfume. I stood in awe as the shards of bright colours danced on the pews from the windows above. It was magical. I realised that Granny was talking to an elegant lady who was going to be my teacher, as a gentle arm guided me to sit with the other children. My granny's voice drifted through my thoughts, "I'll be back to take you home when it finishes."

Home? This is my home! I felt completely at home here. Every cell of my body knew that this is where I belonged. I felt complete; I felt happy in my Father's house.

God's Perfect Timing

By Julie Vance

Turning points in my life seem to begin with struggle. The most recent of these was my decision to retire from my ministry after 25 years of service.

For months, maybe even years, I had felt that I was being guided to take an extended period of time to "dance with the Divine" – my process for listening and following inner guidance – at a deeper level, to explore who I was and what was next for me at this stage of my life.

Letting go of the ministry I had founded and the congregation I had loved for many years was not easy for me. I enjoyed the Sunday services, teaching classes, and sharing in the lives of my spiritual family but felt ready to be free of the administrative duties and the feeling of being on call 24 hours a day, seven days a week.

Frequently, I would ask, "Is this the time for me to leave?" and then immediately follow that question with "I am not ready yet. I can't leave my spiritual family."

My prayer was that when it was the right time for me to leave, I would know without a doubt.

One day in the spring of 2016, I was sitting in the Sanctuary, gazing at the stained-glass windows, feeling the peace and harmony I always felt there. Gently and lovingly, I heard the words from deep within myself: "It is time for you to leave." This time my response was different because I was ready and knew it was time. I simply heard the words: "I know."

Within a year, I retired from Unity of Palmyra. It was the right time. The transition process, although filled with times of joy and sadness, was, for the most part, smooth and easy. A transitional minister was hired, and I completed my time there in an atmosphere of appreciation and love. The church is thriving, I am enjoying exploring new options in my life, and I continue to open to God's perfect timing.

Greg's Gift

By Destrie Sweet Larrabee

Greg had been valiantly fighting the good fight against cancer, doing everything he could to live his life to the fullest, right to the very end. But eventually, he knew that the time had arrived.

As much as we had all prepared for this moment – each of us with our personal relationship, as well as that glorious relationship we had as an amazingly loving, connected family – we couldn't know how it would actually *be* until it came. And, truly, I never could have prepared for the amazing gift I received from my brother-in-law, who became as close as any birth brother ever could have been.

As he left his earthly remains, the entire hospital room lit up with showers of glorious bursts of beautiful sparks of what I knew to be – without question – pieces of Greg's love/Life Force flying out into the Universe and into the hearts of all those whom he had loved and those who love him, starting with my sister – his wife of 35 years and soulmate for 59 years.

When I felt his spark, I thought my heart would absolutely burst with the joy, love, and the absolute sense of freedom I felt. He was finally free, sharing all that he was, is, and always shall be with his loved ones and the Universe.

In that moment, I truly understood that no one ever leaves us. We are all connected by love forever. All we have to do is listen to our hearts with love.

Amen. A'ho. And so it is, has been, and always shall be!

Snow Angels

By Jean Hendricks

A light snow fell one December morning, and the forecast called for even harder snow to the south – the direction I needed to travel for work. Despite the weather, I felt I had to go in because it was the final day of testing prior to a new product launch. There was still so much left to do!

I grabbed my coffee and briefcase and headed to our satellite location, 40 miles from home. As I traveled down the highway, the snowfall grew heavier. Nearing one exit, I felt my car fishtail. I felt that my angels were trying to persuade me to turn around. On top of the dangerous conditions, I was approaching an unfamiliar area without a GPS. Despite my concerns, I decided to keep going, driving a little slower.

Since I hadn't followed their guidance the first time, my angels soon made their point a little stronger. As I neared the next exit, my car fishtailed again. With a sigh of surrender, I said out loud to my angels: "Okay, message received. I'm turning around and going home."

Ten minutes from home, the driver's windshield wiper stopped working. It was hard to see out the window with the snow falling. I used my snow brush to clear my window and realized that if I had taken the exit from the first fishtail, I probably would have been just a few minutes from home. Although I was a little nervous, I believed that the angels were watching over me. I stopped at our local gas station and got a ride home.

I was very thankful for my angels' perseverance, ensuring I acted on their message. They are always with us, watching over us, and guiding us. That day, they showed me how they try using different means to get my attention and deliver their message. They can see the bigger picture. We always have a choice of whether to heed their advice. What a blessing to have angels in our life looking out for us, no matter the weather.

Chapter 8
Messages from Our Hearts to Yours

I magine that you get your "15 minutes of fame" and have the chance to talk to the entire world. What would you say? What story would you tell? What values would you encourage? What inspiration would you offer? What message would you share?

Now imagine that you have to put this message into writing and condense it into a single page. What words would you use?

This is the challenge accepted by the authors in this chapter. In the pieces that follow, these authors share the stories that are nearest and dearest to their hearts. They offer the gifts that they most want to give to others. And they deliver the messages that they feel are most important to them…and to the world.

Some of them offer inspiration for everyday living: how to wake up, stop living on autopilot, and embrace your true calling. Some of them share visions for humanity, messages of peace, and reasons to hope for the future. And some of them encourage you to look within your own heart to uncover the profound messages that lie within.

Some of these pieces will likely resonate with your own inner knowing, while others may awaken you to new possibilities for how you see the world and how you live. Perhaps some of them may resonate so deeply that they change your life forever. But no matter how these messages affect you, we hope that you connect with the hearts and souls who so lovingly offer these messages…and that they touch your heart as much as they've touched ours.

My Wake-Up Call

By Cindy Lyon

I used to live my life on autopilot. What does this mean, you ask? Well, it means that I used to think that life just "happened" to me. I didn't consider myself to be a co-creator in my own life. I focused all my attention outside myself by worrying about what everyone thought of me, measuring my worth by what I had tangibly achieved, and burdening myself with a limiting belief that life was hard and I needed to fight for what I wanted. I was reacting to life. I felt like a victim of whatever came my way without understanding that I was orchestrating all my experiences and relationships. I had no idea of my power and completely no awareness of my magical connection with the Universe.

You see, we are all responsible for being exactly where we are in our life. We write our story every single day, and we are able to change our storyline every single day if we choose to. When we make the decision to just feel our emotions instead of numbing them, to simply look at our relationships as a mirror and listen to our heart's desires, we are free to live our life on "purpose."

I began living my life on purpose after I took complete responsibility for being hit head-on by a transport truck. I learned from Oprah that life whispers to us to create change. If we do not listen, then life throws us pebbles to pay attention, and if we do not feel those pebbles, then life throws us bricks. Because I was not receptive to life's whispers, pebbles, or even bricks, life hit me with a Mack truck, and I am forever grateful.

That one single incident woke me up from my unconscious living and introduced me to myself, my soul, and my relationship with the Universe. This gift helped me get a fresh start on life by releasing me from my job, my marriage, and my home in order to make room for a more abundant life.

What's Your Message?

By Janet G. Nestor

Human beings honor the teachings of many great spiritual leaders and embrace their heart-filled messages. We read books and articles about their lives, and their wisdom becomes part of our culture.

However, messages don't just come from spiritual masters; they also come from everyday people. They flow from the media, social institutions, friends, family, and spirit. They come to us in dreams. We are awestruck by an inspirational cloud formation, touched by a movie plot, or moved by the meaning we find in the words of a song. Inspiration arrives through a stranger's smile or a surprise meeting with an old friend. Each message is important, as is each messenger.

My life turned out much better than it might have because I received important messages from a special uncle, a ninth-grade teacher, and my great-grandmother who gave me permission to use my insight and intuition. But messages don't only come from those we know. Almost anyone can offer us a message if we look for it. Did you ever think the homeless man begging at the stoplight might be a messenger sent to raise awareness of human suffering? Do you recognize that the activists working for human rights are messengers? Did you ever think of your local animal-rescue group as a messenger?

Our children are also messengers. They bring hope for a kinder world. Their presence guides us and often opens our eyes to new ideas and beliefs. Their messages often bring about important social change. And we, as their messengers, have the responsibility to inspire and motivate them to become their best selves. The family we create – loving and supportive or chaotic and dysfunctional – shapes the ideas, beliefs, social views, and life-skills of its members. It impacts the worth, confidence, and worldview of the youngest generation.

Please know that you are a messenger, too. You deliver messages every day, and it is unlikely that you know you've delivered them. Any choice you make and any action you take has meaning to someone. You impact many lives. Your presence is your strongest message, and love is your most precious gift. Your loving presence will change the world for the better.

My Blank Space

By Ayeesha S. Kanji

In the past year, I've learned to manage stress effectively and balance my time while maintaining a full-time job, volunteering, writing, and dancing. During this time, I've found that the trick with stress is accepting what you can control and what is not in your control. Throughout this learning process, I've let go of toxic surroundings, stopped multitasking constantly, and made the effort to live a healthy lifestyle.

A big part of this also included allowing myself to have "blank space" in my life. This means allowing myself to enjoy doing nothing. All too often, we are "busy" or always doing something.

I always remind myself that the only person who stops me from doing anything is actually myself. That means the feeling of being "too busy" or "overwhelmed" is actually on me for feeling that way. When I realized the toll it took on me, I stopped and said to myself, "I need space" – and I decided to create blank space for myself.

It is not emotional space or physical space but "blank" – space just to recharge and rejuvenate. Most people would use exercise to recharge and rejuvenate, but blank space means taking time to just sit with yourself. It can be whatever and however you want it to be because it is your choice how you spend that time.

Time keeps moving and will not come back. Make the time for blank space before the feeling of "busyness" draws you in. The whole world is busy. Take time for blank space before feeling drained from everything around that draws you in. It's worth it because you are worth it.

Light the Way

By Janet Stefanelli

One morning, at the start of a busy shift, I looked at the report and saw that "Mildred" would transition from her beautiful life journey today. Her dedicated husband of 62 years, "Joe," had sat vigil by her bedside since admission, rarely taking time for himself.

When I entered the room, I knew right away that she would die in the next few hours. I then turned to Joe and gently asked him, "Is there anything I can do for you?"

Startled by my question, he began to reminisce about their life together, how he missed her deeply because she had been ill for some time now. Then he whispered, "I just wish I could lie beside her one last time, for I know our time together is very limited."

Wanting to grant his last loving wish and gift to his wife, I raised both side rails up on one side of the bed and gently moved her to that side. Fixing her hair and adjusting her comatose body, I said to him, "She is ready now for you to lie beside her, one last time."

With tears rolling down his cheeks, he asked, "Are you sure?"

I nodded, assisted him into the hospital bed, and granted his greatest desire. I placed the other side rail up, covered them both, closed the door, and wept quietly outside the room. I realized in that moment what being a light truly meant: vulnerable, grace-filled, open, compassionate, and loving.

That scenario has played in my mind often. I felt different. I *was* different. I looked at my perspectives, my thoughts, my goals, and my priorities with a greater sense of worth, wonder, compassion, gratitude, and love.

We are all beacons of love and light, and we never know when we will be called upon to bring that light into someone's darkness. The best gift we can receive is feeling how the love and light we share opens a portal to our own soul. Choose to be a bright beacon of light in this world! Shine on!

Caressing Life with Heart

By Stacy Feliciano

Every day (well, almost every day) I sit with my journal and a colored pen, nestled in my special place I call my heartspace. As I sit with excitement, I can't wait to see what message my heart has for me today, as if hearing a romantic message from my love. It's an adventure of sorts – I never know what will pour out. Some days I begin with a rant, others with a question, and sometimes random words that lead to a heartfelt felt message for me. Most times, the entries end with a voice that speaks *to* me.

As a kid, I never told anyone about this, fearing that I'd be deemed crazy. Now, I've come to appreciate these messages, and I'm ready to share this one that recently arrived. I start to write...

Today may be the best day; today may be the worst day. Whatever it may be, it is a moment in time and will change with each heartbeat of your life. Put one hand on your heart and one hand on your belly and breathe into your life.

Breathe in the bright morning sun, or the darkness of the night, and keep the wind at your back. Today, for each moment, caress the senses of life. Enjoy the warmth of the sun or the cold of the night. Know that you are alive and meant to be here, with me right now, reading this message from my heart to yours.

This challenge of life, the hardness of reality – without this, we will not change our inner condition of life. We must endure what feels unbearable and uncomfortable. This is the very substance that will propel us to change our life.

Your function is to *be* and experience life. Find your heartspace, walk in this sensory-driven reality where we can change our life and our world with connection, courage, and compassion.

This is a message from my heart.

Say a Little Prayer for Me

By Marla David

Lately, while scrolling down my Facebook page, I've noticed a lot of people reaching out for prayers – either for themselves or for a loved one or pet. I'm pleased to see that people aren't afraid to ask for help, and they want others to join in prayer. It's also refreshing to see how people are showing their vulnerability more. That's what being human is all about. We're here in this Earth classroom, and to be our authentic self, we must be raw and honest. It goes with the territory. In a cold, hard, and divided world, this is a ray of light.

All over the world, people pray in their own personal ways and for their own personal reasons. For some, prayer is a way to reach something greater than themselves. Some people pray to express gratitude, such as by using the Ho'oponopono prayer: "I'm sorry, please forgive me, thank you, I love you." And some people pray to convey wishes or ask for something, which is also an important part of life. I believe, as with the yin and yang of life, it's essential to give as well as receive. Also, if you don't ask, how can you receive? Creating the flow keeps things from being stagnant and allows for growth.

Throughout my life, I've prayed in many ways and for many reasons. While visiting the Western Wall in Jerusalem, I pushed a slip of paper with my little prayer into the crevice of the rocks, just as millions had done before me. I've also given slips of paper to others visiting Jerusalem, to place in the wall for me. I do believe, though, that once a message is created in your thoughts, it is sent out into the universe.

People often get disillusioned when their prayers don't come to fruition, but because we don't know the grand scheme of things, we don't have any way of knowing whether the prayer didn't come true for some good reason. This belief requires trust, which can only be achieved by detachment from the outcome. In the meantime, say a little prayer for me, and know I will say a little prayer for you also.

The Secret Guidance of the Heart

By Marina Malmberg

The voice of your heart is the voice of your core that hides the wisdom of your unique path.

In modern life, we are facing a challenge of living through our inner guidance. This difficulty makes us choose logic, trends, fears, biased ideas, and cultural and social conditioning instead. Our mental baggage piles up on our heart's desire and makes it harder and harder to hear the heart's guidance. The mind always takes us the traditional way; the heart keeps whispering the message of our path. The choice is for us to make.

My heart took my life in a way I'd never planned, yet it was fantastic. This path led to my soulmate from another culture and generation. Our love cost my traditional career. We moved to Pakistan, where I had no work permit as a corporate expat spouse. Instead, Lahore gave me yoga and a spiritual teacher with whom I emerged in the art of natural healing, my true passion.

Stark contrasts of cultures enrich us in unexpected ways. Pakistan expanded my heart and gave me the gift of healing. Thirteen years later, I still miss this mysterious country, as well as my friends and other people who surrounded us with so much care and kindness. I am ever grateful to my journey taking a route I'd never planned.

Looking back at my life journey through four very different cultures and countries, I see a completed puzzle where the last piece was the gift of my heart guidance. This was hard for me to grasp, as my mind struggled with it for years, but now I've embraced this all-important piece of my life's puzzle.

My message for you: dare to follow your heart, no matter what route it takes. Only your heart knows what you need and when. Trust it and let the alchemy unfold. When it happens, don't hide; share your unique gift with the world.

Only when we dare to receive our heart's guidance do we start living and working from a place of balance, filling our life with love and joy from the endless well of passion.

Be free to live your dream.

Releasing Fear and Ego

By Karen Stillman

Growing up, I always struggled with low self-confidence, a trait that has been passed down for generations in my family. Unfortunately, with the lack of confidence and belief in myself, I found myself making poor choices a lot, making life that much harder.

As a teenager, I was quite the rebel. I never liked authority or being told what to do. I tended to be a follower, and usually not always with the best crowds. I learned how putting on a tough persona could hide my low confidence. Thank god my mother rode the waves and loved me unconditionally.

After having two kids and working hard to support us, at age 35 I was diagnosed with fibromyalgia. Wow, my world turned upside down and was forever changed. I had to stop working, take endless medications, and try to find a way to live with my new friend, Pain! This only made my confidence and self-esteem drop lower, as daily activities became harder to accomplish, making me feel useless.

In 2009, fate brought a childhood boyfriend and me back together. He is my soulmate, he accepts me at my worst, and through his encouragement and love, he has been a huge part of my journey of spirituality.

In the spring of 2010, I started to understand I was an empath. While mentoring under two very important healers, I honed my gift of intuitiveness. However, it proved to be a tough road, as low confidence and fear were engrained in me. This blocked me from achieving my absolute best.

I started to work with my angels, asking for guidance, which I always struggled with. I am so happy I found the perception to trust and go with the flow of life. I learned to stop allowing ego and fear to take control. As soon as I did this, intentions I've set have been so easy to reach. My hope is to inspire you to let go of your ego and fear and just trust in your journey, as I have.

Beyond the Shadow of Doubt

By Helen Ferrara

Sometimes, totally unexpectedly, things fit perfectly into place, like a series of lenses pointed at a sought-after view, so far away that they show a blurred image at best but then suddenly shift so that the focus becomes crystal clear. This has happened only a few times in my life, but the most recent one was a truly profound experience.

Reflecting on my thoughts and feelings that we are all beloved and taken care of, I was mulling over the differences in my experiences when I have asked for a benevolent outcome as opposed to times when I have just blundered and struggled away on my own. At these times, I've felt as if I were carrying the weight of the world on my shoulders – the opposite of being whisked forward to the best outcome, which has been the result of asking and being open to accepting help. It occurred to me that this didn't seem fair. After all, haven't we been taught as children to be responsible and do things by ourselves?

It was then that the magic happened. All at once I saw us, all the living beings in the world, as part of a great old tree. We humans were the tender new branches at the very tips, where most movement is possible – a dancing tree of life. Yet, from our perspective, we can't see the whole tree and, not even realising our deep connection, we often allow fear to separate us until we're almost cut off.

An unmistakable understanding dawned then that we also have the choice to trust and open to the flow of nourishment that is naturally ours, so that we might thrive.

Having experienced both ways of living, the fearful and the trusting, it's obvious that I would rather always choose to trust. This is easier said than done, as the fearful way seems to be insidiously ingrained in us and in the ways of the world. Yet with clarity comes certainty, even if the image dulls once more. What has been seen cannot be unseen, and the strength of this vision has removed all possible doubt forever.

Creating and Designing for Humanity

By Ayeesha Kanji

With time flying by and the world changing around us, it feels like every day there is something to learn, something to admit, and something to let go of. There is a need to create who we become as human beings, and the desire to design how we become that person. Human beings now focus on "being better" than who they were previously or learning the process of "learning, admitting, and letting go" to shape their individuality along the way. The key is not to design your life as a reaction to the external world's standards of time flying by but to create your life deliberately with your own personal sense of time.

A good friend of mine forwarded me a message stating that everyone has their own timestamp for everything in life. That means that your age is not a determining factor for your goals and what you want to accomplish. You create and design your life based on your own time, not by what everyone is doing around you. Comparisons lead us to feel the "should" of life versus the "could," and we forget to create and design deliberately but just execute based on habit or a sense of obligation.

Executing deliberately is actually tiring. Take a step back, breathe, and realize that your time is what matters. Don't engross yourself in the chaos around you. Take it easy and realize that what "could" become is more important than what "should" have transpired, because the time for that is never coming back. It is okay to take your time, to take care of yourself, because that's what matters. Create and design your life because you want to for your goals, not for someone else. Listen to your mind, acknowledge your heart, and stick to your instinct. Create, live, design, and repeat with your happiness and with your soul as one.

Then smile because that in itself is an accomplishment.

Eyes Are Windows to the Soul

By Sheila Jenkins

Without a doubt, the most soulful message I've ever received was when I looked into the eyes of a complete stranger. At that time, the only thing I knew was that something very profound happened – something that took me over a year to put into words.

It was late May 2011 when I was introduced to my new supervisor at work. As my boss walked away, we looked into each other's eyes. The sound went completely out of the room, and our movements seemed to slow down. There was no such thing as *time*; it just didn't exist. It was a split second that felt like an eternity. At that time, I just scratched my head and thought, "What the heck was that?"

After two years of working together, the light in his eyes intrigued me, along with everything else about him, and I finally allowed my love to surface from under a pile of denial. We decided to start dating, and I knew in the depths of my heart and soul that he would be the man I married.

The very next day, my beloved unexpectedly died of a massive heart attack.

This experience changed me forever. It sent me into deep, raw grief, but it also triggered a spiritual awakening.

I now understand that in the moment I looked into his eyes, it was "recognition." My soul recognized his, and obviously his soul recognized mine, too. I stepped into eternity where time does not exist and recognized the love and wholeness that he and I are.

It is my belief that love never dies and the soul is eternal. It is also my belief that we had spent many lifetimes together, and in this lifetime he was to awaken me out of my slumber so that he and I could add light into the world and carve out a path for others.

We are all sparks of the Creative Source/God/Universe. It is my belief that we are here to express *and* create with Source himself and return humanity and Mother Earth back to their natural state. May God bless each and every one of us as we all ascend in our consciousness and continue to light the path for others.

The Awkward Perfection of Existence

By Mia Lucci

Is anyone truly themselves? Seeing the masks my friends wear, I contemplate my own. Whether thickly caked makeup hiding the "ugly" or flashy clothes only rich people can afford, teenagers apply masks daily. We forget the true beauty of human connection when other, more glorified things float on the surface.

Moving out of my dorm because of an impossible roommate, I find myself alone in a room meant for two. It was every college girl's dream: a walk-in closet, movable beds, and no curfew. I am utterly alone.

Yet, no matter how bright the room, my surroundings feel dark. My body weight is heavier, and my walk to classes feels longer. The sky seems darker, and the cafeteria food tastes even blander (if that's possible). Friends from home feel even farther away. I lug a combination of all the masks I've ever worn.

Staring at the gray walls lined with thumbtacks pinning up smiling faces, I wonder why society teaches that we need someone else to complete us, that our hearts won't feel full until we've made enough money or trimmed off enough fat. Living alone showed me a new way of living.

Friends I thought would be in my life forever – standing beside me at my wedding, lending a shoulder, and spending long nights together – disappeared without closure.

As teenagers, we don't realize how deeply we hurt each other. Focused on our social media image and members of the opposite gender, we forget what's underneath: a longing for connection. A need to be held. Knowing we are loved. It's not until we're out of our comfort zones that we discover the awkward perfection of our own existence. There isn't a particular moment when it hits you. There isn't an abrupt awakening when you realize it. Love it or not, you create your own happiness.

Piling boxes on the tile floor that was somehow always sticky, preparing to move out of my first home away from home, I begin to take down hundreds of pictures. And I see me, the pretty smiling girl in every single one. Yeah, that's me.

Dancing with the Light

By Janet G. Nestor

Something special began happening the summer of 2014 when the book *Yeshua* was written. Each morning, I woke up to a kaleidoscope of white lights dancing behind my eyelids. The lights twinkled from their black or reddish-black backdrop. Today, I continue to anticipate their arrival and the feelings of spiritual closeness they bring.

As the lights dance, a center circle opens and becomes a "movie screen." Unique patterns move in and out of the circle, and sometimes I sense my energy field being cleared. At other times, I feel strong and empowered. The lights always leave me with a quiet joy and gratitude for another day of life.

On the morning of March 14, 2019, the light show was different. Animal after animal walked into the sacred circle and strolled to the left and out through the sparkling lights into nothingness. It was a bone-chilling experience to witness the animals disappear from the circle of life. My passion to save them was at a fever pitch; their time on Earth was ending. My mind was spinning as I felt their urgency and sorrow. How could I help?

Animals are sentient beings with awareness and emotion. They take care of their homes in the natural world, and they understand that their life depends on food, water, and shelter. They need help and continually beg us to save them, yet our human fixation on profit and expansion at all cost causes deep suffering and death. So many humans don't understand Mother Nature, nor do we accept the fact that losing animal habitats, food, and water means the loss of our own habitat and the weakening of Earth's ability to sustain life.

Each part of creation – human, animal, rock, mineral, water, air – is essential. All facets of creation have a role to play. The grass is as important as a tree. A butterfly is as important as a human being. There is an interdependence that can't be denied.

The only solution is a growing awareness that includes love and respect for all forms of life. Heart-centered conscious living creates positive change.

Debunking the "Soulmate" Myth

By Jeanette St. Germain

We've all watched romantic movies with clichéd plot lines and sappy love quotes. We've grown up watching Disney relationships end in marriage with a curly "happily ever after" branded in our minds. Society has taught us that love must be earned, manipulated through gender roles, and understood based on a checklist of conditions to be met by a prospective partner. So when the reality of "you complete me" becomes a vicious cycle of co-dependency and self-sacrifice, we are left feeling unfulfilled, abandoned, and somehow not good enough.

I have experienced the incredible magnetism of a few real-life "soulmates," heartbeams that appear out of nowhere and offer immediate intensity and depth. These bonds defy logic and break all societal rules; they also bring obstacles as opportunities for inner growth. These relationships don't exist to fix anyone; they invite us to remember our true power and challenge us to choose love, no matter what.

The ability to mirror another's thoughts and emotions, to understand what they are saying before they speak, to feel so deeply that the love you share seems to fill the breath in your lungs…it all sounds great in a Hollywood blockbuster, but the truth is far less glossy. Both people must be conscious of their stories and childhood wounds, committed to the understanding that their togetherness has a purpose beyond their individual needs.

Deep soul relationships are a playground for learning the truth of who we are and why we are here; they show us the potential of creation in our everyday lives. Life becomes an adventure when we feel supported and inspired, not because another is responsible for our happiness but because we feel safe to share all parts of the journey.

A true soulmate path has the potential to serve others as an example of higher love, divinity in human form. When two come together in a place of mutual appreciation and wonder, they create a whole new kind of world for us all.

The Inclined Elder

By Ramona Oliver

Who are "Inclined Elders"? We are the women and men who have made a conscious choice to ignore society's negative mindset of "decline" and "over-the-hill" as we age. Instead, we embrace a positive mindset of continuing to "incline" and "climb the hill."

Why, you may ask? Because we intend to live a life of achievement, meaning, and purpose and not allow more birthdays to get in the way.

The metaphor of a hill is an apt one because hills are easier and more enjoyable to climb than steep, lofty mountains, while still allowing for inspiring discoveries and adventures. Some pathways may have twists and turns, and there may be the odd bump, but we continue the ascent. Why? Because the vistas on the trek upward are increasingly breathtaking and exhilarating.

Inclined Elders know that there's no need to rush; it's not a race. We take one step at a time so that we can pause to smile at the waving wildflowers along the road.

Your attitude determines the potential for your altitude, so a shift in mindset is required, regardless of age. As you awaken to each new day as an Inclined Elder, the sunrise will greet you with a symphony of color to applaud your choice to "incline" and "climb the hill." You will continue to broaden your experience and deepen your joy of life.

Serving as vibrant role models, the Inclined Elders I know are leaving their own unique legacies of wisdom and inspiration for future generations. There needs to be more of us to effect real social change, so why not "incline" too? There's an amazing view from up here; come with me and see for yourself.

Miracles Happen for a Reason

By Mohamed (MO) Rachadi

I believe in miracles. I see vast oceans, majestic mountains, dry deserts, and green forests. I am amazed at the sunrise showing up every morning. I am amazed at my own body and how it functions. These are naturally occurring miracles. I have also heard of unseen miracles, but I'd never experienced my own until one warm evening in March 2014 when I was taken to Emory John's Creek Hospital in a coma.

Although I was in a coma, I could hear what doctors and nurses were saying while they tried to revive me. I could feel the pinches. I could hear their speculations and deliberations. But I couldn't open my eyes. My body was there, but my mind was somewhere else.

I could feel the presence of my wife and my daughters near me. I could hear their prayers. I could feel their pain, yet I was not able to open my eyes and give them sign of hope.

While the doctors and nurses were trying to revive me, a miracle was happening. A smile was about to send a sign of hope to many in the room. When I felt my daughters' hands squeezing mine, I knew that I was back with my loved ones.

I opened my eyes. I saw my wife and daughters – their teary eyes and smiles filling the small room. And I knew that God Almighty had just given me another shot at life.

Since then, I have been able to do amazing things for myself and those around me (which I describe in another piece in this collection, "Answering the Call"). By the grace of God, I have been able to make the most of this miracle.

Open your mind, your soul, and your heart. Experience the miracles. They happen for a reason.

What Is Your Platform?

By Shelia Prance

Imagine being able to create a change in society. This change could be in the form of education or influence. Your position may be as an elected official, a celebrity, or a non-profit leader. Who is watching and learning from you? I have always heard that you can either be a mentor or a warning to others by your words and actions. Both positions have their value, but a mentor is the position most desired.

To be effective, you must know who you are and what you stand for. Do you know? Is work necessary before you declare your platform? Have you prepared a list of the goals you want to accomplish? It is important to have a clear path before you start working with others. It is time to put your thoughts into action.

To do this, you will need a notebook, a pen, and time to collect your thoughts. Write down the first 10 items you would change if given the opportunity. To get the brain into gear, I will provide some items for your consideration.

Could you join your school board or other community committee to help make decisions? Have you considered running for political office, either at the federal, state, or local level (such as mayor or city council)? Could you volunteer for your local library, a sports committee, or a church's committee for finance, membership, or hospitality? What do you have to offer? Where could your experience make a difference? Whatever you decide, remember that your words and actions speak volumes about you.

Several years ago, I found a quote that resonates with me so much that I include it at the bottom of all my emails:

"Make your life a story worth telling." – Adam Braun

I challenge you: do you want to be a mentor or a warning to others? What can you do today to create a change in society and make your life a story worth telling?

Soulful Guidance from Above

By Brian D. Calhoun

You are a soul having a human experience. You came down to this planet to enjoy life to the fullest and to live and breathe the three wills of creation into life: the will to love, the will to serve and do no harm, and the will to live while being vitally alive.

You hold the power to create and recreate as you desire. You do so fully knowing, as a soul, that you are created in the exact image and likeness of Divinity. You do so from your perspective of where you are with your limited insights of the potential ramifications of the outcome. But when you surrender to the soulful presence within you, you know that only GO(o)D things will unfold.

Every day, you are allowed to experience all that your world offers to you. If there is something that doesn't serve you further, you can release it with love and appreciation. In fact, you must love yourself to free yourself of what no longer is working or making your heart sing. After all, by staying in a situation that is bringing you pain (in whatever way), you are causing harm to yourself and potentially to the other(s) involved. This goes against the will to love!

Make today the day you look at your life and allow the shift to take place. Choose to do so with love and light leading the way. Let go of the fear and resistance and listen to the central message of your heart. Remember, your soul knows where you are to be and who/what is waiting for you there. Trust and have faith; it will be awesome! Surrender to the forces of creation within.

Often one gets caught up in the fear of the unknown. We are here to let you know that life can indeed be Heaven on Earth. You deserve to live your dreams and let your heart beat again. Get out and enjoy being a soul having a human experience! You only get one life, and you deserve to make it a GO(o)D one! Only you can do so.

My 36 Hours of Solitude

By Hue Anh Nguyen

In April 2019, I had the opportunity to celebrate the grand opening of the monastery we go to in Bonsall, California. Thousands of guests joined the hundreds of nuns and monks gathered there to share the beautiful energy and great sense of peace during two days of teaching and celebration.

In the monastery, the nuns practice what is called *Nhập thất* (solitude retreat). The nuns typically go into solitude for 30-49 days, but some will stay for a year or more as a powerful way to deepen their practice.

I have often wanted to experience a solitude retreat, and on this occasion, I was accepted by the head nun of the monastery. The nuns offered some suggestions and quick guidance. Filled with gratitude and without wasting any time, I gathered my belongings for the next 36 hours.

I had a 10x10 room with only my basic needs met. No phone, no text, no talking to another person. I set my alarm for 36 hours. I meditated, chanted, and did walking meditations. I felt a great sense of peace and renewal in the 36 hours.

Would you like to cultivate some peace and flow in your life? You, too, can try this amazing experience on your own by following these simple steps:

- Choose a day of least disturbance for you. (Why not schedule it right now? With pure intention, nothing is impossible. Everything is lined up for your purpose, even with just a moment's notice.)
- Start with at least three to six hours and build from there.
- You can meditate, walk in nature, and do everything you do as a meditation, even eating or drinking. Know that that's all you are doing for that time.
- Observe your thoughts and feelings, acknowledge them, and let them go without attachment.
- Let go of any outcome of gain from this time.

Experience your own *Nhập thất* and see how your time in meditative solitude transforms you.

Discover Your Core Wound

By Keyra Conlinn

Dive deep and dive hard into the dark depths of your soul. Before you worry about a degree, before you consider dedicating yourself to a shared life with another being, before you hop on a plane to explore the world, before you get caught up in the rat race or start living your passion, discover your core wound.

Core wounds can come from childhood or cycles passed through ancestry and past lives. We're all human, and we all have (at least) one wound buried in our subconscious. And that wound will, inevitably, wreak havoc on what you aim to create and the dreams you work on building. It can create cycles of suffering and loss in your life, bringing you the people and situations that support it.

I've lived out my core wound time and time again, drawing into my life people who've stripped me of my beautiful essence, who've put me down and taken advantage of the inner lack of self-worth I felt from very early experiences in this life and maybe past ones. I've carried for too long the heavy weight of grief and shame from both the experiences themselves and the idea that I allowed them. In a moment of clarity, I understood why these people were in my life and became determined to end the cycle through healing.

Discovering your wound gives you the chance to catch yourself from slipping down the rabbit hole of repeated patterns, and it lights the path to healing. Once you acknowledge it, as I've discovered, you open your world to people who will help you work through it, people who will challenge you to challenge your beliefs. You will call in the right people at the right time to give you the strength you need to become the brightest version of yourself, empowered by understanding our beautiful imperfections and the tragedies they have manifested.

Avoid the repetitive and possibly escalating patterns – the heartache – by bringing awareness early and finding the guidance or healing, in whatever glorious form it may take, for your own sake and for the sake of your family, now and in the future.

Heart and Soul

By Susan M. Lucci

As a child, I played "Heart and Soul" on the piano by heart, solo or as a duet, with endless improvisations.

But then…I forgot it, around the time well-meaning adults said to "stop wearing your heart on your sleeve." I moved on, as most do, competing to master the world of the mind. Wonderful technologies were invented with our big brains, but now we stand at the threshold of destroying our species and our planet.

It's time to remember heart and soul. To learn to listen to Soul as she shares her wonderful wisdom. To feel her rhythm in your heartbeat, let her images and metaphors move you, open to sweet synchronicities, wake up to the wandering web of life weaving around you.

Knowing that our hearts are 5,000 times more powerful than our minds, we courageously wear our hearts on our sleeves. Soul speak, however, is hard to quantify, impossible to point to, prove, or predict. She cannot be bottled, sold, or contained. Soul is wild and free, unpredictable, messy, wonderfully immeasurable, and always present, especially in in-between spaces.

When we reconnect with our innate creativity, go outside in nature, dial up deep desires, and step into synchronicity's flow, we hear her wise voice.

To survive this era, we must slow the pace of our lives to the speed of our souls. Hurry/worry – the pace of busyness – drowns out soul speak. To listen, we must slow, still, and savor. Distractions must be dimmed so we can hear her soft whispers in the wind, sweet singing in the spaces between leaves, catch her in the quiet between heartbeats, and sense her strong shouting on the waves.

Soul leaves messages on journal pages and connects you and me. Soul moves us to what matters most. Just as the mindlessness of living on automatic pilot drove us to mindfulness, so too will this soullessness crisis force a reconnection to that which is most true, most alive in us. This planetary crisis will be rescued by heart and soul – specifically the coming together of many hearts and souls.

Soulful Love and Divine Balance

By Carolyn McGee

Our souls are our truest essence. They are the energetic core of who we are. The information from all lifetimes is stored in our soul for us to access for growth and expansion. Sometimes, it can be easy to get caught up in the physicalness of our body and the world around us. Our bodies see, hear, sense, and know what they experience in the physical world. These understandings can feel more real than our connection to the Divine and our souls' truth.

Our soul is crying out for us to remember what is truly important: *love*. We are surrounded by Divine Love, Angels, and Ascended Masters who are here to support us on our souls' growth journey. Yet at the core of it all, there is love. When we strip away the tangible physical reality and truly talk to our souls, we can feel how supported and loved we are.

Your soul was programmed to vibrate love with all your beautiful skills, talents, and knowledge. Your soul wants you to know that balance is critical in creating a joyful and thriving life. There needs to be a balance between what we perceive as good and bad, right and wrong, shadow and light. All this energy is here to help us learn and see our path more clearly. We need these contrasting experiences so that we can know in our hearts what is best for us. All experiences happen to remind us of our mission to grow and be loving.

Balance is also critical between the divine feminine and divine masculine characteristics. Each soul has divine feminine aspects, such as creativity, nurturing, community building, and spirituality. It also has divine masculine qualities, such as the ability to act, produce, protect, and expand. Understanding when it is optimal to utilize each energy makes our lives flow more easily and with more grace.

When you listen with your heart, you will know which energy is best for you live in. Take a deep breath, be still, and ask your soul what it needs in this moment to help you on your path.

Learn to Create Your Own Miracles

By Lottie Grant Cooper

What is a miracle? Possibly something unexpectedly good that seems impossible or unprovable, such as medical miracles, two people falling in love, a longtime conflict resolved, chronic pain gone, a new job opportunity out of nowhere, an animal saved, a birth, witnessing the most beautiful sunrise and being fully present for it, or a kiss where you fall in love all over again.

I believe in miracles. I see many miracles every day, and so can you. It's a frequency, an alignment, a calling, and it can be learned.

When we trust, listen, have the right information, and connect with unconditional love/source energy, which is the whitest brightest light you have ever experienced, you can tune in to miracle energy. You can access this whitest brightest light through your intention. (I have done this safely with thousands of people.)

Imagine a light within you expanded to make a sphere 8-11 feet wide. Allow your sphere of light to connect to the center of this planet and set it on release. Now you are a sphere attached to a column of light going into the earth. Stretch it up to the cosmos, so you are a sphere floating between Heaven and Earth. Notice the joy in being so connected. Set the intention to release down the grounding column all negative thought forms, feelings, beliefs, other people's negativity, politics, fears, and stresses to transmute into light. This is one of the foundations to prepare you for miracles: releasing and transmuting anything unlike love into light.

Where we place our awareness, we expand into it. So, as you perform this exercise, notice your body relaxing into awareness, your mind becoming quieter (if not silent), and the moment expanding. This ready awareness now attunes to the environment of intention, which we are now intending for miracles. Go deeper and deeper into this whitest brightest light.

What miracle would you like for yourself? Set the intention: feel, see, know, taste, smell, allow, and ask for it with pure heart, and then let go and be still. Trust your intuition to bring you people, places, and opportunities for your miracle. Follow your guidance.

Light After Grief

By Monique Jessica

The day was beautiful. In retrospect, the day was beautifully ominous. I had spent the whole day with my boyfriend. Laughing, walking, and talking about the future. To most, it would seem ordinary. To me, it was peaceful. No cares in the world, and for once, there seemed to be no reminder of his ongoing struggle with addiction. He went home that evening, and I thought everything was right in the world.

Unfortunately, a few short hours later, he lost his battle with addiction. The phone call came, and I was in a fog. This could not possibly be happening. His life was cut short, and mine had been flipped on its head in a blink of an eye.

The journey of grief was the hardest, darkest journey I had ever traveled. Just when I thought there were no tears left inside me, more would flow. The heartbreak was exhausting. The hopelessness numbing.

They say that time heals all wounds. I never believed that nonsense. However, as time passed, something lovely started to happen, and slowly my heart began to heal.

All my broken pieces were finally coming back together, but in a very different way. My true self was blossoming, and my spirit was shining bright. I was grateful for all the little things I had taken for granted my whole life. Whereas money and power had been my motivators in my old life, I now relished the feeling of a deep breath of fresh air in the mountains. I had newfound boundaries that kept toxicity at bay. My connection to my spirituality became strong. My intuition that had fallen asleep so many years ago was now very much awake, and my third eye was open wide. I had become my true, authentic self.

The journey was hard, but there is beauty in seeing how far I've come. Although it seemed so dim and so far away at the beginning of this trek, I assure you, there is a bright light at the end of the tunnel of grief.

December 16

Guided to be Courageous

By Teresa Velardi

Some time ago, I went zip-lining over a desert canyon. I started out being excited, but when I got to the top of the tower where I would have to take a true leap of faith, I sat frozen with fear for a long time.

Then, after a few false starts, encouragement from my team, and the voice of God guiding me, I let go of the fear. Instead of having to climb back down the tower, I experienced tremendous freedom in riding the zip-line with my arms outstretched, completely enjoying the ride. And I would do it again!

Susan Jeffers' book *Feel the Fear and Do it Anyway* gave me a push that day as I was praying for courage. They say courage is fear that's said its prayers, and I guess you could say that I'm living proof of it.

So, what does courage mean to me?

C: Commit to playing full out. Anything less than what you are fully capable of is cheating yourself.

O: Open your mind and heart to new possibilities. Life begins at the end of your comfort zone. Do you want to live or stay in your comfort zone?

U: Understand. Be understanding of others and allow yourself to be vulnerable enough to be authentically seen.

R: Resolve your differences. Practice forgiving others and self-forgiveness. There is great healing in the process.

A: Adjust to the changes you're making. Habits don't change overnight. Take time to absorb new ways of thinking and being as you step into your "new shoes."

G: Gratitude is the key to prosperity in every area of life. Be grateful! Begin a gratitude practice. It's a life-changing gift. The more you acknowledge what and who you are grateful for, the more goodness will come your way.

E: Evolve gracefully, embracing each moment. Trust the process.

Be courageous! There is freedom on the other side of fear.

Learn to Align. Learn to Live.

By Gigi Florez

It's amazing what a little alignment can do to my life.

I've started to realize how powerful it is to listen and align myself with messages communicated by the universe. It wasn't something I've always done. It was something I allowed myself to do.

One day, my mother made a scathing remark to me. Later, a patient I barely knew insulted me at work. Both incidents deeply hurt me. I broke down crying as the words stung, even hours later. But then I drew meaning from these incidents. They weren't unfortunate or unfair events but messages that required me to realign my life. I had to change. I had to move. I had to see these incidents as opportunities to move on to better opportunities and accept better direction coming my way.

When you can perceive insults, arguments, and disagreements as messages that nudge you toward your true purpose in life, you feel a true sense of enlightenment. When I opened myself to the messages sent my way, I found that I was constantly aligning myself to become a better version of me.

One of the first things I realized was that money wasn't nearly as significant as I thought. I was stunned at how I was able to view it merely as an instrument exchanged for goods and services and not something that you need your whole life to revolve around, running a furious rat race to achieve it. When I was able to disassociate the utmost importance I gave to things like money, I was able to see life in a completely different way. A more meaningful way. The way it was meant to be seen.

Aligning myself to the messages I receive will help me find my true purpose on this Earth. It will help me discover why I am here, what I must do, and how I must do it.

Our Lives...Our Choices

By Mohamed (MO) Rachadi

Did you know that, on average, we make 35,000 choices each day? Some choices are as simple as deciding what clothes to wear. Others are far more complex, such as choices about moving to faraway places, getting married, having kids, choosing friends, or pursuing a professional career or a spiritual path. Over time, the choices we make – big and small – shape our lives.

As I approach my 70th birthday, I've become more and more interested in the choices we all make – hourly, daily, during our lifetime – and how these choices shape our lives and affect others. A big part of my own life has been shaped by a single choice I made 50 years ago: saying yes to coming to study in the US. Because of that choice, I've been able to start my own business and live the American Dream. I've also made my share of "interesting" choices, to say the least, and have even made a mess here and there.

Because of my fascination with choices, my daughters encouraged me to write a book about this topic, which I've begun working on. In addition to my own writing for the book, I've invited writers from around the globe to submit and share major choices they've made and how they've dealt with the consequences. During my research, I identified the top 101 major choices we make in a lifetime, their consequences in our own lives, and even more importantly, how these choices affect our loved ones, friends, and others around us. For some of the outcomes, I offer suggestions on how to deal with them and overcome the challenges derived from those choices.

My vision is that this book will be a guide for parents, spiritual leaders, coaches, counselors, mentors, and other professionals engaged in helping others make the best choices to live a joyful life. My hope is that it will be a source of inspiration and way to share the message that our choices shape our destiny – and that great choices lead to great lives!

Carry On – From Generation to Generation

By Marla David

The first stage of life is when we copy our parents and elders. The second is when we have input in our lives, making choices but still not totally independent. The third is when we're totally independent. And the fourth stage is even better because we have a different set of rules when it comes to responsibility. I'm now in the fourth stage, where the main focus of my life is supposed to be doing things I wish to be remembered for – my legacy.

I realize that as another generation is born, there are more loving souls I will one day leave behind. When my grandchildren arrived in this world, I found myself thrust back into the emotion of loving someone more than I love myself, just as it was with my children. When I think about leaving a legacy, I primarily think about leaving one for them. So, how would I like them to remember me?

I would like to be remembered as someone who lived to the best of my ability, someone who lived large, someone who lived my passions every day. I want my grandchildren (and children and others) to know that I loved to the best of my ability, but I would also like to be loved in return, especially after I pass on. There is nothing greater than that, nothing more powerful than pure and unconditional love. Like most people, I would like to think that some of the things I valued have been instilled in my girls, and in turn, in their children. We have always been generous people, and I assume that this will not change, that there will be a continuum with regard to charity and other forms of giving.

It would also be nice if, after I'm gone, someone were to see my picture and have an inkling of who I was, what kind of person I was, and know that I mattered – not only because I existed but because I touched their life in some positive way. And I would like there to be an emotion attached to that memory, one that has been imprinted in their DNA. That is my legacy – what I want to carry on.

Sometimes It's That Simple!

By Donna Godfrey

There is simplicity to this journey called life, though sometimes we manage to turn our experiences into complicated situations. For instance, once I was on a road trip with a friend, and we were discussing our financial situations – particularly, the complications resulting from some changes we were both making in our lives. Then I said that it's amazing how the younger generation just seems to be okay doing whatever they desire, even if it sets them back. I proceeded to talk about how we need to just trust the feelings we get within our bodies and how there really are no wrong choices anyhow; if a situation does not work out based on a decision, simply make another!

Then, shortly down the road, we decided to stop for a walk in the forest. Two young kids pulled up in a car alongside us. They got out and immediately shared that they had both just quit their jobs to take this adventure. They said that they weren't worried because they knew they'd be able to find new jobs when they got back. Well, if that wasn't a validation of our conversation!

Another incident of life simply flowing started at a gathering I was attending. The guest speaker had a table full of small boxes, and I was asked to pick one. I opened it and saw that it was a small puzzle of Bell Rock in Sedona, Arizona. When I got home, I glued it onto a piece of cardboard and, for some unknown reason, hung on to it for more than 10 years. Then my sister Valerie invited me to join her in Phoenix, Arizona. We had no plans or any accommodations booked but decided to stay in Sedona, even though we were told we'd have a very difficult time finding anything. My sister went online and called the first place that popped up. When we showed up, I looked at our view from the front window, and it was exactly the same as the picture on the puzzle, right down to the exact angle and side of Bell Rock!

I understand now how things can unfold at just the right time. So it does not matter if it's hours after or many years down the road, guidance will always show up when you need it!

Your Story Does Matter

By Michele Noordhof

In the fall of 2017, I shared my personal story of walking the dark path of suicide. My friend sounded very interested in attending, but she never came. A couple of weeks later, she was gone.

I was in disbelief that she had killed herself. As the sadness and grief came, I asked myself where I had failed. If I could not even save the life of a friend, how could I ever make a difference? Did my story even matter?

During a conversation with my friend Pamela, I began to come to terms with the loss. Sitting in her truck after the memorial service, she asked me what I thought of the STARS air ambulance service. She asked if I thought they did a good job of saving lives. Then she asked whether they saved everyone. And, finally, she asked the most important questions: What if STARS had given up after they lost their first patient? What would have happened if they had not been there for all the lives they did help save?

In the days following, I wrestled with the aftermath of the tragedy and the realization that my friend's story and journey were hers alone. I realized that my story did matter. I did save the life of someone: my own. I had made a difference. And in that moment, my life was forever changed.

While the circumstances that create our life journeys are not always of our choosing, finding the courage to share our stories can give us a renewed purpose in life, help with our own healing, and let others know that they are not alone.

My message for you today is this: keep going, keep seeking to find your way, don't quit, don't believe the lies this world may be telling you. Remember your authentic truth: you are amazing, you are valued, you are important, you are not a mistake, this world needs you, you are loved, you are perfect just as you are, and your story does matter.

My Peace – A Harmonious Affair

By Marla David

Most people I know, including myself, strive for peace of mind and peace in their life, and this is tantamount only to good health. When your health is in stable condition and most everything in your life is in good order, you're better poised to experience this kind of peace.

As I've aged, I need peace in my life. Times of solitude and quiet don't bore me any longer. I'm always open for new ways to experience peace. Whether through interactions with people or by simply *being*, I'm drawn to everything that doesn't ruffle the feathers of this newfound peace.

I co-create my life in such a way that I can live my best life regardless of circumstance. I'm mindful to make better choices and pay attention to my passions. This helps me experience the balance I need, gives me clarity, and reduces the mind-clutter that comes from everyday living in such a crazy and unpredictable world.

I don't like crazy times any more than anybody else, but the reality is that, as with the yin and yang, with peace also comes its opposite: contrast. There will always be stressful times when certain things steal bits of my peace, but I persevere. I know that life is not static. But I also believe that when we have disharmony or chaos in our life, we have an opportunity to grow in a way that wouldn't have happened without the contrast.

In order to keep things in check, it's important I maintain a balance. When my balance is off, I find myself spiralling out of control and have to reel myself in. Meditation has helped tremendously by grounding me and bringing me to a state of calm, which is necessary to achieving balance.

I am content with this eurythmic life, like this feeling of inner tranquility that warms my soul. I feel at peace – and it's a rather pleasant, harmonious affair.

Choices

By Amy Coppola

"Always go with the choice that scares you the most,
because that's the one that is going to help you grow."
– Caroline Myss

The Denver startup company sought a program manager. I was eating lunch while working at home. The post read, "See yourself working here," so I applied. How could I know that it would be the start of a two-year adventure that would change my life and perspective?

Weeks later, on a trip to Boston, an unknown number called my phone – the Denver startup wanted to schedule an interview.

The position was similar to the job I already had but without the travel and long hours. For 14 years, I'd skillfully climbed several levels and enjoyed a successful corporate career. But on the day I applied, I was feeling run down, thinking that there should be more to life.

The job offer came, along with a promotion and an exciting career challenge! In spite of the scary risk of leaving a mature company for a startup, I looked at the change as a much-needed opportunity.

I'd allowed my previous job to define me; by choosing to leave, my life became anything but routine. The Universe offered the chance to try a new path. Almost a year later, we sold the company, which led to another job offer with the new company. My decision was easy: "No, thank you."

After taking a month off to relax and assess what to do next, a similar position surfaced with a competitor to my original employer. It was an excellent opportunity to leverage my experience and learn from a new organization.

A year later, I accepted an offer from my original company for a position with more responsibility and a higher salary. This two-year series of opportunities helped grow my confidence, build my spiritual awareness, and learn to take chances with my career. And it taught me a valuable lesson: Pay attention to what life brings you and know when it is time for a change. The growth opportunities could be impactful to your life and career with no bounds.

A Message About Technology

By Ayeesha S. Kanji

You may be wondering, "A soulful message about technology – why?" I feel deeply that it is time to relay this message because it has become such a ubiquitous part of our lives. When we look around, we see that technology surrounds us every minute. It affects the way we think, the way we live, and even the way we experience time. When we're immersed in technology, time seems to fly.

Yes, technology has its benefits. It can help us learn, connect, and solve problems. But it is not a solution to everything. Also, because technology is constantly developing and expanding, just trying to keep up with it can feel overwhelming. But nobody is saying you have to know everything. If you don't, it's okay; you're not alone. Remember, technology is there to help you, not to scare you or overwhelm you.

Also, remember that new technology does not have to replace everything we grew up with. For instance, I still love the feel of a printed book in my hand, I look forward to attending group workout classes, and I adore my CD collection – even though all these items are now digital and accessible through a computer, a SmartPhone, or a SmartTV. But I choose to not let new technology replace what I enjoy, and we all have that choice.

We all managed to live without technology up to a certain point. So, even if we can't go back to an earlier age, we can still find balance. Unplug. Take a break. Instead of looking at a TV, your laptop, or your SmartPhone, see people face to face – and remember how to connect on a human-to-human level.

Embrace what technology can do for you, how it helps you learn, and where it can take you. But be sure to balance the role it has in your life because, beyond a certain level, it can become detrimental to your health and well-being.

Most people already acknowledge the importance of work-life balance. Now it is time to make technology balance a priority. When you achieve that balance, pat yourself on the back and remember to maintain it. This will help you maintain the balance you strive for in all areas of your daily life. And it will help you remember what it means to be a soulful human being.

Whisper the Flowers Awake

By Stacey Maney

This is the story of a meditative shamanic journey I had on a women's retreat.

The intention: through meditation, journey to the heart of the Earth for clarity on how I could be of service to the planet with the Great Mother as my guide.

I closed my eyes, and my meditation began. Drums played as I walked down a spiral staircase. At the bottom, an entire scene unfolded: Tribes of people joyfully working to clean the land. Waterfalls rushing all around and luscious green colors filling the spaces in between. The air was fresh, and I was happy to see our Earth Mama being restored.

The Great Mother, tribal and serene, stood next to me. She began to throw blue dust into the air. I found myself pulling this same dust from within my throat, unsure but trusting her guidance. The dust went from blue to yellow to red...a technicolor breeze.

The Great Mother turned me around toward a field of thriving wildflowers. In that moment, I knew that those flowers were born from my soul, watered with my tears, strengthened through my struggles, and brought to life from my intention. They were standing tall because of my efforts. Their presence was proof that I stayed committed to my growth, honored my strength, and let my warrior heart beat equal to this life.

The rest of the field came to life before our eyes. I realized that our multicolored dust was fertilizer. We sang and danced the flowers to life.

It is this story of awakening that I leave for you. A reminder that, just like the flowers, you can root down into love and rise up higher than ever before. Let yourself move, sing, dance, write, and paint the musings of your heart. Your self-expression is the fertilizer for your own awakening.

Inspiring Patients in the Psych Ward

By Catherine M. Laub

2019 has been rough, but after all the storms, I am doing well and inspiring others again.

On March 24, my mother passed away and we emptied her house to sell it. I brought her stuff to my house to sort and donate. My house quickly overflowed.

In April, my husband, Tony, was in the Veterans Hospital due to an intestinal blockage, which turned out to be cancer. I was devastated and the worry began – not only for his well-being but also for my own future. I only own my stuff. Tony owns the house and my car. If he dies, his daughter gets two-thirds of everything, and I won't have much to support myself. I became obsessed with the idea that I would end up with no place to live. In the midst of these worries, I had a minor heart attack and was taken to another local hospital.

While visiting me there, my daughter lectured me about my mother's belongings taking up too much space in my house. I explained the process, but she wouldn't let it go. When she visited on Father's Day, she began all over again and caused me to fall apart. I often speak about getting yourself to the emergency room if you become suicidal, so I followed my own advice. The very next day, I was transported to the psych ward, where I remained for two weeks.

In the psych ward, I met many patients and shared my healing journey, mentally and physically. Tony brought a copy of my book, which is inspirational, and I donated it to the patients. Some read it immediately and were inspired by my accomplishments, including The Celestial Spoon, my podcast where I talk about mental illness.

I believe I was in the psych ward at that particular time to help my fellow patients and share my inspiration to future patients. Many of them read my book while I was there and were amazed with all my health issues and how much I'd accomplished since my last hospitalization in the psych ward. I was there not only as a patient but as a mentor to continue reaching out for assistance in healing.

My goal is to always inspire others to be their best self.

My Twin Flame

By Annie Price

Several years ago, I had a profound soulful message and experience that is still unfolding for me. One day in the spring of 2013, I began listening to a spiritual teacher and was quickly drawn to his message. It didn't seem unusual at first, but as time went on, I couldn't seem to shake the feeling that there was more to it. I found myself preoccupied with this person, but I had no interest in a sappy infatuation. It was troubling, and after a few weeks, it didn't seem to straighten itself out as I'd hoped it would.

I began asking for some higher guidance, wanting to understand what was happening to me. One morning, I woke up with the words "Twin Flame" in my mind. What was this? I didn't remember hearing it before.

Researching this term, I learned that while kindred spirits are people who resonate at the same frequency and soulmates are people we connect with on a deep level, Twin Flames are two people who share the same soul essence. Although aspects of the Twin Flame experience sound beautiful, it can be complicated and is definitely not for the faint-hearted! In a Twin Flame relationship, your twin acts like a spiritual mirror, reflecting back your strengths as well as your weaknesses, helping you heal what is broken within you. This can cause both a lot of pain; however, it's often a necessary part of personal growth and transformation.

When you meet your Twin Flame, there is a deep sense of recognition, meant to wake you up. It's a gift from the Divine that you can only fully appreciate when you've released all the baggage that no longer serves you. This relationship is on multiple levels and may not be on the physical level – it depends on each pair of Twin Flames.

In my case, the other person – my mirror – has a different definition and experience. There haven't been any major changes to my physical life, and I continue focusing on my inner work. It's been challenging to understand this experience, but it's getting easier as I move forward, gain wisdom, and accept what is.

Answering the Call

By Mohamed (MO) Rachadi

When given a second chance, I believe it is the perfect opportunity to do right and do something amazing for you and all around you.

Five years ago, I was given a second chance. With the help of God, the doctors and nurses at Emory John's Creek Hospital brought me back to life from a prolonged coma to be with my wife, my two daughters, my loved ones, and so many more other people (an experience I describe in another piece in this collection, "Miracles Happen for a Reason"). Armed with renewed energy, I felt blessed and compelled to answer the call to do what God wants me to do and follow the new map he has drawn for me from now until the end of my journey in this beautiful world.

Embracing this awesome opportunity, I started the journey of giving back by:

- Volunteering as a Patient-Family Advisor and a member of the Board of Trustees at the same hospital where the miracle happened

- Starting the Rachadi Associates Family Foundation with a mission to build schools and hospitals for needy children

- Sharing my story by writing books and speaking at schools, colleges, corporations, and other community events

- Using my time, expertise, smile, kindness, and whatever I can give to help someone else who needs and is ready to receive my help

I am so amazed at the energy inside me, the desire and the power to do amazing things. I'm still the same person I was before the coma, but I now have a different mindset and different values about what life is or should be.

We have choices in life. I choose to do what's right and just, and that is how I am answering the call. We all need each other to make this world a better place for all.

Live Your Passion

By Ayeesha S. Kanji

On the first day of warm sunshine for Toronto in David Pecaut Square, I was enjoying the warmth. As I turned around, she said to me, "You're coming on stage. We need people, and you're it."

I replied, "Okay, sure. Are we going to rehearse?"

She said, "We'll try but might not be able to."

Next thing I knew, we were on stage, the BollyX Crew, warming up a crowd of 20K+ people before walking for a cause. I ended up in the middle and danced on stage for the first time in three years. I felt amazing. The crowd, the stage, the excitement, the fun, and how much I loved seeing everyone looking up to all of us for inspiration. It was the moment that reminded me how much dancing is my passion and that it brought me back to life.

Dancing has always brought me happiness. It brings out that feeling of being lost in the moment because it reminds me to live in the present – revitalizing that happiness of feeling alive and in tune with who I am and where my passion lies, which has always been dancing.

I've come to realize that your passions do not dissolve; they are always with you. Dancing was always a part of me and who I was, deep in my heart and my soul. Living your passion brings balance to the everyday routine that we get bored with or stress over. Sometimes people feel that "something is missing" or that they don't have enough "me time" to feel content.

Before overthinking or simply trying to fill a void, ask yourself, "Are my passions that make me feel alive a part of my life?" Answer that truthfully and be honest with yourself. Nurture your inner child, find your passion, and live it wholeheartedly.

Dare to Live Your Dreams

By Jenny Ngo

Hi, beautiful soul. I see you. I know that you have a big heart and you want to be of service. You want to make a bigger impact in the world. Wherever you are in your life and/or business, you want to reach your full potential and do the work you love.

You came here with your own unique gifts, passions, and purpose. You are enough. You've been guided, supported, and loved. Remember to reconnect to who you really are and get out of your own way. You are to compare yourself to no one. Trust and follow your heart. Keep dreaming big and shoot for the stars. Don't let your core wounds or your past define who you are meant to be. Your biggest mess is your greatest message. The workshop you are to give is the very workshop you are living. The world desperately needs your gifts and contributions.

Prior to becoming an expert healer and intuitive business coach for entrepreneurs, I was an RN and midwife. I knew I wanted to help people, just like the nurse who saved my brother's life when I was eight.

I'm originally from Vietnam. Growing up, we were poor. When we moved to America, my parents had to work two to three jobs to support a family of seven. This motivated me to study hard, and I went on to graduate with a master's degree.

But even with my high-paying career and the joy of delivering a few hundred babies, there was still a growing sense of unfulfillment. I realized I was just treating my patients' symptoms and not the root causes.

I was unexpectedly let go from my midwife job when I was eight months pregnant with no backup plans. I was at a crossroads, forced to decide whether to find another job or go for my dreams of doing what I love. It was scary, but I followed my heart and took a big leap of faith to start my coaching and healing business.

I've always wanted to help people heal and have lasting transformations. With this mission as my foundation, I went on to grow a successful business to over six figures. I know that anything is possible when you follow your heart, do what you love, and have the proper support and guidance. Dare to live your dreams!

Ready to Soar

By Jodi Chapman

I dreamt the other night that I was leaving. My husband, Dan, was already on the plane, which had thankfully been delayed so I had more time to say goodbye to my friends who had come to see me off. I kept packing and unpacking my bag – making sure I had everything. I didn't have the flight info, and I didn't know where we were going. The only thing I knew for sure was that it was time for me to leave.

We took pictures with one another one last time, using the beautiful ocean as our backdrop. The airport was outside, and we were right at the edge of the waves. As I turned to look at it, I saw eight magnificent elephants in the water, walking toward the shore. I made sure all our pictures included them in the background.

I'm not sure where I was, but it was in a foreign land where the food smelled of spices and the men wore gowns. I reflected on how far I had come with two of the men who had taken quite a while to warm to me but now had tears in their eyes as I prepared to leave. We were now family. They kept trying to get me to eat – handing me plate after plate of food. But we all knew I needed to go.

I turned toward my closest friend, a young woman who I called my little sister, and I gave her a huge hug. She was sobbing, and I asked her to look up at me because I had something important to tell her – something I wished I had known when I was her age. Her big eyes looked up, and I said that no matter when I saw her again – whether it was a few months or a few years – I wanted to make sure she was still this open, that she didn't let the world and all of its madness take away her pureness and her love for life. She promised she wouldn't. Then she asked if there was anything I would have done differently. I said I would have worn more sunscreen and taken better care of my body. We both laughed and hugged one last time, and then I started running toward my gate – trusting that I would find it.

Halfway down the hall, I turned around to look at my friends one more time, and I saw that they were enjoying themselves. They weren't broken because I was leaving. And that made me happy. I turned toward my plane and started running as fast as I could. There was no way I was going to miss it. No matter where it was heading, I was ready to soar.

Conclusion

We created this book to remind us all that we're constantly receiving soulful messages – from our loved ones both here on Earth and beyond and also from our own soul and the divine – and it's up to us to stay open so that when a message appears we'll be able to receive it.

Throughout this book, we've shared story after story of lives being changed because of soulful messages that the authors received. Our wish for each of you is that you'll be on the lookout for your own soulful messages and that you'll take action when they appear – whether it's opening your heart just a little bit more or expanding your confidence in yourself and others or fulfilling a lifelong dream that you've been afraid to pursue. We want you to see that these messages have appeared for a reason. They always come into our lives at the perfect time, right when we need them the most.

If you enjoyed this book and would like to help spread all of the soulful wisdom and goodness that it contains, please share it with your friends and family! We would also be grateful if you left a positive review for us on Amazon, which will help this book's uplifting messages reach even more people. And we would love for you to join us on our Facebook page, where you can share your favorite pieces, connect with the authors, and be part of our wonderfully loving and soulful community: www.facebook.com/365bookseries.

We hope that reading this book has been a positive experience and that your heart is ready to receive all the beautiful messages that are just waiting to flow into it. Because once you open yourself to these messages, you'll find that the messages will come pouring in!

Thank you so much for being part of this journey with us.

Hugs, love, and gratitude,

Jodi and Dan

Contributor Biographies

O ver 200 authors contributed to this book with the hopes that sharing their soulful messages would inspire everyone who reads them to be on the lookout for messages of their own.

The co-authors come from many different walks of life and from many parts of the world, but the common thread that links each of us is our desire to share our words and to inspire others by doing so. That's all, and that's everything.

As you read through each author's biography on the pages that follow, you'll find some who are already bestselling authors and others who are sharing their words in print for the first time, which is such an exciting moment!

It's our hope that you'll enjoy meeting them all through their photos and biographies and that you'll reach out to those you resonate with and let them know how much their pieces moved you. What a gift that will be for them to receive!

About the Editors

Jodi Chapman and Dan Teck are a husband-and-wife team who loves living soulfully and joyfully. Since 2005, they've been living their dream of writing books and creating products that inspire others to connect with their soul and live fully and passionately.

Jodi has a BA in English/Technical Editing and Sociology, and Dan has a BA in Religious Studies and an MFA in Creative Writing. Together, they have over 30 years of experience with editing and publishing and have sold over 50,000 books. They have written over 20 books, eight ecourses, and more than 1,000 blog posts/articles.

Jodi is an award-winning blogger at www.jodichapman.com and the author of *Soul Bursts*, *Soul Speak*, and the upcoming novel *The Breakdown*. Dan is the author of the personal-growth blog *Halfway up the Mountain* (www.halfwayupthemountain.com) and the book *Rewrite Your Story*. They are the co-creators of the bestselling *Soulful Journals Series* and the *365 Book Series* as well as *Your Soulful Book*, a heart-centered writing program.

They live on the Oregon coast with their sweet cat. They enjoy hanging out at the beach and working, creating, and playing together.

They feel truly blessed to be able to spend each day together, doing what they love. It's their hearts' desire that their books and products bring joy to everyone they reach.

About the Contributors

Nikki Ackerman is a holistic business owner and a Master in Usui Holy Fire® Reiki and Karuna Holy Fire® Reiki. She recognizes the rewards are very beneficial for mind, body, and spirit wellness. Her desire is to provide others with peace and balance through a soulful and holistic approach to self-care and well-being

Marion Stoltzfus Alexander is a Family Nurse Practitioner who is passionate about the opportunity to partner with patients to make a positive change in their life through a holistic approach. She strives to develop an authentic relationship with them and work together to accomplish a desired goal.

Rand Allen is a Cosmic Jedi-Macgyver, shaman, master of nine styles of Reiki, reconnective healer, Renaissance man, re/inventor, builder of vibro-acoustic and Ozone Therapy healing devices, and the author of *Fractal Thinking: Zen Intuit*. He's on a journey into self, unlocking the super-conscious mind to experience joyful, exponential learning.

Chris Anderson is a holistic wellness advocate, educator, and bestselling author who has dedicated her life to helping people identify their gifts, initiate soul-level healing, and release fear so they may embrace their divine light and share it with the world. www.1gentleheart.com

Melisa Archer, National Trainer for Tesla Wellness Energy, is certified in Pulsated Electromagnetic Frequencies, BIO Frequencies, Reiki 3, Raindrop Therapy, Vitaflex, essential oils, rejuvenation facials, Emotion Code, and Dolphin Neurostim. Her ability to see and feel energies benefits the clients' sessions. www.TeslaWellnessEnergy.com

I AM Alisa Auger, the Creativity Muse + I AM a Channel. I energetically receive words of Divine wisdom and guidance to help my clients feel free and safe to activate impactful change in their creativity, life, and business. I AM a motivational speaker, singer-songwriter, and course creator. www.alisaauger.com

Joy T. Barican is a life coach who is passionate in assisting you to make meaningful, exciting, and viable choices for yourself based on your individual values, personal strengths, and beliefs. When results matter, contact her via email: jbarican@hotmail.com.

Nora T. Barican loves life and shares her smile, truth, and gratitude. Having a solicitor for a father and teacher for a mother, her various interests were encouraged. Her passion for singing has seen her participate in Messiah and Chorus Oz with Sydney Philharmonia Choirs for 20 years at the Sydney Opera House.

Mauri Barnes lives on Florida's Gulf Coast. Writing stories for this book has opened her heart to the magic and wonder of life's everyday experiences. As she says, "There are so many examples of messages from Spirit. It's exciting to recognize and acknowledge these happenings in stories to share with others."

Keyon Bayani is a lover and student of life. She is not into labels or defining who she is by her formal qualifications or work. She believes that if you follow and honour your own personal truth, and you're kind, you are living your purpose. www.keyonbayani.com

Jill Alman Bernstein is an inspirational writer, intuitive soul coach, Soul Realignment™ Practitioner, writer's coach, freelance editor, deep-sea soul diver, mother, and mermaid. She is the creator of the platform I Must Be A Mermaid, focusing on inspiration, empowerment, and transformation. www.imustbeamermaid.com

With passionate fire in her heart, Michelle Berube shares her love for all through Animal Communication. She offers Reiki sessions and shares the teachings of Reiki with all who choose to develop deeper connections with everything that's around and within. www.MichelleBerube-Animalsspeak.ca

Nicole Black is an entrepreneur, author, and the co-founder of Renaud's Patisserie & Bistro (a French bakery and bistro with six locations throughout Southern California). A native of Southern California, she currently resides in Santa Barbara with her daughter.

Carolyn Boatman has shared the art of "Playful Creation" and promoted its social enrichment for over 45 years. She created the "Soul Process Art Workshops" and "Find Your Ease Meditations" through the last 20 years of living a creative life and learning to "Abundantly Allow." www.soulprocessart.com

Bonnie L. Boucek is an international bestselling author, Fibromyalgia and Chronic Pain Coach, Creative Coach, and reverend whose purpose is to remind people that life is a journey. She lives in South Carolina and enjoys writing, playing N.O. with friends, and being with family. BonnieBoucek@gmail.com

Anne Bradley has always been a writer of one kind or another. Her recent transition from authoring software to memoirs is a welcome and delightful lifestyle change. She loves meeting and hanging out with her readers and author friends at www.facebook.com/annebradleyauthor.

Michael Brewer is on a beautiful journey to discover who he truly is. Love is his light, and he lives each moment of each day in heartfelt gratitude. www.facebook.com/Michaels1188

Jeffrey Brochu is a shamanic energy medicine practitioner, Reiki Master, and healer. He enjoys a soulful, connected journey with his wife, Kimberly, where they appreciate the beach and being in nature's beauty. He feels blessed in life with their five children and growing family. www.lotusandhawk.com

Kimberly Brochu's holistic certifications and life experiences are the foundation for her writing and guiding others through personal transformation. She and her husband reside in Massachusetts, where they devote themselves to their five children, holistic business, real estate business, and each other. www.lotusandhawk.com

Shannon L. Brokaw is a writer and wanderluster who loves the outdoors. She is a seeker of anything that makes her laugh in life and puts a smile on her face. *La Dolce Vita!* www.welliesandwhisky.com

Brian D. Calhoun is a heart-centred international bestselling author, psychic medium, Reiki Master, energy worker, and spiritual teacher who has dedicated his life to being in service to the soul who has sought healing and enlightenment for over 19 years. He is based in Ottawa, Canada. www.BrianDCalhoun.com

Christine Callahan-Oke is a mom, inspirational writer, and positive thinker. Through coaching, writing, and leading an online group of inspired adventurers, she offers practical tips and wisdom to help people uncover their inner treasures, find the beauty in everyday moments, and shine their light brightly. www.ChristineCallahanOke.com

Valerie Cameron is a certified life coach and Reiki Master/Teacher. She has been an entrepreneur for over 40 years, and it is through this and her abilities as an intuitive psychic/spiritual medium that she is able to compassionately assist those who ask for guidance. www.earth-balance-healing.com

Alyssa Canella would spend recess indoors, Word Document open, typing up adventures she'd grown "too old" to keep play pretending. Since then, she's attended Seattle Pacific University to work on her double major in English and Psychology. She divides her time between Las Vegas, Nevada; Boise, Idaho; and Seattle, Washington.

Barbara "Bobbie" Carr is a mother, grandmother, and author who enjoys gardening, choral singing, tennis, and reading. She truly believes in the power and grace of the Spirit in her life. She lives in New Jersey with her husband, Pat.

Angie Carter is a bereaved mother and inspirational author who began writing as a way to cope with the sudden loss of her 19-month-old daughter, Bella. Her blog, A Mother's Journey Through Grief (www.AngieCarter.com) has deeply touched people worldwide with evidence that life is eternal.

Marian Cerdeira is an intuitive channel and medium who also offers soul readings. Her messages from spirit are shared on Facebook at "A Slice of Light" and at www.asliceoflight.com.

Cindie Chavez, Certified Life and Relationship coach, creator of MOONTREAT™, LOA Today podcast co-host, has written for *The Huffington Post*, *The Examiner*, *Confluence Daily*, and *WITCH* magazine. She loves reading, writing, drawing, knitting, glittery nail polish, Tarot cards, magic wands, and moon-gazing. www.cindiechavez.com

Katie Keck Chenoweth, MAEd, LMBT, CHt, a pioneer in wellness, has degrees in training and health and certifications in massage and hypnotherapy. Being an artist, she has the unique ability to fuse art, massage, and past-life regression into radical healing. She can be found offering tranquil touch and meditation on the NC coast.

Claire Chew, MA, kicked stage IV cancer's butt at 19 and now can be found coaching, teaching, cooking, and practicing spiritual psychology. Her favorite mantra is "Let love be your bottom line." She knows her time here is short and empowers women to live fully. www.clairechew.com

Lisa Rachel Cohen, author of *Grace is Born* and *My Grace is Born Companion,* is the CEO of Sparkle Press LLC and InSparkle Media. You can join her on her sacred mission to embrace the heart and grasp the hand of every woman, child, and man at www.InSparkleMedia.com.

Heidi Cohen-Barocas is a spiritual teacher who addresses aging and transitions through her poetry and Divine Dialogue Writing™. Heidi leads meditations and healing programs inspired by the Kabbalah and mystics at nursing centers. Born in Brooklyn, NY, she now calls St. Petersburg, FL home. www.InHarmonywithHeart.com

Joanne Angel Barry Colon has been blessed with a beautiful daughter, is the business owner of Wholistic Fitness, and is a certified personal trainer, intuitive healer, and cosmic energy reader. She is the author and publisher of *Healing Within Meditation* and *The Power To Release Weight*. www.barrycolonfitnessrus.org

Keyra Conlinn is an author, poet, teacher, and lover of nature and culture, promoting choices that support connection to the planet and the beings who walk upon it. She enjoys working with all ages to develop communication and understanding between people across the globe.

Lottie Grant Cooper is committed to healing herself and helping others heal, break free from suffering, and experience miracles. She has an MA in Somatic Clinical Psychology and is a business/relationship/mindset coach, speaker, workshop leader, Cranial/Sacral practitioner, and Advanced Theta-Healer. www.inspirationalcounseling.com

Amy Coppola is a Spiritual Executive Coach specializing in project management with more than 20 years of experience with managing multi-million-dollar projects. She enjoys helping clients master leadership skills and uses her intuition to support clients in developing and sustaining a spirit/mind/body balance. www.amycoppola.com

Terry Corrao is a writer, photographer, and cooking instructor who shares her passion for life through storytelling, images, and food. She is the author of the photography book *Father Daughter*, a 2017 Benjamin Franklin Book Award winner. She lives in Tuscaloosa, Alabama. www.terrycorrao.com

Rev. Jodi Cross is an Interfaith Minister, Reiki Master Teacher, author, stress and sleep counsellor, holistic therapist, hands-on energy healer, wife, and mother of three amazing humans! She lives in England but spends as much time as possible in her beloved sanctuary in France.

Amanda Dale is a Master's-level social worker, spiritual empowerment coach, intuitive life and business consultant, and harmonious integration healing practitioner. She combines academic training, professional experience, and spiritually inspired passion to encourage conscious evolution for her clients. amandadale888@gmail.com

Marla David is a life coach, writer, and co-author of nine #1 international bestsellers. She is an avid reader with numerous personal development certifications and is currently living her life of passion, spending time with family and friends, traveling, and enjoying the arts. She is an animal lover and an advocate for nature.

Netta de Beer is the creator of the successful wedding-events company Delicious and Delightful, which began in 2010. Her great passion is her work as a freelance writer. She enjoys playing with unsaid words and mixed feelings.

Severino Concepcion De Los Santos is a loving son, brother, and father of four. Challenging the impoverished conditions of the Dominican Republic, Severino wakes each morning with passion to follow his dreams. He enjoys fitness, music, and doing a job that is well done.

Demetria is a financial healer and authentic freedom coach who empowers luminaries and wisdom-keepers to discover their divine genius and soul power through healing their finances. She hosts the "Soul Freedom Series" and is committed to empowering all of humanity in accessing internal freedom. www.soulfreedomfirst.com

Dr. Nicole Dolan is a licensed psychotherapist practicing on the Central Coast of California where she lives with her husband, daughter, and newborn son. Nicole describes her life's work as bridging the gap between psychology and spirituality. She is a published author and the owner of Sacred Path, a Holistic Healing Center.

Jody Doty is a writer, intuitive soul reader, healer, and spiritual counselor. Her words are inspired through meditation on the divine. She lives in the Pacific Northwest with her husband, Dave, and three amused cats. www.jodydoty.com

Michele B. Drzymala lives in Marlton, NJ, and is married with two children. She is a second-generation psychic medium who began her training by spending time with professional readers from Philadelphia at the age of 16. www.readingsbymicheledrzymala.com

Dr. Jerri Eddington is the creator of Energy Connections and the co-creator of Lighten Up and Thrive! She loves helping you clear the clutter of your mind, body, and soul. She combines her years in education and the integration of various energy-healing modalities to create powerful transformational programs. www.lightenupandthrive.com

Margot Edge was a primary teacher for 30 years. In retirement, she's exploring her passions for writing, listening to music, playing classical piano, and creating in the garden. She is a proud grandmother and great-grandmother.

Cath Edwards is known as "The Stress Less Coach" and has a passion for supporting people through life's challenges. Her mission in life is to guide people to a place of calm and peace so that they can achieve a healthier and happier version of themselves.

Kimberly A. Elliott is a passionate leader, impacting change for the incarcerated and their families. She's at the helm of the vision and operational objectives of The Four-Seven Prison Ministry to build strategic relationships that help transform lives. She champions the courage to change and experiences grace in full effect!

Kathy Sullivan Evans, a Tampa native, has authored two books: *If Our Table Could Talk* and *It Was One of Those Moments*. She is also a professional photographer with an exhibition forthcoming and is working to complete her first novel, *A Senseless Shame*. www.amazon.com/author/kathyevans

Martina E. Faulkner, LMSW, is a mystic for the modern age. As an author, Certified Life Coach, psychic, and Reiki Master Teacher, Martina guides and assists people on their life path to find more meaning, peace, and joy in their life. Martina can be reached at MartinaFaulkner.com.

Stacy Feliciano was born and raised in Hawaii. She has been on a journey to seek truth. On this journey, she has found her love of expression through painting and writing. Her source of courage and insight is based on her Buddhist faith. www.stacyfeliciano.com

Helen Ferrara, PhD, cares passionately about the world we live in and knows that we are all creative. She has experienced that a holistic perspective strengthens personal transformation. To foster creativity, Helen supports the nurturing of self-knowledge and authentic expression through mentoring. www.creativenurture.com.au

Meredith Fjelsted is a Nationally Certified Health Coach and founder of Dream2bhealthy. She is a professional speaker and healthy lifestyle expert who loves dogs and being outdoors, gardening, going on mission trips, and living healthy. She lives in Minnesota with her husband, Scott; two stepsons, Colin and Aidan; and two dogs.

Scott Fjelsted has been a Certified Personal Trainer since 1998 and is the author of *ForeverFitU: Making Fitness a Lifestyle That Lasts a Lifetime*. He is committed to the wellness of his clients, community, and home. He lives in Minnesota with his wife, Meredith, and two sons, Colin and Aidan. www.dofitanyway.com

Gigi Florez is a lifelong spiritual seeker. She is committed to helping others along their journey and continuously growing with her own. It's her passion for learning and understanding that fuels her ability to explore one's fullest potential. She is a Reiki Master Usui, a distance healer, a fairy card reader, and an intuitive artist. www.facebook.com/gigiflorez17

Stephanie L. Foran is an educator and artist/illustrator. Her love for writing began in early childhood. More importantly, she is a seeker – of knowledge, beauty, wisdom, love, and inner truth. A Connecticut native, she currently lives in New Jersey with her husband and two cats. Her e-mail address is StLyFo@gmail.com.

Elise Forrer is a writer and planner living in Lake Tahoe, California. She was born and raised in San Francisco and lived for several years in the Outer Banks of North Carolina. She is happily married, has two incredible children, and has recently become a grandmother.

Suzanne M. Fortino is a CNA working in the home health field. She has been a student of *A Course in Miracles* on and off for 35 years and is currently working toward her psychology degree. She believes that life is a journey of healing and that love is the path to healing.

Theresa Franson of Effortless Life Operations helps you work *with* your business instead of *in* your business to alleviate frustration, stress, and redundancies – creating ease and freedom for your Genius! www.effortlesslife.ca

Barbara Friedman, MA, LMFT, became a Diplomate in Comprehensive Energy Psychology in 2011. She is an intuitive who coaches highly sensitive individuals, blending energy psychology with clinical psychology and a healthy dose of humor to relieve stress and help people reconnect with their souls. Bf.morepositiveoptions@gmail.com

Catherine Frink loves to dance and paint, and her joy is to spread Don's Writing Mission through telling the story to every person who will listen. She does bunches of push-ups when she feels like it, and once in a while, she'll even do up to 115 without stopping.

B. J. Garcia is an international bestselling author and inspirational teacher. She lives Austin, TX, and loves sharing with others all the many strands of interest and wisdom she has collected, and moved through, in her personal journey for truth. Her deep love is sharing the Gene Keys Transmission. www.bjgarcia.com

Jessilyn Gaylor has a natural way of connecting with others and assessing their needs. She is a teacher at a nature-based, child-centered daycare in Connecticut, where her passions and interests are able to intertwine. In her free time, she loves hiking with her dog, crafting, and cooking.

Carole "Lisa Lynn" Gilbert is a wife, mom, "Gma," and author. Her autobiography, *Unraveled: Time to Tell* by Lisa Lynn (pen name), gives insight of tragedy to truth. Her children's books also tell of encouragement from God's Word. Read more in "The Bookstore" at www.carolelgilbert.com.

Kathleen Gleason is a writer and spiritual guide who has found her connection to the light within. Her mission is to help others reconnect as well. You can find her on Facebook: www.facebook.com/uncoveryourlight.

Lindsay S. Godfree, Author of *Awakening Consciousness: Finding a Larger Version of Self* and Creator of the Consciousness Guide, is an Angel-Oracle and Awakening Mentor. Her 7-Module, 90-Day Consciously Awakening System has changed lives internationally. For monthly newsletter, classes, and blogs, visit www.lindsaygodfree.com.

Donna Godfrey is a wellness advocate, educator, and Reiki Master/Teacher who uses Soul Coach Therapy, quantum energy, hypnosis, and channelled guided meditations. She is very passionate about showing the innate wisdom within all. She owned a Wellness Centre for over 20 years in Alberta but now resides in Creston, BC. dmgodfrey11@shaw.ca

Michelle Anne Gould, Founder of Abundant Spirit Education and BeeHive Woman, supports people who are committed to enhancing their lives by unlocking abundance, wellbeing, and freedom from within by focusing on sacred relationships and activating Divine Christ Bee Templates and Goddess Grids.

Noemi Grace is a psychotherapist, soul healer, and author. She channels new perspectives from God on unconditional self-love, forgiveness, grace, and life's purpose. She also channels answers to people's burning questions directly from the Divine and is delighted to offer you her free self-love ebook: www.noemigrace.com/self-love-ebook.

Leah Grant elevates consciousness as a Master Certified Coach, a metaphysics teacher, and a Certified Master Clairvoyant. She is the creator of Ecstatic Meditation™ and writes fiction and non-fiction. Visit www.leahgrant.com for free items and information on her offerings.

Michelle Griffith is an animal communicator, author, and educator. She facilitates conversations with pets and their people to build a better understanding from the pet's point of view. Her passion is strengthening relationships with clear communication, understanding, and trust. www.ManeRisePets.com

Kimberley Harrington is an animal Reiki practitioner and pharmacist and believes in the magic this world holds. She lives in Pennsylvania with her supportive husband and son (who is studying to be a pilot) and two rescued cats, Walter and Lulu.

Annalene Hart is a Creativity Guide, a poet, and a visionary artist who creates soul journey paintings for individuals. She contributed to the previous four bestselling books in the *365 Book Series*. She's presently working on completing an activity book for teens around creative self-expression. www.enchantedcreative.ca

Ellouise Heather is a creative writer and an accredited Master Coach. She helps sensitive women struggling with their weight to revive their self-esteem and reclaim their power over the scales. She loves anything that sparkles: gemstones, sand on the shore, and particularly souls. www.ellouiseheather.com

Chadi Hemaidan has been working in the field of helping others as a personal support worker for 21 years. In 1981, he first volunteered at a camp for blind and deaf kids. He is a three-time bestselling co-author and enjoys reading books and going on nature walks. He is pursuing his passion for writing.

Jean Hendricks connects with Angels and Guides to receive Divine guidance for all aspects of your life and enjoys channeling messages from them, loved ones, or pets. She feels her intuitive gifts are a blessing. She teaches classes, which include her own divinely created angel workshops. www.sparklewithangels.com

Karen A. Hill received a Bachelor's Degree in Human Services from Union Institute and University in 2009. She has extensive experience working with adults in residential drug and alcohol treatment. She is a co-author in the *365 Book Series* and is very excited to be a part of this journey.

David Hipshman works with conscious entrepreneurs around the world to grow thriving businesses that bring a positive impact to the world. Using proven methods, David helps his clients expand and become more successful and fulfilled so they can create their ideal business and life. www.growandflowyourbusiness.com

Gretchen Oehler Hogg enjoys her passion of studying the healing arts after retiring from a 30-year nursing career. As a #1 international bestselling co-author, she holds certifications as a Clinical and Life-Between-Lives Hypnotherapist, Master Soul Coach, ThetaHealing Practitioner®, and Reiki Master. www.SoulJourneys.Coach

Diana L. Hooker is an accountant, keynote speaker, leadership coach, and author. Inspired by the true stories of her friends and clients, she is following her passion to write an inspirational book titled *Living Your Greatness: How to Find Your Greatness in the Good, the Bad, and the Ugly.*

Alissa Iida is the founder of Intuitive Embassy and S.W.A.N. Academy. She is a bestselling author, intuitive life coach, and Akashic Records Consultant. She enjoys traveling, learning languages, meditating, and relaxing at beach resorts. She is also a school counselor for the Clark County School District.

Katie Jackson is a Quality of Life Coach, Certified Canfield Success Principles Trainer, personal trainer, and inspirational speaker. She has been on a journey of spiritual growth and personal development for 30 years. Katie is passionate about empowering women who are in addiction recovery to live their very best lives.

Susan Jacobi is the podcast host of Conversations That Heal, a healing mentor, and the author of *How to Love Yourself: Hope After Child Abuse.* Her book of poems is due to be released November 2019. Her website is www.SusanJacobi.com.

Debra Lee James, BSN, RN, HNB-BC, assists patients and their families to communicate better with healthcare providers by giving them information, tools, and vocabulary to be able to receive specific answers to specific questions. She lives in Maryland with her husband of 25 years and three cats. www.AngelicTouchHealthandWellness.net

Sheila Jenkins is the author of the #1 Amazon bestseller *The Day Before: Eternal Bonds into the Afterlife.* She is also the author of *Infinite Love: 50 Twin Soul Love Quotes.* She is a certified Reiki Master and the owner of Healing Hands and Hearts. She can be found at www.sheilamjenkins.com.

Monique Jessica is a Tarot reader and aspiring author residing in Alberta, Canada. She loves doing readings and giving people healing messages. Random road trips to the mountains feed her spirit. Monique is also an animal lover and has two rescued kitties. @thetarotgarden

Nancy Merrill Justice is an author, entrepreneur, and Certified Awakening Dynamics Energy Healer. With 44 years of succeeding in business and overcoming personal health challenges, she helps people heal, learn techniques to maintain a "mindset of happiness," and manifest their heart's desires. www.nancyjustice.com

Ayeesha S. Kanji is passionate about writing and dancing. She enjoys reading, dancing, and traveling (and has visited many places, including Africa, China, and Australia). A California Girl chillin' "in the 6ix," she lives a balanced life as a BollyX Instructor, Career Coach, and Technical Trainer.

Cheryl Kedan is delighted to contribute to *365 Soulful Messages*. Her first book, *First You Cry: From Tragedy to Hope*, won a Feathered Quill Award in 2017. After an executive corporate career that included publishing training and educational works, she has turned her focus to storytelling. Connect her at cheryl@cherylkedan.com.

Eva Kettles, a Transformation Alchemist, has helped hundreds of clients truly reveal their Divine Essence to live their lives in balance with nature and all beings. From this place, happiness becomes alive and we return to our natural bliss and become our magic Self again. www.divinealchemy.co

Davalynn Kim is a wife, healer, mother, daughter, friend, and, hopefully, a bright light in this world. She believes that anything is possible when you live from your heart. She believes in magic and miracles. She love animals and all things natural.

Elizabeth R. Kipp, Health Facilitator, specializes in stress and chronic pain management. She helps people unleash the power of their own healing. Founder of www.Elizabeth-Kipp.com, Elizabeth offers help with stress management, addiction recovery, Ancestral Clearing, Bilateral EFT/Tapping, and Kundalini Yoga.

Kara Kissinger strives to lead an inspired life, which she shares with her husband, 16-year-old daughter, two step-daughters, and two crazy dogs. She's a breast cancer survivor, happy introvert, reader, meditator, journaler, crocheter, and weekend napper. She walks barefoot in the grass every chance she gets.

Marci Kobayashi is an intuitive business coach, web designer, and writer. When she is not working with clients, she loves discovering Spirit in all shapes and forms. Look for her upcoming book, *Finding Yoyu*, about living with her Japanese father-in-law as they navigate Alzheimer's together. www.marcikobayashi.com

Karen Koven is an author living in Clearwater, FL. She received first place in the Romeo Lemay Poetry Competition and has had her poetry published in the *Odet Journal*. She has retired from a career as a Senior Consultant with an international training and development company.

Lyn A. Kyrc is an Amazon international bestselling author/motivational speaker. Her upcoming book/screenplay, *Grace*, is an intriguing teen story of faith and love. She resides in Nashville, TN, with her cat, Sparkle. www.lynkyrc.com

Angela Mia La Scala is an inspiring motivational messenger and intuitive Reiki Master Teacher in Western and Eastern lineages. She teaches how to raise one's vibration through the practice of Reiki as a means to heal on all levels: mind, body, and spirit. www.ReikiVibrationsWithAngela.com

Debbie Labinski, Intuitive Angel Communicator, Speaker, and Author, instantly connects with her clients to create a safe place to explore feelings of hope and heartfelt answers, giving them the guidance they need to create positive adjustments in their lives. She is dedicated to empowering others to believe in their own intuitive abilities.

Margaret Jane Landa was an educator for 46 years. Assignments ranged from kindergarten to soldiers of all ages. Locations varied from the Bronx in New York City to SHAPE in Belgium. She resides on a farm in Tennessee, where she enjoys family and friends, watching things grow, meditation, spiritual study, reading, writing, and travel.

Destrie Sweet Larrabee, MEd, lives in Ohio with her wonderful family and cats. She enjoys following her peaceful life path and living close to Lake Erie in a city that honors and celebrates diversity and community. Destrie loves traveling, learning, and participating in her grandson's life experiences!

Catherine M. Laub is a psychic and award-winning author of *Journey of Angelic Healing*. She shares her mental illness and healing journey on her podcast, The Celestial Spoon. Catherine also talks to groups, inspiring them to reach out for care if they require it. www.catherinemlaub.com

Kenneth I. Laws II has been on a spiritual path to understand the unexplainable, his awakening, after a series of life-altering events that occurred in his life in 2013. It was not until then that he started to understand the meaning of oneness with all, accepting all with no judgment. www.simplyindescribable.com

Tara Leduc is a peacemaker, an intuitive, a coach, and a healer who has lived with thyroid cancer for 19 years. You can join her in her mission to change the world, peace by peace, at www.worldpeaceispossible.org.

Greg Lee and his wife, Antonia Van Becker, are the founders of www.SelfHealthInstitute.com, whose mission is to inspire and empower their clients to create optimal health using the body's innate self-healing wisdom. Greg loves to garden, play piano, and sing his original inspirational songs.

Rhonda Lee, MAEd, is the creator of Spirit Mist Smokeless Smudge. She is a Reiki Master, keynote speaker on stress management, and Laughter Yoga leader. She empowers others to take charge of their energy through various modalities. She chooses the path of love to guide her business and life. www.infusionoflife.com

Kianne Lei is a nanny and fitness coach residing in Richmond, Virginia. She has found her passion and purpose by helping others lose their limiting beliefs in all stages of life. She is committed to showing up in her daily life as the most authentic version of herself.

Lorre Leigh is a proud mother of six children and currently works as an office manager for a child-care center. Her interests include movies, books, music, coffee, and writing. She began writing poetry in high school, and it has been her creative outlet ever since. Her Instagram page is @lorleiwrites.

Tanya Levy is a counselor in a community college and an inspirational photographer. She has worked in the human-services field for 25 years. She is a strong and passionate advocate for the healing power of each individual's own learning journey. www.facebook.com/heartladyinspiration

Gena Livings is a visual artist, author, spiritual practitioner of peaceful living, and founder of www.GenaLivings.com. Through her writing and visual artwork, Gena helps people cultivate their awareness so that they can make conscious lifestyle choices based on healthy lifestyle practices and a positive mindset.

Nicole C. Lofton is an anti-domestic violence advocate and certified Christian life coach. After surviving domestic violence and other personal situations in life, Nicole felt led to advocate, educate, and empower others through her story. www.gardenofpurpose.com

Fiona Louise is a nutritional and natural health therapist, educator, and author. Discover her bestselling book, collaborations, and musings here: www.fiona-louise.com.

Lori Love is a Family Nurse Practitioner who loves to encourage and uplift others. Lori has been on a path of forgiveness and thankfulness, journaling her goals and dreams since 2016. She aspires to be a smiling, shining light to those around her. klve2003@yahoo.com

Mia Lucci is a wise fool studying psychology/sociology at the University of Colorado in Boulder, where she also enjoys playing field hockey at the foothills of the Flatirons. She spends her summers managing the busiest lemonade stand in Chicago. https://mialucci10.wixsite.com/mialucci

Susan M. Lucci is a Certified Purpose Guide™ and dynamic facilitator of transformational conversations so that group wisdom, creativity, and engaged action emerge. Passionate about holding soulful Circle conversations to grow healthier communities, this former lawyer is co-creating a sustainable world where everyone thrives! www.pursuepurpose.co

Kimberly Lucht is a life and business coach who helps kickass women make their dreams a reality through workshops, online programs, and one-on-one coaching. She currently lives in New York City. For free resources on how to design the life and business of your dreams, visit www.kimberlylucht.com.

Mary Lunnen, creator of Dare to Blossom, supports you in finding your way home to yourself through Compass Rose life coaching, her Rediscovery Cards, workshops, and online classes. Mary's writing, photography, and artwork are all part of her creative life, based in magical Cornwall. www.daretoblossom.co.uk

JoAnne B. Lussier is a healer, coach, and teacher. Her heart-centered nature attracts people and animals seeking compassion and authenticity. She lives in New England with her beloved cats and spends her free time volunteering, pursuing self-development, and cultivating relationships. www.thewillowconnection.com

Bianca Lynn is a curious traveler who has spent years exploring different paths. Her goal is to help people live with greater joy. Through workshops, writing, and one-on-one work, she guides people to find their way back to their own magnificence, release stress, and live in a way that feels more meaningful. www.biancadisalvo.com

Cindy Lyon is a personal life coach and mentor to hundreds of women seeking personal transformation to live their life on purpose. From one-on-one coaching sessions, workshops, books, and online courses, she helps women around the world improve their lives, learn their worth, and follow their bliss.

Marina Malmberg was born in Russia and lived in four countries that gave her a deep understanding of inter-culture. In Pakistan, Marina met her spiritual teacher who unleashed Marina's passion for natural healing. Today, Marina lives in Sweden and works internationally, helping people restore lost inner balance. www.marinasbachflowertherapy.com

Stacey Maney is an artist, writer, yoga teacher, and mama. She uses spirituality, movement, and creativity as an activation for feminine power and teaches about the magic of interweaving them into your life. She lives in Ohio but will always be a beach bum at heart. www.staceymaney.com

Lori Kilgour Martin is an Angelic Counselor and musical theatre artist from Canada. She is a co-author in *365 Days of Angel Prayers*, *111 Morning Meditations*, and the *Spiritual Leaders Directory 2018*. Plus she feels honored to serve in the entire *365 Book Series*. www.diamondheartangel.com

Veronica Mather is a Reiki Master, writer, and passionate animal-welfare advocate. She shares her world with her husband, Dale; Max and Blaze, two spirited dogs; and three pet sheep in Hamilton, Australia, which is a stone's throw from the majestic Grampians mountain ranges.

Kristy Carr McAdams shares from her "spiritual tool-belt" to show people how to discover their personal gifts. She's a mama, smile purveyor, psychic/medium, artist, Certified Angel Practitioner (ACP), Reiki/IET Practitioner, sound healing facilitator, mandala/art facilitator, author, and hugger extraordinaire. www.EnergyOfAngels.com

Sherry Cheek McBride was raised in Mocksville, NC, and is the daughter of Talmadge and Dorothy Cheek. She currently resides in beautiful Boone, NC (Go APP), with her amazing husband, Kip. She loves to cook, travel, and spoil her grandchildren! Contributing to this book was a bucket-list item for her.

Carolyn McGee has co-authored six bestselling books and is a TV host, sought-after speaker, and blogger who has taught thousands of women how to trust intuitive messages to act and make confident decisions. She specializes in combining Angel and Animal Wisdom to help you to Amplify *Your* Intuitive Superpower. www.CarolynMcGee.com

Iona Meade is a law of vibration teacher, tough-love trainer, mentor, course creator, and Big Money Energy Coach. She teaches soul-guided entrepreneurs to start a movement with their message from scratch and bank 50K in 50 days. Receive her free Masterclass and bonuses: www.SoulLegacyAcademy.com/courses/masterclass.

Giuliana Melo aspires to inspire. She loves life, God, and her family. She spends her days spreading love and light and helping others heal. She is a cancer survivor who is passionate about medicine, non-traditional healing, and angel therapy. She has been married for 30 years and has one 19-year-old son. www.giulianamelo.com

Carol Metz, the Courage Catalyst Farmer, Spiritual Entrepreneur, and Leadership Coach, helps clients ignite their "Why" into their "What" to get to the heart of the matter. She uses her powerful gift of speaking to inspire you to live your life, heart-centered and with possibilities.

M. Lorrie Miller has a master's degree in Clinical Social Work (MSW) with 20 years' experience. She is currently writing a book titled *An Invitation to Co-Creation* about peace, unity consciousness, and soul-purposed living. She is on Facebook and www.mlorriemiller.com.

Melissa Monroe is a poet, writer, and Ayurveda student. She switched law school for Ayurveda school and in the process remembered that she loves poetry! Her first book, *Zen in the City: a Collection of Poems to Guide You Home*, will be released in early 2020. Find your Zen at www.melissa-monroe.com.

Jill Pepper Montz runs her family's business, the Pecan Shed, but secretly wishes she could spend all her days in bed...her flower bed, that is. Recently, she wrote her first book, *My Guru Calls Me Momma*, which is a memoir regarding the ups and downs of being a single parent.

Sonya L. Moore is an entrepreneur. She is the CEO/Owner of Moore Planning & Consulting, LLC. She loves breathing life into new ideas, reading, writing, and being with family. She lives in Cincinnati, Ohio, with her husband Craig and children, Craig II and Shanoah. www.moorepc-llc.com

Candy Motzek, PCC, BASc, is a human *being*, engineer, dancer, dreamer, barefoot leader, and sacred rebel. Candy was a longtime senior leader in "corporate." Now, she's a passionate life and leadership coach who coaches brilliant people to gain clarity, grow in confidence, and take action on what matters most. www.candymotzek.com

Reema Sharma Nagwan holds degrees in Commerce and Law and a post-graduate diploma in Company Secretaryship. Living in Australia and now working full-time as a compliance professional, she juggles her kids, household, and passion for scriptures. Her hobbies are baking delicacies and grooving to her favourite mix.

Lucy V. Nefstead lives in northern Wisconsin with her dog, Sam. She is a retired English, Speech, and Theatre teacher who is co-chair of an animal rescue, president of retired teachers, on Wisconsin's board of directors, and serves on state committees. Spirituality is an integral part of her life.

Sandi Neilson is a personal power and prosperity guide and loves mentoring go-getter types with big hearts who are at a crossroads in their life. Sandi is a lover of everyday miracles, magic, and messages of love, wherever they appear. Find out more at www.sandineilson.com.

Janet G. Nestor is a bestselling author, natural intuitive, licensed counselor, and expert in energy healing and relaxation strategies who is regularly interviewed about mindful living and inner peacefulness. She is passionate about holistic health care and is a co-developer of Radiant Energies Balance. www.mindfulpathways.com

Jenny Ngo is an expert healer, speaker on global telesummits, and intuitive business coach who helps entrepreneurs grow their transformational businesses to six figures and beyond, doing what they love while having the support to navigate the ups and downs of business and life. www.PurposeToProfitsHealing.com

Hue Anh Nguyen, a master healer many lifetimes over, has created a revolutionary process for creating instant shifts in energy fields when people are stuck, feeling off, or are wanting to create the next new experience. Beyond healing, the magic that she creates manifests miracles. Visit www.polarity4harmony.com for your free gift.

Mary Niemi is a mother, sister, teacher, poet, traveller, empath, and artisan. Her magical Nova Scotian hometown is located by the saltwater Minas Basin on powerful ley lines. She loves to walk on the Acadian dikes surrounded by glorious views of Cape Blomidon, home of Glooscap.

Michele Noordhof is an international bestselling author and motivational speaker. She speaks openly about her journey from suicide survivor to life thriver, with the desire that her message will touch the hearts of others and help them through the challenges they face in life. www.thewellspringofhope.com

Ramona Oliver is an advocate of positive aging and lives in Austin, Texas. Rather than accepting a mindset of decline, she is passionate about promoting a life of continuous "incline" and sharing that adventure with others. Her article is an excerpt from her soon-to-be-published book, *The Inclined Elder*. www.ramonavmoliver.com

Mary Cate O'Malley has had a long and successful career leading high-performance teams in the planning and execution of corporate and marketing communications for companies and non-profits.

Wendyanne Pakulsky is passionate about reminding people that with every life shift comes an opportunity for growth and healing into new heights of awareness.

Lisa Anna Palmer, Founder and CEO of the Cattelan Palmer Light Your Leadership Institute (LYLI), is a career and leadership coach devoted to making the world a better workplace and growing a generation of leaders who care about people and the planet.

Patricia Peters is a business strategist, spiritual mentor, and former athlete. In 1989, she discovered the power of energy work when it catapulted her into top 10 world ranking. Since then, she teaches it to women entrepreneurs who want to make a significant change. http://patriciapeters.mystrinkingly.com

Rev. Shelia Prance, PhD, has spent her career as an accounting professional. She has a Bachelor of Science degree in accounting and is an ordained minister with a MDiv and PhD in Religious Studies. Her graduate degrees are based in Native American Spirituality.

Annie Price uses heartfelt, intuitive guidance to empower others in their divine purpose and live the joyful expression of their soul. She is completing her memoir and does a weekly "Tea Reading Tuesday" card reading on her Facebook page: www.facebook.com/SoulSoaring.

Donna S. Priesmeyer is a media professional who works with artists, authors, musicians, healers, and speakers. She enjoys many creative pursuits including writing, art, photography, gardening, traveling, and volunteering. She publishes a website featuring consciousness-raising art, music, and literature: www.LightOnLife.net.

Misty Proffitt-Thompson is a spiritual life coach, a mind/body/spirit practitioner, an author, teacher, and speaker. Her passion is to help those who are struggling with their connection to source because of their grief. She lives in Thatcher, Arizona, and has four children and four grandchildren. www.mistymthompson.com

Mimi Quick is known as the "Prosperity Muse." She is a psychic business mentor and owner of the Spiritual Business Institute – a spiritual coaching and training company that empowers spirited entrepreneurs to create prosperous, aligned businesses and lives doing what they love. www.MimiQuick.com

Mohamed (MO) Rachadi, Ph.D, is a humanitarian, inspirational author, and speaker who holds a BS, an MS, and a PhD in Biology. He lives in Georgia with his wife, Connie. The Rachadis are proud parents of two daughters, Ashley and Jaclyn. Dr. Rachadi volunteers at Emory JC Hospital. www.morachadi.com

Michelle Radomski is a writing and publishing coach, book designer, and bestselling author. She created The Publishing Sanctuary, a safe and nurturing place where authors with tender hearts and tenacious souls will find everything they need to get brave, be seen, and finally birth the book they were born to write. www.OneVoiceCan.com

Nick Rafter is an award-winning journalist, author, and realtor from New York City. Born and raised in Queens, he attended Hofstra University where he was program director at the college's radio station. He recently completed his first full-length novel and hopes to publish it soon.

Amado F. Ramirez, Jr. is a retired police officer from the San Jose State University Police Department. He practices shamanism and makes rosaries, dreamcatchers, and shamanic tools. He and his wife, Maria, reside in Napa, California, and have two children, Estrella and Isaac.

Lupe C. Ramirez uses her experiences with God to inspire others. Time spent dancing, writing, and visiting New York keep her passion alive. She is writing her memoir and shares her life's adventures with her children, grandchildren, and friends.

Cathy Raymond, aka "Crocodile Tears" Raymond, started life as an emotional girl. Through emotional, energetic, and perceptual healing experiences, she discovered a life unburdened by drama and struggle. She helps clients "let it go" using EVOX technology to restore love, balance, and peace. www.changeyourmind-changeyourlife.com

Clare Ann Raymond, a tender-hearted "hubster," connects family and friends around the globe as a gracious hostess. A docent for 36 years at the Museum of Fine Arts in St. Petersburg, FL, Clare is also the cheerleader for authors Lorraine, Cathy, and Lisa Raymond. At 87, this celebrates her first published work.

Lisa M. Raymond has been forever drafting imaginary novels in her mind and has broken through with a short story on gratitude and the power of faith in action. Born and raised in Texas and transplanted to the East Coast, she is a full-time manager, wife, and lover of her overly adorable dog, Oliver.

Visionary teacher Lorraine Raymond's world travels inspire her writing and mentoring. A transformational co-author with five #1 Amazon bestsellers, she encourages women to express themselves through courses, global retreats, and her Divine Dialogue Writing System™. Mentees describe her as "wise, generous, and charismatic." www.LoreRaymond.com

Lori Reeves was born into an Air Force family and moved often as a child. She has settled in Texas and is blessed to have a son, Ty, and now a beautiful granddaughter, Zachary. She has her mom, a poet, to thank for her desire to write.

Joy Resor's gratitude daily overflows so much that she's healed into her name, allowing her to inspire others through her presence and offerings. She writes enlivening books, serves clients as their spiritual mentor, hula-hoops in sunbeams, and shares adventures with her partner, Michael. www.joyonyourshoulders.com

Jacine Rilea is the creator of Orchestree. She helps creative empaths bring their purpose into the world and to those they want to help. She visually helps others find their unique messages from the heart so that they can change the world. You can find out more at www.orchestree.com.

Robyn Ringgold is an intuitive, energy worker, and shamanic practitioner. She is a mother and tree lover and spends a lot of time in nature with Mama Gaia. Robyn would love to assist you with fostering a deeper connection to your divine nature at www.divinesunrays.com.

Pauline Hosie Robinson writes about self-healing through the eyes of love. In her autobiography, *Triumph of Joy*, she utilized nature to help her cope with her husband's PTSD. After her husband's traumatic death, a shaman empowered her to heal herself. To read her healing journey through the natural world, visit www.triumphofjoy.com.

Faye Rogers is an animal communicator, visionary, writer, intuitive healer, and qualified teacher of the Diana Cooper School in Angels and Ascension. She works with animals and people to bring more harmony and awareness. She is passionate about humanity and empowering others. www.animalcommunication-newzealand.com

Isabella Rose touches people's lives and builds community through her creativity, writing, and healing practices. She lives in a small New England town and is a Plymouth 400 Ambassador, Holistic Health Healer, and advocate for those who feel they have no voice. www.bellarosehealinghands.com

Nora Rose is an author, speaker, coach, and teacher with the goal of empowering others to go after their dreams and live their best life. Her books *Gabriel's Journey; Bentley's Week;* and *A Journal, A Recipe, and A Family in America* have all won the Parent-Teacher Choice Award.

Katja Rusanen is a spiritual mentor, success coach, and #1 bestselling author. Katja's pragmatic approach, combined with her spiritual awareness, helps her clients get results fast. She helps spiritual entrepreneurs break through abundance blocks and visibility fears so that they can succeed on purpose. www.katjarusanen.com

Maria Angela Russo, LCSW, is a psychotherapist with a private practice specializing in childhood trauma. She is an author who has contributed to three inspirational books, as well as publishing a memoir, *The Growing Soul: My Transformational Journey from Adversity to the Divine Within.* www.MariaAngelaRusso.com

Debra Sawers lives in Alberta, Canada, where she writes, paints, and facilitates women's empowerment courses and programs.

Jodie Scott, PhD, is an amazing healer who lives in Florida; owns Still Point Counseling, Inc.; and specializes in energy psychology, trauma treatment, spirituality, soul detective, and Pranic healing. She's been in private practice for over 20 years and loves helping people heal. She has three adult children and two amazing granddaughters.

Jordann Scruggs' stories in *365 Soulful Messages* are her first published works. Her life has repeatedly reflected God's power to forgive, protect, guide, and bless. She is currently working on her memoir, *I Know My Father: A Revelation of Truth*. Connect with Jordann at info@cjsoulfulwriting.com.

Kris Seraphine-Oster, PhD, is a coach and strategist who helps creatives and spiritual entrepreneurs create a life and business with pleasure at the center. She has authored two non-fiction books (*Return to Enchantment* and *Unbound*) and is penning her first sacred erotica novel. www.krisoster.com

H. Michelle Spaulding is a creative arts coach and workshop facilitator, artist, and storyteller. Her passion is to encourage and inspire others to tap into their own unique creative spirit. She teaches fiber arts classes and lives in her dream cottage on an island in North Carolina. www.Craftydivacottage.com

Jenny McKaig Speed is CEO, writer, and coach at JennyMcKaig.com; bestselling author and senior editor of *Empowering Women to Succeed*; and an Awakening Coach. She is a business investor and global equality and women's empowerment advocate. Her two daughters, Liberty and Savannah, and her husband, Shawn, are her whole heart.

Jeanette St. Germain is the founder of Radiant Soul Center in Arizona, where she empowers others to embrace their inner radiance. Jeanette's individual sessions and public events often include angelic messages, clarity of life purpose, and deep healing through all layers of the energy field. www.jeanettestgermain.com

Janet Stefanelli lives in Manchester, Maryland. She is an RN by day and a mom, sister, daughter, friend, artist, yoga instructor, Reiki Master, and sound healer in her spare time. Gratitude and mindfulness for life drives her spirit each and every day!

Karen Stillman has been on a spiritual journey for over 10 years. She has been gifted with intuitive and mediumship skills and works hard to continue honing them. Her goal is to inspire others to reach their full potential through angel guidance and self-love. Namaste.

Julie Stygar is a psychic medium, medical intuitive, and Reiki Master who has enjoyed these gifts for a great portion of her adult life. Her ability to connect with Spirit and inspire others is her greatest accomplishment, and she looks forward to every opportunity. Facebook: Julie Stygar Psychic Medium/Reiki Master

Sheila Sutherland is a Life Skills Strategist who believes you can change your life by choosing to shift how you react to your circumstances. She empowers her clients to learn tangible skills to manage their reactions, increase their self-awareness, and regain their personal power to make positive changes that stick! www.ReigniteYourPurpose.com

Joanna Werch Takes is a writer and editor. The former editor of a national hobbyist magazine, she loves dogs, nature, and travel. She also loves to research and is masterful at telling people's stories while letting their voice shine through. Find her at www.linkedin.com/in/joannawt.

Gabrielle Taylor is a psychotherapist and transformational coach. She is passionate about helping sensitive, visionary women reach their potential, make a difference, and live their purpose. She is the founder of Empowered Soul Leader: Birth Your Soul-Project from the Inside Out. www.gabriellebtaylor.com

Connie Theoharis is an artist, photographer, and a writer of poetry and non-fiction. She worked as a commercial photographer in NYC and as a freelance photographer. Supernatural events awakened her to a far greater truth of our existence that she believes we have been intentionally programmed not to see or know.

Lori Thiessen lives in Canada and works as an Architectural Tech. Her passion is for mental health through fitness, nutrition, meditation, and gratitude. She's a writer, trail runner, Toastmaster, certified NLP Practitioner, and mom to five grown-up kids. www.facebook.com/couragefinder

Jamie Thomas is a young man exploring life and nature to discover his deepest calling. Becoming a well-known and beloved author is one of his greatest desires. He enjoys time with his friends, mother, and cats on the east coast, pushing his edge – and always welcoming the return home.

Lori Thomas is a healer, author, spiritual entomologist, and nature communicator. She shares her deep connection with Nature's beings through healing sessions, meditative storytelling, talks, blogs, and social media. Be on the lookout for her upcoming book that will change how you relate to insects forever. www.spiritualecologist.com

Rev. Jamie Lynn Thompson's passion is helping to empower and uplift others to let their "Sparkle Shine and Live Toadily Divine." She is a spiritual ambassador, faith healer, angel practitioner, reflexologist, and spiritual life coach. www.RevJamieLynn.com

Dr. Matthew Tischler, chiropractor and owner of Chiro Care PC in Doylestown, PA, offers patients the ability to have outstanding optimal health and wellness without the use of drugs or surgery. Dr. Tischler is an author, dad, healer, artist, philosopher, scientist, and meditation teacher. www.chirocarepc.com

Liz Uhlaender lives in Austin, TX, with her amazing four-year-old son, Otto. A former professional bodybuilder, Liz works as a personal trainer, caregiver, and OsteoStrong session coach. She is working toward a career in occupational therapy and thoroughly enjoys helping people achieve their goals. lizuhlaender@gmail.com

Antonia Van Becker and her husband, Greg Lee, are the founders of Self Health Institute, Inc., inspiring and empowering their clients to create optimal health using their body's innate self-healing wisdom. Antonia also loves to write fiction, sing and write songs, and garden at Hummingbird Farm in Northern CA.

Julie Vance is an ordained Unity minister, inspirational speaker, writer, workshop and retreat facilitator, and avid ballroom dancer. Committed to trusting her own inner spirit in her "dance with the Divine," her mission is to gently guide others to discover their own unique dance. www.facebook.com/julievance.106

Teresa Velardi is an author, speaker, and publisher. She is committed to making a difference in the lives of others while using her gifts and talents with passion and purpose to help people get their stories told in books. Email dailygiftbookseries@gmail.com for info on her upcoming book series.

Valerie R. Vestal, MSN, PMHNP-BC, has spent the last five years enjoying her work as a Psychiatric Nurse Practitioner. She is also a high-energy speaker whose greatest influence is her ability to give practical solutions to difficult problems.

Lindsey Gaye Walker is a professional recording artist and part of an award-winning music duo called Unleashed Dreams. She also has a BA [hons] in Psychology, is a transformational life coach, NLP practitioner, and Holotropic Breathwork facilitator [GTT]. She lives in Ontario, Canada. www.UnleashedDreams.com

Julie Wheeler is a spiritual mentor, holistic health coach, author, and retired project manager. Stroke, cancer, and triple grief led Julie to retire from corporate work in 2011, leading her down a spiritual path that has evolved from survival to serving others in an empowering way. www.thesacredacre.org

Heather Wiest is beyond blessed to love, serve, and inspire the community as a Registered Yoga Teacher, Reiki Master, and Licensed Clinical Social Worker. Her holistic yoga sessions are engaging and rejuvenating, leaving one feeling balanced and inspired. Restore your body. Renew your mind. Refresh your spirit. www.loveserveinspire.com

Stephanie Williams is 35 years old and has been married to her loving husband, Jeff, for 10 years. She is currently a stay-at-home mother to her two beautiful daughters, Rylee and Alexee. She has always wanted to be a writer and is excited for this opportunity.

Jan Wilson is an intuitive empath with training in various formats of holistic health. She is dedicated to empowering others to believe in their abilities to connect to themselves and the world around them, to be who they truly are, and to trust themselves. Reach Jan at Every.Body.Matter@gmail.com.

Janet Womack is a breast cancer survivor and holistic life coach who inspires and empowers women to live their lives on purpose and recreate a fulfilling life after loss. She's madly in love with cats, life, laughter, and personal growth. Visit her at www.janetlwomack.com.

Jody Wootton embraces a heart-centered life. Her motto is "gift gratitude and create meaningful relationships." Being a home-based travel agent with Goldrush Getaways, LLC, she believes the value of taking vacations with family creates memories and are worth the investment.

Julie Wylie uses her eclectic background of Nia Technique and t'ai chi to create comfortable, safe spaces for individuals to find health, healing, and well-being. She contributes to the greater good by facilitating movement, creative writing, and public speaking classes to incarcerated women in Texas. www.JulieAnnWylie.com

Karen Wythe is dedicated to living life with passion. She enjoys traveling through life with her husband, best friend, and soulmate, Bill. A lifelong Spiritualist, Karen is an ordained minister, certified medium, healer, life transformation coach, workshop presenter, writer, and fiber artist. enrichingliferesources.com/AboutKaren.php

Barbara Yager, former corporate attorney, is a skilled and gifted transformational life coach who specializes in helping people realize their true potential by recognizing and capitalizing on their personal strengths. Barbara offers an invigorating approach to life, believing if you can conceive it and believe it, you will achieve it.

Chanin Zellner is a Certified Master in Reiki and the Vibrational UPgrade™ System. She didn't know how extensively she'd been affected by trauma. When she truly cleared it, her life magically transformed for the better. She learned these techniques so she could help others. www.thelightvessel.com

Jenean Zunk, BDiv, is an emotional mastery coach and energy healer for empaths and highly sensitive souls. She assists others in mastering their emotions and turning their unique makeup into their superpower. "Learning to master your emotions allows you to be the calm within any storm."

Contributor Index

For your convenience, we have listed each contributor in alphabetical order by last name and have included the page number(s) of their piece(s). We hope that this makes finding your favorite co-authors easy!

Acknowledgments

This is the fifth and final book in this special series, and we wanted to take a moment to thank each author who contributed to this book or to any of the previous four. We're so grateful to each of you for being so authentic and brave and vulnerable and honest. We're so grateful that you shared stories that only you could share – true-life moments that you experienced that have inspired us all in such profound ways. This series never could have existed without you, and we'll forever be grateful to each of you for being part of it. We love the community of soulful authors that's grown around this series – we've become friends, and we love seeing you support one another. It's rare to find such authentic sharing – in books and also online – so thank you for that as well. We're so grateful.

From Jodi:

This year hasn't been an easy one for me. We had to say unexpected goodbyes to two of our precious cats, Elsie and Monkey, and my health took a nosedive. I've had to rely on Dan much more than normal, and he's been amazing at taking such great care of not only me but also the authors in our communities. He's had to carry a lot on his shoulders, and he still shows up every day from a place of love, devotion, and a huge heart. So, Dan, thank you from my whole heart for your love. You're everything to me. While I believe that the sun will shine brighter next year for both of us, thank you for being the sunlight during my darkest days.

And Elsie and Monkey, know that Mama misses you both every single day. Thank you for blessing us with your love and your silliness and for bringing us both so much joy. While I wish we had more time with you both, I'm so grateful for the time that we had. You'll both be in my hearts forever.

Thank you, also, to my mom for helping me get through such a difficult year, for listening to me cry day after day, and for just being there whenever I needed some extra love. I love you. And thank you so much to everyone who sent their love and prayers to us. We felt it all and constantly feel so blessed that we're surrounded by so many heart-centered and kind people.

From Dan:

First and foremost, thank you, Jodi, for the heart, soul, brains, and energy you bring to this series, to this community, and to my life! These books would never have seen the light of day without your inspiring vision, beautiful spirit, and countless hours of work – from figuring out behind-the-scenes technical aspects of launching the book to the thousands of emails and Facebook posts you write, respond to, and share with our soulful community to help bring us closer together. I admire you every day, I love you every day, and I thank my lucky stars every day that I won the love lottery and get to have you as my wife, my best friend, and my forever everything.

I also want to thank the numerous authors, teachers, thought leaders, and other amazing souls – in this series and beyond – who have offered inspiration, enlightenment, wisdom, technical know-how, and personal upliftment. You will never know how much you have shaped me, informed my worldview, and allowed me to become more fully myself – simply by being your true self. Thank you for sharing your gifts and shining your light.

Also, we would like to thank you, the reader. Your loving emails and reviews mean the world to us. When we hear how someone has been inspired by one of the pieces, we all cheer together as a community. It's our intention that these books will uplift – that each person who reads them will feel better after they've put the book down. It's a writer's dream to know that our words mean something to someone else. So thank you so much to each of you who have reached out over the years and shared what these books mean to you. Thank you for believing in us, in this series, and in our vision to put loving kindness into our world.

Other Books in This Series

This is the fifth and final book in our bestselling *365 Book Series*, and we would love to invite you to learn more about all of the books!

365 Ways to Connect with Your Soul

In this #1 international bestselling book, over 200 beautiful souls came together to share how they connect with their own souls with the hopes that it will help you connect with yours as well. It's a wonderful addition to your spiritual practice!

365 Moments of Grace

This #1 international bestselling book contains 365 personal stories of grace, miracles, and transformations from beautiful souls all around the world to show how magical our world is and how connected we truly are. Moments of grace are presents from the universe!

365 Life Shifts: Pivotal Moments That Changed Everything

In this #1 international bestseller, over 250 beautiful souls came together to share life shifts that they've experienced that opened up their world, inspired, uplifted, shook them to their core, got them back on track (or onto a new track altogether), and led them toward their true selves.

Goodness Abounds: 365 True Stories of Loving Kindness

In this #1 bestseller, over 275 beautiful souls share their stories of goodness and loving kindness. These stories will lift your spirits, restore your faith in humanity, and remind you that goodness truly does abound.

You can learn more about the books from this soulful series here:
www.365bookseries.com.

An Invitation

If one of your dreams is to write a book that inspires others, then we hope you'll sign up for our program! In it, we include everything you'll need to write, publish, and market your own book!

This program includes monthly live sessions, monthly workbooks, over 30 videos, one-on-one time, a private Facebook community, tons of advice from experts, and so much more! We support you during each step of your outer and inner journey of being a writer, offering concrete writing/marketing tools while guiding you through the emotional highs and lows that you'll experience throughout the process of bringing your soulful book to life.

You've already got the book inside you. Now it's time to get it out of you…and into the world. Now is the time to share your gift, answer your calling, and write your book! Your words matter. Your message matters. Your book matters! It can change the world, touch hearts, and inspire thousands…but only if you write it! If you're ready to bring your soulful book to life, we would be honored to support you on this life-changing journey!

To learn more, visit www.yoursoulfulbook.com.

Made in the USA
San Bernardino, CA
01 December 2019